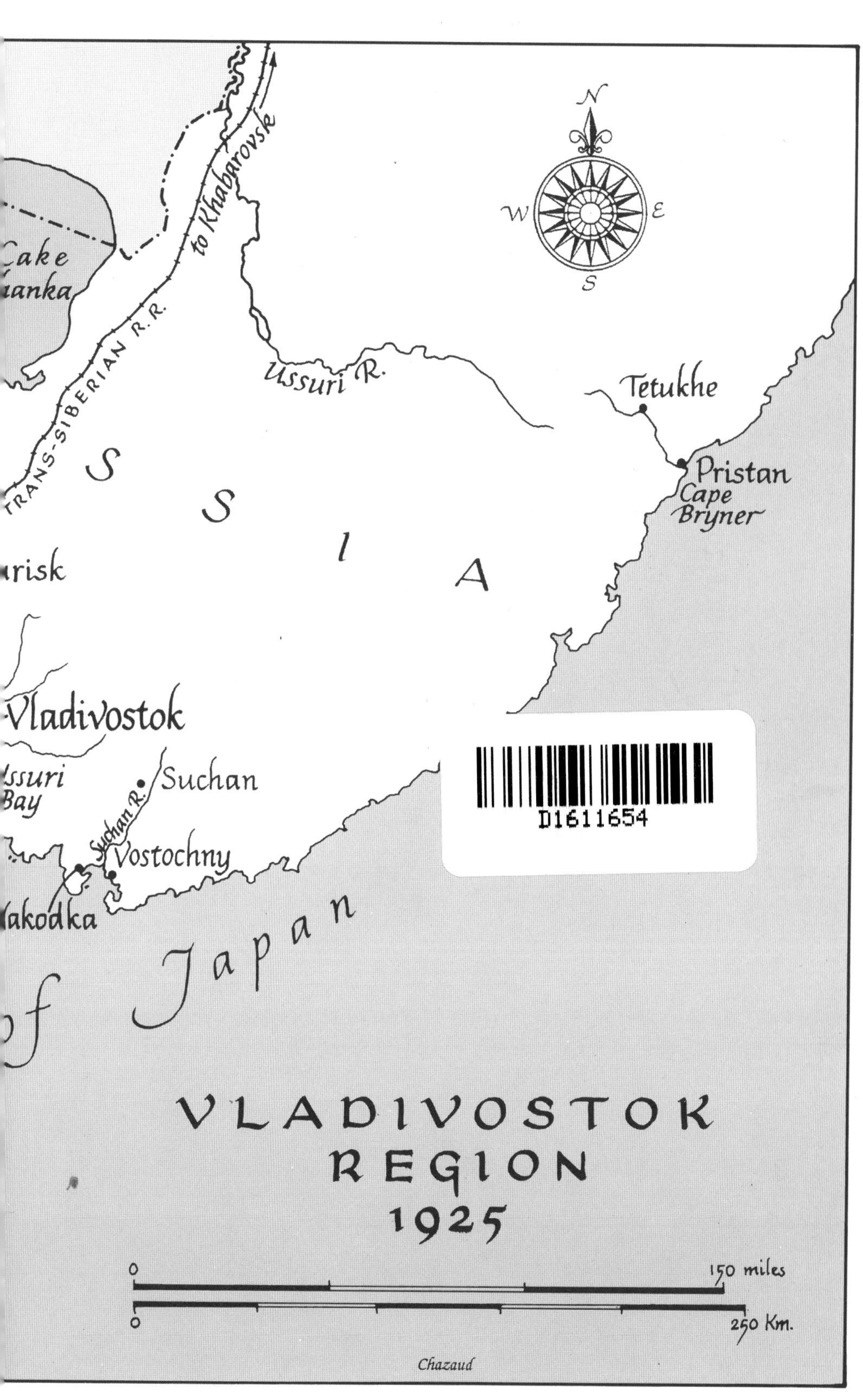

N
W
E
S
to Khabarovsk
TRANS-SIBERIAN R.R.
Ussuri R.
Tetukhe
Pristan
Cape Bryner
S
S
I
A
Vladivostok
Suchan
Suchan R.
Vostochny
Japan
VLADIVOSTOK
REGION
1925
0
150 miles
0
250 Km.
Chazaud

EMPIRE &
ODYSSEY

Jules (Juli Ivanovitch) 1849–1920

Boris (Boris Julievitch) 1889–1948

Yul (Yuli Borisovitch) 1920–1985

Rock (Yuli Yulievitch) 1946–

EMPIRE & ODYSSEY

The Brynners in Far East Russia and Beyond

ROCK BRYNNER

STEERFORTH PRESS
HANOVER, NEW HAMPSHIRE

Library of Congress Cataloging-in-Publication Data

Brynner, Rock, 1946–
Empire & odyssey : the Brynners in Far East Russia and beyond / Rock Brynner. — 1st ed.
p. cm.
Includes bibliographical references and index.
ISBN 1-58642-102-6 (alk. paper)
1. Brynner family. 2. Bryner, Julius Josef, 1849–1920. 3. Bryner, Boris Julievitch, 1889–1948. 4. Brynner, Yul, 1920–1985. 5. Brynner, Rock, 1946– 6. Industrialists — Russia — Vladivostok — Biography. 7. Actors — United States — Biography. 8. Russia — History — Nicholas II, 1894–1917. I. Title: Empire and odyssey. II. Title.

CT1217.B79B79 2006
929'.20973–dc22

2005036507

Book design by Peter Holm, Sterling Hill Productions

FIRST EDITION

To Olya Vigovskaya
and all my friends in Vladivostok

Contents

Acknowledgments

Alexander Doluda first invited me to Vladivostok, and but for his persistence this story would never have been told; I owe him my never-ending gratitude. Equally, Public Affairs Officer Tara Rougle at the U.S. Consulate in Vladivostok was determined to bring me to Far East Russia as part of the State Department's Speakers Tour Program and, together with Consul General Pamela Spratlen, went to great lengths to make my trip there as valuable as possible.

V. V. Veeder, Queen's Counsel of King's College, University of London, has spent years studying Boris Bryner and the mines at Tetukhe. His generosity with his research and advice has been invaluable, along with the assistance of Sonia Melnikova. As well, Bella Pak and her father, Professor Boris Pak, respected specialists in Russo-Korean history, provided two unique documents relating to Jules Bryner's business in Korea that they found in their extensive research at the State Archives in Moscow. Birgitta Ingemanson, who teaches Russian Culture and Film at Washington State University, provided me with her valuable writings on early Vladivostok, and took time to redact my manuscript. So did the preeminent specialist of the Russian Far East, Professor John J. Stephan, to whom I am deeply indebted.

The interpreters and translators who made my research, lectures, and speeches in Russia possible include Professor Evgenia Terekhova, Valery Osavlyuk, and Evgenia Mironets in Vladivostok; in Moscow, Natasha Fedorova of the Moscow Art Theatre School and my editor at Eksmo, Max Nemtsov. They are all good friends. In St. Petersburg, I received assistance from many at Smolny College, St. Petersburg University, starting with Professor Gennady Shkliarevsky (also of Bard College), Director Valery Monakhov, and his assistants Philip Fedchin and Elena Nasybulina. Olga Voronina, then with the U.S. Consulate, welcomed me warmly to St. Petersburg and helped coordinate my lecture at the American Corner, Mayakovsky Library. Jeanna Polyarnaya, director of the St. Petersburg Mining Institute Museum, was of great assistance, as was translator and guide Kirill Fedorov.

Paul Rodzianko has provided enormous assistance, including an introduction to Ludmilla and Hodson Thornber; together, they made my second lecture tour in Russia possible. My third and fourth tours were sponsored by the Vladivostok International Film Festival with the kind assistance of Larisa Belobrova and her husband, Sergei Darkin, governor of the Primorye Region. The Arsenyev Museum in Vladivostok has an extensive archive of Bryner photographs; its director, Natalya Pankreateva, and scholar Iraida Klimenko have both been enormously helpful. Vladimir Khmel, of the Primorye Business Initiative Association, shared wonderful historic photographs, as well as his yacht for traveling to Sidemy. Vasily Usoltsev, the chief of Dalpolymetall and member of the regional Duma, made it possible for me to visit the Bryner mines at Tetukhe.

Elena Reznitchenko, my personal representative in Vladivostok, has devoted much time to locating historians and translating documents; her help has been crucial. Through Elena, I have had assistance with the Uspensky Cathedral's registry from Tatiyana Kushnareva. As well, local historians Professor Maria Lebedko and Nelli Mis have made valuable contributions.

From Australia, Catherine Bryner, daughter of Boris, was especially helpful in offering eyewitness accounts of the life she and her mother led with my grandfather.

In the United States, my dear friends Peggy Troupin and Carol Anschuetz provided fluid and meticulous translations of key documents cited here. My sister, Victoria Brynner Sullivan, contributed her time and effort with the reproduction of many of the photographs. I am grateful for permission to use those photographs; in a few cases I have not been able to identify the photographer.

My special thanks to Chip Fleischer of Steerforth Press for understanding my intentions, and to Kristin Sperber, Peter Holm, and Bronwyn Becker for helping me to realize them.

We shall not cease from exploration
And the end of all our exploring
Will be to arrive where we started
And know the place for the first time.

— T. S. Eliot, *Four Quartets*

Introduction

> History is neither to be considered as a formless structure, due exclusively to the achievements of individual agents, nor as . . . the work of some superior force variously known as Fate, Chance, Fortune, God. Both these views, the materialistic and the transcendental, must be rejected in favor of the rational. Individuality is the concretion of universality, and every individual action is at the same time superindividual.
>
> —Samuel Beckett, "Dante, Bruno, Vico, Joyce" (1929)

This work began with an invitation I received in June 2003 at my hilltop home in upstate New York, asking me to come to Vladivostok in Far East Russia. The message concluded with these words: "In Russian, your name, Rock, means 'Destiny,' and it is your destiny to come to Vladivostok."

I was intrigued, of course, because Vladivostok is where my father, Yul, and grandfather, Boris, were born; it is also the city that Jules Bryner, my great-grandfather, helped to build as he established his own empire in the Far East just at the twilight of the Russian Empire. Since childhood I had assumed that I would never see Vladivostok; for most descendants of the Russian diaspora, visiting the Old Country behind the Iron Curtain was never an option. Besides, one was told, after Stalin, you wouldn't care to: not after the very souls of its towns had been extinguished by totalitarian terror and then expunged from history, removed from the map, or renamed. For many emigrants, "the Old Country" was not a place at all, but a long-gone era that lived on only as a frame of mind.

I did not reply to the invitation at first. As a history professor, I didn't see how I could reconcile my lecture schedule with the travel plans that were proposed. And I was still badly wounded by the deceit and disregard of a woman who had moved through my life like bad weather; I was still too haunted by pain to put on a happy face and travel through fifteen times zones to the other side of the world. But then another invitation arrived, and another, until I finally replied with the one word required to launch the adventure that led to this book: "Yes."

With that, I was carried away by events that have transformed my life and restored my soul. Ever since, it seems I have been in the thrall of forces that I could not even identify, and that have guided me in a benign and generous way through the story of my family. I gradually came to understand that these were forces of history and that their impact was both a matter-of-fact phenomenon *and* a spiritual experience; that is, belonging in the realm of the human spirit. The only way I know how to untangle these historical forces and identify them is by writing this book. As it happens, I am a historian and a writer with the experience for the job.

As a historian, I reject the notion of Destiny because it presumes that all the choices before us have already been made, and that individuals are helpless pawns, preordained to play out their scripted roles in some great, unfathomable chess game. Nor do I believe for a moment that genetics is destiny. Human history, in my view, is at least partly the result of individual and collective free will, and while that may be influenced by ideologies, ambitions, and trends, events are not predestined, because the future has not yet been written. Nevertheless, I felt almost *compelled* to travel to Far East Russia, not by Destiny, but by curiosity. And once I arrived, I did feel a powerful affinity for Vladivostok, but that may be because I was welcomed so warmly that anyone in my shoes would have felt the same.

As the son of an American-born mother and a Russian-born father, it seemed as if my childhood embodied the Cold War: the place my father and his family came from was the mortal enemy of the place that *I* came from. I could not make sense of that fact. I was not so much at war with myself (come to think of it, I was, but those battles came on other fronts) as I was keenly aware, from a young age, of the distinction between Russia and the Union of Soviet Socialist Republics. I knew by the age of six that Russian culture was magnificent and soulful when I was transfixed by Prokofiev's *Peter and the Wolf*, and later by Tchaikovsky's First Piano Concerto. I also understood that Soviet authorities were soulless totalitarian monsters who slaughtered their citizens in labor camps as surely as Hitler's henchmen did, by different means and wearing different uniforms. So I grew up loving the many Russians I knew, while despising the Soviet Union the way all other American kids did in the 1950s. But over the next decade the reality of Mutually Assured Destruction gave such chauvinism a hollow, baleful quality. Who, after all, is the winner when, after the war, the survivors envy the dead?

For most of my adulthood, I kept my Russian heritage stored in the attic, as it were: it simply wasn't a part of my daily life or my professional interests. Only after the Soviet regime ended in 1991 had it become possible to visit, and I had my hands full then with other undertakings.

Today, thanks to my five visits to Vladivostok and extensive research, Russia has become part of my daily life *and* my professional work, as the Russian and the American within me are becoming reconciled.

The worldwide epic of the Brynners consists of four successive lives that make up a single story, whose themes and leitmotifs provide a chronicle of their times and, in so doing, provide a silhouette of modern Russian history, with which it is closely entwined. Each of these men, including myself, was given the same name at birth (though, to be precise, my grandfather had only the patronymic middle name, "Julievitch").

Of course, for my father's millions of fans, there will forever be only one Yul Brynner. His overpowering presence on stage and screen, his starlight, has naturally outshone the other members of the family, including his father, who endured the Russian Revolution, and his grandfather, who created jobs for hundreds of thousands of working men, though his accomplishments were consigned to obilivion by the Communist regime. But Yul's contribution to world culture was to become the most exotic movie star of all time, a man whose origins could never be ascertained. With this persona he brought forth a new style of acting born, like himself, in Russia.

Next to my forefathers' accomplishments, my own seem meager indeed, despite my eclectic assortment of adventures. Yet many of their achievements would never be recognized had I not acquired the skills and the passion to research and write this book. Even Yul's most righteous work, for the United Nations, has gone largely unnoted. I did not inherit Jules' vast, industrial vision, or Boris's courage in the face of totalitarian dictatorship, or Yul's irresistible charm and heroic strength. The heritage I did receive from them, apparently, was a passionate curiosity, and a yearning to take a big bite out of life and let the juices run down my chin.

It fell to me to complete our family's odyssey by returning to Vladivostok. It is a city whose population reached three-quarters of a million people, founded by a handful of men, including my great-grandfather, whose name is on my birth certificate. And it also fell to me to research our collective saga: it is only because this is my family's story that I have been offered documents and photographs that other historians could not have unearthed. That is why I felt obliged to chronicle my family's achievements in Russia and beyond, lest this story go untold.

Visiting my father's birthplace almost twenty years after his death did seem like a return of sorts, as well as a balm, for myself and for others: this reconstruction of the Bryner empire and odyssey has become important for many of my friends in Russia, from Vladivostok to St. Petersburg. Some have spent many hours helping to uncover documents and facts, out of the goodness of their hearts. But they had also lived for decades with the *need* to recall the region's pre-Soviet culture, and to take pride in having kept that history alive in their families, secretly, even as Stalin did his worst to amputate modern Russia from its history. By relaying that culture to me, they have fulfilled an unspoken commitment to their own ancestors.

It is altogether fitting that I should begin writing this history here, at the Hotel Versailles on Svetlanskaya Street in Vladivostok, where I am presently staying. In 1921, not long after Yul was born around the corner, this hotel was headquarters for the fearsome Cossack leader Ataman Semyonov, the last self-proclaimed "Supreme Ruler of Russia," during the bitter resistance to final Communist rule.

I would like to ask a favor of the reader: to withhold judgment of the individuals you will soon come to know. It is my experience that as soon as we begin judging people we stop understanding them. Only with a generous spirit can we see the world through others' eyes. I, too, will try to keep this counsel and present the clear-eyed truth about these four lives and the many others that touched them. While pointing out the galaxies of facts that I have culled, I will leave it to readers to connect these dots of light and discern whatever constellations they will.

With that, I shall start where our odyssey began, in Switzerland. . . .

NOTES ON SPELLING

"Jules Bryner" and "Yul Brynner" are the same name spelled differently: in Russian it is "Юлий Бринер" or "Juli." My great-grandfather's full Swiss given name was "Julius," as in Caesar, and pronounced "Yulius." In writing, the two spellings have been transliterated differently, first into the Cyrillic alphabet (Swiss-German to Russian), and then from Cyrillic back to the roman alphabet.

When writing about Jules and Boris, I use the spelling "Bryner" as they themselves did, while for Yul and myself, I use "Brynner." When referring to the family collectively, as in the title of this book, I have used "Brynners": present usage encompasses the past, not vice versa. My father certainly made this spelling more familiar, and it is the name I was born to.

In the text, I have used the system of Cyrillic transliteration I am most comfortable with: apostrophes denoting hard and soft signs are omitted; ***в*** is represented by *v; ii, ia, io, iu* and *e* are written *y, ya, yo, yu*, and *ye*. Familiar names, like Nicholas, have been anglicized.

Calendar dates follow the conventional Western calendar except where noted.

The Bryner Family

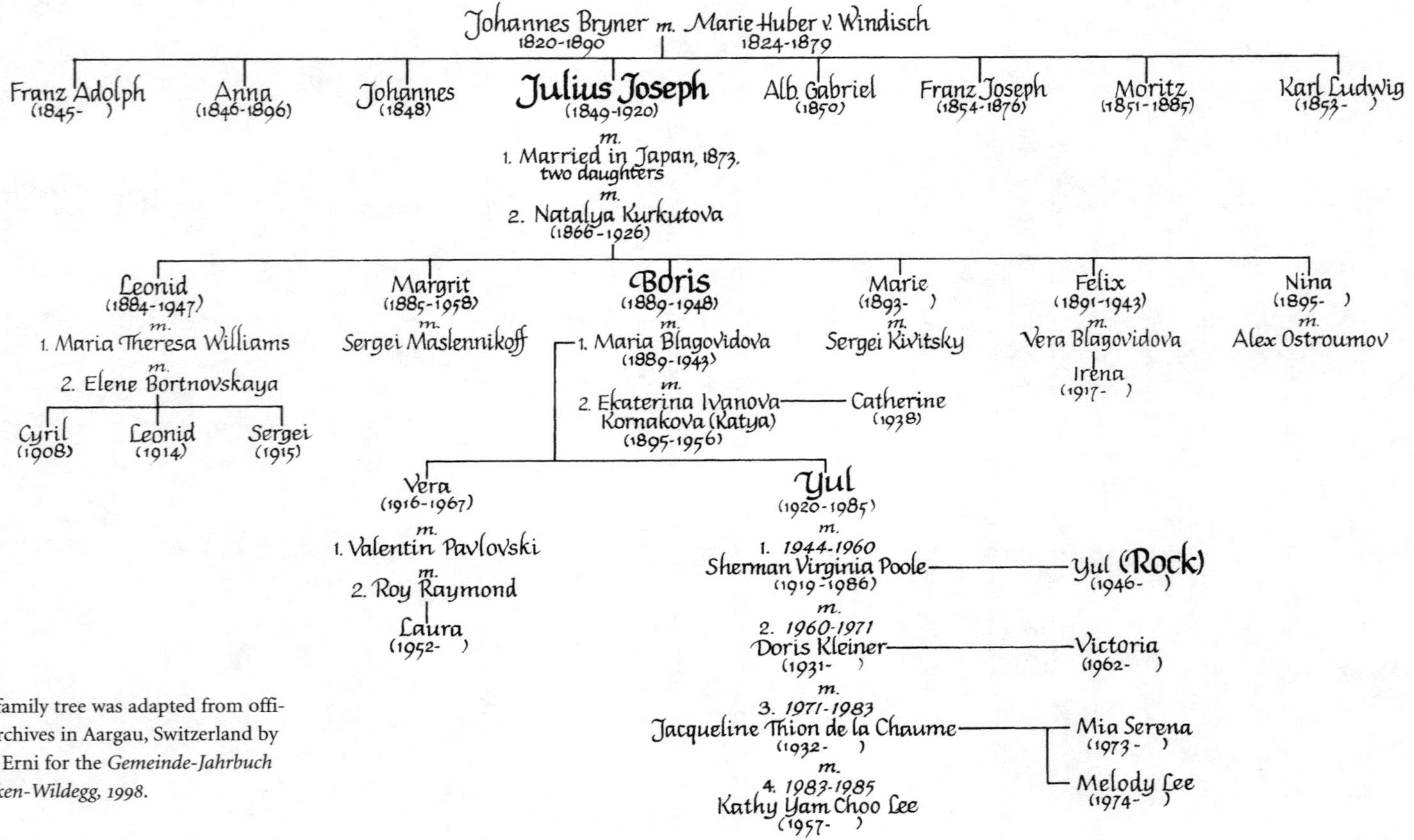

Johannes Bryner m. Marie Huber v. Windisch
1820-1890 1824-1879

Franz Adolph (1845-)

Anna (1846-1896)

Johannes (1848)

Julius Joseph (1849-1920)
m.
1. Married in Japan, 1873, two daughters
m.
2. Natalya Kurkutova (1866-1926)

Alb. Gabriel (1850)

Franz Joseph (1854-1876)

Moritz (1851-1885)

Karl Ludwig (1853-)

Leonid (1884-1947)
m.
1. Maria Theresa Williams
m.
2. Elene Bortnovskaya

Cyril (1908)

Leonid (1914)

Sergei (1915)

Margrit (1885-1958)
m.
Sergei Maslennikoff

Boris (1889-1948)
m.
1. Maria Blagovidova (1889-1943)
m.
2. Ekaterina Ivanova Kornakova (Katya) (1895-1956) — Catherine (1938)

Marie (1893-)
m.
Sergei Kivitsky

Felix (1891-1943)
m.
Vera Blagovidova

Irena (1917-)

Nina (1895-)
m.
Alex Ostroumov

Vera (1916-1967)
m.
1. Valentin Pavlovski
m.
2. Roy Raymond

Laura (1952-)

Yul (1920-1985)
m.
1. *1944-1960* Sherman Virginia Poole (1919-1986) — Yul (**Rock**) (1946-)
m.
2. *1960-1971* Doris Kleiner (1931-) — Victoria (1962-)
m.
3. *1971-1983* Jacqueline Thion de la Chaume (1932-) — Mia Serena (1973-); Melody Lee (1974-)
m.
4. *1983-1985* Kathy Yam Choo Lee (1957-)

This family tree was adapted from official archives in Aargau, Switzerland by Hans Erni for the *Gemeinde-Jahrbuch Möriken-Wildegg, 1998.*

PART ONE
JULES BRYNER

I can say with good conscience that I have never met an individual who is more observant or more curious about practical matters.

— Secret Agent Pokotilov to Finance Minister Sergei Witte (1896)

Julius Josef Bryner was born in 1849 in the village of La-Roche-sur-Foron, thirty miles southeast of Geneva, Switzerland. He was the fourth child of Johannes Bryner, a professional spinner and weaver, and his twenty-five-year-old wife, the former Marie Huber von Windisch. Although they had been in the Geneva region for a time, the Bryners were citizens of Möriken-Wildegg, a village northwest of Zurich, where they soon returned. The Bryners were Protestants, like most families in the surrounding canton of Aargau, though their doctrine probably owed more to the German Martin Luther than to Switzerland's own Jean Calvin or Ulrich Zwingli. The Bryner home in Möriken-Wildegg was a spacious two-story thatched farmhouse, but barely large enough for Johannes's eight offspring, including four that followed "Jules"; he was always known in the family by the French variant of his name.

Jules was born during the first year of the modern nation of Switzerland, in which the centralized New Federal State united the twenty-two previously independent cantons. The country had long been divided between its liberal, Protestant regions and its conservative, Catholic districts, but at the end of the Sonderbund War, the Federal State was founded upon a constitution so ideologically progressive that it helped spark revolutions in Vienna, Venice, Berlin, Milan, and finally France.

The year Jules was born, His Imperial Majesty Tsar Nicholas I, Autocrat of All the Russias, was preparing to conquer the Ottoman Empire and gain control of Constantinople's Golden Horn, the waterway that would give Russia access to the Mediterranean for the first time in its eight-hundred-year history, vastly enhancing its power throughout Europe and the world. But Russia's Holy Alliance with Austria collapsed, and in 1855, Britain, France, and Austria defeated Russia in the Crimean War. By then Tsar Alexander II had succeeded Nicholas I upon the Romanov throne.

Now the only direction for Russia to advance its restless, aggressive imperialism was eastward, where the contest was on for colonial domination of the Far East. China in that era was a helpless, pitiful giant from which pieces were being carved off: by Britain (in Shanghai and Hong Kong); France (in Laos, Cambodia, and Indochina); and Japan (in Manchuria and Korea). Soon Russia, through a treaty with China, would secure a new naval outpost on the Pacific, well to the south of its frozen ports in Kamchatka and Sakhalin. Even the name given to this navy base projected Russian strength: "Ruler of the East," or "Vladivostok."

When he was fourteen years old, Jules struck out from Möriken-Wildegg to make his way in the world. This is not as surprising as it may seem. Apprenticeship provided a boy his age with the opportunity to learn a craft or a trade while relieving his family of his upkeep. But it is also clear from the choices Jules made over the next few years, and over his lifetime, that he was both diligent and extremely adventurous in spirit. He was quick to master new skills, especially languages, and swiftly adapted to the unfamiliar circumstances that his curious nature sought out.

Growing up in the 1850s, Jules knew that one of the most famous men in the world, Johann Sutter, had set out from a small town just near Möriken-Wildegg, and that, in the very year that Jules was born, Sutter's Mills in far-off California became the center of the greatest gold rush in history, drawing ambitious prospectors from all across the globe. Whether or not Jules was inspired by Sutter's story, he had to be well aware of his compatriot's adventures and gold mines, and knew beyond doubt that such rewards could come to those who dared to seek them. Jules probably was not aware that Sutter later lost everything he had earned on his adventure.

As a young teenager, Jules received an internship with the Danzas Company in Zurich, a shipping agency where his uncle Moritz Bryner worked. And through this agency he learned of opportunities on the high seas for young men like himself. By the time he was sixteen, Jules was earning his way as galley boy on a privateer that sailed out of the Mediterranean, bound for the Far East.

The ships that plied the trade routes in the 1860s were still sailing craft, two- or three-masted brigantines and well-armed schooners, sloops, and corvettes with cannon belowdecks. Steam-powered paddlewheels were soon added to push the sailing ships forward when the winds betrayed them, but most of the shipping that circled the globe was still powered by sail, barely evolved from the bellying canvas that propelled the Greeks three thousand years before. Aboard his privateer, Jules discovered a passion for the sea that lasted his whole life. Switzerland, of course, is landlocked; when Jules discovered how attached he was to the bays and oceans of the world and the style of life they entailed, he must have known that he would never again make his home in the shadow of the Alps.

During the next few months, as the winds carried the craft eastward, Jules was periodically locked in the galley, "for his own safety," he was told by the crew. On these occasions, as their ship approached others and tied up alongside them, he heard fierce scuffles and cries on deck, sometimes lasting for hours. His crew were experienced buccaneers who grazed upon the sea lanes, collecting all the bounties traveling westward, which could easily be plundered from the ships they overpowered and boarded. Silk, mahogany, tea, opium, and sometimes even gold and gems were the treasures to be had for the taking by these skimmers of the sea. Only a few of the opium traders were protected by fast-running clippers that fired thirteen-inch shells from mounted guns.

When it dawned upon Jules that he was himself a brigand, feeding the crew of a pirate ship that forcibly seized cargo, the teenager also realized his shipmates would brand him a turncoat if he left without warning and without a plan. He would have to disembark in a large city where he could find work and protection.

Since the 1840s, the city of Shanghai had been under the jurisdiction of the British throne, which needed a deep-water mercantile port in the region. Some one hundred thousand pounds of tea passed through the city each year, along with fifty thousand bales of silk and the thirty thousand chests of opium brought down from the neighboring mountains and stored in the hulls moored along the Bund, the embankment in the heart of the city. Once gaslights were installed, the tireless business district was alive with rickshaws and clatter day and night. Because Shanghai was the only deep-water port in the north, virtually all Chinese-European shipping had to pass through the Bund, where goods were transferred from river junks to three-masted schooners. The first steamers were also plying their way along the nearby Yangtze River, and trade figures were poised to skyrocket.

When the seventeen-year-old Jules Bryner disembarked in Shanghai in the mid-1860s, the Taiping Rebellion had been suppressed, and the exodus of Chinese refugees left thousands of jobs and homes available. Jules had already learned some Mandarin, and quickly found work in the office of a silk merchant who obtained raw silk locally to sell overseas. Over the next few years, the Swiss youth became very knowledgeable about silk — perhaps because his father was a cloth spinner and weaver — as well as trade generally throughout the region. While running errands, he developed a workable fluency in different Chinese dialects, and before long he had also learned how to run the company. He added efficiency to what had been a lackadaisical operation, and brought an attention to detail that was his lifelong hallmark. Most of all, he could conduct business with English, French, and German customers of the Chinese company that employed him.

For British residents who made up the majority of the three thousand foreign settlers in a city of four hundred thousand, Shanghai was a little spot of England, re-created with a splash of colonial whimsy. Wherever Englishmen go, it was said, they take their church and their racetrack; true to form, by the 1860s the city had five Christian churches and three racetracks. The city also boasted the Royal Asiatic Society, as well as libraries, amateur theater groups, a Masonic Lodge, and, of course, the exclusive, newly built Shanghai Club. In later decades Shanghai became known as the "Paris of the Far East," the first of many Asian cities to claim that title and the only one to earn it; but when Jules worked there in the 1860s, Shanghai culture was largely the British Raj with chow mein instead of curry. Not surprisingly, the Chinese population became increasingly hostile to these Anglo-Saxon intruders, the well-meaning no less than the rapacious: in 1869 Prince Kung, in Peking, declared to British Consul Sir Rutherford Alcock, "Take away your opium and your missionaries, and you will be welcome."

It was in this very cosmopolitan atmosphere that Jules groomed himself for management, acquiring the habits and manners of an international *homme d'affaires*, learning the niceties of society among British colonials and how to appear interested in cricket. Meanwhile he concentrated upon studying the businesses of the Far East and how they could cooperate to develop the region.

On behalf of his employer, he also became engaged in local English political machinations concerning two issues that would directly improve regional shipping: dredging the mouth of the Yangtze River, and building the first railroad in China, from Shanghai to Woosung. For both these efforts, a group of foreign merchants, mostly English and American, had formed a company. There was much official and public opposition to the plan for a railroad, but the merchants were permitted to construct a tramway; instead, they used wide-gauge locomotive rails and presented the Chinese with a *fait accompli*. All this, Jules took in.

Tensions were rising between Chinese residents and foreigners in the Shanghai settlement by the beginning of the 1870s. In the turbulent years to come, the restive Chinese under foreign rule began a series of riots culminating in the Boxer Rebellion in 1900, and its unambiguous motto: PRESERVE THE DYNASTY, EXTERMINATE THE FOREIGNERS.

Jules' Chinese employers periodically dispatched him to Yokohama, Japan, to deal directly with customers. Shanghai had thus far rejected any telegraph connection because of popular concern that telegraph poles would disturb the feng shui of the region. During a business trip to Yokohama, where raw silk from Shanghai was dyed and then exported, Jules became acquainted with an elderly English gentleman who ran a one-man shipping agency throughout the Pacific region, and who soon invited Jules to become his assistant and protégé. Perhaps because of the lack of opportunity to advance within his Chinese-owned company, and perhaps because of the growing threat to foreigners, Jules left Shanghai behind and followed the trail of silk to Yokohama, the largest port in Japan.

Less than twenty years earlier, Commodore Matthew Perry had come ashore near Yokohama carrying a letter from the president of the United

States, Millard Fillmore, to the new mikado, Mutsuhito (1852–1912), demanding that Japan engage in foreign trade. Perry then departed for a year, obligingly, to give the mikado time to consider his options. When Perry returned in 1854, Japan signed the Treaty of Kanagawa, opening its doors for the first time to international commerce. Five years later the modern port of Yokohama was inaugurated.

A decade later, Jules settled there, having been taken under the wing of the English shipping agent. Jules was in his early twenties. He had been studying Japanese before he arrived, and soon the Swiss lad who could negotiate in French, German, English, Mandarin, and Japanese, all in the course of a morning, was put in charge of the agency's meetings and correspondence.

A shipping agency did not own ships; it leased them (or space upon them) according to the best contracts that could be obtained to transport cargo efficiently. It was easy enough to arrange for large items to travel from one place to another, but very challenging to make that arrangement profitable — especially with privateers lurking along the coastline, as Jules knew all too well.

An established young businessman, Jules was by now well acquainted with the principal powers in the region, which he approached with a detached, empirical focus that gave him a reputation as a problem solver. He came up with creative new solutions to chafing old problems in the shipping business: maximizing capacity, loading and unloading, transporting goods efficiently by land, and navigating rampant corruption among dock officials. A few months after arriving in Japan, Jules fell in love with a young woman to whom he was introduced, and the following year they had a daughter, and before too long a second daughter. Jules' Japanese descendants still live near Yokohama today, where his grandson, Etoh Naoasuke, became a successful paper manufacturer after World War II.

In the 1870s, Jules' English patron passed away, leaving the ongoing business contracts — which *were* the business, along with a few assets — to his young Swiss associate. Still in his mid-twenties, Jules now had his own small, successful shipping agency.

Exactly why Jules then chose to leave his family in Yokohama and move the headquarters of his shipping business to a Russian frontier village remains unanswered, but for his business there were several benefits. He had already witnessed the infancy of Shanghai, and of Yokohama; the Russian port of Vladivostok offered an opportunity to help develop a modern city. That would mean railroads, telegraphs, and buildings, and Jules had solid, established banking relationships by this time. And there were significant tax advantages to relocating his headquarters. But the greatest attraction may have been that Russia was a European country that stretched, uninterrupted, more than five thousand miles to the Imperial capital of St. Petersburg in the west. And from the growth of railroads around the world — especially in the western United States and Canada — Jules must have figured that someday he would be able to ride to Europe from the new Russian port.

The sea gave birth to Vladivostok.

The new naval outpost was established under the benign reign of Tsar Alexander II, at about the time that he emancipated millions of serfs across Russia in 1861. The tsar and his ministers intended to move a large part of the Russian population eastward, beyond Siberia to the coastal regions of Ussurisk and Amur ("Love"), because they wanted to demonstrate to the other powers in the Far East that Russia was fully committed to developing the region. The governor-general of East Siberia, Nikolai Muraviev (later Count of Amur), had himself explored Peter the Great Bay aboard his U.S.-built corvette, the *America*, a swift, three-masted, steam-driven paddle-wheeler. By signing the treaties of Aigun and Peking with China, Muraviev had assured Russian control of the maritime region known as Primorye.

The first Russian sailors and officers arrived upon a transport schooner, the *Manchur*, and stationed themselves at the southern tip of a narrow, finger-shaped peninsula, twenty miles long, between Amur Bay and Ussuri Bay, with little more than a cow path to connect them to the mainland. The sailors discovered a natural harbor carved into the peninsula, a wide inlet that they named Golden Horn Bay (Золотой Рог), after the waterway in Constantinople that had eluded the tsar's forces five years earlier. Whether this name was bestowed as a tribute to imperial ambition or a mockery of its failure is still uncertain: it is such a small waterway that the name seems like deliberate hyperbole.

Small clusters of native people still lived at the edges of these bays, tribes of short, swarthy hunter-gatherers that ethnographers trace back to the Paleoasians and Tungus-Manchurians who predated the pyramids of Egypt. The Udege, Nanaïs (Goldi), Orochi, and smaller tribes had been almost eradicated by centuries of Chinese control, followed by the sweeping destruction of Genghis Khan and his Mongol tribes, but remnants of those cultures still existed in the communities that clung to the shores, producing unique and beautiful art and design, wearing clothes fashioned from cured fish-skins.

"Temüjin" was the name he was given when he was born in the Altai Mountains of Mongolia in 1162, but "Genghis Khan," meaning "universal ruler," was the title he adopted at the age of forty-two. His was the first empire to unite the Far East with Europe — a far greater empire than the Romans ever dreamed of — and it devoured most of China and southern Russia. Through the prodigious and relentless rape of women by himself and his hordes, a people known as the Buryat came to exist, described traditionally as "descendents of Genghis Khan." That notion was scoffed at as myth until very recently, when DNA mapping by genetic anthropologist Spencer Wells established this history as essentially correct. Khan himself kept a harem of five hundred women collected from all the lands he had conquered; he and his subordinates, many his own sons, deliberately fathered thousands of children from eastern Europe to the Pacific Ocean. Many of those children went on to rule the Far East as well, including his own grandson Kublai Khan, first emperor of the Yuan Dynasty in China.

Now a nation of tigers ruled the endless virgin timberland known as the *taiga* (pronounced "ta-ee-GA"): the Siberian tiger, the unchallenged champion of the food chain, is the largest feline on earth, measuring as much as thirteen feet; each one consumes a hundred pounds of flesh every night. Thousands of Siberian tigers stalked the dense forests surrounding Amur Bay, prowling hungrily among the sailors' barracks after dark and dragging off livestock. Each night there were gunshots around the naval post, and each morning the anxious residents counted up the carnivores they'd seen or heard coming down from the crest they called Tiger Hill.

A Russian visitor to the base described the forlorn scene in the first year:

> We saw the officers' house on the northern shore [and] a wooden barrack where the crew of forty-eight men lived. Behind the barrack were a kitchen and an animal farm on the steep bank of a ravine. A tiny brook ran at the bottom of the ravine, where they drew fresh water. North of the barrack a

> church had just been started. . . . There was much drinking and abuse among the soldiers. Most of them had been transferred from army regiments for misbehavior.

The first civilian, Yakov Semyonov, settled there the following year, when the commanding naval officer granted him land on which to build a home and graze livestock. Semyonov, at thirty, was a merchant of the third guild — the lowest order of government-endorsed merchants — who traded in sea kale, which was abundant in the Amur and Ussuri bays. A large, portly man with a Vandyke beard and solemn demeanor, Semyonov may have been lured there by an edict approved by both the finance and the foreign ministries, which, in a rare moment of unanimity, had declared Vladivostok a *porto franco,* or duty-free port, allowing businesses established there to conduct trade without any taxation whatsoever. Soon enough, Semyonov's business flourished. As the city's first honorary resident, he would remain a respected figure there for the next half century and rise to "merchant of the first guild," which meant that throughout Russia his signature was as good as a check.

The early structures in the settlement were all wooden, little more than docks, boat sheds, and log cabins, while the sailors gradually dug wells and cleared land for planting with help recruited from Chinese and Korean camp followers, male and female, who built mud homes for themselves. Before long there was an infirmary, and in 1863 the first child was born in Vladivostok. Soon after, the main street in the village was named Amerikanskaya Street, in honor of Muraviev's ship. Before long, crew members of the schooner *Aleut* cleared a passage perpendicular to Amerikanskaya Street; the new road was called Aleutskaya Street.

In the next few years the first trickle of refugees from the overpopulated cities and farms in western Russia drifted eastward over makeshift roads and frozen tundra to the more tolerable climate along the Siberian maritime, where the ocean reduced the chill. Vladivostok was not, however, a warm-water port, as the Imperial government had hoped: in winter, the port was partially frozen and would require ice-breaking ships that hadn't been designed yet to allow traffic in and out.

In 1864, while the rude shantytown was under threat of a massive Chinese invasion, two dapper German businessmen arrived. Gustav Kunst and Gustav Albers had met in China, though both were from Hamburg; together they had come to this outpost to open a major trading house. Before leaving Europe, each had established extensive credit agreements with different companies that supported their venture, while Deutsche Bank provided them with capital. In time "Kunst and Albers" became what today would be called a department store, selling a wide variety of goods and products from Asia and Europe. Initially they operated out of a small wooden cottage, but the subsequent growth of their business reflected the rising good fortune of the region.

As more sailors and fisherman arrived, along with many Korean and Chinese workers who provided cheap labor, something resembling a town began to arise. By 1867, passing geographer Nikolai Przhevalsky wrote that he saw "about 50 public and private houses and two dozen Chinese huts. The population, including the troops but excluding the Chinese, amounts to 500 people. Private houses are largely owned by retired servicemen who settled here and by four merchants who keep shops but trade mainly in sea-kale." There were also barracks, warehouses, and a shipyard.

The first city council was formed in 1869 and chose as its leader Yakov Semyonov, the kale merchant. Under his chairmanship, and with the energy and European connections of the German merchants, the Danish Great Northern Telegraph Company was persuaded to connect Vladivostok by cable to Shanghai, and by underwater cable to Nagasaki. This innovation probably convinced the Imperial navy to move its Pacific Command from Nikolaevsk to Vladivostok. It also increased Kunst and Albers' trade with silk merchants, whose orders came through a shipping agency in Yokohama owned by another German-speaking European, Jules Bryner.

Jules Bryner first came to Vladivostok in the mid-1870s, an energetic and self-assured twenty-five year old. A well-built man of short stature — no more than five and a half feet — he had straight, neatly-parted dark hair and a full mustache. He was meticulous in manner, dress, and planning: a Swiss perfectionist, by all accounts, and driven by adventurous curiosity.

What he looked for, every direction he turned, was a fresh opportunity for growth, and where he saw potential, he took risks. In the best sense, he was a speculator; and though an ambitious man, his ambitions were well attuned to the social needs he saw around him. Whether this was a characteristic he brought from Switzerland, or something he had acquired as a young businessman, Jules always sought enterprises that would be assets to the community he was helping to establish. But it was clear to Jules from the start that, to help build a modern city in these wilds, he would have to build a business empire.

This well-experienced Swiss traveler arrived among a collection of wood shacks set along a sleepy harbor that received only two dozen vessels a year. Although he did not yet speak Russian, he learned about the region quickly from Gustav Albers (Kunst had returned to Germany to coordinate the export end of their burgeoning business from there) and his other partner, Adolph Dattan. Jules knew from the start that a thriving new community would make an ideal port for his shipping company, and would offer an opportunity to put into action all he had learned about developing a city. The *porto franco* status of Vladivostok would free him of substantial tariffs in Japan, giving him a significant advantage over his competitors, but to qualify he would have to relocate his headquarters — and himself. Yet this frontier town was certainly no place to bring up his Japanese-born daughters. Jules left his family behind in Yokohama. At first he made frequent trips back to Japan, and he continued to support his family there long after he resettled in the new Russian port.

The handful of fascinating and determined Europeans who had already come to Vladivostok — and the impressive business and banking connections they had — helped persuade Jules that this was where his shipping headquarters had to be. The first mayor of the city, M. K. Fedorov, was elected in 1875 by the 165 members of the city council, and in subsequent discussions, all of the men agreed upon a central ambition: to build a thoroughly European city.

By no coincidence, this was precisely the ambition of the Imperial government. The argument for Russian hegemony over the East was best voiced by Prince Ukhtomsky, who wrote ardently: "We have nothing to conquer. All these people of various races feel themselves drawn to us. . . . this great and mysterious Orient is ready to become ours." It may be that the Imperial government's consistent misreading of Asian geopolitics had its origin in Prince Ukhtomsky's optimistic misrepresentations.

Ministers in Moscow still intended to populate the region with Russians, despite barely passable roads from Europe. Six months was considered a swift crossing then, owing to the absence of villages along most of the way; few of the millions of freed and displaced serfs were heading east. Northern Korea, just one hundred miles south of Vladivostok, was in dire economic straits, as was eastern China one hundred miles to the west; as a result, in 1877 four out of five residents of the city were new arrivals fleeing Korea or China. Clearly, it would require a deliberate effort to make Vladivostok a culturally European center.

In the mid-1870s discussions began in earnest in St. Petersburg about the feasibility of a railroad that would cross all of Russia. Earlier estimates of the technological difficulty and cost had been so daunting as to stifle the most ardent proponents for years to come. But looking at the inexorable development of railroads in Africa, the United States, and Canada, as well as the government's show of power in Vladivostok, Jules and the other city fathers must have reckoned that a railway directly linking the Far East to Europe was coming sooner or later.

In 1875, Jules made his first visit to Switzerland, seeking to establish strong business relations with European banks in Zurich (where he had apprenticed with a shipping company) in order to expand his shipping agency. His trip was something of a victory lap: staying at the city's most expensive hotel, the Baur au Lac, he presented a gift to the government of Aargau, with a note signed, "Julius Bryner from the Communities of Möriken and Japan." The boy who had left home at fourteen had become a very wealthy businessman at twenty-six.

What stimulated Jules to diversify his business interests throughout his career was the need to fill empty space on ships that he leased. The growing community of Vladivostok, for example, had to import shiploads of commodities and industrial materials regularly to survive, but since nothing except sea kale was being exported, Jules' ships were leaving Golden Horn Bay empty, effectively doubling the cost of shipping the imports. So he was well motivated to create businesses that would fill his ships' holds on return voyages to Yokohama, Shanghai, and Hong Kong.

Jules invited a local trader named Kuznetsov, a merchant of the third guild with whom he had done business, to become his partner in the shipping agency, thus allying himself with an established Russian businessman, and in 1880 they launched their new enterprise: Bryner, Kuznetsov and Co., proprietors of the Far East Shipping Company (FESCO). After consulting with Kunst and Albers, they chose a renowned Russian architect, Babintsev, to design a baroque, three-story stone office building among the unpainted, wooden structures. Jules had already secured long-term commercial tenants to share his prime location, including the Siberian Trade Bank, and he had his own apartment there for a time. Their building was the center of town, at the intersection of Aleutskaya and Svetlanskaya Street (formerly Amerikanskaya Street). From that intersection, the rest of the streets had been laid out in city blocks.

Two years later Kunst and Albers Trading House moved into its enormous new edifice down the street from Jules. Designed by a German architect named Junghändel, this vast three-story building was almost on a scale with Harrods in London, already famous by then. Kunst and Albers was (and still is today) an art nouveau structure with baroque decor harking back to Dresden in the time of Bach. Wotan, the Walkyrie, and other Germanic legends guard its facade. "It was an encyclopædic store," wrote a visitor in 1889, "where one could buy everything from a needle to a live tiger." Nowhere in all of Russia was there anything like Kunst and Albers, and its reputation enhanced that of its location. "The clerks were multilingual," wrote historian John J. Stephan, "and offered Swiss watches, German condiments, wine from Bordeaux, robes de chambre from Paris, and suits from Savile Row."

In 1883 the Russian Volunteer Fleet began delivering refugees — mostly former serfs who had collected in the port of Odessa on the Black Sea — aboard Dobroflot ships, and with that the population of the Far East took off. Soon there were seventy buildings and five hundred homes where some five thousand Europeans resided (with a ratio of five men to every woman), along with educational, medical, and charitable institutions.

Jules became close friends with another extraordinary European, an adventurer and a central personality among the early *intelligentsiya* of Far East Russia. Count Mikhail Ivanovich Yankovsky of Poland was a larger-than-life figure who transformed Jules Bryner's life. Charged with treason in the 1863 Polish uprising, Yankovsky had been captured, condemned to hard labor, and sent to exile in the Far East; five years later he was released in a general amnesty. Yankovsky, in partnership with a Swedish whaling captain from Finland named Fridolf Gek, laid claim to a peninsula of eight thousand acres, half a day's sail across Amur Bay from Vladivostok, which he named Sidemy, or "The Seat." There he began raising the rare spotted sika deer, whose antlers are highly valued in Chinese medicine as a remedy for impotence, and soon became very wealthy.

A tall, powerfully built man, handsome and serious with a full, broad mustache, Yankovsky went on to produce his own breed of Far East horse, larger and more powerful than those from Mongolia or Korea. In 1900 he was awarded a government contract to supply the Russian army in Vladivostok with its horses, and for that venture he sent his oldest son, Yuri, to study horse breeding in California. He also tended a successful plantation of wild ginseng, a precious commodity that could not be cultivated methodically in those days. Much later he started a mink farm, and then a barge business for hauling sand by tugboat to the city's beaches.

Along with all his other activities, Yankovsky spent decades cataloging flora and fauna, identifying more than one hundred new butterflies, of which seventeen varieties still bear his name, along with the swan *Cygnus jankovskii* and two other species of birds. He was as well an ardent conservationist who wrote passionately about the destruction of natural resources and the need to protect a wide variety of species — certainly a far-sighted concern in the nineteenth century.

But enemies surrounded Sidemy. All about the houses built by the Polish count and the Finnish skipper, Siberian panthers competed with Siberian tigers, but neither of them posed the greatest threat. Nor did the packs of

Mongolian wolves, though they were terrible enough: originating in Siberia, these were the largest wolves in the world and would have slaughtered a dozen of Yankovsky's deer every night (or goats, sheep, cows, or even a horse) had he not built and manned watchtowers and barriers. Even these, however, did not guarantee safety for the village that Yankovsky had established for the growing workforce in his private fiefdom where children and livestock were at particular risk, but attacks were a constant possibility for everyone.

The most dangerous predators were gangs of Chinese brigands known as the *hunghu'tze*, or Red Beards, the seeds of a bandit army that had spread throughout the taiga. In 1878, soon after purchasing the estate at Sidemy, Yankovsky and Gek returned one June afternoon from Vladivostok to find that the hunghu'tze had brutally slaughtered Gek's wife and children, along with his servants. Skipper Gek, distraught, returned to live on his whaling ship.

Jules Bryner had met Yankovsky and spent weekends at the enormous stone fortress that the Polish count had designed and constructed at Sidemy. In fact, he was already enchanted with the peninsula when Yankovsky offered to sell him Gek's section. Jules accepted. It was a uniquely beautiful spot, with a good pier and an ideal headland for a lighthouse to make the crossing from Vladivostok safer in the fog.

Together, Jules and Yankovsky launched a private war against the bandits for the safety of their homestead. One historian wrote, "As Yankovsky, Bryner, and Shevelev [another neighbor] worked together, they hired more men to help guard the land and tend the herd — men who came to be known as 'Yankovsky's subjects.' Yankovsky turned his 'subjects' into a private army, recruiting exclusively Koreans — whom he believed he could trust — to search out and destroy the Red Beards." They eventually ran all the bandit leaders to ground, "exterminating them," according to one account. In the next few years the count and his vigilantes continued to ride out on many nights, and soon the hunghu'tze no longer threatened the immediate region.

Jules had become impressed with the family, including Yankovsky's Russian wife, Olga; but it was Olga's cousin, Natalya Kurkutova, who swept Jules off his feet. A substantial young brunette with a strong mind of her own, she had grown up in Irkutsk, on the edge of Buryatskaya near Lake Baikal, a thousand miles to the west. The granddaughter of a half-Buryat merchant from Siberia, Natalya was thirteen when her father died of consumption, in debt and some disgrace. For the next three years she was raised by her cousin, Olga Yankovsky, and the Polish count.

Jules Bryner, a declared Lutheran, married Natalya Iosiphovna Kurkutova at the Uspenskaya Orthodox Church in Vladivostok on November 1, 1882. He was thirty-three years old; Natalya, at sixteen, was his child bride. From their apartment they proceeded by boat to the Bryner summer house at Sidemy, where the couple spent their first night together in the stone "honeymoon cottage" that Jules had designed on a bluff over Amur Bay.

A year before Jules and Natalya were married, Tsar Alexander II, the "great liberator" of serfs and most liberal of all Russia's emperors, was assassinated by a bomb thrown between his feet. A half-dozen previous attempts on his life had failed, but this time he died, hours later, in agony. Beside his deathbed stood his son and successor, Alexander III; there too, trembling, was his grandson, thirteen-year-old Nicholas, who now ascended to the title of *tsarevitch*, or crown prince, also destined someday to become "Tsar of All Russias."

For Alexander III, the murder of his father reinforced the belief that any participation by the people in the governance of the Russian Empire spelled disaster. Russia could only be governed by absolute autocracy at home and by the show of force abroad.

For Nicholas, the sensitive young tsarevitch, the vivid lesson was that tsars can be maimed and killed by their subjects.

By the time their first child was born in 1884, Jules and his bride, Natalya, had settled in a new house on Svetlanskaya Street in Vladivostok, taking their place among a handful of elite families. The city now had eight thousand inhabitants, of which almost half were with the Russian navy. In just twenty years the rude naval outpost had become remarkably cosmopolitan: there were residents from North America, France, Sweden, Turkey, Italy, Serbia, Germany, Denmark, Switzerland, and Great Britain, along with many from nearby Japan, Korea, and China. But now the Volunteer Fleet was regularly delivering refugees from western Russia, who settled throughout the Amur and Maritime regions. Overland, the new arrivals included many Cossacks, the fierce horsemen chosen by the Imperial government to enforce the law across most of Russia. All told, the Cossack people amounted to two and a half million, and in the Far East the clans made up much of the population, policing the resettled peasants and anybody else in the way of their cavalry.

Jules strived relentlessly for efficiency. One bit of advice that passed down from him in the family for three generations was that "you should always leave the dinner table feeling a little bit hungry." Such an abstemious outlook came naturally to a Swiss-born businessman, and suggests a measured approach to life as a whole.

To keep cargo flowing in both directions between Vladivostok and Japan, Shanghai and Europe, Jules invested in businesses that could fill the Far East Shipping Company's outbound ships, and soon he was starting new ventures of his own. As he looked about the region, he saw what everyone else saw: the taiga, endless forests of larch, spruce, pine, maple, ash, oak, and birch. In a matter of months Jules launched a successful timber business, which not only filled his cargo holds, but also created many new jobs: lumberjacks, wagon builders and wheelwrights, millers, rope makers, accountants, and many others — all were needed for Jules' new business. At the same time he invested in coal mines on Sakhalin, the Russian island north of Japan where prisoners were sent into exile; later he had a share in gold mines to the west and began to acquaint himself with mining engineering. All the while FESCO was handling large industrial and government contracts, and transporting timber and coal from Jules' other interests as well. By virtue of his years of residence, Jules was qualified to become a Russian citizen. In doing so he did not lose his Swiss citizenship, though the Russian government would henceforth regard him only as a Russian.

And with that, Jules was named merchant of the first guild, a title that guaranteed his capital worth. By the eighteenth century, Russian society was among the most precisely stratified in the world. In 1769, under Peter the Great, the law "On the Middle Class of People" was adopted, outlining the rights and status of the new bourgeoisie. The urban population was divided into six groups, one of which was merchants. As a class, the merchants were divided into three "guilds," or classes, according to their wealth. Merchants who had capital of more than ten thousand rubles belonged to the "first" guild, those with five to ten thousand rubles were in the "second" guild, and those capitalists with just one thousand rubles were in the "third" guild. First and second guild merchants had the right to own industrial enterprises and large estates, and they could not be subjected to corporal punishment.

As population and business in Vladivostok grew dramatically, so did the city's sophistication. Directly across Svetlanskaya Street from Jules' offices, developer Ivan Galetsky had built the two-story Central Hotel; then in 1885 he added a 350-seat European theater, the only one within thousands of miles, known as Madame Galetsky's Theatre. The city's roads were still hazardous bogs most of the year, but after the city inaugurated its telephone system in 1884, one no longer needed to dispatch a messenger across town. The Bryners' phone number was 14.

As his businesses grew, so did Jules' family. Over the next twelve years, Natalya safely delivered three boys and three girls after a first died in infancy, leaving her in deep melancholy; as a result, every few winters the Bryners moved to a larger home. Their summers were spent at Sidemy, where Natalya could visit her cousin, Olga, who rarely left the Yankovsky stone "fortress." The Bryners' third child, Boris, was born on September 29, 1889. He seemed clever from the first, but then so did his siblings. Perhaps Boris stands out for me only because he was my grandfather.

3

Throughout the reign of Tsar Alexander III, planning for a railway across Siberia demonstrated Russia's imperialistic ambitions, but also highlighted the infighting among its ministries. (Like the secretary of state and other equivalent U.S. cabinet members, ministers were personally appointed by the tsar to "ad-minister" the country.) It was often said in the nineteenth century that "Russia has ministers, but no government." Mostly because of endless disputes between the ministers, construction of the railroad had only just begun when Alexander died in 1894. These ministerial disputes were not all trivial, but often centered upon divergent views of governance: should momentous decisions obey sound economics, or merely the will of the tsar?

To the reader it may seem a foregone conclusion that profit provided the motive for building the Trans-Siberian Railway, as it had in America's Wild West. But that was not the case in the "Wild East," as Far East Russia has often been called: the Trans-Siberian was never a viable capitalist venture *because it could not hope to turn a profit.* Simply put, people weren't going to line up at a window to buy tickets to Siberia.

The government, however, was not planning to give them a choice; it planned to resettle *millions* of peasants from western farms and industrial cities to the unpeopled plains, tundra, and taiga of the East. In fact, this was the largest exercise in demographic engineering in all of human history; its intent was to relieve a West overcrowded since the freeing of the serfs. But it was also aimed at assuring the "Russification" of the Far East. As Governor-General Unterberger explained it, indelicately, "We didn't occupy this region just so that it could be colonized by yellows." The railway's most insightful biographer, Steven G. Marks, put it best: "The Trans-Siberian Railroad was built for the purpose of bringing to the East a population that would need a railroad." And, he might have added, an army to protect that population.

The Trans-Siberian Railway was an iron bridge across Russia; it was also proof that Russia was preparing for the military domination of Asia. This system could deliver soldiers and matériel from western Russia that would easily overpower the small (or, in China's case, dysfunctional) nations of Asia. Such a monumental military advantage might even avert the need for war with Japan: once the Trans-Siberian Railway was rolling, the mere threat of an overwhelming attack by Russia would achieve victory.

The Russian Empire's national pride and ambition had still not recovered from its abject defeat in the Crimean War of 1855. But this was the Age of Empire, described as "the frantic post-1880 jostling by the Great Powers for additional colonial territories in Africa, Asia, and the Pacific, partly for gain, partly out of a fear of being eclipsed." England had been colonizing the Orient since the 1700s, and Germany, France, and the United States also had footholds there, seeking out natural resources they could plunder, using limitless local labor, cheap and pliant.

But after controlling the sparsely inhabited Siberian region for three hundred years, Russia's only claim in the Far East was Vladivostok. There were other towns, including Ussurisk and Khabarovsk to the north, but no other city. And worse, this region was part of contiguous Russia, not some distant colony; yet that meant nothing if it remained inaccessible and indefensible. Vladivostok would be helpless if attacked by the European powers in Asia, and its defeat would represent a loss of Russian soil, not a mere colonial holding. Thus, even as Vladivostok was being developed by a handful of civic-minded individuals during its first thirty years, it had already acquired enormous strategic and geopolitical significance far beyond its modest realities.

From the start, the city's long-term survival hinged on whether or not the Imperial government chose to build the Trans-Siberian Railway. By the 1880s, Vladivostok seemed threatened by developments thousands of miles away in Canada, oddly enough. With the completion of the Canadian-Pacific Railroad by the British government, the average journey from England to Japan would be reduced from fifty-two days (traveling east by way of the Suez Canal) to just thirty-seven days (traveling westward across Canada). "London expected to make use of it," wrote Marks, "to concentrate its forces against Vladivostok."

By any measure, the construction of the Trans-Siberian Railway was an audacious undertaking; the enormity of the project is difficult to grasp, even today. Almost six thousand miles of largely inaccessible terrain had to be crossed — a decade before the first automobiles and trucks — some of which was frozen solid for months at a time. It was estimated that the western and central sections alone would require eighty thousand men, including thirty thousand navvies just to dig and move earth — there were no bulldozers — as well as two thousand skilled stonemasons. One leg of the Russian-owned Chinese Eastern Railroad was so isolated that in 1896 the Russian ministries decided to build a thoroughly Russian city in China to house all the railroad workers and their families. They chose a spot along the Sungari River and built a few houses at the place they named Harbin. By 1910, the city was home to some forty-four thousand Russians and sixty thousand Chinese.

The Russian merchant marine was created for the very purpose of building the railroad. One hundred fifty million pounds of pig iron would be required. Hardened U.S. steel was imported for just a dozen of the hundreds of railway bridges. Many of the rails would be delivered from English factories in batches of six thousand (sixteen miles' worth) and loaded onto barges — which sometimes sank under their weight. The total rolling stock required was more than thirty thousand railroad cars and fifteen hundred locomotives.

The man remembered as the "Father of the Trans-Siberian Railway" was not Tsar Alexander III, but the urbane and thoughtful minister, Sergei Witte. Witte's career, rising through the Department of Railroad to become minister of transport and finally minister of finance, put him in a position to understand all aspects of the gargantuan project, and to see it through to completion. In fact it was for years the principal component of Russia's entire economic policy under Witte. Before him, ministers had argued about the enormous cost of the project; Witte argued that it would benefit Russia at *any* cost, just by its prestige and power. The mercantile possibilities alone would achieve "economic imperialism" — the subjugation of Asia through trade policy rather than military might.

A tall, broad, and heavyset man, Witte "suggests something that might have been shaped by an axe," according to A. P. Isvolsky, a former Russian minister of foreign affairs, "a fracture of the nose . . . gave him a certain resemblance to the portraits of Michelangelo." Others noted his pumpkin-shaped head. Senator Albert Beveridge of the United States — an unabashed imperialist from Indiana — said Witte's eyes had "an expression of patience and weariness about them which reminds you of what you have read about the eyes of Lincoln." Historian John Albert White observed that, as minister of finance, "Witte's projects absorbed a major portion of the state budget, the grasp of his power touched the lives of increasing numbers of people, and he became the master of what amounted to a state within a state." "One may say," wrote Isvolsky, "that for some ten years he was the real master of the 160 million inhabitants of the Empire."

A single decision that Witte made under Tsar Alexander III effectively guaranteed the eventual completion of this monumental project. In 1891, Witte appointed Tsarevitch Nicholas, twenty-three years old, as the first chairman of the Committee of the Siberian Railroad. In so doing, Witte was able to "ingratiate himself" with the future tsar by "finding an outlet for the latter's initiative," as one member of the government put it. In fact, this was Nicholas's first undertaking in the adult world, and with his prestigious participation and nominal leadership, Witte knew the venture could never be abandoned, no matter what challenges arose.

Tsarevitch Nicholas came to Vladivostok on May 31, 1891, a ceremonial occasion fraught with implications for the fledgling town, and ultimately for Nicholas himself and his foreshortened reign. It demonstrated to the world that the next tsar was genuinely interested in the region, and of course he was greeted by the founding fathers of the city, including Jules Bryner. Nicholas, who (by the estimate of one contemporary) was only 1/128th Russian by blood, most likely spoke German with Jules — who was 100 percent Swiss, though now a Russian citizen, and so a subject of the royal family.

The tsarevitch had just visited Japan, where he was nearly assassinated by a sword-swinging assailant who bloodied Nicholas's scalp; the event had left him understandably distressed. And he was probably not impressed by the hardscrabble city in its early incarnation. Though it boasted a few gilded parlors, Vladivostok was still a navy port in a remote setting where most of the population lived in ramshackle shantytowns. According to the biographer Robert K. Massie, the tsarevitch found Vladivostok "a desolate frontier town of muddy, unpaved streets, open sewers, unpainted wooden houses, and clusters of mud-plastered straw huts inhabited by Chinese and Koreans." First, Nicholas attended an outdoor service next to the Orthodox Uspensky Cathedral. Then Jules Brynner and the other city fathers escorted him beside Tiger Hill to Aleutskaya Street near Golden Horn Bay, where the tsarevitch "wielded a shovel to fill a wheelbarrow with dirt," wrote Massie, "trundled it along for several yards and emptied it down an embankment of the future railroad. Soon after, he grasped a trowel and cemented into place the first stone of the Vladivostok passenger station." In that moment, Vladivostok was officially designated the last stop on the longest stretch of rail in the world. By planting that stone personally, Nicholas was committing the honor of the Empire to the completion of the railway, even though it would do little to benefit the Russian subjects who paid for it. And while it projected the threat of military power deep into the Far East, it also gave Russia's enemies years of preparation to thwart that power.

It was a dozen more years before the first Trans-Siberian trains pulled into that station, and a dozen more before they arrived reliably. The whole project, so closely identified with Nicholas, had long-term costs that would only become apparent much later, to historians. "Witte's spending pushed the budget into deficit," wrote Marks, "forcing him to overtax," requiring "large sacrifices on the part of the Russian population" that added significantly to Russia's dire conditions in the years leading up to the revolution of 1905, which Trotsky described as a "dress rehearsal" for the Bolshevik Revolution of 1917.

When Alexander III died of illness in 1894, Nicholas became tsar. Exactly one week after his father's funeral, Nicholas married Alexandra, his German fiancée, a granddaughter of Queen Victoria. "One day in deepest mourning, lamenting a beloved one," Alexandra wrote to her sister, "the next in smartest clothes being married. There cannot be a greater contrast."

Three years later, Tsar Nicholas II and Jules Bryner were more closely involved in another venture together, with more ominous consequences for both their empires.

By the 1890s, life in Vladivostok, for the well-to-do, was civilized indeed. A little like San Francisco after the gold rush, there were unexpected items of sophistication and culture embedded in a crude metropolitan infrastructure. Whereas other colonial powers had only grafted European neighborhoods onto existing Asian cities, the architects in Vladivostok had succeeded in giving the whole city an unmistakably European flavor with its first major buildings. There was never another place like it in the Far East, and that remains true today.

Jules Bryner and the other founding fathers made continual efforts to enrich the city's cultural life. They remembered vividly its rough-and-tumble beginnings as a log-built frontier town: now much of Svetlanskaya and Aleutskaya streets were lined with stone-built structures, three stories high and built to last. Madame Galetsky's Theatre (also called the Golden Horn Theatre) soon attracted renowned actors and actresses from Moscow and St. Petersburg, as well as musicians and performers from around the Pacific Rim.

In October 1890, a year before Tsarevitch Nicholas visited, Anton Chekhov came to Vladivostok. Then just thirty years old and not yet an immortal author, in the next decade Chekhov would become Russia's soul-searching tragicomedic genius of theater and fiction, and his works of drama would illuminate the stage under the direction of his nephew, Mikhail, and Konstantin Stanislavsky. Chekhov had earned his license as a medical doctor, and it was primarily in that capacity that he had made a heroic humanitarian fact-finding trip to the grim prison camps of Sakhalin Island, already in operation for decades. His published account of the visit was a revelation to most Russians.

Chekhov particularly wanted to stop in Vladivostok while returning to western Russia, because, curiously enough, from Moscow he had been following the newspaper *Vladivostok* all through the 1880s; it is an indication of how powerfully the Far East played on the imagination of people in the metropolitan region, much as the Wild West had an allure for East Coast city folk in the same era.

During the three days Chekhov spent in the city, he paid a visit to *Vladivostok*'s editor, for whom he expressed high regard, and he enjoyed the view of Amur Bay from Tiger Hill. He also had tea with the Bryners and, with Jules, participated in the official stone-laying for the Amur Society Museum building. The Society for the Study of the Amur Region, founded in 1884, was the first organization to focus attention upon the region's flora and fauna, ethnography and history; the museum began a collection of specimens, which, to this day, displays the area's natural history. Jules personally paid for exquisite color prints of botanical species, rendered by the finest printing house in Germany in a manner no less meticulous than those of the Royal Botanical Society in London. Two months later, when Chekhov returned to Moscow, he visited his brother Alexander and saw his infant nephew, Mikhail, for the first time. Forty years later, Mikhail Chekhov would play a decisive role in the Bryner odyssey.

Jules gave of his time as well as his money in developing the educational resources of Vladivostok. After years of investment and preparation, the Oriental Institute opened in 1899, intended to become Russia's major academic center for Asian studies. It soon became a magnet for ambitious Western academics specializing in the East, and taught the histories of China, Japan, Mongolia, Tibet, and Korea. Students were required to learn English, Chinese, and one other Asian language. From the first year, Jules served as chairman of the scholarship committee, while contributing generously to the fund. His children were among the first to attend the Vladivostok high schools (called *gymnasiums* in Russia) that prepared young men for universities in the West, and young women for clerical jobs.

Thanks to a local resident, Eleanor L. Pray, a bountiful journal of everyday life among the wealthier residents of the area exists in English. Mrs. Pray was born in Maine, but settled Vladivostok with her husband in 1894. They rented a summer house from the wealthy Goldenstedt family on the DeVries peninsula, much like Sidemy, four hours to the south. For thirty-five years she wrote letters almost daily to her family in the United States, describing all aspects of her life. The Goldenstedts' farm provided the city with cows, bulls, pigs, chickens, guinea fowl, turkeys, and geese; as well as milk, butter, sour cream, potatoes, and cabbage; and oysters, crab, and fish. They bottled tons of sauerkraut — literally — along with jams and relishes (peach, raspberry, black currant, marmalade, crab apple, sweet pickle, and piccalilli). For a celebration at the summer house they would serve "cold salmon with mayonnaise, chup-chup, Danish salad, potato salad, hot boiled potatoes, gravy, horseradish sauce, cucumbers, lettuce, radishes, rhubarb jelly, ice cream and coffee." In January 1900, Mrs. Pray wrote: "The Bryners gave a dinner night before last and Mrs. Hansen told me about their dining-room. She says it is magnificent — about as large as four of our drawing-rooms, and lighted from the roof, with the exception of one big window. A narrow gallery runs around it, and this was filled with camellias and other plants."

In Vladivostok, Kunst and Albers had become a truly grand department store. In 1893 it became the first building in the city to have electric lights — powered by its own steam-driven generator, which was quite a novelty — and soon was equipped with the first electric elevators in Asia. The well-heeled customer could find many manufactured goods, a haberdashery, hardware, saddler's goods, books (including scientific editions), pianos and other musical instruments, and jewelry. The *very* wealthy could order anything in the world from Kunst and Albers.

Sidemy, where the Bryner children spent every summer, was only thirty miles from the northern border of Korea — the Hermit Kingdom as it was then known. In his search for further businesses that would also advance the cause of Russia in the Far East, Jules had agents in northern Korea scouting out timber resources, which were soon found in great abundance along the Yalu and Tumen rivers: he needed only to persuade the king of Korea to give him the timber concession in the area. So Jules set out for a protracted business trip to Seoul, capital of (then undivided) Korea.

By 1896, Korea was dominated and occupied by Japan, while neighboring Manchuria to the west had fallen under Russian control. King Kojong of Korea, an indecisive leader of diminutive stature and uncertain authority, was in fear for his life: the year before, his wife, Queen Min, had been assassinated by Japanese agents to stop her intrigues against the occupation after Japan declared Korea its "protectorate." At that point, unsafe in his own palace, King Kojong sought sanctuary in the Russian embassy in Seoul.

There, on August 28, 1896, Jules met with Kojong, the twenty-sixth king of Korea (he declared himself emperor the following year), and formalized an agreement giving Jules' new Korean Timber Company the right to harvest trees on 1,800 square miles of land around the Yalu and Tumen rivers in northern Korea — a vast area that provided absolute strategic control of the entire Korean peninsula. (A translation of this contract is provided in the appendix.) Also specified in their agreement was the right to "do whatever is necessary to create roads and horse railways, and to clear rivers . . . and also to build houses, workshops, and factories . . . either on the Russian bank of the Yalu River, or on the Korean side, whichever is more convenient." By implication, he was entitled to bring a whole army of security forces if he deemed it necessary to protect the lumber crews from the hunghu'tze. Fully a quarter of the document addressed the care needed "for the growth and re-development" of the forest. Finally, the contract allowed Jules to "transfer this contract to any trustworthy Russian individual or organization." In exchange, King Kojong would receive one quarter of the net income of this vast operation, whose headquarters was the Bryner office on Tiger Hill in Vladivostok, at the corner of Aleutskaya and Svetlanskaya streets.

Of course, Jules knew that the Imperial government was aware of his timber concession from the beginning, since his negotiations with the king of Korea took place at the Russian embassy. What Jules probably suspected but did not know for certain was that Sergei Witte had taken a personal interest, or perhaps, alarm, in Jules' activities. The director of Witte's office, Petr Mikhailovich Romanov, had requested that one of its agents in Seoul, a man named Pokotilov, report to him everything he could learn about the Swiss-born merchant's activities in Korea; Pokotilov sent the complete text of Jules' four-page timber contract to the ministry of finance, noting that "Bryner's efforts were crowned with complete success." Pokotilov also reported to Romanov that, during Jules' month-long sojourn in Korea:

> Mr. Bryner began to make a thorough study of questions relating to the revitalization of relations between Korea and our Pacific region. In addition, I can say with good conscience, that I have never met an individual who is more observant or more curious about practical matters. Aside from his forestry business, he was, it appeared to me, quite seriously interested in the possibility of organizing the export of rice from Korea to Vladivostok. . . . In addition, Mr. Bryner paid serious attention to the possibility of importing kerosene into Korea — at present an exclusively American product that can only be obtained through the Japanese. With this in mind, Mr. Bryner had one of his new acquaintances in Chemulpo search for and buy him a spot in that port for the construction of cisterns.

The agent charged with spying upon Jules had become enthralled with the entrepreneur from Vladivostok and his far-sighted interests.

> In informing Your Excellency about Mr. Bryner's activities in Korea, I would like to be so bold as to express the opinion that his efforts to institute direct trade relations between this country [Korea] and Vladivostok should be met by the Ministry of Finance with the greatest sympathy, and I am positive that the communication to him of Your Excellency's approval would strengthen even more his zeal for this undertaking, which is unquestionably sympathetic to the Russian government's point of view. In November of next year, Mr. Bryner . . . will be in Petersburg, and at my urging, will not fail to present himself to Your Excellency.

The agent also reported, with unease, that Jules' concession raised alarm "in both the Japanese and Japanophile Anglo-Japanese presses, which interpreted the whole affair as a new step by Russia to try to spread its political influence to the Northern provinces of Korea." So, from this moment, Japan was concerned with Jules' intentions regarding the Yalu River Concession and the Imperial government in St. Petersburg knew it. One look at a map of Korea explains why: together, the Yalu and Tumen rivers virtually amputate the whole of the Korean peninsula from the Asian mainland. And Jules' contract, allowing him to do "whatever is necessary," could serve as justification for moving whole divisions of Russia's army onto his 1,800 square miles — all of which was under Japanese military control.

Vladimir Gurko was working at the Imperial Chancellery in St. Petersburg in 1897; some years later he wrote an insider's account of Jules Bryner's visit to the Imperial city that November, and its calamitous consequences. "When we were increasing our activity in Korea, a Vladivostok merchant, Bryner, had arrived in St. Petersburg with an offer to sell a concession for the exploitation of the enormous forest areas covering the entire north of Korea." Jules met with an adviser of Witte's named Rothstein, who represented the Rothschild banks in Russia; he was not interested. Jules then met with a personal adviser of Tsar Nicholas II's named Alexander Michael

Bezobrazov, a former officer of the guards and well-known stock-market speculator whose father had been a wealthy marshal of the nobility of St. Petersburg. Bezobrazov, according to his associate, Vonliarliarsky, was endowed with "ill-balanced faculties — in which imagination predominates — and a morbid hankering after fads."

Regarding the Bryner contract with the Korean emperor, Gurko recounted that "Bezobrazov had then composed a detailed report on the subject and . . . had succeeded in presenting it to the tsar. The report was designed to persuade Nicholas II to acquire Bryner's concession as his personal property." At the same time, Minister of Finance Witte — contemplating the enormous national deficit produced by the Trans-Siberian Railroad — advised Nicholas against involvement in the Bryner timber concession.

There were numerous arguments in favor of Nicholas making use of the Bryner concession, whose location, wrote historian White, was "itself the key to its strategic significance. . . . an area of 1,800 square miles stretching across the northern frontier region of Korea." Bezobrazov pointed out that a mountain range "was a natural barrier protecting the concession territory from a Japanese advance," which would also protect the coastal cities of Port Arthur and Dairen to the west that Russia had just acquired from China, allowing Russia to assert control over Manchuria and build another new railroad there. The Koreans themselves certainly preferred Russian domination to that of the Japanese, with whom they had made war for centuries.

Although Nicholas remained cool to the project, writes Gurko, Bezobrazov "persuaded the tsar to send an expedition to examine the territory of Bryner's concession," led by the privy councilor of Nicholas's cabinet and financed out of Nicholas's personal treasury; "It pleased His Majesty to issue a command that a contract be signed for the conditional acquisition of the lumbering concession of the merchant Bryner." The arduous twelve-thousand-mile expedition and the tsar's personal contract show how important this was to Nicholas. When the expedition's members returned, "their enthusiastic description of the region and its strategic value (they brought back a detailed, topographical map) in protecting our portion of Manchuria from Japan excited the lively interest of Nicholas II. Bezobrazov did everything he could to keep this interest burning bright." On May 11, 1898, the Yalu River Concession was purchased from Jules Bryner "with money from His Majesty's private funds." The price was sixty-five thousand rubles —roughly $650,000 in today's dollars.

What were Jules' motives in the Yalu River affair? This sophisticated, subtle man, who had lived throughout the Far East, could not have been oblivious to the strategic implications of his contract with Emperor Kojong. Yet he was clearly not acting as an agent for the Imperial government, which was initially uninterested in his offer. Had Jules gone to these lengths just for the sale price? Had he intended from the start to sell the Yalu concession to the tsar? Or did he travel to St. Petersburg merely seeking government approval and perhaps assistance for the project, with which to attract other investors? Jules was paid an enormous sum for a piece of paper signed by the captive Korean emperor. But Jules was known more for prudence than for avarice, and he never failed to consider the effect his dealings would have on others. He had lived in Japan, and undoubtedly knew that if the Japanese perceived the sale as a Russian provocation, the mikado might well launch a war in the region that would threaten everything Jules had been working for in the last twenty years — including his family, his business, and the city of Vladivostok. Could it have been his concealed intention all along, to help Russia seize Korea from Japan?

In the course of my research, a remarkable document came to light in which Jules explains his motives in his own voice, and describes how his interest in the Korean forests began. The three-thousand-word manuscript, recently discovered in the Moscow Archives of the last Imperial government, is a first-person account of Jules' interest in Korea, describing its value for potential investors and government officials; with this document, Jules proposed the Yalu River concession to Tsar Nicholas II. It begins:

> As I had been occupied in commerce, including the lumber trade, in the Far East for 20 years, I had paid some attention to the forests of Northern Korea. Well before that country was opened to European trade, a large quantity of thick logs appeared in the markets of Chifu and Tienzin and amazed

> travelers with their size. This was wood from the river Yalu (Jalu-kiang). The precious root ginseng, which grows exclusively in thick woods impenetrable to the sun, is frequently found in North Korea. Finding that root there increased my interest and speculation about the probable richness of her centuries-old forests. Later by chance I encountered some magnificent wood columns of a type of wood [from Yalu] similar to teak in one of the temples of Kyoto.

Seven years earlier, Jules explained, the price of timber in Japan had risen by 50 percent; thereupon, he "gathered reliable and detailed information about the condition of the timber along the Tumen River," and, through the services of a Russian representative in Seoul, began negotiations with the Korean government for the timber concession. "Concerned that owners of the Yalu River and Dazhilet Island forests would be dangerous competitors for my lumber from the Tumen River in the Japanese and Chinese markets," he added, "I attempted and succeeded in obtaining all three forest areas for my use." The Yalu River timber was clearly secondary to his Tumen River plans. And, far from anticipating war with the Japanese, he expected them to be his customers.

Jules did not anticipate any military threat to his work force. "The only thing that could disturb the population," he wrote, "are Chinese drifters (mostly runaway soldiers), who launch attacks with the purpose of looting. But usually the presence of even one or two Europeans keeps these drifters at a respectful distance." He examined in detail the varieties of timber available and how it should be transported, along with market comparisons for price and quality with lumber from around the region and from the United States. These are not the perfunctory observations of a man trying to mask some ulterior motive.

Clearly Jules hoped to establish a profitable timber business with government cooperation; indeed, without Imperial approval, it might prove difficult to obtain the significant financing this project would require. His own property at Sidemy was only a day's travel from the Tumen River, and he may have hoped for a Russian border patrol that would buffer his summer home from possible attacks by Koreans or hunghu'tze, and provide government security forces for the timber concession from the beginning.

It is utterly improbable that Jules was acting as a freelance *agent provocateur*, but that is the implication made by historian White when he observes that "Bryner's official connections appear to have been close, since he received the concession through the Russian minister in Korea. Furthermore, at the time he received it, he was serving on a border commission. . . . From the very first, the concession was closely associated with official circles if not official policy."

It was always Jules' intention to travel to St. Petersburg and seek government approval for the Yalu River project; that intention was mentioned in the letter from Witte's secret agent, Pokotilov, to the finance ministry a few weeks after Jules' agreement with the Korean emperor. Doubtless, Jules had expected the concession to appeal to Sergei Witte's economic imperialism: after all, this was a Russian industry taking control of Korean land legally. But from the first, it seems, Witte identified the plan with a political foe, Bezobrazov. After dismissing Jules's proposal, however, the finance minister changed his mind; eventually, as Alexander Solzhenitsyn wrote, "Witte, contradicting himself again, agreed to the annexation of Manchuria, and even to the opening-up of a timber concession in Korea."

But what was Nicholas's intention in purchasing the Bryner concession — and paying for it out of his own pocket? According to Solzhenitsyn, Bezobrazov had persuaded the tsar that "Russia's commercial venture in Korea, especially the timber concession, would shortly begin to yield fantastic profits, and that the East would pay its own way." But that is unpersuasive, given the vast stretches of taiga available on Russian soil. Besides, the tsar only showed interest in the strategic location of Jules' concession, not in its flora and fauna, which Jules had dutifully chronicled during his personal expedition along the Yalu River. For the Russian government, this was a thinly disguised grab for land — not for trees.

Bezobrazov's plan, as outlined by White, was that "the Bryner concession be put into operation by the organization of a semi-official 'East Asia Company' modeled after the British East India Company. This company was to be so organized and managed that it would not be forced to concern itself about dividends, but rather was to concentrate on serving the Imperial interests. The company would control both local affairs and *Russia's entire Far Eastern policy*."

Everyone agrees that Bezobrazov was the active force who brought this arrangement about — but what was his interest in the whole thing? According to Gurko, "he was deluded by dreams of grandeur. The idea of playing adviser to the tsar captivated his imagination, and the thought of influencing cardinal issues of state policy befogged his weak brain, hid from him the general condition of the country, and led him to conjure up before his mind's eye the chimera of Russian supremacy, perhaps over the whole of Asia."

That was exactly the ambition that alarmed Japan. In sharp contrast with Witte's doctrine of economic imperialism, Bezobrazov gradually succeeded in persuading the tsar that Russia needed to demonstrate its military power in the Far East, to make clear throughout the region the absolute dominion of the Imperial government over the "Yellow Peril." Witte's sway with Nicholas had diminished as the national deficit grew from the ongoing construction of the Trans-Siberian Railway; cost overruns were now approaching 150 percent. As Witte's influence faded, Bezobrazov's voice grew louder in Nicholas's ear . . . and so did the drums of war.

For the next several years Japan sought clarification of Russia's intentions in Korea, even as the slaughter of foreigners during the Boxer Rebellion brought all practical development in the region to a halt. "The Japanese Prime Minister, Marquis Ito,[a] had learned that we had acquired a Concession in northern Korea," wrote Gurko, whereupon Ito declared that Japan needed continental territory for its growing populace. "The part of the continent that Japan had in mind, said Ito, was Korea, and preferably its northern part," because it was so unpopulated that it could accommodate a large Japanese resettlement. Marquis Ito traveled to St. Petersburg — a journey of more than eight weeks, through the Suez Canal — and waited there for months, but no one in the Imperial government would meet or speak with him. Whatever the intentions of Nicholas's government, this was a prolonged, cowardly, and dishonorable failure of Russian diplomacy, for which a steep price would be exacted.

Witte traveled to the Far East on an inspection tour and, in October 1902, he visited Vladivostok for a series of meetings with business and civic leaders, including Jules Bryner. Witte was especially concerned with any increase of foreign businesses based in the Russian Far East; for that reason, he had canceled the *porto franco* privileges for foreigners that had first enticed Jules away from Japan. Now that he was a Russian citizen, Jules probably supported this decision.

Mutsuhito, the mikado of Japan, was still seeking some agreement with Russia, but the situation continued to grow more ominous. Soon the Trans-Siberian Railway would begin to operate and could, in theory, deliver Russian regiments to the East with just a few weeks notice, though at this point, a detour around Lake Baikal — the largest freshwater lake in the world — was not yet started, so troops and other passengers still had to cross the lake by ship before continuing by rail. Moreover, the Chinese Eastern Railroad (a wholly Russian enterprise, despite its name) had just come into operation, crossing Manchuria all the way south to Port Arthur, and these rails could deposit Russian troops within a hundred miles of the Yalu River. Most threatening from the Japanese perspective, the timber concession began operating in March 1903, thereby justifying armed guards under the terms of Jules' contract with Emperor Kojong.

By this time the uncertain hand of Nicholas II was being directly influenced by the imperialistic ambitions of Bezobrazov, who had traveled to Port Arthur in January 1903 with two million rubles ($40 million today) available to him from the tsar's personal fund, "for a use known to His Imperial Majesty." He also had a plan to reorganize Manchuria and its environs into a viceroyalty — literally, a vice-kingdom, or quasi-independent monarchy — in charge of all troops and enterprises in the Far East. So as not to appear self-serving by seeking the title for himself, Bezobrazov enticed Admiral Alexeiev, head of Kwantung Province, to be a candidate for the post of viceroy. "Drawn on by ambition," wrote Gurko, "Alexeiev curried favor with Bezobrazov and supported him in the matter of the Yalu Concession."

At one point St. Petersburg backed down and ordered Alexeiev to evacuate troops from southern Manchuria; amazingly, Alexeiev disobeyed, while Bezobrazov wrote to Tsar Nicholas that an additional thirty-five thousand Russian troops should be moved into the region, along with a mounted detachment of five thousand to proceed directly to the Yalu concession. Further, Bezobrazov formed and financed his own bands of hunghu'tze (comprising, possibly, some of the same Chinese bandits who had survived Yankovsky's "private war" at Sidemy, twenty years earlier and a hundred miles north), and sent them into Korea to destroy Japanese units scouting the region. The Russian minister of war, Kuropatkin, was outraged to have his authority appropriated, but failed to shake the tsar's confidence in Bezobrazov. Before long, Nicholas appointed Admiral Alexeiev the viceroy of Far East Russia; he also created a new cabinet office in St. Petersburg in charge of all matters relating to the Far East, and named as its chairman none other than Bezobrazov.

Massie offered this crisp summary of the events that ignited the Russo-Japanese War:

> Although Japan clearly regarded Korea as essential to her security, a group of Russian adventurers resolved to steal it. Their plan was to establish a private company, the Yalu Timber Company, and begin moving Russian soldiers into Korea disguised as workmen. If they ran into trouble, the Russian government could always disclaim responsibility. If they succeeded, the empire would acquire a new province and they themselves would have vast economic concessions within it. Witte, the Finance Minister, vigorously opposed this risky policy. But Nicholas, impressed by the leader of the adventurers, a former cavalry officer named Bezobrazov, approved the plan, whereupon Witte in 1903 resigned from the government.

In Japan, there were massive demonstrations in Tokyo, Kyoto, and Yokohama, where the throngs were outraged that Russia was occupying Manchuria, and where the press had been inflaming public opinion about the Yalu River concession since Jules signed the agreement seven years earlier. Japan had indeed been very patient with Russia's provocations, *if* one accepts the absurd premise that Japan was entitled to Korea. By this time, the Japanese military command was planning war, and many young men were being forced into the Japanese army, as was occurring across all of Russia: the oldest son of Jules and Natalya, Leonid, was nineteen and, while studying at St. Petersburg University he was also a military cadet facing possible battle duty.

By the beginning of 1904 preparations for war accelerated in both countries. Viceroy Alexeiev requested permission from St. Petersburg to mobilize troops throughout Manchuria to advance on the Yalu River. Still, the tsar was fully expecting the mikado to back down: as late as February 1, 1904, at a dinner party in the Winter Palace, Tsar Nicholas II proclaimed, "There will be no war."

But on February 6, Russian troops crossed the Yalu River from Jules' original concession and invaded northern Korea. Within hours, Japan broke off diplomatic relations with Russia.

On the evening of February 8, Jules and Natalya Bryner attended a gala *soirée* in Vladivostok hosted by municipal leaders to honor an official representative from Tokyo. The next day telegraph reports revealed that Japan had launched a surprise torpedo attack overnight upon the Russian navy *inside* the harbor at Port Arthur, decommissioning two battleships and a destroyer. The next day the Japanese crippled the Russian fleet leaving the harbor of Chemulpo, later renamed Inchon, forcing crews to scuttle their own ships. Two weeks later, when another destroyer was sunk leaving Port Arthur, the Russian commander of the city, Stoessel, ordered his sentries to shoot any suspicious Chinese seen "signaling." After his order went out, "Chinese civilians were shot like partridges."

The Russo-Japanese War was a catastrophe for Russia from the first day to the last, and its cost, in blood and treasure, directly fed the roots and the rage of the Russian Revolution. At the outbreak of hostilities, Lenin's early Marxist mentor in exile, G. V. Plekhanov, wrote with prescience that the war "promises to shatter to its foundations the regime of Nicholas II."

Imperial arrogance and racist contempt for Asians had blinded both the ministries and Nicholas to the remarkable advances that Japan had made during years of preparation for this moment. In fact, no one in the Imperial government had ever believed that Japan would go to war at all, much less launch a preemptive attack on ships at harbor. Russia had been rattling its saber in the Far East since 1860 when it bestowed that threatening name upon a naval outpost of just forty-eight sailors: Vladivostok — "Ruler of the East." Now, in 1904, the mettle of the Russian Empire would finally be tested, its population primed and eager for war. Even as Japan sank two more Russian ships near Port Arthur, Russians turned out *en masse* to cheer the tsar. This terrible moment, a direct result of Nicholas's indecisive, mismanaged governance, also marked the very peak of his popularity.

Russia seemed invulnerable, with an active force of 1 million men and another 4 million reserves; Japan had only 180,000 troops, with 400,000 in reserve units. The Russian navy was almost twice the size of Japan's — but most of the fleet was near Finland in the Baltic Sea, thousands of miles to the west; in the Pacific, Japan had twice as many torpedo craft as Russia, and used them (and floating mines) to devastating effect. The tsar mobilized the Empire's vast, clumsy military machine as quickly as possible in the west, and prepared to carry it eastward aboard the most critical element of the Imperial government's strategy: the Trans-Siberian Railway. This, after all, was the war for which it had been built.

• • • • • • • •

But the railroad was not ready in time for Japan's attack. Tracks had not yet been laid along the hundred-mile-detour around Lake Baikal. Minister of War Kuropatkin had implored the government to delay the war until the tracks were finished, but he was consistently overruled by Far East Committee Chairman Bezobrazov, by Viceroy Alexeiev, and by Tsar Nicholas himself. Witte, the "father" of the railroad for the past fifteen years, had already returned to private life.

Meanwhile Japanese agents at Lake Baikal were reporting regularly to Tokyo that the railway could not possibly deliver the full force of Russia's military superiority; they also reported that the ice on the lake was more than three feet deep. Japan initiated the war deliberately, "at the very moment when Russia was most vulnerable — when the ice on Lake Baikal had reached the depth at which icebreakers could no longer function." At that point, the eastward flow of thousands of troops began backing up at the edge of the lake, overwhelming the city of Irkutsk.

In sheer desperation, the Russian Command improvised an outrageous solution. Using five hundred laborers, they laid thirty thousand rails *directly on the ice* for twenty-five miles to cross Lake Baikal. But the first locomotive shattered the ice and sank. So instead they used horses to tow more than three thousand railway cars, one at a time, over the frozen lake, while the soldiers were marched across the ice, or ferried by sleigh, stopping every few miles at heated barracks that had been erected in these excruciating conditions. Thousands of men were incapacitated by frostbite. One regiment of six hundred men lost their way in an ice storm, and all were drowned or frozen. Still, five trains a day were able to cross the lake, along with a total of more than sixteen thousand passengers and nine thousand tons of freight. This, however, was far below what the military plan required, and much less than what was needed to withstand Japan's withering attack.

Four weeks later, the Japanese navy bombarded Vladivostok. At 2 P.M. on March 6, 1904, as the first rockets struck near Golden Horn Bay, Jules and Natalya took their five children (Leonid was still at university) to the basement. By this time the whole city was under military law, and sixteen thousand Russian soldiers were stationed there, commanded by Lieutenant General N. P. Linievitch: it was their barracks that were targeted. However, a small Russian fleet with two cruisers was in port and succeeded in driving the attackers away before more extensive damage was done.

Two days later the demoralized Russian Pacific Navy took heart from the arrival in Port Arthur of the well-respected Admiral Makarov, who took command of the fleet aboard the battleship *Petropavlovsk*. A month later the Japanese lured the *Petropavlovsk* out of the harbor and sank it, killing Admiral Makarov and his crew of seven hundred men. By this time the Russian Pacific Fleet had been decimated, and sailors' esprit de corps had collapsed, but reinforcements were a long time coming. It was another six months before St. Petersburg ordered its Baltic Fleet from near Finland on the long voyage around South Africa and across the Indian Ocean to support the Russian army in the Far East. It was also apparent that, once they arrived, the addition of eight battleships, twelve cruisers, and nine destroyers to the Sea of Japan would make this the greatest naval engagement the world had ever seen.

Before the sailors left, Tsar Nicholas and Tsarina Alexandra rode out from the Winter Palace to encourage the troops and wish them victory. But the captain of the battleship named after Nicholas's father, the *Alexander III*, retorted publicly, "You have wished us victory, but there will be no victory. . . . [If the ships arrive in the Yellow Sea], Togo will blow them to bits. His fleet is infinitely better than ours, and the Japanese are real sailors. I can promise you one thing, however. [We] shall at least know how to die."

At the Bryner concession, 42,000 Japanese troops crossed the Yalu River on April 30, 1904. By the following day they had routed 14,000 Russian soldiers, leaving some 3,000 dead. In the words of one historian, "The Russians were outnumbered by their opponents, but they were also outwitted and outmaneuvered, and the result was an overwhelming victory for the Japanese." Russia was humiliated all across Manchuria: at Sha-Ho, 200,000 Russian troops suffered 41,000 casualties. Japan lost almost 60,000 men in the siege of Port Arthur, but they took the city after four months; it cost almost 30,000 Russian lives and led to the enormous anti-war demonstration in

St. Petersburg. Finally, at Mukden, in the largest land battle in human history to date, Russia suffered 90,000 casualties among its 350,000 troops; Japan lost "only" 75,000 men. This was a gargantuan war, and a colossal defeat for Russia.

But the humiliation was not yet complete. After a seven-month voyage, the twenty-nine ships of the Baltic Fleet finally reached the Straits of Tsushima between Japan and Korea. Admiral Togo was waiting, exactly as the captain of the *Alexander III* had forewarned. The "greatest naval engagement the world had ever seen" lasted forty-five minutes. Twenty-one Russian ships were torpedoed and sunk, including all eight battleships, seven cruisers, and six destroyers. In less than an hour, 4,830 Russian sailors were lost and 6,000 captured. Japan lost just 117 men.

President Theodore Roosevelt had been offering for months to mediate peace talks. Ten days after Russia's navy was effectively eliminated, Tsar Nicholas agreed to send a high-ranking envoy to Portsmouth, New Hampshire, to negotiate peace. The tsar's emissary to the United States was none other than Count Sergei Witte, formerly scorned by Nicholas and now newly titled. Witte's egalitarian posturing in New Hampshire might "partly account for the transformation in American public opinion toward Russia," he wrote. "I treated everybody, of whatever social position, as an equal. This behavior was a heavy strain on me as all acting is to the unaccustomed, but it surely was worth the trouble." The peace talks proceeded even as Japan stormed Sakhalin Island, and Admiral Togo considered playing Vladivostok as a bargaining chip. This was exactly what the people of Vladivostok had been dreading, especially after the *Japanese Times* wrote that, "with Mamiya Strait in our grasp, the blockade of Vladivostok will become a very effective undertaking." For Jules' Far East Shipping Company, the notion of an armed blockade was especially chilling.

By the time the Portsmouth Treaty was signed in September 1905 (incidentally winning a Nobel Peace Prize for Teddy Roosevelt of "big stick" acclaim), Russia had accepted all but one of Tokyo's demands: the tsar refused to surrender Vladivostok as an "international city."

• • • • • • • •

By then the Imperial government faced an even greater threat, not in the Far East, but at the tsar's front door.

After the war had begun, a growing anti-war sentiment in Russia arose out of the initial Pavlovian knee-jerks of nationalism fed by eloquent rabble-rousers in the press and in the parks, standing on soapboxes, exhorting the labor unions to strike against the war. As early as June 1904, the Sixth National Zemstvo Congress (a gathering of the country's local governments) addressed Tsar Nicholas directly: "Sire, Russia has been drawn into a disastrous war by the criminal abuse of your councilors. Our army is incapable of defeating the enemy, our fleet is annihilated. More menacing than this external danger, civil War is flaming." This same sentiment was expressed by demonstrators across Russia. By January 1905, "the number of working days used up by strikes . . . rose to the unprecedented and since unequaled figure of 920,000," more than double the *annual* total for 1903.

And on January 22, 1905, an estimated 120,000 of his subjects converged upon the Winter Palace, Tsar Nicholas's official residence (though he was at his country palace that day) to protest the war. The crowds were singing "God Save the Tsar." When they found all the major intersections blocked by the tsar's regiment, including mounted Cossacks, the anti-war demonstrators surged forward, and the troops opened fire. At least ninety-two protesters were killed by the tsar's palace guard, and hundreds more were wounded.

"'Bloody Sunday,'" wrote Massie, "was a turning point in Russian history. It shattered the ancient, legendary belief that the tsar and the people were one. . . . But it was only the beginning of a year of terror," the aim of which was to end Nicholas's reign. Nine months later the entire nation was in the grip of a general strike, without trains, electricity, hospitals, or newspapers.

Finally, on October 30, 1905, Tsar Nicholas relinquished some authority, together with the title "Autocrat of All the Russias." In his "Imperial Manifesto," Nicholas decreed that under a new, elected parliament named the Duma, Russia would become a semiconstitutional monarchy, with certain rights and freedoms guaranteed to the people. The tsar and the ministers he appointed would retain control of foreign policy.

For the more extreme partisans, it was far too little, too late. By December the soviet (council) of Moscow brought two thousand workers and students together to barricade the streets around the Kremlin, where they proclaimed a new "Provisional Government." That December, Vladimir Ilyitch Lenin, the Marxist revolutionary, secretly returned from exile for the first time in a decade.

Lenin, then thirty-five years old, had been exiled to Siberia in 1897 for inciting unrest among workers and had then removed to Europe to publish *Iskra*, his periodical dedicated to unifying the fractious revolutionary forces within Russia; he lived much of the time in Switzerland, first in Geneva with his mentor Plekhanov, and then in Zurich (where the teenage Jules Bryner had worked before his early life at sea). In July 1903 the exiled Russian Social Democratic Party, of which Lenin had been a member since 1898, held a meeting of forty-three delegates in Belgium, where the Plekhanov group that wanted a broad, collectivist leadership for Marxist Russia proved to be the "Minorityites" or Menshevik Party; Lenin's followers, who wanted an elite, restricted party of leaders, were the "Majorityite" or Bolshevik Party, and won the day.

Gradually, though, the initial surge of revolutionary fervor across Russia dampened and faded. The chance for self-government under an elected parliamentary Duma was tantalizing enough to undercut the tepid appeal radical socialism held for the bourgeoisie. Besides, the massive demonstrations and strikes that had lit the nation had been aimed at stopping the war. Once the war was over, the workers returned to their jobs, and V. I. Lenin returned to exile in Europe for twelve more years. But by this time he was closely associated with Leon Trotsky, and in Finland he had already met twenty-six-year-old Josef Stalin. The "Triumvirate of the Soviet Empire" had been brought together by the war with Japan.

The "failed" revolution of 1905, like the victorious Bolshevik revolution in 1917, began as an anti-war movement abetted by famine, and ended unexpectedly with a new form of government.

In his magisterial study, *The Rise and Fall of the Great Powers*, historian Paul Kennedy observed that, "if a state overextends itself strategically — by,

Marie Huber Bryner (1824–1879), wife of Johannes, mother of Jules and seven other children.

The earliest photo of Jules Bryner (1849–1920), at age forty-three, was taken in Vladivostok.

he farmhouse of Johannes and Marie Bryner in Möriken-Wildegg near Zurich, where Jules lived ntil 1863, when he sailed with pirates to Shanghai.

The corvette *America*, built in Boston, in which Count Muraviev first explored Amur Bay.

This photo was taken in 1866, just six years after the Russian Navy first stationed forty-eight sailors in the wilderness, surrounded by tigers, wolves, and bears. The outpost was named Vladivostok, which means "Ruler of the East."

Vladivostok in 1874, about the time Jules made his first visit.

ladivostok a decade later. Jules had moved his shipping business to the city four years earlier.

Natalya Bryner was married to Jules at sixteen. She was a cousin of Mikhail Yankovsky's wife, and her grandfather was part Buryat.

The Bryners in Vladivostok: Leonid (age 8), Natalya (26), Marie (1), Jules (43), Margrit (7 and Boris (3).

Built in 1882 with bricks imported from Hamburg, Kunst and Albers was "an encyclopaedic store where one could buy everything from a needle to a live tiger"; it boasted the first elevator in Asia.

The main summer home at the Bryners' Sidemy estate on Yankovsky Peninsula, a half-day's sail across Amur Bay from Vladivostok.

Aleutskaya Street, where Jules built the Bryner Residence in 1910, was still primitive twenty years earlier; telephone poles were erected in 1884.

Tsarevitch Nicholas worshipped at the Uspensky Cathedral in May 1891 before proceeding to the site of the Vladivostok Train Station.

In 1896, Jules was forty-seven; his Far East Shipping Company was expanding, he had opened the silver mine in Tetukhe, and he had signed the fateful Yalu River timber contract with the emperor of Korea.

Tsarevitch Nicholas at the time of his visit to Vladivostok. This photo was presented to notables of the Amur society, established by Jules Bryner.

King Kojong, later emperor of Korea, lived in the Russian embassy in Seoul when Jules met with him in 1896 and signed the timber contract.

Alexander Bezobrazov, who urged the tsar to acquire the Yalu River concession from Jules as a challenge to Japan, was a man of "ill-balanced faculties in which imagination predominates."

Finance Minister Sergei Witte, "father of the Trans-Siberian Railroad," assigned secret agent Pokotilov to spy on Jules Bryner in Korea.

Vladivostok Train Station, the last stop on the longest railroad in the world. Tsarevitch Nicholas laid the cornerstone in 1891 with Jules and other city fathers (here the station is shown after it was enlarged).

More than fifteen hundred locomotives were ordered from Europe for the Trans-Siberian; hundreds were shipped to Vladivostok and assembled beside the port.

Governor-General Unterberger encouraged the forced relocation of Russians to the Far East.

Statue of Mikhail Yankovsky, erected in 1991 to honor Jules' closest friend and relative by marriage: tiger hunter, zoologist, ginseng pioneer, warrior, and early environmentalist.

Tsar Nicholas II and his wife Alexandra (in carriage) in front of the Winter Palace, reviewing troops bound for Korea in 1904.

After losing history's greatest sea and land battles to date, the Russian Army retreated from Korea. The war with Japan produced the Revolution of 1905, which stripped the tsar of autocratic rule.

The Bryner Residence, built by Jules in 1910; Yul was born in 1920 in the upper-right room.

Initially, Trans-Siberian trains started out along Aleutskaya Street, passing directly in front of the Bryner Residence.

The first lighthouse Jules built, on Rabbit Island in front of the Bryner estate at Sidemy.

Jules' second lighthouse, at Cape Bryner, the port that served the Tetukhe mines.

The silver, lead, and zinc mines that Jules created at Tetukhe grew to a complex operation employing three thousand miners.

The monk Rasputin, whose power over Imperial policy contributed to the end of the Empire.

Cossack Ataman Semyonov led a private army of Interventionists financed by Japan and used his own armored train to maraud along the Trans-Siberian route.

By 1919, Interventionist troops from six countries marched down Svetlanskaya Street, including the American Expeditionary Force seen here.

By 1910, Jules' business empire was nearing its zenith, and he had no reason to expect that it would ever be in danger.

By 1919, World War I and the Bolshevik Revolution had undermined everything Jules had achieved in his career.

The extended family in 1914. Boris, seated opposite Jules, is wearing the military cadet uniform of the Mining Institute of St. Petersburg.

By the end of Jules' life, the rough frontier town he had helped to create was a metropolis that reached beyond the hills surrounding the harbor.

The Bryner family crypt that Jules designed five years before his death in 1920. His remains were moved before Bolsheviks despoiled the tomb.

say, the conquest of extensive territories or the waging of costly wars — it runs the risk that the potential benefits from external expansion may be outweighed by the great expense of it all." That is how all empires have eventually imploded, if they have not first been conquered by other empires.

One-quarter of the earth's circumference lies between St. Petersburg and the Trans-Siberian's terminus in Vladivostok. When Tsarevitch Nicholas laid the cornerstone for the railroad station in 1891, he was planting the seed for a revolution that would destroy him a quarter-century later. That year also marked the beginning of a terrible drought and subsequent famine that cost thousands of Russian lives, even as Russia borrowed money to construct the railroad — not for the tsar's subjects, who paid for it, or even for industries that might develop the region: this railroad was a weapons-delivery system aimed at Asia. It was also a perfect example of "a state overextending itself strategically," in Kennedy's words. *The sea gave birth to Vladivostok*; it did not need the railroad. With the limited technology of the 1890s (fifteen years later, trucks would be available), the willful determination to span Russia with an "iron bridge" was a costly, arrogant effort in which Russia's ambition overreached its capability out of ministerial hubris sanctioned by Imperial hubris. Oh yes, such a railroad *could* be built — the Imperial government proved that much. But would it be fully operable when it was needed as a *critical component* of Russia's geopolitical strategy? Would it be reliable? Or would its cost devastate the nation's confidence in the tsar and the very institution of monarchy?

Because there was a larger question posed by the construction of the railway: *Who* is entitled to determine whether or not the cost was too high: the people of Russia who filled the national coffer, or the tsar and his ministers who emptied it? Or the historians, perhaps: the retro-spectators, if you will, who, with the benefit of hindsight, can trace the consequences that flowed from every decision and then argue about it with each other unto eternity?

The war with Japan was the unintended consequence of a passive-aggressive Imperial policy that began with the tsar's purchase of the Bryner timber concession. Nicholas was a genuine, warm, and humane individual raised by military martinets and schooled in unapologetic dictatorship — a sensitive gentleman trained for insensitive tyranny, and easily misled by such persuasive courtiers as Witte and Bezobrazov — and later, Rasputin. Russia didn't need a railroad to the Far East *yet* — except to intimidate Asia; Nicholas knew that. And with its thousands of miles of taiga, Russia didn't need timberland in Korea; Jules knew that. Nonetheless, my great-grandfather chose to bring his concession from the emperor of Korea to the tsar of Russia.

Any simplification of the Russian Revolution is a distortion; still, historians agree that the ill-conceived and disastrously prosecuted war with Japan marked the beginning of the end for Imperial Russia. Even empires, *especially* empires, overreach. The Bryner concession in Korea marked the very spot where Russia's territorial ambition exceeded its capability, when the "iron bridge across Russia" became a bridge too far.

Through the war, the Bryner family — three boys and three girls, between ten and twenty-one years old — struggled with the circumstances, but of course their wealth gave them many more options than most residents of Vladivostok. To begin with, Bryner & Co. (Kuznetsov was no longer a partner) now owned ships — and an extensive shipyard — that could, if the city were targeted, spirit the family out of harm's way. And if tensions within the city became too threatening, they could cross Amur Bay to Sidemy in a few hours — even at night, if necessary, since Jules built the lighthouse. But Sidemy was just a few dozen miles from the northern edge of Korea; if Japanese troops ever marched on Vladivostok, they would arrive at the Bryners' property — and the Yankovskys' — with no warning. Needless to say, Mikhail Yankovsky had well-equipped patrols of his private army scouting the region, and probably paid for protection from the hunghu'tze bandits as well.

"Wartime Vladivostok contained ample ingredients for unrest," wrote historian Stephan, given the flow of sailors and soldiers on ships and trains. But the restless anger after the war proved even more alarming, when martial law was lifted. With the peace came a massive demobilization of ninety thousand troops, most of whom passed through the city, and outbursts of mob violence erupted periodically as sailors and stevedores mixed it up with infantry garrisons. Sections of the Trans-Siberian were periodically shut down by strikers, creating dangerous bottlenecks, and unexpectedly filling towns along the railway with whole regiments of penniless, frustrated soldiers for weeks at a time. Hundreds and possibly thousands of prisoners had been freed from jails and camps throughout the region during and after the war; they too collected in Vladivostok, mostly around the many opium dens in the long-established Korean and Chinese quarters. Poppies were still grown routinely by isolated Chinese farmers in the northern part of Primorye, and opium dens were generally tolerated throughout the Far East, in decadent neighborhoods like Millionka in Vladivostok. But it was vodka at thirty cents a pint that fueled the brawls between dockers, soldiers, prisoners, and sailors.

"Complete anarchy" exploded in Vladivostok on November 12, 1905, after Nicholas's Imperial Manifesto was read aloud at the nearby cathedral, according to the military governor: over the next three days thirty-eight people died in street fighting, some right in front of the Bryner house on Svetlanskaya Street. This eruption was purely political, between those who supported an elected Duma and those loyal to the ideal of absolute autocracy. Over the coming years, this political polarization would develop into civil war.

As turmoil from the revolution of 1905 slowly waned, Jules Bryner, now fifty-seven years old, focused his attention on a new business — one that would play a meaningful role in the next era of Russia's history. This was an enormous project that he had initiated at just the time he was meeting with the emperor of Korea nine years earlier, but had not yet been able to put into operation. Delayed first by the Korean concession, then the Boxer Rebellion, then the Russo-Japanese War and the 1905 revolution, he would now launch one of his most valuable and enduring industries, and with it a new town, built from scratch in the wilderness.

In 1896, Chinese ginseng traders had visited Yankovsky to trade their medicinal root for *panti*, the "remedy" for impotence made from the antlers of the Sika deer that Yankovsky raised; they had also brought some ore found in the hills three hundred miles north of Vladivostok. They showed it to Jules, thinking it might be silver, and offered to take him to its source. The sample did indeed contain silver, as well as calamine, a high-grade zinc oxide. After having it assayed, Jules called for the assistance of a talented Russian explorer named Sergei Maslennikov, who later became his son-in-law. A few months later, the small party, including a renowned German geologist, set out overland to a valley with the ancient Chinese name of Tetukhe, deep in the dense taiga of the Sikhote-Alin Mountains.

The Chinese traders led them on a harrowing trip, on horseback for the last leg, fending off attacks by wild boar, then on a perilous climb eight hundred feet up. There, a small hole had been carved through the undergrowth, and a cave dug into the mountain wall, exactly where the ore sample had been found. After a protracted survey, the German geologist declared that the potential yield of the site was well worth the cost of extraction. In 1897, after obtaining mining rights from the Russian government, Jules erected a fifteen-foot-tall metal sign identifying the first site as the "Upper Mine" (Рудник Верхний). The first calamine came down the hill that year, though at the negligible rate of one thousand tonnes per annum. Meanwhile, a seventeen-year-old named Feodor Silin helped Jules' party locate sites at different altitudes on the mountain that promised rich deposits of zinc and lead. There, assigned crews would dig by pickax the terraced opencast mines. Later, seven lower mineshafts were opened up, which Jules named after his wife and six children: "Natalevsky," "Leonidovsky," "Borisovsky," and so forth; these were sulphide mines with a high content of lead, zinc, and silver.

In 1897, while traveling to St. Petersburg to offer the Yalu River concession to Witte, Jules began planning the future mechanized operation. Although he had invested in coal mines on Sakhalin, and in a gold mine to the west near the Russian-Chinese border, he had never before launched such an enormous and complex business — in an unapproachable location, with no local workforce and no town to house one. He had already determined that carrying the ore overland through the mountains was not feasible: it would have to be transported to the coast, twenty-five miles away. A natural cove on the Sea of Japan would provide the operation's port; there, the ore would be loaded onto ships and transported to industrial ports in Europe.

But transporting the ore twenty-five miles to the sea was itself a daunting prospect. Jules was going to have to build his own railroad. The apparent cost involved could exceed possible profits for years to come; however, since it wouldn't have to accommodate passengers, this needn't be a full-size railroad. He had been thinking about trains ever since the issue of the trolleys and railroads had come up in Shanghai thirty years earlier; and now he and the city fathers of Vladivostok were discussing a trolley system there.

Finally, Jules decided he would build a light-gauge rail system at Tetukhe, narrow enough to carry wagons deep inside the mine shafts to be loaded with ore, yet stable enough to come all the way down the river valley to a pier in the port. He knew that in Switzerland, where he had ridden on his first train as a child, some systems used track that was sixty centimeters in width (about twenty-one inches) for transport in mountainous regions, much narrower than the gauge for passenger trains. All of this had to be powered by steam engines.

Projecting the costs of the Bryner mines accurately was a challenge. By providing all the heavy mining equipment on credit, Humboldt-Kalk A. G. of Cologne, Germany, became a significant investor in the company (of which Bryner & Co. were majority shareholders); they also built the enormous, steam-driven power plant for the whole operation (and the town), supplied jaw crushers and rolling mills, and created a concentrating plant so the operation ultimately could produce refined ore. A Bremsberger inclined railway brought the ore down three hundred yards from the Upper Mine to the main rail line. All the materials for this scheme, including the railroad and a steel pier strong enough to support wagon-loads of ore, would be delivered by ship from Europe to Cape Bryner, where Jules erected a lighthouse over the harbor, different in design from the first he had built at Sidemy.

Operating the mines would require an enormous workforce; eventually, as many as three thousand men went to work every day at the Bryner mines. But first these miners and their families would have to be relocated to the region, housed, and fed; that is why Jules built the town of Tetukhe (renamed Dalnegorsk in the Soviet era). And near the small harbor, a village of stevedores and sailors also sprang up, which they named Brynerovka.

Jules' standing as a merchant of the first guild was indispensable: this *ne plus ultra* of mercantile achievement in Russia was critical for industrial capitalization. In the previous forty years Russian industry had grown fivefold, thanks in large part to the policies of Sergei Witte, who had encouraged foreign capital investment; Jules was seeking a million rubles in foreign capital for Tetukhe (roughly the equivalent of $10 million today). By 1907 he had secured the balance of the necessary capital from a German investor named Aron Hirsch. With his oldest son, Leonid, as his associate, Jules began bringing all the elements together. In April 1908, three hundred tonnes of zinc ore from the upper mine were transported to Pristan Harbor by horse and cart along a rough trail, and loaded onto the steamship *Selun*, bound for Germany. That September, construction began on the Bryner railroad, which was operating by the following spring — with considerable security forces at hand; in this region, too, gangs of hunghu'tze were a continual threat, along with Siberian tigers. Jules requested Imperial troops to patrol the region, but they were almost useless on the bandits' home turf.

He also went to great lengths to keep his workforce (initially about one thousand men) happy, well fed, and focused on their jobs; a century later, families in Tetukhe still remember the consideration Jules showed to their grandparents. Once a week Bryner & Co. delivered bags of vegetables, potatoes, and flour to the miners' doors. He provided a free clinic for his employees and their families. And he offered money-saving options: if the miners chose, they could take a percentage of their pay in the well-made clothing that Jules brought in by ship — knowing that, otherwise, new clothing would hardly ever reach this isolated community.

In about 1910 a new power arose in the region, and across Russia. Partisan fighters with a stronghold in the village of Olga, not far from Tetukhe, led by Communist hero Sergei Lazo, were intent upon overthrowing the tsar's exploitive government at the local level, as well as capitalist industries. Eventually, partisan forces grew to some fifty thousand men in two hundred independent groups. "The word 'partisan' embraced a heterogeneous and changeable constituency," wrote Stephan. "Criminals called themselves partisans whenever they wanted to confer a patina of legitimacy on plunder. . . . Some partisans professed to believe in 'freedom' and 'democracy' and regarded Bolsheviks as meddlesome outsiders." It was the Bolshevik Lazo, the brash, handsome, tough enforcer who, in the coming years, would unify the splintered Communist groups in the region between Tetukhe and Vladivostok.

The Marxist ideology espoused by the partisans offered a new society adapted specifically to the well-being of miners and other proletarians; therefore the partisan Reds, as they were called, spent a lot of effort trying to strong-arm miners into the Communist movement and turn them against Bryner & Co. But their message was largely lost in Tetukhe, where the workers seemed genuinely content with their lot, despite harassment by the partisans. On one payday in early winter, a miner leaving the Bryner office, pleased with the new gloves he had received along with his pay, was accosted by two partisans, who wrested the gloves away and cut the fingertips off them. "Look at the shit material Jules Bryner gives his miners," spat one of the partisans, throwing the gloves on the ground. "Bryner will continue to exploit the people until the day his mines belong to us." Such attacks increased steadily over the next decade, even as attacks by Siberian tigers came less often.

In 1910 the Bryners moved into their new home on Tiger Hill, at 15 Aleutskaya Street, halfway between the Bryner offices and the train station. The train that was just a five-minute stroll from his house could deliver Jules to St. Petersburg a week later; that very notion was a novelty for someone born in 1849. The Bryner Residence, as the house has been known ever since, was designed by the same German architect, Junghändel, who had already designed many of the city's stone buildings in a wide variety of architectural styles. But this three-story townhouse was like no other, displaying a stunning, fresh, art nouveau mode, with playful detail, instantly brightening the stretch of buildings overlooking the main port. Mrs. Pray was impressed and wrote that "yesterday afternoon I went to call on Mrs. Bryner as she is now settled in the new house, which is very nice. The old dining-room has two big alcoves now and looks like something in the L.H.J. [*Ladies' Home Journal*]: from one alcove the staircase goes up and it is all so pretty and cozy."

That year Vladivostok celebrated the fiftieth anniversary of its founding, when tigers still roamed Tiger Hill. The rough-and-tumble port first settled by forty-eight intrepid sailors had become a cosmopolitan center. By 1897 the population of all Far East Russia had reached about three hundred thousand, of which about 30 percent were Chinese and Korean residents. By 1914 the total population of all Siberia reached fifteen million, mostly migrants resettled in the nearby fertile corridor of southern Siberia. Now, horseless carriages from Baltic Machine Works puttered among the horse carts and, and before long, Belgian trams started clattering along Svetlanskaya Street, which now had electric streetlights. There was a Japanese consulate, many new churches, and a cinema named "Illusion," where Charlie Chaplin's films were soon the rage. A fearless Russian flyboy successfully demonstrated heavier-than-air aviation over Vladivostok just seven years after the Wright brothers first flight in North Carolina; at a shipyard in the Golden Horn Bay, some of the earliest effective submarines were being designed and tested.

Also in 1910, Mikhail Yankovsky left Sidemy and abandoned his wife, Olga, for a much younger woman; he passed away two years later in the Crimea. His son Yuri, then thirty-one, inherited the vast estate adjoining the Bryners', including the horse-breeding business and the deer farms. The Bryners remained closely involved with Yuri Yankovsky, who is still famous today as Asia's greatest tiger hunter. A remarkable and fearless sharpshooter, in his time Yankovsky must have killed hundreds of tigers. In those days the Tiger Balm Company in China, whose camphor balm for sore muscles was advertised as having tiger cartilage in its ointment, had purchasing agents who traveled through the Amur region, offering a generous sum for carcasses. The Yankovsky family could not have imagined that today the Siberian tiger faces near-certain extinction.

Still that same year, Jules' second son, Boris, was preparing for university. Both Jules and Leonid knew a great deal about business, but almost nothing about engineering or geology, so Boris decided to earn his degree at the Gorny [Mining] Institute in St. Petersburg, in order to grasp all the technical aspects of the mines at Tetukhe — and future mines. Doubtless my grandfather Boris was also delighted, at the age of twenty, to escape the confines of Vladivostok's small society for the breathtaking sophistication of the Imperial city.

And perhaps to escape the confines of his mother's overbearing temperament as well. Natalya was, by all accounts, a chronically angry person. By this time Leonid's first wife, Maria Theresa Williams, an American, had fled her marriage and the close-knit Bryner family. She was driven away, it seems, by the behavior of her mother-in-law, whose possessiveness toward her three sons she found intolerable. Jules, preoccupied with work and revolution, was emotionally disengaged. He apparently wafted above the disputes in the family, played out mostly in French, which was the primary language used in the Bryner home. (In fact, at home he was called by his preferred name, "Jules," though in Russian he was always "Juli.") Leonid soon remarried and moved into his own house, at about the time that Boris, at twenty-one, boarded the Trans-Siberian Railroad for St. Petersburg.

• • • • • • • •

There, at the Winter Palace, Tsar Nicholas and Tsarina Alexandra were in the thrall of Rasputin, the mad monk. Gregory Efimovitch (or Rasputin, which means "dissolute," a childhood nickname that Gregory kept as a badge) was a peasant and healer, an overpowering personality who used his hypnotic powers for good and for evil, to cure the ill and seduce the innocent. As his influence over the Imperial couple expanded, so also did his debauchery and his notoriety.

Since childhood the crown prince, Alexis, a hemophiliac, had periodically endured numerous medical crises during which minor wounds became life-threatening events. Alexandra, the German-born tsarina, was a devoted and desperate mother who spent sleepless nights caring for her boy, as did the tsar himself. So when Rasputin visited the Winter Palace and, merely by his presence, stopped Alexis's medical crises on several separate occasions, Alexandra submitted to the belief that this monk had the very will of God at his personal command, as she made clear in her voluminous correspondence with her husband. Even as Rasputin began insisting upon major changes to governmental policy with Nicholas, relayed by his credulous yet strong-willed wife, the tsar viewed Rasputin's governmental advice as God-given and his life as saintly. This admiration says a great deal about Nicholas's catastrophically poor judgment of character, because when Rasputin wasn't influencing the course of history, this unsaintly degenerate was a reckless hypocrite in a monk's cloak, known for his many romantic conquests, accomplished, it was said, by his hypnotic powers. That may be the best explanation, since he was also renowned for his poor hygiene. Rasputin spent stretches of time in hermit-like isolation, followed by periodic binges of deranged drunken behavior. Yet "no one dared speak to the tsar about Rasputin. No one even dared arrest the monk when he smashed up night clubs. . . . About this time I first began to hear talk of a revolution," one contemporary noted.

When he was in Moscow, Rasputin often visited the fabled Gypsy village of Mokroie to the south, depicted by Dostoyevsky in *The Brothers Karamazov*. Mokroie had been a Gypsy enclave since the reign of Catherine the Great, when her friend Count Orlov introduced the nobility to the music of the Russian Gypsies, or "Tzigani." By the late 1800s, Mokroie had become a retreat where the unleashed revelry in its bars and brothels and gambling dens was accompanied by Gypsy guitars and voices. The best-known musician in Mokroie was a Tzigan named Ivan Dimitrievitch, who played the seven-string guitar and sang mostly in Rom, the Gypsy language. Ivan tried to murder Rasputin one night in Mokroie, and having failed, he and his clan, or *kumpania*, set out in about 1915 for the safety of Paris, according to his son, Aliosha; there, twenty years later, the Dimitrievitch family played a pivotal role in the life of Yul Brynner.

In August 1914, the assassination of the heir to the Austro-Hungarian throne, Archduke Ferdinand, triggered World War I. For the record, the Austro-Hungarian Empire declared war on Serbia; Germany declared war on Russia and France; Britain declared war on Germany; Austria declared war on Russia; Serbia and Montenegro declared war on Germany; France and Britain declared war on Austria; Austria declared war on Belgium; and Russia, France, and Britain declared war on Turkey. Summarized so succinctly, the effect would be comical were it not for the millions of deaths in the trenches from bombs and bullets, mustard gas and disease.

World War I brought Russia to the fore against Germany, highlighting Alexandra's Teutonic origins and putting Nicholas in a progressively more untenable position with his people, especially as Russia lost battle after battle against the highly mechanized German military machine. The Duma, which had no constitutional role in foreign affairs, watched helplessly as the army blundered again and again. Gradually, public anger focused upon Alexandra, who was widely believed to be working for Germany's victory. With the outbreak of the war, Nicholas made every effort to appeal to Russian patriotism, even changing the name of his capital city from the Germanic "St. Petersburg" to the Slavic "Petrograd." But while Nicholas was spending most of his time with the military command away from the capital, Alexandra — apparently under the complete control of Rasputin with regard to ministers, policy, and even military strategy — took a more and more active role in the Imperial government. Socially isolated, she did not understand that she was the object of widespread loathing.

The Great War — as it was forever remembered by most who lived through it — had an immediate impact in Vladivostok. The Far East Shipping Company now faced the threat of torpedoes. The Bryner mines closed overnight because their key engineers and technicians were Germans, expelled immediately from Russia. Many of the Russian miners were drafted, and thousands of small towns like Tetukhe were reduced to populations that could not feed themselves: women, children, and old men. Although Jules did his best to help the miners' families, he could not support thousands of people from his own pocket indefinitely.

Much of the new anti-war agitation that arose came directly from the sentiments that had erupted twelve years earlier on "Bloody Sunday," and mostly from the same population against the same tsar — though with new contempt. What was particularly different now was the enormous organization that had been prepared by labor unions, workers' soviets, and local governments, or *zemstvos*. This resentment of the war and the political fervor it inspired did not arise from an abstract pacifism, nor from a failure of patriotism or courage, both of which the Russian people possessed in abundance. For three years anti-war sentiment grew from a smoldering ember to a bonfire as a desperate, visceral reaction to the intolerable suffering that World War I inflicted upon villages and towns that could no longer function. Across rural Russia hay could not be harvested to feed livestock, meat could not be hunted, roofs could not be repaired, and criminals acted with impunity.

All this suffering, it seemed, just so that Tsar Nicholas II could join with one of his cousins, King George V of England, to defeat another cousin, Kaiser Wilhelm II, when the pompous German monarch decided that France was his for the taking. As Russian casualties rose, public expressions of loathing for Empress Alexandra became commonplace, even in the press, along with wild tales of debaucheries with the dissolute Rasputin, to whom the German princess had handed all the powers of Russia, it was said, while Nicholas was off "playing soldier" at army headquarters. Every time Nicholas reaffirmed his love for Alexandra, public disgust with him mounted.

In 1916, Rasputin was murdered by one of the many aristocrats who thought the mad monk was destroying the monarchy — especially in the appointment of new ministers that Rasputin had insisted upon, and which Nicholas had carried out. The parliamentary Duma was by now a seething cauldron of collective anger, ideological polarization, and personal animosity. Anti-Tsarist rhetoric in the Duma became so inflammatory that Nicholas simply removed or outlawed some members, making a mockery of the only achievement of the 1905 revolution.

The Russian Empire came to an end on Monday, March 12, 1917, with the creation of a new Provisional Government, and on March 15, Nicholas II, the last tsar, abdicated his throne. He went further, and abdicated as well on behalf of his ailing teenage son, Alexis. With that, Nicholas ended three hundred years of Romanov rule. In November 1917, the Provisional Government was deposed, and the All-Russian Congress of Soviets assumed power under Lenin's forceful leadership of the Bolshevik Party, reinforced by the secret police, or Cheka (from *Vecheka*, an acronym for the All-Russian Extraordinary Commission to Combat Counter-Revolution and Sabotage). Their ice-chief, Felix Dzerzhinsky, was the most passionate and dedicated of revolutionaries, and Lenin considered him his personal hero. Over the coming years, the Cheka created by "Iron Felix" would evolve into the GPU, and then the OGPU, the MVD, and then the KGB.

The Imperial couple and their children were taken as prisoners to the city of Ekaterinburg, ostensibly to await exile to England. Instead, they were held under house arrest for a year in increasingly dire conditions. On July 16, 1918, Nicholas and Alexandra, Alexis and his four sisters — Olga, Tatiana, Marie, and Anastasia — were taken to a basement and murdered by a Cheka firing squad. Anastasia, seventeen years old, "recovered consciousness and began to scream," according to a contemporary. "She was bayoneted to the floor by eighteen thrusts." She died with her spaniel, Jimmy, in her arms. The mangled bodies of the royal family were dumped in a mine shaft and later found in a shallow grave.

Jules Bryner was sixty-eight years old when the Russian Empire collapsed, and with it, much of his own. Two of his sons had returned from university in Petrograd with brides and babies, and were living in the separate apartments of the Bryner Residence, next door to his home with Natalya. Boris Bryner had just graduated from the Mining Institute, and now there were no mines: the entire Bryner industry at Tetukhe had become the property of the Soviet government, along with every other business in Russia. As the result of a "Special Board" hearing by the Provisional Government, Jules was removed from the mine's board; when the Provisional Government fell, the mines were left without a legal owner. However, the import-export business remained the Bryners', because Jules had had the foresight to register the Far East Shipping Company and its ships in the British colony of Hong Kong, assuming rightly that the new Soviet government would not choose to provoke Great Britain.

Natalya, at fifty-two, often succumbed to deep fits of depression that had begun decades earlier with the death of her first daughter. In 1916, when Natalya's younger sister died, she was left distraught and morbidly preoccupied; she had cared for Antonina since they were little girls. She prevailed upon Jules to build a Bryner tomb at Sidemy, where her late sister would be the first buried. Jules acceded with the construction of a stolid, soulless twelve-foot-high Greek archway with four grand pillars and no suggestion whatsoever of religion. This must have been a concession to Jules' Lutheran commitment, because all the family's religious rituals — weddings, baptisms, and funerals — transpired at the Uspensky Orthodox Cathedral. Still, Natalya often unleashed her tempestuous anger.

Meanwhile, there was a tempest outside, growing daily in Aleutskaya Street, in front of the Bryners' cheerful art nouveau facade. The abdication of Nicholas signaled the start of five years in which, almost month by month, a different political party ascended to power in Vladivostok only to be brought down by a successor: Partisans, Mensheviks, Bolsheviks, Moderates, even pro-Tsarists vied for control over Primorye. With each new ascendancy, supporters and troops would arrive at the Vladivostok Train Station and march in formation, or stroll, or run, or fight their way to the center of town. Once again, the Trans-Siberian Railroad was key to Russia's history, because "the ribbon of steel linking the Far East to the Center," wrote one historian, "served as a lightning rod for revolution," the main artery for civil war to reach Vladivostok.

Had the Russian Civil War been simply a contest between the Red Army and anti-Communist Whites, the outcome might have been very different. But resistance to the Bolsheviks was divided among incompatible factions, from moderate socialists to extreme monarchists, and could not agree on strategies or policies. Atrocities were committed by Reds and Whites alike, though many of those by the Reds were later covered up. And "unlike the Reds," wrote Stephan, "who killed methodically in the name of a higher principle (class struggle, revolution, human progress), Whites murdered in a wild fury at everything and everyone whom they thought had destroyed their pre-Revolutionary world."

Atrocities were also committed over the next four years by multinational troops of the Siberian Intervention, which grew directly out of World War I. Ostensibly, the Interventionist nations, including Japan, the United States, Britain, and France, intended to restrict Soviet authority (which was under Lenin's absolute control) to western Russia, and thereby secure independence for Siberia and Far East Russia. Although this was decades before U.S. diplomat George Kennan recommended "containment" as a policy toward Communism, in fact containment began with the Intervention.

Beneath their stated goal, however, all of the allied nations had their own motives, revenge not the least of them. Because the new Soviet government had suddenly signed a separate peace with Germany and Austria (the Brest-Litovsk Treaty), leaving its allies — France, England, the United States and others — in dire straits strategically, even as World War I raged on.

As the Russian Empire collapsed upon itself, it left a vacuum of authority across the vast continent. Every political office at every level was up for grabs between a half-dozen major political parties that often recruited with threats and violence. At the same time, as a condition of its peace treaty with Germany, the Soviet government was obliged to release *2.3 million* foreign prisoners of war. That produced a flood of bitter, desperate, hungry men for the Interventionists and partisans alike to recruit from. Many of the former POWs were passionately pro- or anti-Bolshevik; others simply couldn't get home. That is what happened to forty-five thousand Czech troops traveling toward Vladivostok when the Bolsheviks, who controlled all the towns along the Trans-Siberian Railroad through local soviets and workers' unions, stopped the trains and left the Czech Legion stranded in the middle of Russia. Thereupon, they decided to fight their way eastward and join the Interventionists in Vladivostok.

So too did a fearsomely cruel Cossack leader, Ataman Grigori Semyonov, who declared his own independent Buryat Mongol Republic in Chita. He was, in the words of a contemporary, "a man of medium height, with square, broad shoulders, an enormous head, the size of which is greatly enhanced by the flat, Mongol face, from which gleam two clear brilliant eyes that rather belong to an animal than a man." White described at length the Cossack's "career of torture, murder, and robbery" as he "moved about in his famous armored railway cars":

> One of them, the *Destroyer*, had fifty-seven men and officers aboard. . . . It had ten machine guns, two three-inch guns, and two one-pounders. . . . Cars often carried off large parties of unfortunates. In a single day, according to one report, 1,600 people were carried off and killed at Adrianovka station. . . . In his more practical moments he robbed banks, stole from the customs station at Manchuli, and took what he wanted in goods or money from travelers. . . . His activities, moreover, had the complete support of the Japanese.

It is easy to see just how gravely the White Russian cause discredited itself in the Far East, where Semyonov was its principal warrior against the Bolshevik revolution.

The ataman (a Cossack title) had served as an officer in the tsar's Cossack forces of the Great War. The Japanese financed Semyonov's independent army, using him as a means of slowing down the Red Army, but also of sowing discord among the White Army, the Czech Legion, the Kadets, the Socialist Revolutionaries, the partisans, and other members of the Intervention. Japan's perceived interest lay in preventing *any* of these factions from achieving supremacy over the region for as long as possible, while trying to establish a foothold there for the mikado, who most especially did not want a Communist neighbor for Japan.

In principle, White Russian resistance to the Red Army was led by Admiral Alexander Kolchak, who, in an overstatement rarely equaled outside asylums, declared himself the "Supreme Ruler of Russia." That was in Omsk, some two thousand miles east of Moscow; from there Kolchak tried to build a credible government from scratch across the East, with the uncertain assistance of Interventionist troops. Kolchak had received numerous medals for valor during the Russo-Japanese War, but like most of Russia's war heroes, he was now a declared enemy of the Soviet state. More importantly, it was known by his enemies *and* his treacherous allies that Kolchak was traveling with *the entire treasury of the Russian Empire* hidden in train cars filled with three hundred tons of gold, somewhere along the six thousand miles of the Trans-Siberian Railroad. Of that estimated total, it seems that Kolchak shipped twenty-two crates of gold to his Japanese "allies" to pay for weapons he never received. And while each of the Interventionist nations had a separate agenda, they were all hoping to hijack Kolchak's gold; none hoped so more than Japan, which poured troops through the Golden Horn Bay and along Svetlanskaya Street to spread out across eastern Russia.

Stephan described the setting:

> Vladivostok was a world unto itself, a unique blend of provincial Russian, treaty-port Shanghai, and the American Wild

> West. A dozen languages reverberated in the lobby of the Versailles Hotel, and more than a dozen currencies circulated. . . . By 1918 there were eleven foreign expeditionary forces of varying sizes, sympathies, and agendas. Leading the list were 73,000 Japanese, followed by 55,000 Czechs, 12,000 Poles, 9,000 Americans, 5,000 Chinese, 4,000 Serbs, 4,000 Rumanians, 4,000 Canadians, 2,000 Italians, 1,600 British, and 700 French . . . clustered around Vladivostok.

Konstantin Kharnsky, a professor at the Oriental Institute, depicted the social landscape:

> Morphine, cocaine, prostitution, blackmail, sudden riches and ruin, dashing autos, a cinematic flow of faces, literary cabals, bohemian lifestyles, coups and countercoups, Mexican political morals, parliaments, dictators, speeches from balconies, newspapers from Shanghai and San Francisco, "Interventionist girls," uniforms from every kingdom, empire, republic, monarchist clubs, leftist rallies, complete isolation from Moscow.

Added to these was the broader panoply of Russian factions — Bolshevik, Menshevik, Socialist Revolutionary, Monarchist, Kadet — along with portside roustabouts by the hundreds, each one bruising for a fight. All this and more unfolded daily in front of the already tense Bryner Residence near the train station; at one time or another, all those foreign troops marched within fifty feet of the front door.

The nine thousand men of the American Expeditionary Force (AEF) were under the command of Major-General William S. Graves from Kansas City, and they paraded down Svetlanskaya Street upon their arrival. Americans were for the most part warmly welcomed; indeed, 6 percent of the AEF married Russian women. But the U.S. doughboys were also targeted by partisans. At an encampment near the village of Romanovka, that brash, partisan commander, Sergei Lazo, and his men from the Tetukhe region — some of whom had no doubt worked in the Bryner mines —

ambushed two hundred sleeping American soldiers, killing most of them in their tents. A year later Lazo himself, one of the great Soviet heroes of the Civil War, was captured by Japanese troops and delivered to the Cossacks' Trans-Siberian train, tied up inside a canvas mailbag. Lazo was still alive when the Cossacks stuffed him into the furnace of the locomotive they were riding on.

By way of retaliation, Russian partisans killed 136 Japanese prisoners along with 4,000 Russian men, women, and children of Nikolaevsk, for having "collaborated" with the Interventionists. The Civil War went on like this for four years; but unlike the American Civil War that pitted only Americans against Americans, the Russian Civil War was fought by ten foreign nations on Russian soil — most of which were intent upon *capturing* their ally, Admiral Kolchak, or at least the Imperial treasury he was transporting.

But the White Army had failed to mobilize the masses under the self-styled "Supreme Ruler of Russia," Kolchak. By its arbitrary brutality and commandeering thievery, the White movement discredited itself everywhere it went, even among those Russians sympathetic to the capitalist traditions of the bourgeoisie. The Kolchak "regime" lasted a year. After a number of successes pushing westward in early battles, his troops began abandoning him, and forced recruits resisted him by any means they could, including self-mutilation. Desperate, Kolchak finally fled toward the last stronghold of resistance, Vladivostok. But in Irkutsk the Czech Legion captured him; and while they should have been his allies, they too needed safe passage to Vladivostok. The Czechs turned Kolchak over to the Bolsheviks, who promptly shot him dead.

Some White Russians were not pro-Tsarist at all, but workers from the Urals — by the thousands, many with their families — who followed General Vladimir Kappel eastward across Siberia and Lake Baikal in December 1919 on what is remembered as the Ice March, or "Lednoy Poshod." Along this bitter trail hundreds died, including Kappel himself, and thousands more endured severe frostbite and amputations. In January 1920, the survivors joined forces with the Cossacks of Ataman Semyonov. But by that time most of the European Interventionists had left Russia, and on April 1, the last American troops departed Vladivostok aboard a steamer.

That still left tens of thousands of Japanese troops in Primorye. The Soviet government in Moscow — Lenin had just moved the seat of government there from Petrograd — was now facing military challenges in the Ukraine and Crimea. Rather than "tolerate" Japanese troops for a prolonged stay on Russian soil, Lenin tacitly approved the creation of a separate eastern state that Moscow might still control, if only through the Bolshevik Party in the region. The new state was named the Far East Russian Republic. Its flag was composed not of a crossed hammer and sickle against a red background, but a crossed plow and anchor against blue.

Jules Bryner died in March 1920, a month before Vladivostok became the principal city of the new Republic. He was seventy-one years old. It had to have been a dizzying experience for him to reflect upon his childhood in Switzerland, adolescence as a brigand, apprenticeship in Shanghai, the family he abandoned in Yokohama, and his first view of Golden Horn Bay, when tigers still roamed the hill where his art nouveau home now stood in the midst of revolution. Jules had outlived most of his contemporaries: Gustav Albers, Mikhail Yankovsky, Sergei Witte . . . and Tsar Nicholas. But he could not lie easy upon his deathbed when he considered his family's future. Bolsheviks murdered industrialists and their families. Still, Jules knew that he was leaving his heirs with a considerable fortune, and that, if they felt threatened, his sons could walk the family down to the port and board one of the Far East Shipping Company steamers for any destination they chose.

Jules' remains were taken to the large tomb he had built at Sidemy and were buried there. But with the approach of Bolshevik forces, his remains were removed and cremated by loyal Korean workers and scattered to the wind, so that they would not be desecrated if the tomb were raided, as it soon was. Jules left behind his child bride, Natalya, now 55, and three daughters and three sons who had already produced five grandchildren. Then, four months after Jules died, Boris's wife, Maria, delivered a second child, a boy baptized "Juli" who, as a child, began writing his name "Yul."

Two more years of intense chaos in Vladivostok followed before the Russian Civil War ended and the Far East Russian Republic was absorbed into — not exactly Russia anymore, but the Union of Soviet Socialist Republics. During those years, people "kept two flags, one red and one tricolor, to hand out as the occasion demanded," wrote historian Canfield Smith. "Government in Vladivostok was paralyzed, because nobody was certain who constituted the government." In June 1921, Ataman Semyonov suddenly commandeered the Hotel Versailles as his headquarters and declared himself the successor to Kolchak; so for anyone who believed him, the "Supreme Ruler of Russia" was now living on Svetlanskaya Street. But the White government that was in power briefly would not tolerate the cutthroat Cossack in their midst, and before long neither did Semyonov's Japanese sponsors.

The flood of families fleeing Bolshevism from towns great and small had begun as early 1917; by this time, a deluge of Russian émigrés was pouring into Western Europe. Many were willing to take a big gamble and travel on to the United States, but the Russian diaspora also carried families to South America and Australia, Korea and Shanghai. In China, Harbin's population ballooned: in less than thirty years it grew from zero to half a million. For those able to escape Russia with their wealth intact, the destination of choice was almost invariably Paris.

When the Red Army marched down Svetlanskaya Street on October 25, 1922 — to liberate the city from White Russian capitalists like the Bryners — its arrival marked the final triumph of the Communist revolution all across the country, soon followed by the official creation of the Union of Soviet Socialist Republics. For the next seventy years, that date would remind the people of the Soviet Union that Vladivostok had been "the last city in Russia."

PART TWO
BORIS BRYNER

Though Vladivostok is a long way off, it is after all one of our towns.

— Vladimir Ilyitch Lenin (1922)

Boris Julievitch Bryner grew up as a prince of Primorye, with all but the formal title. From the day he was born, September 29, 1889, until the twilight of the Russian Empire, he led a charmed existence. Unlike his Swiss-born father, he was a Russian child, and one for whom privilege and luxury came naturally in an era when it was still respectable to be wealthy in his homeland.

But idle wealth was never an option. His father was a man to whom hard work was a matter of character not choice, and who believed that much must be returned from those to whom much was given. He wanted his three daughters to marry well, but he hoped that his three sons would share his passion for work, and deliberately groomed them to take over different aspects of his industrial empire, according to their interests. Leonid, five years older than Boris, and their youngest brother, Felix, shared that ambition naturally; Boris, however, might have chosen a different path in his life, but he was also a dutiful son, who recognized his responsibilities as a scion of their industrial and shipping empire.

So in 1910, having sent his trunks on ahead, the twenty-one year old walked one block down from the Bryners' home to the Vladivostok Station and boarded the Trans-Siberian Railroad for the one-week ride west, to attend the Mining Institute of St. Petersburg. By the time Boris graduated five years later, the name of both the capital city and the Institute had been changed — to Petrograd — and so had almost everything else in his world.

Boris attended secondary school at the Vladivostok Gymnasium, but Jules sent his youngest son, Felix, to school in Lausanne, Switzerland, not far from Geneva and the village where Jules himself was born. Leonid, the oldest, had by then returned from St. Petersburg University, where he had gone to study law and to become an officer cadet in the army, as other well-to-do children from Vladivostok did. Boris, no less a patriot, chose to attend the Mining Institute, which was also a military academy that provided officer training; he too would be wearing a tsarist uniform in the growing pre-Revolutionary tumult.

The Mining Institute was the finest geological institution in the world, and vastly different from any grimy tunnels the name might conjure up. It was founded in 1773 by Catherine the Great with the encouragement of her friends in France, Voltaire, patriarch of the Enlightenment, and Diderot, the first encyclopedist. As part of the institute's magnificent home near St. Petersburg University beside the Neva River, the empress included a museum to house a collection of rare minerals and geological samples from around the world that was, and still is today, unequaled. The collection included the largest gold nugget ever found — roughly the size and shape of a baby hippopotamus — purportedly one of the national treasures that Admiral Kolchak later carried on his "train of gold" during the Civil War. The dozen or so vast halls filled with displays under glass were — and still are — decorated with large frescoes, gilded trim, and oak paneling.

Though one might expect that the institute was a narrowly focused professional school, the course requirements included history and literature in French, German, and Russian, as well as geology, chemistry, and engineering. Boris had a definite advantage in that all three languages were regularly spoken in his home. In 1915, after four years there, he submitted a forty-page thesis for his master's degree, entitled "Strata of Lead, Silver, and Zinc in the Mines of Tetukhe." In this published study, Boris briefly recounted his father's development of the mines, then detailed the mapping of the estimated ore and the most modern techniques of detecting and extracting nonferrous metals. The following year he defended his thesis, whereupon he received a master's degree with honors in mining engineering, the 2,824th degree awarded in the institute's century-old history.

During Boris's first few years in St. Petersburg, the city was relatively calm on the surface, despite growing whispers about Rasputin and the German-born tsarina. Most of the political turmoil was confined to the Duma, which was often deadlocked by the polarized party politics, and occasionally by the unconstitutional interference of Tsar Nicholas II. Meanwhile, in the halls of the workers' unions and the conference rooms of soviets (councils) around the city, organizers and agitators like Leon Trotsky talked up a storm that seemed to many like hot air.

In the streets and along the canals, the city sparkled with culture, wealth, and high society. Before and during the eighteenth-century reign of Catherine the Great, St. Petersburg was transformed into a majestic capital with more than 120 palaces in the heart of the city, many built along the embankment of the Neva River. Grandest of all was the Imperial family's Winter Palace, formerly the principal home of the tsar — until the assassination of Nicholas's grandfather, Alexander II, in 1881. Between 1910 and 1916, the years that Boris was at university, Nicholas and Alexandra rarely stayed at the Winter Palace (which later became the Hermitage Museum). They felt happier living a modest family life at their country estate, Tsarskoe Selo — and, after "Bloody Sunday" in 1905 — safer as well.

But there were many other social figures in the city for Boris to meet and mingle with. In the thin oxygen of those cosmopolitan heights, many among the aristocracy were living beyond their means, though some did not realize it yet and others did their best to ignore it. Nonetheless, as the son of a merchant of the first guild, Boris had entrée among all the industrial elite; this was a heady experience after a lifetime in the remote, provincial world of Vladivostok — where he still returned most summers to visit his parents at Sidemy.

He also made several trips to western Europe, including London and Paris; and though he never visited his ancestral home of Möriken-Wildegg in Switzerland, Boris and all his siblings were entitled to Swiss passports. The Russian government regarded dual-nationals as *exclusively* Russian citizens, but for the Swiss, citizenship is an inherent right and an inalienable fact, like the color of your eyes, not something that could ever be renounced as it is for Americans and others. What's more, the male descendants of any Swiss father are automatically Swiss wherever they are born for the next four generations. This only operates along the male line, described frankly under the law as "paternal privilege": the right of a Swiss father to pass his nationality down to his sons, his grandsons, and even his great-grandsons.

Boris had been raised by Jules to be diligent and meticulous; he was also sociable, witty, soulful, and carefree, with a fine tenor voice that he occasionally let out at parties. The first thing women invariably noticed was that Boris was stunningly handsome, which remained true even as his demeanor became weathered by age and ordeal. He was taller than his father, trim and very athletic, with close-cropped hair that he grew somewhat longer in later years.

Boris was just preparing to write his master's thesis when World War I erupted, and everything in Russia changed overnight. Patriotism ruled the day across the country, and people proudly displayed their loyal support for the emperor and his troops. When Nicholas II made his formal declaration of war in August 1914, throngs of people lined the Neva to greet his yacht, the *Standart*, as he made his way to the Winter Palace where tens of thousands teemed in the palace square — the largest public gathering there since Bloody Sunday nine years earlier. From the palace, Nicholas and Alexandra stepped out on a balcony and were greeted by a roaring rendition of the Imperial anthem. Just four years later, after Nicholas had sent fifteen million citizens to war, their mutilated corpses would lie in a mine shaft.

From that first day there was also powerful opposition to the war, even among the aristocracy and the ministries. Count Sergei Witte could hardly restrain himself. "This war is madness," he wrote. "Our pious duty is to help our blood brothers? That is a romantic, old-fashioned chimera. . . . What can we hope to get? An increase of territory. Great Heavens! Isn't His Majesty's empire big enough already? . . . My practical conclusion is that we must liquidate this stupid adventure as soon as possible."

Toward the end of his university career, Boris fell in love with a young woman named Maria Dimitrievna Blagovidova, a tall, stately, and demure young lady with dark hair that fell almost to her knees, the daughter of a doctor in Vladivostok, Dimitri Evgrafovich Blagovidov. Boris and Marousia, as she was usually known, were the same age, and had first met as teenagers in the Far East. They became romantically involved now, while she was studying at the Conservatory in Petrograd to become a singer and actress in light opera, and planning for a life in the theater.

The Blagovidov family belonged to a social class specific to Russian culture: the *intelligentsiya*, different from the intelligentsia of other countries in that Russian society actually identified and admired such individuals as members of this class. The intelligentsiya was not restricted to the wealthy or titled, as in most European countries, nor were its members merely intellectuals or academics. Rather, they were "Renaissance men" — and women, too, for whom Catherine the Great had been a liberating icon, if not exactly a role model. Marousia's sister, Vera, was a shining example of that class of intelligentsiya: the first woman licensed as a doctor in the field[a] of psychiatry in Russia, she was at the same time a noted concert pianist. Soon after Marousia accepted Boris's marriage proposal, *her* sister, Vera, fell in love with *his* brother, Felix.

But as Boris looked ahead, he could anticipate trouble — especially if the wedding were held in Vladivostok. He did not expect his mother, Natalya, to appreciate his bride-to-be. Natalya neither admired nor aspired to the intelligentsiya, and the fact that the Blagovidova girls' maternal grandfather had been Jewish (a Dr. Shari, who changed his name after converting to the Russian Orthodox Church), may not have endeared them to the Bryner matriarch either. But what Natalya disliked most about Marousia and Vera was their modernity: they were free-spirited women in their speech and their actions, unconstrained by most Orthodox teachings; Marousia was even training to be a *performer*, which was hardly respectable for the wife of an industrialist — especially in a small city like Vladivostok, where they would have to make their home.

Because now that Boris had his degree, he was committed to reopening the mines at Tetukhe once the Great War ended. Jules was in his late sixties, and before long he would not be able to tolerate the difficult two-day trip there from Vladivostok. There was no one else to manage the mines, and Boris could not do that from Petrograd or Moscow, where the whole repertoire of Marousia's beloved Russian light operas was performed regularly. To marry Boris, Marousia would have to renounce the career she had been working toward since she was a girl.

It was a very painful decision. Marousia's family had made great sacrifices to pay for her costly tuition and travel far from home. Worse, Boris insisted that their wedding take place *before* they returned to Vladivostok, to present Jules and Natalya with a *fait accompli*. That meant that, apart from her sister, Vera, none of Marousia's own family could attend her wedding. To the conservative Orthodox social world, it seemed very much as if the son of a merchant of the first guild was eloping with a would-be actress.

But Marousia was hopelessly in love with Boris and acceded to his every request. They were married in Petrograd while Boris was still a student, and by the time they boarded the Trans-Siberian Railroad to return to Vladivostok, they were expecting their first child. By this time, Vera was living openly with Felix in Petrograd, disregarding the hypocrisy of social dictates in spite of the fact that Felix was an officer in the tsar's army. Boris was certain that his mother was going to be furious with him and with his younger brother.

He was right. Natalya despised the sisters Blagovidova, a fact she made clear the moment she met them. She especially hated Marousia, perhaps because Boris was her favorite son. It might not have been so difficult had Boris not made their home in the Bryner Residence, but this was wartime, and with growing social and political unrest, it was best that they stay close together. All except Natalya, who profoundly resented the intrusion of this free-thinking actress who had entrapped her son. Her loathing was exacerbated by the birth of Boris's child, a daughter, born at the Bryner Residence on January 17, 1916, whom he and Marousia named after her sister, Vera.

In March 1917, shortly after Boris and Marousia settled in Vladivostok, Tsar Nicholas II was forced to abdicate after the Winter Palace fell to the revolutionaries, along with all of Petrograd; meanwhile, across the Neva, Vera and Felix learned that they too were expecting a child. Felix asked her to marry him, but Vera did not accept at first out of concern for her career as a doctor at the psychiatric hospital, Panteleimon; she was determined to keep her independence, and avant-garde enough to dispense with the niceties of marriage.

But then, on April 9, Vladimir Ilyitch Lenin returned to Russia upon a special train provided by Kaiser Wilhelm II, who was counting upon Lenin's anti-war sentiments and leadership to end the war. As an inspirational rabble-rouser, Lenin was unparalleled, and when he was not immediately welcomed by all the Communist factions, he began speaking in public venues around Petrograd. Felix later described to his daughter how he had encountered Lenin personally, "in his capacity as a Tsarist army officer; during one of those political meetings, he tried to pull Lenin off the podium."

Lenin was an unlikely personality to launch a bloody revolution; then again, he never acknowledged launching anything. In 1919, the English author Arthur Ransome, a left-leaning journalist with the *Manchester Guardian*, spent many hours with him in private conversation and emerged impressed by his modesty.

> Lenin struck me as a happy man. Walking home from the Kremlin, I tried to think of any other man of his caliber who had had a similar joyous temperament. I could think of none. This little, bald-headed, wrinkled man, who tilts his chair this way and that, laughing over one thing or another, ready any

> minute to give serious advice to any who interrupted him to ask for it, advice so well reasoned that it is to his followers far more compelling than any command. Every one of his wrinkles is a wrinkle of laughter, not of worry. I think the reason must be that he is the first great leader who utterly discounts the value of his own personality. He is quite without personal ambition. More than that, he believes, as a Marxist, in the movement of the masses, which, with or without him, would still move. His whole faith is in the elemental forces that move people, his faith in himself is merely his belief that he justly estimates the direction of those forces. He does not believe that any man could make or stop the revolution, which he thinks inevitable.

In the subsequent weeks, as the strength of the revolution and the political chaos grew, Vera and Felix decided to have their baby in Vladivostok. With that prospect, Vera accepted Felix's proposal, and they were married on April 29, 1917. After a tumultuous trip on the Trans-Siberian Railway, upon which millions of émigrés mixed with millions of soldiers as the Great War raged, Felix and Vera joined Boris and Marousia at the Bryner Residence beside the larger building where Jules and Natalya now lived. Soon, the Blagovidovas' mother, known as Baiga (from *babayaga*, a witch), was also living with them to help with Marousia's baby girl. Now the Blagovidovas outnumbered Natalya on her own property, leaving her outraged and inconsolable. On December 1, 1917, Vera delivered a baby girl at the Residence, whom she and Felix named Irena.

With the October Revolution of 1917, Lenin's Bolsheviks led a successful coup against the post-Imperial provisional government: PEACE, LAND, AND ALL POWER TO THE SOVIET was the slogan with which they seized control. But those famous "'ten days that shook the world' only ruffled the Far East," wrote historian Stephan. The Bolsheviks in Vladivostok had been developing a strong organization among railway and port workers, sailors, troops, and miners. On November 18, they temporarily took control of Vladivostok and most of Primorye.

ɔris Bryner, raised as a prince of Primorye, shown here in Imperial Cadet uniform in 1914.

Jules and Natalya Bryner's children; photographed in 1897: Margrit (age 12), Leonid (13), Nina (3), Felix (6), Marie (4), and Boris (8).

Jules and Natalya with their children and nanny at Sidemy in the summer of 1901. Boris, then twelv is at the bottom left.

In 1912, Boris rode the Trans-Siberian Railroad to study mining engineering in St. Petersburg, in order to take charge of the Tetukhe mines.

Marousia Blagovidova, who was studying to be a classical singer at the Conservatory of Music when she met Boris.

Marousia (on right) had been trained as a soprano in light opera; Vera was the first licensed female psychologist in Russia, as well as a respected concert pianist.

Soon after Boris fell in love with Marousia, his brother fell in love with her sister, Vera. Both couples soon married and moved Vladivostok, spending their summers at Sidemy, where Vera and Marousia were photographed on the beach.

Marousia and Boris had their first child, Vera, at the Bryner Residence in 1916. Jules and Natalya had settled upstairs in the larger adjoining building, above the offices of the Far East Shipping Company.

A family gathering in 1918 at Sidemy that included Boris and Marousia, Vera and Felix (with nephew Cyril).

Conscious of being photographed, Boris struck a pose that came to him naturally, and which reappeared with Yul some thirty years later.

Marousia and her son, Yul Bryner, at Sidemy in 1921. Boris was often away in Moscow negotiating the restoration of the Bryner mines.

n the living room of the Bryner Residence, Marousia and Boris played with their nephew, Cyril. This is the last photograph of them before the end of their marriage.

Valery Yankovsky was the grandson of Jules' partner and the son of Yuri, "the world's greatest tiger hunter." Yuri, a close friend of Boris, was cousin of Katya Kornakova, Boris's second wife.

In October 1923, on the first anniversary of the Soviet regime, the Red Army paraded through Vladivostok, up Aleutskaya Street from the train station on the right and past the Bryner Residence a hundred yards up on the left.

Katya Kornakova was a teenager when she ran away from home to become an actress at the Moscow Art Theatre with Konstantin Stanislavsky.

Her first important role was in Dostoyevsky's *The Village of Stepanchikovo.* Years later she was best remembered in Gorky's *The Lower Depths.*

Boris and Katya (front row) spent much of their free time with the company of the Moscow Art Theatre.

The Taming of the Shrew was one of Katya's last roles before settling in the Far East with Boris.

Boris negotiated with the government of Lenin (left) to reopen the Bryner mines. Boris continued to operate the mines during the regime of Stalin (right) until 1932, when he first faced arrest.
(Corbis Images)

Felix Dzerzhinsky, founder of the Cheka secret police, was also in charge of foreign concessions. In July 1924 Boris and Dzerzhinsky reached the agreement that reopened the mines at Tetukhe.
(Corbis Images)

Boris personally supervised the restoration of the Tetukhe mines, idle since World War I. Production resumed in 1926, saving the desperate mining town.

Stalin's economic policies crippled the mines, which were taken over by the Soviet government and providing an important source of lead for bullets in World War II.

The desolation in the faces of the family Boris left behind lingered for years. The only pictures of Yul smiling as a boy are those taken with his father.

Boris occasionally visited Yul (here, age twelve, in Harbin, China), but when he moved to Manchuria with Katya, Marousia took Yul and Vera to Paris.

In the summer of 1934, Boris visited Yul (14) and Vera (18) in Deauville, where Yul worked as a lifeguard on the beach.

In 1932, when Boris was forty-three, he and Katya settled in Harbin, China, and managed the Bryner offices. He used his training as a mining engineer to open a construction company.

By the age of fifteen, Yul was already living an independent life in the circus and nightclubs of Paris, and only joined his mother and sister for summers in Deauville.

Catherine, the daughter of Katya and Boris, was born in Harbin in 1938.

Boris and Katya were adoring parents.This photo was taken shortly before the family's Soviet incarceration.

Boris continued to be sportive in Harbin, riding his mare, Venus, almost daily.

Whenever Yul visited Boris in Harbin, they rode together along the Sungari River — Yul's only experience in the saddle until his first western, *The Magnificent Seven*.

Boris with his niece, Irena. The three Bryner brothers, Leonid, Boris, and Felix, ran the Far East Shipping Company offices in Shanghai, Harbin, and Port Arthur, respectively.

Boris had hunted since his childhood with the Yankovskys; he and Katya kept a dacha at their hunting lodge in North Korea well into the 1940s.

his prince of Primorye was ill prepared for the hardships he and his family would endure when
ized by the Soviets soon after this photo was taken in 1944.

The Bund in Shanghai in the 1930s, where the Brunner office at No. 18 had already been operating continuously for decades. The

Now the Bryners were in imminent peril from Bolsheviks. Their only real protection was the massive Japanese Interventionist occupation of the city. For the foreseeable future, the Bryner property on Aleutskaya Street would periodically be home to large numbers of Japanese troops, camped out in the garden and sometimes sleeping in the halls and stairways — the same Japanese troops that had defeated Russia just fifteen years earlier. Their presence inside and around her home could make Natalya nearly hysterical with rage, especially as Jules' health started to fail. But the fact was that the Interventionist troops billeted in their home provided the Bryners with the security the family needed. As the city's most successful capitalists, the Bryners' extended family (six children with spouses, and five grandchildren) were obvious candidates for the Bolsheviks' new system of labor camps: the gulags.

The labor camps, which would come to define Soviet totalitarianism, were first created as an emergency measure during the Civil War. "Three weeks before the October Revolution [1917]," according to gulag historian Anne Applebaum, "Lenin himself was already sketching out an admittedly vague plan to organize 'obligatory work duty' for wealthy capitalists." He later wrote that he looked forward to "the arrest of millionaire-saboteurs traveling in first- and second-class train compartments. I suggest sentencing them to half a year's forced labor in a mine." Applebaum concludes that "from the very earliest days of the new Soviet state, people were to be sentenced not for what they had done, but for who they were." For a time, the Far East Shipping Company shielded the Bryners, because it provided a crucial link between Vladivostok and the outside world, along with some of the few jobs still available.

Jules and his family had no way of guessing which way the wind might blow between partisans, Bolsheviks, and Cossack Interventionists: between 1917 and 1920, Vladivostok had *seven* successive governments, each one fiercely hostile to its predecessor. Across Russia, capitalists like the Bryners, along with the *bourzhouy* (bourgeois), were being rounded up and shot. Jules' grandchildren, including Yul, grew up hearing stories about partisans swinging infants by their feet and bashing their heads against walls in front of their parents, who were then shot.

Jules and Boris struggled to salvage the Tetukhe mines even as the Soviet government confiscated and nationalized *every* industrial enterprise in the country, along with private real estate, in strict accord with the Marxist precept that "private ownership is theft," and the credo that the State must own and control all the means of production. Under the nationalization decree of June 28, 1918, factories were seized and assigned to directors loyal to the Communist Party who instituted forced industrialization in urban regions, while millions of private farms were declared collective property and assigned to cadres.

But when Admiral Kolchak declared himself the Supreme Ruler of Russia and leader of all anti-Communist resistance, Jules appealed to Kolchak's government in Omsk, asking that the Bryner mines be restored to the Russian shareholders and directors on patriotic grounds. Kolchak agreed, and at a meeting of the Tetukhe shareholders in June 1919, Jules was returned to the board of directors, and Bryner & Company took over management. "The Tetukhe mine, however, remained abandoned," wrote V. V. Veeder, Queen's Counsel, University of London. "The Company's financial affairs were in disarray; its goods and materials had been requisitioned for military purposes; its buildings had been looted; its port facilities at Pristan, next to Cape Bryner, had been blockaded and shelled, with its steam-driven tugboat, the *Rynda,* taken and sunk by the White Siberian Fleet." As well, the upper mines had now been exhausted, and further underground exploration below would require a whole new production plant. Since no investors were forthcoming in the midst of such chaos, the Bryners were now barely keeping the moribund company alive with personal loans. Ore could never be produced there again without a large infusion of cash and expertise, neither of which was available; foreign capital had fled the country the moment Lenin's government began seizing properties.

For the thousands of desperate mining families in Tetukhe, this was the dead-end conclusion, apparently, to their thwarted hopes of resuming jobs they once had with Bryner & Company — the only work within hundreds of miles of uninhabited taiga. The Bryner mines had succumbed to the ravages of civil war.

In October 1918, Felix Bryner, then twenty-seven years old, traveled to

Omsk to serve Admiral Kolchak in his anti-Communist cause, even though, after the assassination of the Imperial family, there was no empire to fight for. Felix's daughter, Irena, later wrote that:

> as a White officer in the Tsarist Army, my father was assigned to General Kolchak. . . . Many foreign countries pretended to want to help Russia, but in reality they were only interested in grabbing Russian gold, which Kolchak was transporting on the train. A French general, Renan, tried to negotiate a deal with Kolchak. My father was an interpreter in those negotiations and was witness to Renan's words: "To hell with Kolchak, let's get the gold." Soon after, the French and the Czechoslovaks together betrayed General Kolchak and delivered him to the Bolsheviks.

Unlike Kolchak, Felix was lucky enough to escape Irkutsk alive, but what followed was almost worse than death. "Father was then assigned to another White general, Kappel, who led the remaining White Army through the Siberian taiga on foot," wrote Irena. "This was the 'Ice March,' which few survived. Every morning there were piles of corpses because of typhus and frost. . . . Exhausted, and with frost-bitten feet, he was happy to return home to his family."

Boris had been frustrated since returning to Vladivostok, but just keeping the business alive required a lot of work. He and Leonid were coping with the Bryner shipping company: for an import-export company, the political sea changes, fluctuating currency values, and shortages of coal to fuel the steamers made it a trying time. But their immediate concern was establishing numerous business bases outside Russia. Because of Jules' perspicuity in registering FESCO as a Hong Kong company and in keeping an office on the famous Bund in Shanghai, the company was still a going concern. Now all they needed was to establish shipyards outside Russia and a wide array of new clients. Leonid and Boris, and soon Felix, too, traveled all across the Far East, opening new offices, enhancing older ones, and cultivating personal ties with local officials. They went to Port Arthur and

Dairen, Chinese cities that (like Korea) were now under Japanese control. The brothers also opened offices in Peking, Hsingking, and Tientsin in China, as well as in Mukden and Harbin in Manchuria, which was under Chinese authority. It was an enormous operation to oversee, but it gave them a flexible set of alternatives if they needed to flee Communist Russia. The brothers knew they would not be destitute, even if they lost their industrial dynasty.

Boris was never idle. Just months after settling on Aleutskaya Street, he began organizing the first technical school in the Far East. Building a staff from experts and engineers of the port and the military, and raising funds everywhere he could find them, including within his family, in November 1918 he launched the Higher Polytechnic School of Vladivostok. The chairman was chosen from the Oriental Institute, which Jules had helped establish twenty years earlier. The school had two faculties, one for economics and the other for mining, mechanics, and construction engineering. Boris also used his positions as board member of the Amur Society and as the Far East representative of the Russian Geological Committee to attract teaching talent. He taught several mining classes, passing along exactly what he had learned at the Mining Institute in Petrograd, and he contributed his own extensive collection of rare minerals to form the core of a Geological Museum at the Far Eastern State Technical University in Vladivostok.

Boris was easily the most sociable and athletic of the Bryners. Something of a sportsman and *bon vivant*, he had been a member of the Imperial Society of Lifeguards and of the Vladivostok Yacht Club because, like his father, he was always passionate about being out on the water. He regularly took Marousia to the theater and concerts, as well as to sporting events. But as the Civil War deepened, most such activities disappeared, and it became difficult to travel safely around town.

Jules' death in March 1920, though not unexpected, was a terrible blow to the family's badly battered world, leaving Natalya more emotionally isolated than ever. She had been a girl of sixteen when she married Jules, thirty-eight years and seven children (one deceased) earlier. With the death of her husband, Natalya inherited most of his property. She made it clear to the family that she had no intention of letting *any* of it reach her daughters-in-law, and drew up her own will accordingly: if she were predeceased by her sons — a real possibility in the midst of civil war — the Blagovidovas would go begging.

Three months later, the newly formed Far East Russian Republic gave its citizens ten days in which to exchange all their rubles for a new Far East Russian currency, worth 1/200th of the rubles exchanged, effectively reducing everyone's saved wealth by 99.5 percent. This caused an uproar; even the large and menacing Japanese Interventionist force objected, and, by boycotting the new currency, effectively devalued it. Using their dominant position and powers of persuasion, the Japanese volunteered to disengage completely from the Transbaikal area *if* the Far East Russian cabinet would include members of the *tsenzoviki*, or "qualified bourgeoisie." Four such members were chosen for the cabinet, including Boris Julievitch Bryner,[a] who thereby became the minister for industry in the Far East Russian Republic.

The following month he met regularly with members of the Communist, Menshevik, Socialist Revolutionary, Kadet, and Popular Socialist parties, who had all initially refused to sit at the same table with a capitalist. The meetings deadlocked repeatedly, adding to the enormous stress that Boris was under. Because at that same moment he was preoccupied with the arrival of his second child, a son, born on July 11, 1920. Yul was baptized on November 29 at the Uspensky Cathedral, where his grandfather had attended Mass with Tsarevitch Nicholas thirty years earlier.

Once the Soviet Union took control of the Far East in 1922, the Bryners' situation was even more tenuous. "As entrepreneurs with a foreign background," wrote Veeder, "their existence was in daily jeopardy from the Soviet authorities in Vladivostok, particularly the OGPU (the Unified State Political Administration). Felix had been a Tsarist officer who had also served as a French interpreter with the White Kolchak regime; and the Bryners' middle sister, Marie, was married to Sergei Hvitzky, a White officer in the Siberian Fleet, captured and imprisoned by the Reds." (When she was younger, Marie had been briefly engaged to Kostia Sukhanov, who died a youthful Red hero of the Civil War.) Now the fear and disorder of brigades of foreign troops outside their door were replaced by the terror of sudden arrest by Soviet authorities, with or without orders from Moscow.

Over the next two years famine swept across the Soviet Union as the agricultural and economic structures for production and distribution broke down and were replaced by failed theoretical plans. The nationalization of private business and industry was soon recognized as unworkable, and in 1923, Lenin announced his New Economic Policy, for which this period is remembered as the NEP Era. Private ownership of small businesses was restored, though *all* large industries — mines, for example — remained strictly under the control of the government. Recognizing the country's desperate need for foreign capital, Lenin's comrades-in-leadership also launched a new trade policy that would allow foreign entrepreneurs with cash in hand to receive government concessions for mining.

By 1922, industrial production in the Soviet Union had been reduced to one-fifth its 1913 volume, and as a result of grain requisitions by the government, famine had taken millions of lives; in effect, the Bolshevik government was starving its citizens. Since the government had already become desperate enough to return confiscated businesses under NEP,

Boris and his brothers resolved to deal with Lenin's new government in Moscow in still another attempt to resurrect the Tetukhe mines.

After all, the site still had enormous proven reserves of ore, for which the world had a growing market, and the Soviet treasury urgently needed foreign currency. If, as Russian citizens, the Bryners could not *own* Tetukhe, perhaps they could restore and operate the business on behalf of some foreign concessionaire. Would Moscow look favorably upon such a scheme and enter into agreements with Bryner & Company? Because if so, the family would no longer have to fear the sound of the secret police — the Cheka — stopping in front of their door.

Foreign concessions were so important to Lenin that he had assigned responsibility for them to the chief of the Cheka, the dreaded Felix Dzerzhinsky. In fact, the Soviets' foreign concession strategy "fulfilled a political as well as an economic purpose," Stephan pointed out, because "Lenin regarded Far East concessions as a means of gaining *diplomatic recognition*." Many nations were still reluctant to acknowledge the Bolshevik revolutionaries as constituting the legitimate government of the country even as others that bought timber or railroad rights (the United States, for example, in Kamchatka and Nikolaevsk) were granting *de facto* recognition. Many foreign countries were divided on this point: in Britain, for example, the Conservative Party would not agree to recognize the Communists' authority in Russia, whereas the Labour Party would, and did. That is why, explained Stephan, "foreign concessionaires proliferated . . . and included familiar names such as Bryner & Company."

Boris would have to spend a great deal of time in Moscow, seeking official assurance that Lenin's government really would do business with him for the sake of the overall economy. The venture would entail leaving his wife and two children behind in the most fearful of times. But only Boris could serve as the front man for the mining operation, while Leonid held down the offices and handled the hard contracts and legal fine points, and Felix traveled the region recruiting qualified labor. It was Boris, after all, who had earned his master's degree by researching Tetukhe. And as minister of industry during the short-lived Far East Russian Republic, Boris had already demonstrated his ability to work closely with revolutionary socialists. Besides, Lenin's government knew that the Bryners had a proven ability to attract European capital. (Their last investor, the German Aron Hirsch, had lost most of the money he had put into Tetukhe: the Bryners had discharged their legal responsibilities to Hirsch, after a fashion, by repaying him in the sharply devalued "rubles" of the Far East Russian Republic. Understandably, Hirsch continued to seek satisfaction from the Bryners for some time after, but the underlying truth was that they had all lost out to the Revolution.)

Perhaps Boris's most useful talent, according to his associate, C. A. Kidd, was in making himself popular, even among the dedicated Communist leadership. This "prince of Primorye" navigated smoothly between the paradoxical cadres of the political elite in an anti-elitist political culture. Boris emerged as "a man of both charm and tenacity," wrote Kidd. "In spite of his connections with the capitalist world, Boris was well thought of in Soviet Moscow, and . . . he achieved a remarkable degree of success in these dealings." That charm and tenacity, perhaps as much as his technical knowledge of mining, was why Boris *had* to leave Vladivostok for Moscow and negotiate personally with "Iron Felix" Dzerzhinsky.

Dzerzhinsky was the truest believer in the Communist revolution; he lived by the mantra "the end justifies the means." Polish-born, he had spent much of his early adulthood as a political prisoner, and for his role in the Revolution of 1905 was sent to a Siberian labor camp from which he escaped twice, settling finally in Poland. In 1917, when Dzerzhinsky returned to Russia, Lenin appointed him commissar for internal affairs. During the years that Boris dealt with him, Dzerzhinsky was minister of the interior, chief of the Cheka and the OGPU, and minister for communications.

For the first six months of 1923, Boris "commuted" on the longest railroad in the world. When he was in Vladivostok he was an adoring father to his daughter, Vera, now seven years old, who wanted to be an opera singer (just as her mother had) and to his son Yul, who even at the age of two was alarmingly independent and willful; and he gave Marousia all the warmth and support that she needed. When in Moscow, Boris was an urbane figure with an understated elegance, even in a time of famine and despair.

On May 3, 1923, the USSR's Council of Labor and Defense decreed that

Bryner & Company could resume mining in Tetukhe "on a lease basis." There were many foreign mining concessions, but what was unique in this case was that the Bryners were Russians; however, the basis of the agreement was that the financing would be foreign. Projecting annual production of one hundred thousand tonnes of ore, Lenin's council required foreign financing of 250,000 gold rubles (about $2.5 million today), which, Boris pledged in writing, would be available from "one group in England to finance the business on a large scale." The British Engineering Company of Siberia, Ltd., or Becos, offered their guarantee that the Bryners were well-placed to obtain such capital, though Becos themselves would not provide the full amount. That gave Boris the authority to move forward and deal with Iron Felix.

In his negotiations with Boris, Dzerzhinsky was acting as chairman of the Supreme Council of National Economy. A thin, intense man whose ethics reflected his prison-camp years, Iron Felix could be expected to despise the well-polished son of an industrial capitalist; and while negotiating with Boris, he never gave up for a minute being chief of the Soviet secret police as well. So the meetings between Boris Bryner and Felix Dzerzhinsky were fraught with opportunity and danger. The future of the Bryners in the Soviet Union hinged on success. Boris knew that at any time the chief of the secret police could summarily accuse him of some abstract crime such as "individualistic tendencies" — which the Cheka had done with thousands of others — and send him directly to a labor camp in Siberia to die, together with Marousia, Vera, and Yul. And Dzerzhinsky probably would have liked doing that better than sending Boris off to mingle with European bankers and other capitalists. But the Soviet Union needed foreign investment to obtain the ore from Tetukhe, which it needed in order to earn foreign currency, which it needed to obtain food, seed, agricultural equipment, and everything else that the country lacked in the third year of famine. That included diplomatic recognition from foreign countries, which in turn would unlock loans from foreign banks.

At this juncture the survival of the Soviet Union as a viable government was in grave peril. In 1922, Vladimir Lenin had suffered the first of several debilitating strokes possibly caused by tertiary syphilis. As the singular founding father of the Communist revolution, his death could topple the whole shaky Soviet experiment after its years of famine and starvation caused by bureaucratic excess and idiocy. Severely weakened, but not incapacitated, Lenin modulated his opposition to the capitalist structures that might save his government, along with millions of Russian lives. Doubtless he was personally aware of all the foreign concessions under discussion in 1923, including the Bryners', because of the *de facto* diplomatic recognition that they might garnish. But as his health deteriorated, Lenin spent his last days trying to insure that Leon Trotsky would be his successor — even as Josef Stalin prepared to seize the government.

On July 25, 1924, six months after Lenin's death, Boris Bryner and Felix Dzerzhinsky — in his role as chairman of the USSR's Supreme Council of National Economy — signed a concession agreement for the Tetukhe mines. The other signatory was Georgi Chicherin, another Bolshevik true believer who had returned from exile with Trotsky as his loyal aide, and now succeeded him as foreign affairs commissar. In that capacity Chicherin had personally negotiated with Germany the mutual dismissal of war reparations in the Treaty of Rapallo. The uniquely prestigious Soviet names of Dzerzhinsky and Chicherin would convince foreign bankers that this was an agreement the shaky Soviet Union would respect.

The broad terms of the agreement gave Bryner & Company a thirty-six year mining concession, with stipulations: the Bryners had to bring in the foreign capital and begin work within a year, and the projected yields of ore that Boris had specified would have to be met. The agreement allowed the Bryners to assign the concession to foreign operators, and it included an arbitration clause — but one that pertained only to the foreign investors selected. That clause came to have great significance later.

Boris had prevailed in his negotiations with the most fiercely ideological and intimidating Communist leader alive. As a result, the mines created by Jules in Tsarist Russia would be resurrected by his sons in the Soviet Union . . . and the town of Tetukhe would be saved. Now Boris had to find an investor willing to risk a large capital investment inside an avowedly anti-capitalist country.

• • • • • • • •

In the meantime, during his many months in Moscow, Boris's life had undergone a revolution of its own. He had fallen in love.

Ekaterina Ivanova Kornakova was a star. Five years younger than Boris, she was twenty-seven when they met, and an adored actress in the Russian theater. Katya, a stunning petite blonde of immense talent and renowned beauty, had been born in 1895 in Kyakhta, along the Russian-Mongolian frontier, where Genghis Khan originated. Her father, a wealthy landowner, bred racehorses, and her mother was a renowned sociologist who later received the Order of Lenin for her study of Mongolian peoples. Katya had decided at an early age that she belonged on stage, which her parents forbade absolutely. So, at seventeen, she ran away from her home to become an actress in the big city. Five years later she was a star, appearing in an adaptation of Dostoyevsky's *The Village of Stepanchikovo* with Konstantin Stanislavsky, cofounder of the Moscow Art Theatre. By 1922, when she met Boris, she was celebrated for her performance in Gorky's *The Lower Depths.*

At the time, Katya was also married, without children, to an actor named Alexei Diki, though she was miserable living with his emotional and alcoholic turbulence. Katya had been ardently courted by her director, mentor, and co-star, Stanislavsky himself, thirty-two years her senior; some still insist that she was the one great love of his life. Be that as it may, Katya walked away from both Stanislavsky and Diki to devote herself to Boris.

They met in Moscow by way of the Yankovskys in Sidemy, who were Katya's cousins by marriage. Boris's easy, self-assured manner and handsome elegance earned this mining engineer a warm welcome among Katya's artistic friends. He himself was quickly dazzled and absorbed by the intensely creative world of the Moscow Art Theatre in the early 1920s. There, a revolution in the theater was unfolding even as the Communist revolution proceeded at the Kremlin, half a mile away; in the decades to come, the Bryner family would be affected as much by the former revolution as by the latter.

The Moscow Art Theatre had been founded twenty-five years earlier by Konstantin Stanislavsky and Vladimir Nemirovich-Danchenko. It was the first ensemble theater in Russia in which the actors trained and worked together on each production, and thereby developed shared principles.

"The program for our undertaking was revolutionary," Stanislavsky later wrote. "We protested against the old manner of acting and against theatricality, against artificial pathos and declamation, and against affectation on the stage, and inferior conventional productions and decoration, against the star system which had a bad effect . . . and against the sorry repertoire of the theatres." Their aim was to communicate to the audience emotions that were *genuine* as well as ideas that grew out of real-world social experiences, and to explore every conceivable dramatic innovation toward that end. A wave of exceptional new Russian playwrights, led by Anton Chekhov, provided the material for this new school of social realism. But how does an actor achieve genuine emotions in the artificial setting of a hall filled with attentive strangers? Stanislavsky, it seems, was the first director even to pose that question, and his answer became the basis of acting theory for the next four generations.

Some of Stanislavsky's closest colleagues disagreed with central techniques of his "system," especially with his insistence that his actors make use of specific memories from their personal lives to trigger genuine emotions on stage. One of these colleagues was Mikhail Chekhov, nephew of the late playwright, Anton, and an actor and director with the Moscow Art Theatre. Between 1919 and 1922, Mikhail Chekhov created a separate repertory company, the independent Moscow Art Theatre Studio. Like others, he could not abide Stanislavsky's embrace of the rising Stalin government. An outspoken critic of both sides of the Russian Revolution, Chekhov had been spared arrest by the personal intervention of Lenin, who admired his socially minded theater, and soon after Stalin enshrined Stanislavsky's "system" as the model for all Soviet theater: social realism became Socialist Realism. Stanislavsky withheld any criticism of Stalin's regime, and thrived; by contrast, Mikhail Chekhov felt compelled to flee his homeland, and eventually joined the burgeoning White Russian community in Paris, where he started a new repertory ensemble and an acting school.

These were the personalities who peopled Boris's new, metropolitan life, and who were much more exciting than his friends from the Mining Institute or his provincial peers in Vladivostok. Even outside the theater,

Katya was far more impulsive, spirited, and expressive than Marousia, who had settled into her matronly duties exactly as Boris had expected when he insisted she renounce her career in the theater.

After months of delirious love with Katya, and several postponed or canceled visits to Vladivostok, Boris decided that he would not, could not, leave Katya to return to his wife and two children. He sat down and composed the following letter, the impact of which would reverberate through the Bryner's lives for decades.

Moscow, October 13, 1923

My dear Mamulinka,

I am writing you this letter with great anguish, but not to write it to you would be impossible and unfair both to you and to me.

I am so tired, so worn out with inner discord, that I can't endure it any longer, and I want you, as my best friend until now, as my wife and as the mother of my dear children, to know everything I am going through, and I [hope] that you will understand [me] and [forgive] me.

If I haven't written you everything until now, it is because I thought I would overcome the feeling that I am experiencing and which now seems entirely to have engulfed me, and [because I thought] I would be able to regain my emotional balance; but that has turned out to be wrong. It turned out to be beyond my reason and beyond my strength.

Of course it all came about partly because of the environment, the circumstances in which I happened to find myself in Moscow, far from you, Mamushalka, and from all my loved ones.

The only person in whom I immediately felt a kindred and a [illegible] fine spirit was Katya. She radiated such warmth to me, from the very first, that I literally rested only when I was with her and I didn't suspect that that feeling of friendship might become warmer than it ordinarily is, or that it could change into something more.

But that is what happened. She and I both felt it more acutely when she made the trip to Kharkov. Only then did I feel how attached to her I have become, how I miss her when she isn't there. Not long ago she fell so ill there that at times she was not able to perform.

Mamushalka, my beloved, I was terrified, literally terrified, to realize that I have come to love Katya, and now for a whole month I have been suffering unbearably from the thought that it is so, and from fear of killing you by telling you; yet, at the same time, I was aware that there is no other person to whom I must open my heart than to you. That is true and I knew that I couldn't do otherwise: it would go against my nature, against that [illegible], that [illegible] which always existed between us, Mamulichka.

I know what pain I am causing you and that thought alone weighs so heavily on me that I don't know what to do with myself but, dear Mamulichka, what is happening to me — what I am going through — is stronger than I am.

My greatest wish now is that you might understand me and not judge me too harshly.

I have already gone through a great deal since I began to feel as I do and evidently I will go through a great deal more in the future. I would like to talk with you now, Marinka and, as it is, my heart is heavy. Now I've written to you but I don't know whether I will send the letter. I've written it, [illegible] sitting here in my room, and I couldn't have done otherwise.

If you can, write me even just a few words.

For the moment I won't write any more. I embrace you and our dear, wonderful children.

By the time the letter was aboard the Trans-Siberian mail car headed toward Vladivostok, Boris and Katya were no longer keeping their romance a secret. Katya had left her husband, and now she began accompanying Boris to business functions and charming the various Soviet authorities who needed to be charmed for the Tetukhe mines to be revived. Boris's concern a decade earlier about associating with an actress now proved to be inoperative.

Early Soviet ideology disdained the bourgeois institution of marriage; in fact, the government actively discouraged marriages and encouraged divorces, with new provisions making it a quick procedure that could be accomplished by either spouse, acting alone. Accordingly, Boris received a divorce from Marousia Blagovidova in Moscow on May 20, 1924, and four weeks later, on June 18, he married Ekaterina Kornakova. He was thirty-five years old, and she was twenty-nine.

The letter dealt a blow to Marousia from which she never recovered. Boris wrote that he suffered from "fear of killing you by telling you": after eleven years together, he well knew she really might not survive this betrayal. In fact, a large part of her identity did not survive. "I remember how she paced the floor," her niece Irena wrote later, "twisting her arms and moaning, 'It hurts, it hurts, what pain, it hurts.' . . . I could feel how brutally she was wounded by the man she loved so much. This pain remained with her always." Of the many photographs later taken of Marousia together with her children Vera and Yul, there is never another in which they are smiling. "For Marousia, it was as if her husband had declared her dead," according to Irena, "and in her heart, she obeyed his wish."

Everything about Marousia's situation was unbearable: she was still living at the Bryner Residence next door to her mother-in-law, Natalya, who, without Jules' moderating influence, gloated openly at the pain and humiliation that Boris had inflicted. While completely dependent upon the Bryners, Marousia was suddenly cast in the role of a single parent for which she was too badly damaged, by shock and rejection, to fulfill. She went for days at a time without speaking at all, barely coping with minimal responsibilities. And all this was unfolding in the fearful uncertainty of the post-Revolutionary era: Marousia received Boris's letter on the first anniversary of the Red Army's march past the family's front door. To commemorate that march, Aleutskaya Street had just been renamed Twenty-fifth October Street, transforming the Bryners' home address into Communist propaganda.

The only salvation for Marousia was her sister, Vera, and brother-in-law Felix, who took charge of her and her children as Boris must have known they would. Together they all moved into a house on the outskirts of Vladivostok, in a neighborhood called Nineteenth Versta, because it was that distance (about ten miles) from the city center. They created a new family as best they could, with Felix as the head of the household. He was a remarkably even-tempered man: angry as he was with Boris's actions, he did not shirk his responsibility. Marousia remained too deeply unbalanced and distracted to care for her children, both of whom were exuberant and willful. Her mother, Baiga, provided a steady, stable, comforting presence, "always ready to assist anyone who needed her," wrote Irena, and otherwise entertaining herself, quietly crocheting enormous shawls or playing solitaire, but it was Felix and Vera who provided young Vera (age eight) and Yul (four) as much love as they did their daughter, Irena (seven), raising the double cousins as siblings in their sudden, tempestuous exile from the home where they had been born and raised.

After their wedding, Boris took Katya on a tour of Europe for their honeymoon, including London, a city they both loved. There they spent several months, during which time Boris succeeded in securing the capital for the Tetukhe mines. With that, he brought his new bride back to his old home in Vladivostok, where his mother warmly welcomed his second wife.

Now Boris needed to remain in the Far East, since it fell to him to supervise the complete reconstruction of the system his father had first devised in 1897; occasionally he might visit his children, too. For Katya, this meant relinquishing stardom in the theater capital of the world. Though leaving the Moscow Art Theatre was a terrible loss for her, she knew that she would have had to retire soon anyway, given the duplicity and discomfiture of appearing to have supported Stalin's cruel leadership through Stanislavsky. She considered joining Mikhail Chekhov's Moscow Art Theatre Studio, but his "individualistic tendencies" put him in grave jeopardy, and he was soon forced to flee the Soviet Union. Katya was passionately in love with Boris, and wouldn't have dreamed of being apart from her husband. Besides, she loved horseback riding, and the outdoor recreations around Vladivostok — by now a city of 150,000. Nonetheless, the couple kept her apartment in Moscow for their frequent trips there; it is evidence of her star status that this was permitted, given the city's housing shortage.

The investment capital for Tetukhe came from Sir Alfred Chester Beatty, an American-born original. Trained at Columbia University's School of Mining, Beatty first worked for the Guggenheim family's mining empire, assisting in the prospecting, acquisition, and development of gold, silver, and copper mines in Mexico, the United States, and the Belgian Congo. By 1910, Beatty was sharing his offices as a consultant with another mining engineer named Herbert Hoover. They became fast friends, and the following year Beatty and Hoover traveled together to visit mines in Siberia, where it would seem they must have met with Jules Bryner. Their close professional association lasted for years, until Hoover was elected president of the United States in 1928. When Beatty formed a new private company, Selection Trust Ltd., its first venture was a diamond expedition in Gold

Coast (now Ghana) and Sierra Leone. Its second was the mining business at Tetukhe.

The negotiations for the concession took less than six months (during which a life-threatening winter survey of the mines was conducted by a technical team), thanks to Beatty's forceful style of management and Boris's diligence and tenacity. Together they formed an English company, the Tetiuhe Mining Corporation, in May 1925, capitalized at £250,000 (approximately $2.5 million in today's dollars, a figure that later doubled), which included a payment of £150,000 to Bryner & Company for the transfer of the thirty-six-year concession, pre-approved by the Soviet government. Boris was appointed the resident director in Russia (Leonid was also a director), and the Bryners' office in Vladivostok was the appointed agent, in charge of procuring all necessary supplies, labor, and technical expertise. Their lawyer was Shura (Alexander) Ostroumov, who was married to Boris's youngest sister, Nina.

A year later, in May 1926, the mines began operating again: after more than ten years of decay, Jules' sons had restored his creation. According to Veeder, the new company had:

> rebuilt the old facilities, installed a new mill, power plant, and lead smelter, greatly extended the underground workings, renovated the railway, and effected a large number of technical improvements using 20 or more British, German, and U.S. resident engineers (many accompanied by their wives and dependents) together with a permanent labor force of about 1,000 rising to 2,400 comprising of Chinese (from Mongolia and Manchuria), Russians and Koreans. In July 1930, the Soviet government advanced a loan of two million rubles to match increased capital investment from London. . . . By August 1931 the Company had expended £682,000. Sales of ore concentrates, other than to the Soviet Government, were conducted from London; and shipment to Europe, a voyage taking three months, was made by cargo-ships, mainly of the British Glen Line.

In the first fifteen months of operation, the Tetukhe mines sold ore worth £107,000; by 1930 sales had tripled, totaling 136,300 tonnes of milled ore.

"Boris spent quite a lot of time at the mine and took great interest in technical as well as administrative affairs," wrote Kidd, who worked with Boris in the early 1930s. "Not unnaturally this was sometimes not altogether appreciated by the general managers, who felt that their authority was being eroded. He was quite a frequent attender of board meetings in London and kept up an extensive correspondence with London while he was in Russia."

Obviously, Boris and Katya spent an enormous amount of time traveling, much of it on the Trans-Siberian Railroad. Each trip of more than six thousand miles to Moscow took more than a week, and it was another day to Leningrad (as Petrograd had been renamed, four days after Lenin's death). London was several more days away, depending upon the season and the route taken. Between Tetukhe, Vladivostok, Sidemy, Moscow, and London, with occasional trips to continental Europe, Shanghai, and Harbin, the couple was rarely in one place for more than a few weeks at a time during the first years of their marriage. Whatever they planned, they were usually in Vladivostok only for hasty business meetings, so there was little or no time to spend with Boris's children. Many planned get-togethers were canceled at the last minute, or simply forgotten.

Joseph Vissarionovich Dzhugashvili was an escaped political prisoner in 1910 when he adopted the name "Stalin," meaning "man of steel." By 1917, he was at Lenin's side during the October Revolution, and by 1922 he was general secretary of the Communist Party. From that vantage he was able to prepare a base of political support that would carry him into leadership after Lenin died in 1924. Once in power, Joseph Stalin concentrated upon the extermination of millions his own citizens and became the greatest killer in human history. He offered a dry explanation for his mass slaughter: "A single death is a tragedy; a million deaths is a statistic."

By his fiftieth birthday in 1929, Stalin had effectively consolidated his power in Moscow. With Trotsky exiled (and later assassinated in Mexico), he ruthlessly purged the ranks of the government and the military bureaucracies, liquidating *any* possibility of political opposition. In 1928, with the first of his economic Five-Year Plans, Stalin had begun reorganizing the entire countryside through the collectivization of private farms. Peasants who resisted, along with any political opponents, were sent to the harshest labor camps on earth: the Siberian gulag of Magadan and Kolyma, hundreds of miles north of Vladivostok, where temperatures dropped to –30°F and a third of the prisoners died each year. By the 1930s, millions had died under collectivization.

A typical anecdote about Stalin's peculiar cruelty was recounted by his propaganda chief of the Soviet Red Army, Dimitri Volkogonov. Stalin had the secret police arrest the wife of his closest assistant, Poskrebyshev, but whenever he pleaded for her release, Stalin insisted there was nothing he could do, and that only the secret police could release her. She was held in prison on trumped-up charges for three years before being shot. Yet throughout this time Poskrebyshev was forced to work at Stalin's side for twelve to fourteen hours each day, bringing his mail, scheduling appointments, and organizing his paperwork. It seems that Stalin took special pleasure from such situations.

Working relentlessly with a hand-picked elite leadership whom he kept off balance and in constant fear, the "Red Tsar" was nonetheless adored by much of the population. As Volkoponov put it, "No other man in the world has ever accomplished so fantastic a success as he: to exterminate millions of his own countrymen and receive in exchange the whole country's blind adulation." And historian Laura Detloff wrote that "the Stalin myth was so built up by propaganda that he was considered to be a sort of demi-god in the eyes of the people. He was portrayed as the total embodiment of absolute good." The Soviet people knew that Stalin was working day and night for the fatherland; they could not know how many comrades perished at the hands of the autocrat they called Uncle Joe.

Even after Stalin abandoned the pretense of collective leadership, the socialist dream of an egalitarian society served as workable camouflage throughout Stalin's quarter century of dictatorship. Equality was fine, but as Orwell put it, some were more equal than others. Beneath Stalin, a pyramid of cronies made up a vast, wrongheaded, and often self-defeating bureaucracy

— something Russia had been accustomed to for centuries. Setting aside all the slaughter, arguably the greatest failure of Russia's experiment with Communism originated with Stalin's Central Planning, whereby the Politburo (governing council) in Moscow laid out production quotas for every segment of society and punished mercilessly those who failed to meet them. Since those quotas were usually off-hand, optimistic guesses, many people were punished mercilessly if they were unable to bribe their superiors. "Repression is a necessary element" without which socialism could not advance, Stalin declared at the Sixteenth Party Congress in 1930. By the time his purges were over, nearly every family in Russia had been affected by the Terror. Better that nine innocent men be punished, Stalin believed, than for one guilty man to go free. Meanwhile, critical supplies of coal, food, and clothing were diverted, stolen, and misplaced.

It was in this political climate that Boris and Katya made their frequent trips to Moscow. Despite the initial success of the mines, enormous problems were created by local political and labor officials from Vladivostok and Khabarovsk who harassed the management constantly, frequently shutting down production because of supposed violations of the ever-changing codes, violations for which the general managers were sometimes subjected to *criminal* prosecution. At a Tetiuhe board meeting in London in 1928, Beatty declared that, "while I fully appreciate the sympathetic co-operation of the central authorities in Moscow, the interference of the local authorities and trade union officials with our staff and workmen has caused and is still causing us a great deal of trouble and cost."

But by now, under Stalin, "there was a movement against foreign concessionaires," wrote Kidd. Even after the Soviet government had loaned the company two million rubles, "the attitude of the central authorities seemed to change, they became less and less disposed to help the Corporation." Every trip that Boris made to Moscow became more unsettling and less productive. Before long, he knew he was being stonewalled by Stalin's government.

His first insurmountable problem was the shortage of coal to drive the power plant for both the mines and the town of Tetukhe. It took two thousand tonnes of high-grade coal per month to raise a sufficient head of steam to drive the power plant. Even when Bryner & Company could apply political pressure to the collieries, the company was still obliged by law to use state-owned shipping lines for the coal — and that brought innumerable delays and no-shows. But the government had made it impossible to import foreign coal, in an effort to stanch the flow of rubles abroad. For that same reason, Chinese and Korean miners — about half the employees — were suddenly forbidden to send their earnings back home to their families, and with that, they left. Overnight, absenteeism rose to 40 percent.

"Clothing was in short supply for the whole period," wrote Kidd, but British technicians were "restricted in the amount of clothing they could bring into the Soviet Union, and any excess was liable to be confiscated by Customs." And with the first Five-Year Plan came the first peacetime food rationing, as peasants across the country slaughtered their herds rather than deliver them to collectivized farms.

The values of zinc and lead dropped by half on the world market by 1927, a result of overproduction; two years later after Wall Street crashed, their prices were halved again. In 1930, output from Tetukhe actually doubled, but with falling prices revenues stayed flat. Finally, the full impact of the Depression struck industries everywhere. On May 31, 1931, the Tetiuhe Mining Corporation's published accounts showed a bank balance of one pound, twelve shillings, and sixpence; in reality, it was in debt for £222,000. Chester Beatty pulled the plug and started to liquidate the company by returning the Bryner mines to the government. "The U.S.S.R. agreed to compensation of £932,000," wrote Veeder, "spread over eighteen years." The Soviets, Beatty reported at the company's general meeting, "have acted very fairly during the negotiations and in carrying out all the detailed payments." And in letters to the *Times* of London, the company's British attorney denied that the Soviet government had forced the company to abandon the concession. The fact that Beatty was a former associate of the sitting U.S. president, Herbert Hoover, may have contributed to Stalin's relative cooperativeness.

The Bryners' position was less certain. As far as the Soviet government was concerned, Veeder wrote:

> Boris was a Russian-speaking Russian mining engineer who had lived all his life in Russia; but like his father he was also a resourceful entrepreneur who had proved many times that he could work the Soviet system, most recently with a two million ruble loan secured from the Soviet government. . . . Time and again for almost thirty years Bryner & Co. had successfully approached Tsarist, White, Red, and Soviet authorities to argue the case for the Tetukhe mines — on their terms. Moreover, it was not hard for Bryner & Co. to pose as patriotic pioneers under pre-Soviet rule, creating and supporting the Tetukhe Mine for the common good — because it was widely known to be true.

But without the Tetukhe mines, the Bryners were disposable. As a "qualified bourgeois," Boris had been allowed to go abroad on business; but the rules were changing so quickly in Stalin's Russia that whatever privileges the family had enjoyed could be revoked in a heartbeat, followed immediately by arrest and internal exile. The Trans-Siberian Railroad, which had operated first as a weapons-delivery system, then as an artery for Revolution, now provided one-way transport to the gulag.

In the seven years since Boris had divorced Marousia, the Bryner family had been transformed. In 1927, Marousia and her family moved to Harbin, China, just two hundred miles inland from Vladivostok; the city built by Russia during the construction of the Chinese Eastern Railroad had good Russian schools and a Bryner & Company office. Marousia was set up in a new home with little Vera (age eleven) and Yul (seven); Felix remained with his wife and daughter in Vladivostok, but their life there became easier the year before when Natalya passed away at the age of sixty.

By the time the mines closed in the spring of 1931, the situation had become too threatening for the family that remained in the Soviet Union. As Leonid Bryner later wrote:

> The attitude of Soviets in Vladivostok toward business people generally had strongly changed, and became more aggressive

> than before. Having felt such change of attitude ourselves as well and having lived there during nine years under nervous strain owing to constant reprisals and arrests of people belonging to the intellectual and 'well-to-do' classes, such changes toward ourselves prompted my brother Felix to escape from Vladivostok as soon as possible, while I was away on business trip in Manchuria. . . . He had always been denied by Soviet authorities the freedom to leave that country when he wanted, which [left] an impression on [him] that he was treated by Soviet authorities as a hostage.

Felix had meticulously prepared secret plans for escaping with his family to freedom without compromising the associates who remained behind. The secret police suspected that the Bryners were preparing to flee, and had assigned neighbors to watch their apartment. But their cook found a Chinese boatman willing to row them out to a British ship in exchange for his own safe passage. On May 31, 1931, Felix, Vera, and their daughter, Irena, age thirteen, sneaked away from their apartment at five o'clock in the morning, leaving everything they owned behind. Together with Felix's sister, Nina, and her husband, attorney Shura Ostroumov, and their children, they set out from Golden Horn Bay in thick fog. On Russian Island, they met with a peasant who had a goat to sell them — or at least that was the cover story for their trip. After paying the man, they set out again, saying that they would return for the goat.

"The waves were higher now," Irena later wrote,

> the wind was stronger. . . . We waited for five hours or more, until we began to wonder if the ship had missed us in the thick fog. Finally, we heard the deep horn of the ship. . . . The huge, marvelous ship appeared out of the fog, like a glorious vision. . . . Later we found out why the ship was delayed. The secret police were so sure that father was using this boat for escape that they had searched for him everywhere, even in the double hold.

The ship was the *Glinifer*, of the Glen Line, which had plied the seas for years from Tetukhe to Europe, carrying zinc ore for Bryner & Co. Its skipper, Captain Baker, had prepared a written confession to exonerate his ship's crew in the event they were apprehended, taking sole responsibility for the Bryners' escape.

The ship left them off in the Chinese port of Tsingtao. From there, Felix took his family to Dairen, the commercial harbor near Port Arthur where a Bryner office was waiting for him to take charge. They disposed of all their Russian documents and registered with Chinese authorities using their Swiss passports. From the flagpole over the Bryner building, they lowered the hammer and sickle for the last time, and raised the white cross over a red field — the flag of Switzerland.

Boris and Katya were now the last Bryners in the Soviet Union, and they were rightly becoming very anxious about their safety. "Whilst in Moscow," wrote Kidd, "Boris heard that his life would be in danger if he returned to Vladivostok." In July 1931, when they received word that Felix and his family had made it safely to China, they boarded the Trans-Siberian as planned, so as not to arouse suspicion. But in Irkutsk they disembarked surreptitiously and boarded the Chinese Eastern Railroad instead, to Harbin.

Because the Bryner office in Vladivostok was now defunct, Boris needed to conclude business in London to ensure that the Bryners would continue to receive annually the substantial payments still due to them for the Bryner mines. In late 1931, in the midst of the Dust Bowl and the Depression, Boris and Katya traveled across the Pacific, and the United States, and sailed to London.

More than half a century would pass before any Bryner set foot on Russian soil.

Like millions of other Russians, the Bryners were now refugees; but unlike almost all others, they had Swiss passports, along with a successful import-export business with offices throughout the Far East. Of course, this had nothing to do with mine engineering, Boris's singular specialty, and if somehow the Bryners fell into Soviet hands, their Swiss passports would count for nothing. But in the midst of Stalin's Terror, Boris rated among the more fortunate of Russians, even if he was no longer a prince of Primorye.

Boris and Katya remained in London for a year, traveling to Normandy and the rest of France while they considered their options. Future payments owed to the Bryners by the Soviet government for Tetukhe certainly could not be relied upon. As for other jobs, in 1931 the mining industry worldwide had been devastated by collapsing prices, the industrial slump, and the Depression. Boris's expertise came from just one zinc, lead, and silver mine, and he was unlikely to find reliable work as a consultant in the face of both coal shortages and a weak market.

Boris knew that his brothers needed his help urgently with Bryner & Company. Given the turmoil in global markets and the new trade concerns of nations neighboring the Soviet Far East, there was a constant flow of decisions to be made daily just to keep the business afloat. By this time Felix was running the Dairen office and Leonid was stationed in Shanghai. Boris and Katya decided to settle in Harbin and, in 1932, it was there that they made their home.

Built from scratch in 1896, Harbin had been created at the behest of the tsarist finance minister, Sergei Witte, during the construction of the Russian-owned Chinese Eastern Railroad. By 1922, Harbin had half a million residents, of whom a quarter were Russian. The city's social life was organized largely around the imposing, wood-built Russian Orthodox cathedral at the heart of the well-to-do neighborhood of Novy Gorod.

It was in that quarter that Marousia had settled with Vera and Yul when they fled Vladivostok in 1927. But the arrival of Boris and Katya was more than she could bear. And there was talk of war in the region again; Marousia was far too frail, emotionally and physically, to withstand life under another military occupation. Soon after Boris arrived, Marousia and her two children, armed with their Swiss passports, took the Chinese Eastern Railroad to Dairen to visit Felix and her sister. From there they boarded a ship for Le Havre in France, via the Suez Canal, and proceeded to Paris.

But in September 1931, while Boris and Katya were preparing to move into Manchuria, so was Japan, which swiftly seized control of the region from both China and Russia. Japanese *agents provocateurs* in the Manchurian city of Mukden — not far from the Yalu River in Korea — had staged an "incident" to justify sending in their troops, who fanned out across the countryside. In February 1932, Japanese troops marched unimpeded into Harbin — where they were greeted by jubilant crowds of White Russian émigrés — because Japan's presence assured the refugees that a Soviet invasion would not threaten them any time soon. In fact, when the Japanese seized Mukden, the only opposition that the Soviet Far East Navy could come up with were a few antique rust-buckets.

"To cover the fruits of aggression with a fig leaf of legitimacy," wrote Stephan, "Japan created the puppet state of Manchukuo, and installed as its sovereign the last Manchu emperor." If Boris and Katya made it safely to Harbin, they would be a Swiss married couple in a Russian city of the independent Manchurian Empire currently under Japanese occupation inside China. It was the best option they had; besides, Boris had an obligation to Bryner & Company.

And so in 1932 Boris and his wife continued the Bryner odyssey from England across France, where they spent a week in Deauville, north of Paris, with Vera (sixteen) and Yul (twelve), and from there eastward across Austria, Hungary, and Romania to the Crimea, where they boarded a ship for Port Arthur in the "Manchukuo Empire."

Though he and his wife were lucky to be safely out of the Soviet Union, the fugitive life was not what Boris was cut out for. Now, he and Katya were content to settle down and live. By 1932, they had been together nine years through relentless turbulence — some of it of their own making — but they remained undeniably, passionately in love with one another, and now that they had a chance to settle, Katya badly wanted to have a baby. So did Boris, notwithstanding his two children in France. Such separation was not entirely Boris's fault, since he had just moved to the city where his children had been living, but his presence with Katya in the same city had proven intolerable to Marousia, as much as had the Japanese occupying force.

After the Bolshevik Revolution, the population of Harbin had swelled with Russian refugees who struggled to maintain their traditions, along with shared delusions that Communism was a passing fad and that Imperial Russia would soon be restored. "Like excised tissue preserved in formaldehyde long after the parent body has perished," wrote Stephan, clinically, "the émigrés of Harbin persisted, a lifelike fragment of the pre-Revolutionary era." In the cafés and clubs of Harbin, arguments erupted between supporters of Nicholas II's doddering uncles, competing for the throne of a long-gone empire. And everywhere in the Far East there were aimless bands of Cossack families, formerly the tsar's cavalry, now slumped forlornly in vacant meadows like lost sheep.

Bryner & Company continued to thrive, providing import-export contracts for large businesses and industrial development. Despite the global slump of the 1930s that made the fluctuations in demand, fuel prices, currency values, and other variables challenging, the 1930s were a period of relative tranquility for the family.

To relax, Boris rode his large black mare, Venus, around the outskirts of Harbin. He also went out with friends hunting for duck and pheasant with his two dogs, a black Labrador called Taigee and a red setter, Jan (Katya had a cairn terrier named Sedka). Before long Boris also bought a family-sized motor launch, which they took on day trips along the Sungari River.

Major theater companies from Europe that toured China and the Far East invariably performed in Harbin, which now rivaled Vladivostok in stature and size. The two cities were just three hundred miles apart, but now they were divided by the "Iron Curtain," a phrase that was in use more than twenty years before Churchill supposedly coined it (see note). Katya organized a young group of actors in Harbin and regularly produced performances of Shakespeare and Dickens, as well as special events when friends from Moscow visited the Far East. The renowned Russian opera star, Fyodor Chaliapin, came through Harbin and visited with the Bryners. He had known Katya while he worked with Stanislavsky on acting technique; he was admired more at the time for his acting than his singing.

The Bryners renewed another old friendship — with the Yankovsky family from Sidemy. Yuri Yankovsky, "Asia's Greatest Tiger Hunter" and son of the family's Polish patriarch, had made a daring decision a decade earlier, when the Bolsheviks were approaching Sidemy. His son Valery described their trip more than eighty years later.

> We left on our ice-breaker *Prizrak* that pulled two 200-ton barges on tow-lines. There were eight Holland cows and about seventy people, with bag and baggage. Father had driven sixty horses south along the coast to Posyet; there he loaded them onto the barges and crossed the border into Korea. About a hundred caged deer were waiting on the bank at Sidemy. But the *Prizrak* was late with the second run, and the Bolsheviks had already occupied Primorye. The *Prizrak* just barely escaped, but the deer remained behind at Gek Bay. If father had not taken horses with us, we would have been penniless. Later we bred four wild deer from the forest, and eventually produced a profit.

The Yankovskys steamed slowly south from Sidemy with their chattel, hugging the coast, and traveled sixty miles before they were safely out of Russian territorial waters. From there they proceeded down the Korean coast as far as Ch'ŏngjin.

Within weeks, Yuri and his wife, Daisy — the cousin of Katya who had originally introduced her to Boris — purchased a considerable property in the Paektu-san foothills near the Chu'ŭl River, where they could continue breeding horses and deer. But Yuri Yankovsky had something more ambitious in mind.

The Yankovskys created a hunting resort for White Russians that they named "Novina," which incorporated architectural and pastoral features from Sidemy. "There were orchards for apples and pears, fields for vegetables, and hives for honey," wrote historian Donald Clark, "while the mountain forests furnished abundant venison, pork, and pheasant. Evenings at Novina featured dinners with as many as twenty people seated at the dining table, followed by vodka and storytelling by the fireplace." Over the next twenty years, hundreds of White Russians came to stay at the barrel-shaped lodge and hunt Siberian tigers with the celebrated hunter. Boris and Katya traveled there almost every summer from Harbin, where it was much hotter. Together with other guests, exiled members of the intelligentsiya, Katya staged plays and readings. One winter, when eighteen-year-old Yul was visiting Boris from Paris, they went together into north Korea on a week-long hunt for tiger, bear, and wild boar with Yuri Yankovsky.

The life Katya and Boris led together was happy and relatively secure in this era. Boris established himself as a valuable ally to other businessmen in the region, finding some consulting work with mining operations and then opening a construction firm, which dovetailed well with Bryner & Company, which imported timber and other elements of construction. By this time Leonid had turned the Shanghai office into a smoothly run and expanding shipping business from its headquarters on the Bund, the port-side business district where Jules had worked in the silk trade as a teenager in the 1860s.

Felix, in Dairen, was also doing well. Since the early 1930s, he had held a second job there as a consular agent for Switzerland's Department of Foreign Affairs, which had asked Felix to assist Swiss visitors in the Port Arthur–Dairen area of Manchukuo. Soon, Boris was also appointed Swiss consular agent for the Harbin region, this despite the fact that neither one had ever lived in Switzerland, much less had diplomatic training. However, as few Swiss ever ventured into Manchukuo — apart from the Bryners — the brothers were not fraught with responsibilities. In fact their assignments were a diplomatic anomaly: since Switzerland regarded the "Manchukuo Empire" as a fiction of the Japanese occupation rather than as a legitimate nation, the Swiss embassy in Tokyo was technically responsible for visits by its citizens to Manchuria. But Boris's peculiar commission as a consular agent would later save his life.

As happy as Katya and Boris were together, the years they remained childless were a source of deep frustration. That, together with the stress of their fugitive lives, had taken a toll on Boris's heart: he began suffering painful bouts of angina. But in 1938, Katya at last became pregnant. She was forty-three years old, and it seemed to her that she had been given this one last chance at what turned out to be a difficult pregnancy. She had already hired a nanny, named Nadenka, to help her. She was carrying twin boys, and she managed to bring them to full term. But they were delivered stillborn.

Katya was devastated — all the more so when she was told she had lost any chance of delivering another child.

Within weeks, Boris and Katya adopted a baby girl in Harbin and named her Catherine. Though little is known beyond her birth date — December 18, 1938 — it appears she was born to a Swiss woman. They also agreed *never* to let Catherine know that she was adopted. Only a handful of people were aware that Katya had not given birth to Catherine, and since she had in fact been pregnant, no one was ever the wiser.

Nine months after Catherine was born, Hitler invaded Poland in violation of his treaty with Stalin, who was taken completely by surprise. Now, with World War II underway, few doubted that the Nazi Army would soon overrun France, where Vera and Yul lived with Marousia.

Boris's vivacious, twenty-two-year-old daughter had married Russian pianist Valentin Pavlovski, permanent accompanist to the USSR's renowned cellist Gregor Piatigorsky, who had left his homeland in the 1920s. Now, as Piatigorsky moved to the United States, his accompanist moved with him, along with his wife.

Yul, then nineteen, had made himself very much at home in Paris, as had Marousia; but about this time she was diagnosed with leukemia. With the imminent threat of Hitler's invasion of France, the Bryners were refugees yet again. Yul took his frail mother back to Dairen by ship, sometimes carrying her in his arms, so that Marousia could be cared for by her beloved sister.

Marousia and Yul's year in the Far East gave Boris an opportunity to spend a good deal of time with his son. Yul visited with him in Harbin, and together the two traveled to Shanghai, Peking, and to Novina, as guests of the Yankovskys. That Yul was genuinely fond of his stepmother was a source of additional pain to his mother, and the fact that he was interested in becoming an actor made her very angry. It made Boris even angrier: he was counting on his son to work for Bryner & Company, and eventually to take it over. At one point Boris invited Yul to Shanghai, but by the time his son arrived, Boris had left. Although only one of many canceled reunions between father and son over the years, this was the one that broke Yul's heart. He never really forgave his father for it, and he made certain that Boris understood that.

Soon after, Yul took the ailing Marousia to New York, where his sister cared for her until her death two years later, on February 4, 1943. Marousia had been bitterly unhappy for most of her adult life. Her ashes were buried in Cold Spring, New York, a long, sad way from Vladivostok, where she was born.

Boris and Katya remained committed to Harbin, and given the chaos that now raged around the world, it was a safe enough retreat as long as Japan controlled Manchuria; besides, the Bryner business still needed them there. Catherine had contracted meningitis as a child, and then survived tuberculosis. Nonetheless she was, for the most part, a happy girl, treasured by her parents. She spent most of her time with her spaniel, Mollie, or in the enormous dollhouse that Boris built in the garden, large enough for her to walk around in and entertain her many dolls.

The Great Patriotic War, as World War II is still known in Russia, cost some twenty million Russian lives, including seven million men in uniform. The Imperial City of St. Petersburg that had dazzled Boris thirty years earlier was now Leningrad under siege. For two and a half years, the former capital of Russia was ringed by Hitler's army, and of its four million citizens, one and a half million perished from disease, starvation, and German artillery. The war demanded sacrifice and commitment from every citizen, every day, across the country, and that is what the Russian people gave to the cause. The human loss and suffering, added to those millions lost in Stalin's purges, is incomprehensible as anything but a statistic, confirming Stalin's cynical dictum. Indeed, he and Hitler, from opposite ends of the ideological spectrum, validated each other's bleak totalitarian worldview, as historian and philosopher Hannah Arendt famously pointed out — and almost annihilated each other over the next five years.

Felix had been the fully appointed Swiss consul for the region for some time, as well as acting consul for France and Sweden. (Leonid had been acting Swiss consul in Vladivostok — at least for some formalities — and now Boris was acting Swiss consul in Harbin.) After the Japanese attacked Pearl Harbor in December 1941, he was immediately appointed by the Swiss government to protect British and American citizens as well, and to assist in their evacuation now that they were deemed enemies of Japan. Switzerland's long-established neutrality in international affairs gave it unique prestige for those who sought sanctuary. Felix was now the sole diplomatic representative in the region for the citizens of five Western nations — an awesome responsibility for a Russian-born businessman who was not a trained diplomat. At the end of May 1942, after escorting members of the U.S. and British consulates to their ship, Felix was stricken with severe chest pains; the next morning, as Vera and Irena tried to save him, his heart stopped.

Jules Bryner's youngest son was buried beside the Orthodox church in Dairen. His wife and daughter went to Harbin to stay with Jules' youngest daughter, Nina, and her husband, Shura Ostroumov, the longtime lawyer for Bryner & Company. Ostroumov quickly took charge of all their affairs, including the $20,000 that Felix had left for his family in a bank in Shanghai.

With every bloody battle the United States won in the Pacific, the Japanese occupying forces in Manchuria became more menacing to foreign residents. By 1944, as U.S. and Soviet allies began closing in on Japan, the occupying forces in Harbin became unbearably threatening, and for safety this Bryner contingent moved to Tientsin, where they lived for a year, spending part of their time in Peking. By August 1945, when the United States dropped the atomic bomb on Hiroshima, Stalin's army was poised to seize Manchuria, where Boris, Katya, and Catherine still lived.

The invasion of Harbin by the Soviet Army in 1945 was announced by rocket and machine-gun fire, and flares lighting up the city," wrote Catherine Bryner more than sixty years later. "I remember being in the garden and crouching under a tree with Nadenka and watching the sky light up. We thought the house might be bombed."

Then came the sound Boris had dreaded ever since the Bolshevik Revolution almost thirty years earlier: Soviet jackboots outside his home. On September 13, 1945, "I was in my nursery," Catherine wrote, "and was told by Mummy that high-ranking Soviet army officers came to our house and put us under house arrest. This happened to all European-Russian citizens in Harbin. These officers told Mummy at a later date that she would be repatriated to Russia with me, and that she could return to the Moscow Art Theatre." The fact that the MVD — the secret police that succeeded Iron Felix's — knew about the family in such detail was no reassurance. Katya was "really terrified when she heard this."

"The Soviets questioned my mother and father many times, always in the middle of the night," Catherine continued, "accusing Daddy of collaborating with the Japanese. He said he never did so, because the Swiss were neutral during World War II." But of course, the Soviets did not acknowledge that Boris was a Swiss citizen, much less a diplomat, given his background as a Russian industrialist. In any case, many such diplomatic officials really were spies.

The Bryners were held under house arrest in Harbin for three months. Catherine described what happened next.

> On New Year's Eve, in the dead of night, they came to get us and took us to the airport where a plane awaited us. I don't remember anyone else being with us except Russian military.

> We boarded the plane — it was bitterly cold — and we took off for Russia. The officers offered us champagne, as it was New Year's Eve, and they had "Katusha" playing on the radio, a very popular song during the war. That is my name in Russian.
>
> We didn't know where we were going but it was somewhere near Vladivostok. We were taken to a refugee camp, which had lots of tents and was full of people. We stayed there about two days. It was very cold. I had just had my seventh birthday. After two days we were taken to a detached house in a village called Voroshilov [Ussurisk]. My parents were told that we would be staying there for a while and that a Japanese Admiral had been executed to make room for us. The house had two bedrooms and we had one, while the cook, who was KGB and who was our keeper, had the other one. There were two soldiers with semi-automatic guns who guarded us as well. The house had no bathroom and we were only allowed to bathe once at the local bath about three months later, when we were told we were being taken to Moscow.
>
> During our stay food was very scarce. We had to dig in the garden for frozen potatoes and cabbage stalks which the "cook" made into soup. We were given black bread, which tasted like it had sawdust in it and was horrible. There was a wood stove in the kitchen and in the sitting room — when it went out, then it was freezing cold. We did receive one Red Cross parcel during that time, which was wonderful.

The Primorye prince was now helpless to save his family. It was all they could do to stay alive.

In Shanghai, Leonid was working frantically to save his brother, knowing full well that most prisoners in the Far East ended up at the Kolyma gulag, whence few returned. On November 2 he wrote to the Swiss consul general for China, also in Shanghai, regarding "the abduction by force of my brother, Boris Bryner, from Harbin to the USSR." Leonid outlined the Bryner family's history in the years since "the Russian Far East was occupied by the Soviets"; describing it as an "occupation" after a full quarter of a century displayed Leonid's unreconstructed disdain for the Revolution. "I cannot think of any other grudge which the Soviet authorities might have had against my brother Boris, but one," he wrote, "his remaining abroad instead of returning to Vladivostok in 1931," fourteen years earlier. At the same time, Leonid was writing at length to the Swiss Department of Foreign Affairs in Bern, pleading for help from the government of Switzerland — the nation that Jules had left more than eighty years earlier. "We were always considered Swiss by birth," he wrote, "and are still Swiss citizens."

In March 1946, the Bryners were taken to the Vladivostok Station to board the Trans-Siberian Railroad, passing in front of the Bryner Residence as Soviet prisoners. Boris wondered who was living in their home now; later he learned that it had been taken over as a printing house for the Communist Party. "We now had two officers looking after us," Catherine wrote. "The train was full of the military and I remember that soldiers, and once even a general, were very kind to me and gave me sweets and cakes. The train had good food, after what we had lived on."

It was still not clear what was happening to them. The Soviet apparatchiks continued to disregard the Bryners' Swiss nationality, and Boris understood that the Soviets considered this principle too important to overlook. That is why he feared that the worst possible forms of interrogation awaited them in Moscow; for Katya and Boris, this might include watching their little girl be tortured, a common strategy. Instead, upon their arrival in the capital, they were treated as "honored guests" of the Soviet Union, and escorted to one of the city's finest hotels, the Savoy.

It was not until Boris met with a Swiss envoy that he made sense of it all. The Swiss government, having failed to convince the Soviets that Boris Bryner was entitled to diplomatic immunity, had offered to exchange six Soviet private citizens and a military pilot being held in Swiss jails for the Bryners' freedom. As soon as the exchange was effected, Boris, Katya, and Catherine were "repatriated" to Switzerland, their unfamiliar homeland.

They left Moscow for Berlin on a bus, since the Soviets had canceled all passenger trains to Europe indefinitely. "I remember our arrival in Berlin,"

Catherine wrote. "It was at night, and it was like a ghost town. Everything was in ruins, and it was pitch black with an occasional candle burning in the shell of a house — crumbling walls and buildings without roofs." The defeated city, divided into sectors controlled by the United States, the Soviet Union, Great Britain, and France, was the very spot where the Cold War began, on the very day World War II ended. There, where American-sponsored West German democracy rubbed shoulders with Soviet-sponsored East German communism, the Bryners were released at the only exit point permitted from the Soviet Sector, later known as Checkpoint Charlie.

The Bryners had been Soviet prisoners for six months: interrogated, intimidated, and starved. Throughout most of that time, Boris and Katya could not have expected to survive, when so many others in their situation did not. Their relief upon release must have been beyond imagining. Leonid's labors had saved his brother from near-certain death, thanks to the enormous diplomatic efforts of the Swiss government, efforts based solely upon the Swiss citizenship that Boris had inherited from Jules Bryner.

The extent of the Holocaust was just then becoming known, and had not yet been widely reported in the press. In Berlin, wrote Catherine, "Journalists came to see Daddy, and gave him horrifying photos of the extermination of the Jews to take to Switzerland, so that German atrocities could be known."

In Bern, Boris was debriefed by the Department of Foreign Affairs, the government agency that had arranged for the exchange for prisoners. Catherine, who was suffering a relapse of tuberculosis, was first sent to a sanatorium in Locarno; a few months later the entire family traveled to England, where Katya's sister bought a house in Surrey with help from Boris, and opened a restaurant.

Boris was anxious to return to Shanghai, where Leonid had been shouldering all the responsibilities of Bryner & Company for too long. So traveling west around the globe instead of east on the Trans-Siberian Railroad, in early 1947 he took his wife and daughter to the United States. There he had the stunning experience of visiting with Yul and Vera, both of whom were fulfilling their wildest dreams after only a few years in New York.

• • • • • • • •

By this time both Yul and his sister had added an *n* to Bryner, so that people would not mispronounce it "Breiner." Yul, at twenty-six, having barely mastered English, had already starred on Broadway in *Lute Song* and then toured the United States with the play. Boris met Yul's wife of two years, the young movie star Virginia Gilmore, and visited their tiny apartment over a dry cleaner's on East Thirty-eighth Street. There Boris spent a day with Virginia and her four-month-old baby. Boris's grandson, like his son, was named after his father, Jules. In grade school, Yul Brynner, Jr., took on the nickname "Rocky." Boris received a warm reception from Virginia, but was treated with cool correctness by Yul, who continued with his busy routine, unable or unwilling to spend much time with his father. But the most amazing experience for Boris was with Vera, his thirty-one-year-old daughter.

"We went to see Vera sing *Madame Butterfly* at the Metropolitan Opera House," wrote Catherine. What an astounding night that must have been for Boris! He had not seen Vera in a decade, and now he was watching her perform one of the greatest soprano roles at one of the world's greatest opera houses. Boris, who himself always loved to sing, had been furious with both his grown children for choosing to become performers, even as Katya had encouraged them. Now, they had both launched themselves on stellar careers. But Boris must have also remembered that their mother had sacrificed her career as a singer and actress for her husband, only to be abandoned by him for the love of an actress.

Still another thought must have crossed his mind that night watching *Madame Butterfly*. It is, after all, the story of a visitor to Japan from the West, Benjamin Franklin Pinkerton, who marries a Japanese girl and after spending an idyllic time, leaves her, together with their child. Of course, Boris knew this mirrored the story of Jules as a young man in Japan; the similarities were too haunting to overlook. And Boris must have considered the fact that, had his father not made the same choice as the scoundrel Pinkerton, then he himself would never have been born.

Yul was also at the opera that night, "dressed in a black Cossack shirt and boots," Catherine recalled. "And he brought his guitar, because he was singing in nightclubs at the time." How inexplicably strange and wonderful that they found themselves together on the opposite side of the planet from their birthplace, with Yul dressed in the signature costume of the Cossacks who had patrolled the streets of Vladivostok when he was a boy, while they listened to Vera's triumphant performance.

Yul was brisk with his father even as they said goodbye. Though they had no particular reason to believe this would be their last meeting, neither could they have foreseen when or where they would meet again.

From New York, Boris, Katya, and Catherine proceeded to Palo Alto, California. There they stayed with Leonid's oldest son, Cyril, who had moved from Vladivostok to San Francisco soon after the Bolshevik Revolution.

Boris, however, was impatient to return to Shanghai to join Leonid, who had recently been diagnosed with stomach cancer. "Mummy was very much against it," Catherine wrote, because of a "strong premonition that something bad was going to happen to us, and begged him not to take us there. But he wouldn't listen and said that everything would be fine. . . . So we sailed for Shanghai."

Bryner & Company still had its offices on the Bund, at Number 18 where Boris and Leonid had located the business in 1930. Boris and Katya rented an apartment in the European section, and Catherine recalled that "there were many of my parents' friends in Shanghai and a large Russian colony."

A few months after they settled there, Leonid passed away at the age of sixty-three. As the last of the Bryner brothers, Boris knew that Jules' empire would come to an end with his own death. In spite of excruciating attacks of angina, which grew more frequent in the hot, humid atmosphere of Shanghai, somehow Boris had to plan for the future. Although his brother-in-law, Shura, was also in Shanghai and was familiar with the company's legal standing, he was a lawyer and unfamiliar with the operation of the business. Obviously, Yul could not have been prevailed upon to take over Bryner & Company.

Returning from school one day, Catherine found her mother dissolved in tears. "When I got home in the afternoon," Catherine wrote, "Mummy was completely distraught and told me that Daddy had died of a heart attack." It was July 9, 1948; Boris was fifty-eight years old.

As a young man, Boris had supervised construction of the Bryner tomb on Sidemy, where he had expected to be buried someday; instead, he was laid to rest in Shanghai. Katya remained utterly inconsolable, as did Catherine. "We had been very close," his daughter wrote recently, "and I didn't get to say goodbye to him."

With the last of Jules Bryner's sons dead — all by the age of sixty-five — Shura Ostroumov assumed responsibility for dissolving the residual property of Bryner & Company, and promised to send Boris's share of the proceeds — the remainder of Jules Bryner's empire — to Katya in England, where she took Catherine to join her sister in Surrey.

Boris, like Jules, had led an unimaginably full life, but the circumstances they lived through were different at every stage: Jules, born to a wool-spinner, and Boris an industrialist, a prince of Primorye. Jules had thrived in the freedom of the early "Wild East," while Boris had grappled all his adult life with oppressive dictatorship. Both men had abandoned their first families before becoming devoted husbands and fathers. And both men had produced remarkable sons.

PART THREE
YUL BRYNNER

Yul Brynner must be mad to imagine that he could be Yul Brynner.

— Jean Cocteau (1956)

On July 11, 1920, Juli Borisovitch Bryner was born into an industrial empire that was crumbling in the chaos of revolutionary Russia, which had made its way into the Bryner Residence on Aleutskaya Street; Interventionist troops slept in the hallway outside the room where the infant was delivered. When he was three years old, turbulence of a different nature reached deep into his family after his father's desertion damaged his mother beyond repair: four years later his family became displaced persons, albeit reasonably wealthy for a short time. He nonetheless grew up within a ring of adoring females, assisted by his steadfast uncle Felix. From a very early age, Yul was accustomed to being the organizing principle in any roomful of people.

A variety of languages swirled around his crib: Marousia spoke Russian and French with Boris, who sometimes spoke English on the telephone or with his brothers, and inside the house he heard Chinese, Korean, Czech, and Japanese. This polyglot society obliged everyone to find extra-verbal means of communicating. Yul grew up speaking Russian with Vera, his sister, who was four years old at his birth, and with Irena, his cousin, who was three. His mother spoke Russian, although only rarely after Boris left her: she moaned and wept for months, and then fell almost completely silent. But his aunt Vera, uncle Felix, and grandmother, Baiga, instilled in the children Russian cultural traits — a forthright emotional expressiveness, for example, and boundless admiration for dominant virility — mitigated by the artistic and intellectual sensitivity of the intelligentsiya, and the Swiss attention to detail that Felix and Boris had learned from their father, Jules.

Strictly speaking, young Yul was not born in Russia, but in the Far East Russian Republic for which his father served as the minister of industry. During the thirty months of its existence, the republic issued passports, but only a handful of countries officially recognized its nationhood. The only certain thing was Yul's Swiss nationality, but that was not recognized by Russia. The name given at his Orthodox baptism, Юлий, was transliterated in his Swiss documents as *Yul,* which reflected the correct pronunciation and the fact that the *i* in *Juli* was dropped in his childhood.

Yul was an independent spirit from the start, encouraged by his aunt Vera, a devout free-thinker. He was cheerful and mischievous, musical and imaginative, with a total intolerance for authority in any form: *whenever* discipline was imposed upon him, he pushed back. That could prove dangerous, say, in a Trans-Siberian railway car full of Soviet apparatchiks.

Even as a baby he loved the sea and the coast where the estate at Sidemy spread out along Amur Bay. He was still an infant when the family took him there by boat, and his first six summers were spent on its rocky beach beneath the cottage where he and his family stayed; where his grandparents had once spent their honeymoon, looking out at the Bryner lighthouse on Rabbit Island. Yul's grandmother Natalya was so hostile toward his mother that he rarely visited the old lady up at the main house. Instead he skipped rocks and caught crabs on the beach below.

Yul was just six when his family left Vladivostok, but his love for the seaside and his sense of a city and of a busy, multicultured port had first developed in that diverse world, where a wide variety of uniforms filled the streets and a dozen nationalities coexisted in mutual cooperation and/or disinterest. By then Kunst and Albers was struggling: founded in 1864, just four years after the original naval base, its ornate, baroque building was soon taken over by the government store, GUM, where the shelves would often be empty in the coming decades. Most of the other foreign businesses soon disappeared under the Communist regime, too: National City Bank, International Harvester, the YMCA, the Knights of Columbus, the American Red Cross, the Chicago Café, and many European businesses succumbed, under the corrupt oppression of local authorities.

Yul was aware early on that his family had been privileged and that their special status was quickly eroding: the Bryner children were suddenly "undesirables" in the public schools, because they were *bourzhoys* (bourgeois). Yul was sensitive to the tension, anxiety, and terror that events in the street produced in the household from time to time, but he also had a personal connection to the whole world by virture of the railway beside his home that stretched all the way to Europe. Like most boys he was fascinated by trains, their sounds and shiny parts, and the sheer power of the enormous black locomotive. He had always wanted the model train set from Europe that Boris had promised to bring to him, but apparently never remembered to buy when he visited Harrods in London; in fact, Soviet customs would have confiscated any such ornate thing.

After Boris signed the Tetukhe agreement with Dzerzhinsky in 1924, he and Katya moved to the Far East. While spending most of their time at the mining town four hundred miles northeast, when they stayed at the Bryner Residence, they had visits from Yul and his sister. Though the emotional climate for the children's meeting with their stepmother did not bode well, Yul and Vera adored Katya from the moment they met her. She was vivacious, theatrical, clever, and charming, and the excitement of her career in Moscow still wafted about her; Katya seemed to be everything that their dismal, wounded mother was not. And in fact, this same woman who played the central role in the destruction of Yul's family also inspired him to become an actor.

It was about this time that Yul first ran away. "He declared that he no longer wanted to live at home," wrote his cousin Irena, "that he loved the oldest daughter of family friends and wanted to go live with her. He was five years old, she was over twenty. Marousia said, 'Fine, I will help you pack your bags.' She took a suitcase and put in pajamas, a shirt, and a chamber pot, carried it to the gate, kissed him goodbye, closed the gate, and walked away. Yul was fine until then. I think he must have heard something final in the sound of a closed gate. First he looked puzzled, then he started to cry. His mother came back and asked what was wrong. 'I want to go home, she lives too far away and I am hungry.' So ended Yul's first love affair."

Not long after, Yul moved with his mother, sister, and grandmother to Chinese-controlled Harbin, beyond the threat of Soviet arrest. Felix took them there, to a house he had rented in the Russian neighborhood of Novy Gorod. By this time, "Yul was a lively and naughty boy," Irena wrote, "and there was no end to his mischievous inventions. He always had a solution for everything. When he wanted something and his mother told him that she had no money to buy it for him, he would say, 'Just go to the bank and *buy* some money.' He had many fights with boys and girls, and his teachers constantly complained to his mother." But when Marousia was forced to rouse herself and punish him, her sister Vera often came to his defense, and so, early on, he devised different strategies for playing authorities against each other.

And while growing up in the midst of military chaos and family trauma, then fleeing to China, Yul was forced by circumstance to develop an internal support system, to consciously construct and *become* his own role model, his own hero, his own organizing principle.

Harbin was celebrating its thirtieth anniversary when six-year-old Yul settled there. Many volumes have been devoted to the uniqueness of early Harbin, and to the abstruse debate of whether the city's character was predominantly Russian or Chinese in 1910, and 1920, and 1925. Founded in 1896 by Finance Minister Sergei Witte to provide housing for the laborers constructing the Chinese Eastern Railroad, most of the population was Chinese and Korean, but they controlled only a tiny fraction of the wealth. In the 1920s, according to Stephan, about a quarter of the city's half million inhabitants were Russian. "Harbin remained a major center of the Russian diaspora until the late 1940s," he wrote. "Chinese (300,000) predominated, followed by Koreans (34,000) and Japanese (5,000). There were also pockets of Baltic Germans, Poles, Ukrainians, Armenians, Tartars, Georgians, and Estonians who had fled the Bolsheviks, and about 13,000 Russian Jews, some of them longtime residents and leaders of Harbin's business, religious, and scholarly communities." In fact, with the Chinese Eastern Railroad complete, Harbin "challenged Vladivostok's regional preeminence. Russian and foreign firms alike opened branches in Manchuria," among which Bryner & Company was prominent, with its Swiss flag above the entrance.

The YMCA school that the Bryner children attended was a much beloved institution for generations of students. Although Headmaster Haig was American-born, the school's syllabus and method copied those of the Russian gymnasium, and the elementary school classes, which Yul attended from the ages of six to eleven, were preparatory for a traditional, Old Russian education. Its reputation was such that graduates were admitted to American universities without entrance exams.

Classes at the YMCA began at nine o'clock — after a half hour of prayer in the auditorium — and finished at three, whereupon the Bryners had their main meal, after which Yul had piano lessons or practice with his aunt Vera (who had continued to give occasional concerts after her medical career in Moscow), followed by homework. He and his sister — who broke the hearts of all the boys at Harbin High School — also took singing lessons, and it soon became apparent that they both had exceptional voices; since Marousia and Boris sang beautifully, music had always played a large part in all of their lives. Perhaps that is why, when Yul asked his father for a guitar on his tenth birthday, Boris actually produced an instrument for him, and soon Yul began studying classical guitar instead of piano.

In Harbin, Yul had his first experience at the theater. He was seven years old when the Soviet Opera Company toured the Far East, performing Rimsky-Korsakov's *The Snow Maiden* with the renowned tenor Lemishev. He came home with his eyes twinkling and his imagination thoroughly captive to the combined force of a well-staged, brightly costumed musical drama enhanced by a powerful live orchestra. Not long after, wrote Irena, "when Yul had a fever, he all of a sudden jumped up in his bed singing from *The Snow Maiden*, 'Wait, Snow Maiden, wait!' after which he collapsed to his pillows. All through his life those little signs of an actor within him came out." This introduction to the performing arts was soon followed by other operas, plays, and ballets that toured the Soviet Union.

By that age Yul was already exploring Harbin for whole afternoons in the spring, often skipping piano and homework. The staid, civilized Russian community wasn't as exciting as the Oriental parts of town with all the strange foods and smells in their marketplaces, ubiquitous gambling in the Chinese neighborhood, tournaments of *Gō* among the Japanese, and opium dens never far away.

Opium was universally tolerated in Manchuria, and its tincture was available from apothecaries (Dr. J. Collis Browne's "Chlorodyne" was sold throughout Europe for decades), taken regularly by adults and given regularly to infants for colic, or to help them sleep. Opium dens degraded neighborhoods, but they also earned large profits for everyone involved, including police and other authorities who took bribes — everyone except the addicted smokers, who earned only pipe dreams. Yul tried smoking opium on more than one occasion, and after the nausea passed, he enjoyed it immensely.

In early 1932, when Yul was eleven years old, Japanese troops began moving across Manchuria toward Harbin. "There was panic among the residents," wrote Irena, then fourteen, "after we were told that in the night Chinese troops would depart and the Japanese Army would come in. Everyone was afraid that the Chinese soldiers would loot or attack the white population. Some people armed themselves for protection and put sand bags against the windows. When the night came we were all awake. . . . On wooden carts, pulled by small horses or mules, the Chinese soldiers sat in their dirty quilted jackets, looking frightened and miserable. Nobody looted anything; all they wanted was to get out of their uniforms, to hide from the Japanese. We felt sorry for them."

This was more pressure than Marousia could bear, and now that Boris had also moved to Harbin with Katya, "every time her ex-husband . . . came to see his children, it was a major tragedy for her." As well, Yul's sister was determined to continue her studies at the Russian Conservatory of Music in Paris: Vera especially wanted to study light opera — as Marousia had done at the St. Petersburg Conservatory. Yul would be enrolled in one of the finest traditional boarding schools in France, and Marousia would have the excitement of Paris to perhaps reawaken her soul and the enormous White Russian community among whom she could find friends.

So in the autumn, Marousia, Vera, and Yul set off by rail to Dairen, and then by ship to Shanghai. This was the most modern and exciting place that Yul had ever been: it was also a city that his father loved, and it would forever hold a certain fascination for him. There they boarded an American ocean liner for the six-week trip to Marseille, stopping at a half dozen ports of call along the way: Hong Kong, Saigon, Singapore, Rangoon, Calcutta, Madras, Bombay, and then finally through the Suez Canal to the Mediterranean. They stopped in each harbor for a day, and Yul explored all the port towns, soaking up the distinctive atmosphere of each and when he found opium, buying small amounts, which he hid inside his guitar. Meanwhile, as they traveled, he devoured the works of Dostoyevsky.

There had long been a cultural affinity between Russians and the French, even as the two nations waged war upon war with each other. But as Paris became the undisputed mecca of the European arts in the late nineteenth century — due in no small part to Cézanne, Renoir, and the other masters of impressionism — Russian artists as dissimilar as Chagall and Goncharova came to Paris. Waves of Russian immigrants settled within walking distance of the Russian Orthodox church on the rue Daru, near the elegant 8th arondissement. Since Marousia attended church regularly, family friends had found an apartment a few blocks from the church in rue Catulle-Mendès, which would remain their home throughout most of the 1930s.

White Russian refugees lived all across Paris, from maids' rooms on the Left Bank of the Seine to fine *salons d'art* and *hôtels particuliers*, and some of these émigrés were transforming European culture. Sergei Diaghilev had brought innovation to Paris with his Ballets Russes, as well as the dancers Anna Pavlova, Vaslav Nijinsky, and Serge Lifar; but most of all he brought from Russia the works of Igor Stravinsky, and then Stravinsky himself, who made Paris his home between the two world wars. "Astonish me!" (*Étonnez-moi!*) was Diaghilev's famous challenge to Jean Cocteau, some years before their collaboration with Picasso on the ballet *Parade*. That challenge expressed better than any other motto the "banquet years" of cultural experimentation in the concert halls, galleries, publishing houses, theaters, and cinemas of Paris during Yul's adolescence.

From the day they arrived, Yul spent hardly any time at home; by the age of twelve he was determinedly independent. At first he was sent to École des Roches in Normandy, a traditional "old school tie" institution for boys in a beautiful country setting eighty miles north of Paris that offered an intensive summer course in French for foreign-language students, in which Yul had been enrolled. His French was still limited and his accent Slavic, but he quickly became fluent; like his father and his grandfather, he had an exceptional facility with languages.

From the start, Yul made little effort to conform to expectations. The very first day of school he got into a fight, and he was regularly caught smoking cigarettes because he refused to hide. Unlike the coteries of other foreign students, his unusual background — a Russian-born Swiss citizen raised in Asia — made him a singular figure, and thus a target for the tougher, older students. But Yul had grown up in a culture of chaotic cruelty and violence that these schoolyard bullies could not have imagined. His retaliation against any attack was so fierce and his disregard for authority so complete that he earned a reputation as one of the tough kids, as well as a ringleader of sorts among his peers.

He did not last the whole summer at Les Roches, and by the fall he was enrolled at the Lycée Moncelle in Paris. Boris was providing for their financial needs in France, including young Vera's tuition at the Conservatory, where her unusually rounded soprano voice had earned her a place; but he was often late sending money, and Marousia, with nowhere else to turn, had to ask her sister and Felix to help them out. This added to Yul's mounting disdain for his father, and for authority figures in general. He did not dispute their authority per se — only that it applied to him. So, when he took a dislike to his Latin teacher, he persuaded his classmates to turn their chairs to face the back of the class when the teacher arrived. His attendance at school was minimal, and Marousia's limp efforts at disciplining him were unsuccessful. Nonetheless his teachers, recognizing that he was gifted, lazy, and headstrong, did not expel him, even when he was gone for days at a time.

By then Yul had found the world he was looking for, and the key to admission was his guitar.

It was Vera, then almost seventeen years old, who first took Yul to a Russian restaurant in Montmartre where the Dimitrievitch family of four performed Gypsy songs nightly. She had gone there for dinner one evening with Rostik Hoffmann, private secretary to Serge Lifar, the ballet dancer. Vera had chatted with the *Tzigani* — Russian for Gypsies, known to themselves as the Romany or Roma people — and she had sung a Russian folk song with them. The patriarch of the troupe was the same Ivan Dimitrievitch whose failed attempt on the life of Rasputin in Mokroie twenty-five years earlier had required his family to flee Russia. Aliosha Dimitrievitch, his nineteen-year-old son, was instantly smitten with Vera and invited her to return as his guest. When she did, she brought along her kid brother; Aliosha was not thrilled at that, and he and Yul had at least one serious fight before they became fast friends.

Yul was seven years younger and much stronger than the diminutive Gypsy, but with Aliosha for the first time Yul had a fraternal bond, an older brother who could show him the ropes and teach him the folk songs. Felix was the only male with whom Yul had had close regular contact, and while his uncle was always a reliable and caring figure, he was not a lot of fun; Yul's camaraderie with Aliosha was an entirely new experience.

The Dimitrievitch clan welcomed Yul into their *kumpania* as a family member. Given the choice between the Gypsies and the dreary company of his mother, there was no contest; Yul spent almost all his time with the Dimitrievitch family, grabbing sleep wherever he could as he learned to play the unusually small, seven-string Gypsy guitar and developed a repertoire of traditional Russian folk songs he could play with the Dimitrievitches. Most of the time he was just a member of the Dimitrievitch ensemble led by the patriarch, Ivan, with Aliosha and his two sisters, Marukha and Valentina, and family members who played other instruments. Aliosha gave him helpful tips: "Not too loud, Yul," he once advised, "only to the horizon." On rare occasions they collected a veritable orchestra, thirty guitars strong. For the rest of his life, Yul would commemorate June 15, 1933, as the date he began performing professionally — one month before his thirteenth birthday. That was at the club Raspoutine, named in ironic tribute to the mad monk who had helped bring down the Russian Empire.

The first Russian nightclub in Paris had opened in rue Pigalle in 1922, financed by a wealthy refugee from St. Petersburg; by the mid-thirties there were dozens of clubs, restaurants, and bars in Montmartre that could, with enough vodka, help refugees forget that the Empire had been overthrown. Many *bourzhoy* Russians who had escaped with their wealth intact now spent it heedlessly in these dark, expensive dens of nostalgia, struggling to recapture the world that had evaporated like a mirage. The doormen and *maîtres d'hôtel* at these establishments were often former Russian aristocrats whose wealth had remained behind; now, down at the heels, they had chosen capitalist poverty over Communist famine.

The decor in most of these clubs leaned heavily toward dark velvets, gilded candelabras, and tsarist mementos: swords, photos, military ribbons, and silver samovars. The menus tempted Parisians and refugees alike with traditional Russian dishes and an array of strongly spiced vodkas and high-priced champagnes. Balalaika and accordion provided the dinner music before the artists performed: the Dimitrievitches were the stars of the evening, every evening, in a half dozen clubs within a few blocks' walk of each other.

Yul was an asset to the Dimitrievitches and to the clubs: by the age of sixteen, he was often the handsomest man in the room. When he spoke flawless Russian with wealthy dowagers and widows who flirted with him, they invariably offered to buy him a drink, and he invariably ordered "my usual": the waiter would bring Yul a tumbler the size of a small fish tank supposedly filled with vodka, charging the customer an enormous sum and giving Yul a kickback. The Gypsies always shunned serious involvement with non-Gypsies, whom they called *gaje*.

The Dimitrievitches spoke Russian and French, badly, but to each other they spoke Romany or Rom, the language of the Kaldaresh Gypsies and of most of their songs. As with the "tinkers" of Ireland and England, and the Spanish *gitanos*, the Tzigani adapted local folk songs to their liking, blending Russian with Rom. Over a year or two Yul learned the lyrics to fifty or more Tzigani songs along with dozens of French *ballades*, and enough of the Romany language to communicate with his friends; "The truth can only be spoken in Rom" was an oft-repeated maxim. The gaje could never be trusted to speak the truth; that is why the Gypsies always tease the gaje.

But even more than the language, the worldview of the Romany resonated perfectly with Yul's repeated experience as a refugee. He was quick to see himself as a permanent vagabond who, like Aliosha, would live his life by the rules of the road, not by the rules of the homebound gaje. It already seemed clear that the world of European gypsies would soon come to an end, as prophesied in the song that became a trademark of Yul's: "The End of The Road," or "Okonchen Poot."

In this nightclub setting, Yul came into his own. By his reckoning, he began his independent adult life in those restaurants, *boîtes*, and *bistros* (from the Russian word *bystro* or Быстро, for "quickly"). His baritone voice was rich and powerful, and for a time he studied operatic singing with one of Vera's coaches; at eighteen he even appeared in a Conservatory concert, performing an aria from *Don Giovanni*. In the clubs, his presence as a musician demanded the full attention of all the customers, who offered generous tips after he sang beside their tables; decades later Yul encountered many of these customers again in radically different circumstances.

For half the summer each year, Marousia had the loan of a small house outside Deauville, near the beaches of Normandy, where Yul and Vera usually spent a week or two. During their first vacation there, Boris also visited for a week, staying at the Casino Hotel looking out at the English Channel. In every photograph that remains of Yul as a boy, his expression is unalterably gloomy when he is beside his mother, and invariably cheerful when he is with his father. Knowing that Boris had been in the Imperial Society of Lifeguards as a young man in Vladivostok, Yul found a job as an assistant and soon became a senior lifeguard on the Casino's beach — which also raised his romantic prestige among the "older women" of seventeen or eighteen. He already had a number of advantages in that department: he was well-groomed and spirited, sophisticated, and a passionate, self-confident lover, even by that first summer in Normandy.

In Paris, the Dimitrievitches usually met up at a café near the circus, where the trapeze artists also gathered. Bantering with them one evening when he was fourteen, "I pretended to be an old hand on the trapeze," Yul later explained, so the aerialists invited him to give a demonstration; but, of course, "I was bluffing, and when I had climbed up to the take-off platform, about fifty feet above ground, I looked down and nearly fainted. . . . They all roared at me; but they gave me a few months training and took me into the troupe. It was the happiest period of my whole life."

Trapeze aerialists had originated in France, among swimmers and divers who used pools in lieu of safety nets to practice their stunts. The first trapeze artist was Jules Léotard, celebrated in the song "The Daring Young Man on the Flying Trapeze," who wore the garment that still bears his name. In 1859, Léotard had made his debut at the Cirque Royale in Paris, establishing a tradition that lasted there until 1917, when the circus building near Place de la République was transformed into the Cinématographe for silent movies; that is where Yul and Vera had seen Charlie Chaplin's *The Gold Rush* when they first arrived in Paris. But in 1934, the four Bouglione brothers took over the large hall and raised a tent inside, restoring it to a one-ring circus that operated only during the winter months; hence the name the Cirque d'Hiver. Two years after it opened, Yul went to work there, first as a general apprentice, then as an apprentice clown, then tumbler and acrobat, then as a trapeze catcher, and finally as a flying trapeze artist, right on the spot where the sport had been born.

In those years trapeze acrobats were stars, thanks largely to the elusive triple somersault. Circus audiences stood in long lines for the chance to witness any flyer attempt the "World's First Triple." Yul, ever quick to accept a challenge, had set his sights on the triple even before he'd made his first flight from the release bar to the hands of the catcher dangling upside-down from another swinging bar.

Yul performed his stunts as a melancholy flying clown in a tramp costume and a fright wig, with lugubrious makeup. "I flew and cried," he said later. With this comical figure, he could attempt the triple as often as he liked, incorporating his failures into the routine. His plucky clown character kept trying to throw a triple, and fell spectacularly in a variety of poses to the safety net twenty feet below. In the small world of circus aficionados, Yul had already made a name for himself.

He was also a man about town, even at the age of sixteen. In 1936, after his aunt Vera and cousin Irena moved to Lausanne, Switzerland, they came to visit Marousia in Paris and found that Yul had become "a handsome young man with wavy dark hair," Irena later wrote. "He loved to dress up, and was very elegant. When he took us somewhere for a walk, he insisted on choosing what we were going to wear. It was important to him to have an elegantly dressed companion." His connection with the Cirque d'Hiver and the Dimitrievitches only became known to the family much later, and "the surprise element of it was not easy for his mother, who was not well." But in fact, by the age of sixteen, the most reliable social institutions Yul had ever known were a circus and a Gypsy nightclub.

He was seventeen when he had an accident. Landing off-kilter in the safety net, he was flung to the ground and landed on a pile of scaffolding pipe, shattering numerous bones on his left side, from his leg to his shoulder. It was not clear that he would be able to walk normally again. In fact, he was immobilized for months at Marousia's apartment, where he spent much of his time preparing to enter the Sorbonne and playing guitar. Although he returned to work with the Dimitrievitches and played a few sets each evening, Yul remained hobbled by pain for another year. During that time he smoked opium regularly — easy enough to find in Paris, where France's colonial rule of Indochina assured a steady supply. As late as the 1950s, many sailors in the French merchant marine, centered around Marseille and Le Havre, happily accepted opium in lieu of their pay. Gangsters moved large quantities to the *métropole*, where regular consumers were generally aging aristocrats who had used the drug for some ailment, real or imagined, for years.

Many artists in Paris also used opium in the 1930s. One evening, after performing at a Russian club named Tsarevitch, Yul was approached by an unusual poet in his late forties who had heard that the young performer might have access to some opium. Yul recognized him right away, of course: it was Jean Cocteau, the writer, filmmaker, and artist, whose image appeared almost as often on the society page of *Le Figaro* as it did on the arts page; Yul had seen Cocteau's recent film, *Le Sang d'un Poète* (*The Blood of a Poet*, 1932), and had read his novel, *Les Enfants Terribles*. So, loosening two strings on his guitar and reaching into its cavity, Yul produced a wad of the tarlike substance wrapped in wax paper. With that unusual beginning, they formed a lifelong friendship.

Cocteau had been widely recognized as an innovative poet since the first decade of the century, then as a playwright, then as a designer (with Diaghilev's Ballets Russes), and finally as a cineast, especially for his seminal masterpiece, *The Beauty and the Beast* (1945), pillaged by the Disney organization half a century later. He had been friends with Marcel Proust, enemies with André Gide, and by the 1930s, Cocteau was a proud but battered figure, known as *l'enfant terrible* of French art. He was, by his own description, unsynchronized with the world. Belonging neither to the mainstream culture that he rejected nor the avant-garde subcultures that rejected him, he was often regarded as a frivolous society figure, a *poseur* masquerading as an artist. He endured considerable scorn, especially from Marcel Duchamp and his Dadaists, who mocked him publicly. Perhaps by comparison with the stellar reputations of the company he kept, especially his long, ambivalent friendship with Picasso, Cocteau seemed like a lesser figure in the art world. His homosexual proclivities, thinly disguised, and his self-centered aesthetic did not enhance his popularity with either the art world or the general public.

Nor did his addiction to opium endear Cocteau to the world. By the time he met Yul in 1937, Cocteau had already published a memoir, *Opium, Journal of A Cure,* filled with anguished drawings, that he had kept during his first detoxification. Obviously, the cure did not take, and he continued to smoke opium for the rest of his life. Often in the year that they met, Jean procured his drug from the teenage nightclub singer, leaving as an unlikely historical footnote the fact that in his youth,Yul Brynner was Jean Cocteau's opium supplier.

For a time Yul controlled his own use of the drug, mostly by heeding an old French "truism": if you never use opiates (including morphine or heroin) on three consecutive days, you will not become addicted. Like so many truisms, this wasn't true at all, and soon enough Yul found that he was uncomfortable and mean-spirited every third day, whereupon he discarded the truism rather than the opium. But not long after he was in trouble, physically and financially: the more strung out he was, the more money his suppliers were charging him. Finally, after persuading them to advance him a considerable quantity of the drug on consignment, he failed to pay and fled Paris.

Determined to break opium's grip, in 1937 Yul sought out the only real maternal care he had ever known — from his aunt Vera, who had settled in Switzerland for four years so Irena could study art history at the Université de Lausanne while Felix managed Bryner & Company in China. They had chosen Lausanne because that was where Felix had been sent to school as a boy to learn French, just a few hours' travel from where Jules had been born. And that is where, on his first visit to Switzerland, Yul spent three months in detoxification. The family's medical alibi was that Yul was suffering from a hormonal imbalance of the pituitary gland. In fact, he admitted to his aunt that there were some very tough guys hunting for him in Paris.

Nonetheless, Yul returned to Paris after the opium had worked its way out of his system. But by this time he was possessed by an ambition so strong and clear it could best be described as a calling: he had decided to become an actor. At seventeen, Yul was already a seasoned performer, "showcased" every evening in the clubs with one solo and a duet with Aliosha; he was also welcomed back to the Cirque d'Hiver to work, not as a trapeze flyer, but as a clown. His makeup and skullcap evoked Europe's long-reigning "King of Clowns," Grock (Swiss-born Karl Adrien Wettach), but his own persona as a clown was more sad-sack than slapstick. That paycheck allowed him to rent a tiny studio apartment, or *garçonnière*. But it was the possibility of acting — and eventually, perhaps, in the movies — that captivated him. His father was furious at this notion, but since Yul was living independently, Boris had little sway, especially since Katya had been encouraging Yul to go into the theater for years. Now, to Boris's chagrin, she recommended him to Mikhail Chekhov, who after leaving the Moscow Art Theatre had established a company in Paris.

By the time Yul was ready to join Chekhov, however, the director had moved his company to England. Yul joined the theater company of Georges Pitoëff instead, working there as an apprentice and carpenter, and occasionally taking small walk-on parts. Georges and Ludmilla Pitoëff, White Russian émigrés, had recently been appointed the directors of the Theâtre des Mathurins, where they had been mounting innovative productions for a decade, including French premieres of works by Luigi Pirandello, George Bernard Shaw, and Ferenc Molnar.

This was Yul's introduction to the theater: a close-knit repertory company where everyone pitched in to bring fresh, thoughtful, and often experimental works to life on stage. The Pitoëffs, including son Sasha, about Yul's age, were disciples of both Stanislavsky and Mikhail Chekhov, giving Yul his first exposure to the underlying concepts that had evolved at the Moscow Art Theatre. For theater in France as in the United States, these were "the fervent years," as Harold Clurman of the Group Theatre described the 1930s. The friends Yul made in that era included such superlative artists as Jean-Louis Barrault, already a theater actor and film director, and soon the star of Marcel Carné's *Les Enfants du Paradis* (1945), widely considered the greatest French film of all time; and Marcel Marceau, who, like Barrault, had been a student of Etienne Decroux, and who was developing "Bip," a character the world's greatest mime would continue playing for sixty years.

But by late 1938, Marousia had been diagnosed with leukemia, and despite her frail condition she wanted more than anything to see her sister, Vera. Dutifully, Yul accompanied his mother by ship back to Port Arthur, and then north across Manchuria to Harbin, carefully skirting the Soviet Union. Meanwhile his sister, Vera, married pianist Valentin Pavlovski and set out to make a home in New York City.

At eighteen, Yul found himself back in the Far East for the first time since he was eleven, in the city where he had attended the YMCA school and first smoked opium. And now he also had the opportunity to visit with his father in Shanghai, a city that remained as exotic and full of excitement as it had been for his grandfather Jules, who had also disembarked there as a teenager, from a pirate ship seventy years earlier.

Yul took real pleasure from his own strength and prowess: while in Shanghai, he added the sport of jai alai to his stints as a lifeguard and trapeze acrobat. The game that had originated as handball and then become pelota in the Basque country had evolved into jai alai ("merry festival" in the Basque language) and traveled with Spain's imperial ambitions to the Philippines; from there British gamblers had imported it to Shanghai. At eighteen Yul was not quite six feet tall and still visibly underweight, but his shoulders had been powerfully developed by hundreds of hours on the trapeze, which served him well in the *fronton*, the three-walled arena for "the fastest game in the world."

Boris admired his son's physical strength, but continued to admonish Yul for his ambitions as a performer even as Katya continued to encourage them. Nonetheless, they had a great time together. Perhaps the happiest time that Yul ever spent with his father was on their trip to Novina, the Yankovsky's hunting retreat in northern Korea. Yuri Yankovsky, the great tiger hunter, personally took them out on the track of Siberian tigers and bears; decades later Yul described their adventure there as "a magical time." But it was also during that trip to the Far East that Yul lost all patience and tolerance with his father when Boris failed to show up in Shanghai for one last visit together. The cumulative effect of the many canceled get-togethers with Boris finally broke Yul's heart. In years to come Yul often recounted that, from that time on, he had wanted to kill his father.

This complete emotional break — the first of many over the course of Yul's life — was a psychological defense mechanism with well-defined cultural roots. "Russians have long been possessed by the urge for a clean slate," wrote historian and journalist Andrew Meier, who identifies this characteristic as *otrecheniye*, which means "renunciation." But it may also be used to mean "denial or abandonment — in this case, of one's past." Historian Aleksandr Panchenko considers otrecheniye "a fundamental Russian trait. We've done it for generations. . . . We've insisted on denying who we are for so long, this denial may just make us what we are."

In the spring of 1939 Yul took Marousia back to Paris before setting out for England, where he hoped to join Mikhail Chekhov's theater company at Dartington Hall. This fourteenth-century castle in Devon belonged to Leonard and Dorothy Whitney Elmhirst, of *the* Amiercan Whitneys, devout and active patrons of the arts who, during the 1930s, transformed their outsized, historic barn into a theater. Their daughter, Beatrice Straight, was an aspiring young actress in New York who saw Chekhov's one-man show, *An Evening of Anton Chekhov*, on Broadway in 1935, and promptly invited his troupe to her family's Devonshire castle.

But by the time Yul had arrived at Dartington Hall, Chekhov himself was preparing to leave. As an attack on England by the Third Reich became more likely, Chekhov now accepted the Elmhirsts' invitation to move his company to a large home they owned in Ridgefield, Connecticut. Chekhov went on ahead to arrange a series of Shakespeare productions to provide the company with some income in the United States. The rest of the troupe remained in Devon for the time being, and welcomed Yul as a new member of the company during his three-month stay.

It was Yul's first visit to England, and not a particularly auspicious introduction. Dartington Hall was an unheated medieval cavern of a place, damp and frigid throughout his stay. But the work that the company did, in rehearsals and acting classes, was a revelation. The classes were conducted by Chekhov's partner and associate, George Shdanoff, a Russian actor and director a little older than Yul who had worked with Chekhov at the Moscow Art Theatre Studio before they both fled Soviet Russia in the 1920s; he had worked in Germany with Meyerhold before joining Chekhov again in England, where he began offering creative guidance to Yul's acting technique.

Yul also made his first forays into English culture. Among other plays, he saw a production of *Macbeth* by Donald Wolfit's repertory company, which toured England starring Wolfit in all of Shakespeare's greatest roles. Wolfit was carrying on the theatrical tradition of the actor-manager, demonstrating to Chekhov and his troupe, just as they moved to the United States, that this was a viable means of survival. Four decades later, Yul too would be an actor-manager.

In the early spring of 1940, Yul returned to Paris, and the Chekhov Company left England for the United States. By this time it was clear that Hitler would soon invade France, and once more the Bryners were refugees, as they had been from Vladivostok and Harbin. Yul's sister and her husband had settled in New York City, awaiting Marousia's arrival for treatment of advanced leukemia, so Yul and his mother packed up their most necessary and treasured belongings, including the dwindling collection of possessions from their early lives in the Far East — little more than mementos now of a world long gone. Then Yul took Marousia to Le Havre, where they boarded an ocean liner bound for Manhattan just weeks ahead of the Nazi army's march on Paris.

Yul Bryner disembarked in New York City with his mother in the summer of 1940. Both Russian-born, and they might have been refused entry into the United States, but they were traveling as Swiss citizens by virtue of Yul's grandfather's nationality. Curiously, Swiss passports provide the individual's "place of origin," not their birthplace. Both Yul's and Marousia's "place of origin" was listed as the Swiss village of Möriken-Wildegg, where their citizenship derived from.

They were met at the Westside pier by Vera, while her husband was on tour with cellist Piatigorsky. They went to her apartment, where she had prepared a comfortable bedroom for Marousia, whose condition after the Atlantic crossing was perilous. Though Yul remained a dutiful and attentive son, he had long since insulated his own feelings from his mother's intense, unending melancholia, using the same defense mechanism he had used with his father: the emotional abandonment of otrecheniye. After less than an hour of settling his mother at Vera's, Yul set out to see midtown Manhattan for the first time, and to find Grand Central Station, where he boarded a train to Ridgefield, Connecticut.

Yul's English was still barely functional, despite some lessons at the YMCA school and his recent time in England. His Russian and French were both excellent, of course, and he retained smatterings of Mandarin, Cantonese, and Korean; but negotiating around New York City and Connecticut was difficult. Fortunately, Michael Chekhov (as he spelled his name in English) sent one of his company to the Stamford station to pick Yul up and convey him to the Whitney home where the Chekhov Players were now installed.

Yul would at last begin studying with Michael Chekhov, half a century after his grandfather had welcomed Michael's uncle, Anton, to tea in Vladivostok. This training provided the basis for Yul's future, together with his cultural education among the Russian intelligentsiya, his intense concentration, vivid imagination, expressive powers as a performer, and physical prowess as an acrobat.

Michael Chekhov was a small man of enormous spirit. As an actor he could transform himself completely, it seemed, into any character he chose; and as a teacher he could evoke from his students dimensions of expression they had never dreamed of. Doubtless, the greatest influence upon his creative life had been his uncle, Anton, whose stories and plays had radiated throughout Russian culture well before the Soviet era, and whose gentle humanism had contributed to the founding of the Moscow Art Theatre in 1898, which had opened with the world premiere of Chekhov's most enduring work, *The Seagull*, under the direction of Konstantin Stanislavsky.

Michael Chekhov had begun his career as one of Stanislavsky's actors and had established his reputation in a number of roles before founding the Moscow Art Theatre Studio and separating himself from his mentor's commitment to "the feeling of being true to life" in the theater. "I never stopped wondering," Chekhov later wrote, "what was so imaginative and creative about merely copying life around us in every detail, photographically as it were, and I regarded it as one of the beclouded facets of Stanislavsky's many-sided talent." Chekhov nonetheless always credited Stanislavsky as "the first to break the land that opened up the new fields which all of us later tilled in our own distinctive ways."

This was the difference that divided the two directors' aesthetics, and one that continues to reverberate in the theater almost a century later. For Chekhov, the paramount consideration in every drama and comedy was the imaginative creation, not *re*-creation, of human emotional and intellectual experience. It was not enough, he insisted, for actors to reproduce their own genuine feelings; that was not art, it was "merely copying life." The actor, rather than searching for the character he is playing *within* himself, must inhabit the character he has thoroughly conceived in his imagination, which is "like asking the character himself to show you how to do it." He differentiated between his own approach and Stanislavsky's as "the supremacy of the character's ego (mine) against the actor's ego (Stanislavsky's)." Through concrete techniques for training his imagination and empathy, the actor can grasp and highlight the character's most essential aspects by teasing them out of the dialogue and action.

But how does the actor *communicate* the many subtle, internal qualities that compose a complex, well-rounded character? By learning to use his body, his voice, and his spirit as expressive instruments. "When you are a pianist," Yul later wrote, "you have an outside instrument that you learn to master through finger work and arduous exercises. . . . As an actor, you the artist have to perform on the most difficult instrument to master, that is, your own self — your physical and your emotional being." It was through concrete techniques and exercises that Chekhov taught his students how to develop an extreme "*sensitivity of body to the psychological creative impulses*," as he emphasized. "The body of an actor must absorb psychological qualities," wrote Chekhov, "must be filled and permeated with them so that they will convert it gradually into a sensitive membrane, a kind of receiver and conveyor of the subtlest images, feelings, emotions, and will impulses." From the trapeze and the nightclubs, Yul had learned the power of virility; from Chekhov he learned the power of gentleness.

Chekhov's techniques for actors included a variety of imaginative aids. The actor might begin by determining the character's "psychological center" — perhaps at the tip of the nose for someone who is very curious, or in the legs of a lifelong sailor, or behind the head of a nervous, haunted character. The "center of the stage" will also be different for every character: for the thief, it will be the box of jewelry on the table, which he will be drawn to and yet never look at directly lest he be noticed; for the lover, it might be the photograph of his beloved on the mantelpiece. But the overarching technique that Chekhov proposed was the "psychological gesture": a posture or simple movement involving the whole body that the actor chooses as an emblematic, essential expression of his character. It is an action or a pose that the actor never actually reveals during a performance, and yet which informs his every move.

The emphasis that Chekhov put upon the physical performance was a perfect match for the physicality that Yul radiated. He had also perfected vocal expression, as well as the physical delivery of a song, learning to gauge the immediacy and the degree of "presence" that was called for, whether from a small raised stage or right beside a table. Soon, in fact, he went into New York City, sixty miles by train, and auditioned for nightclubs, where he began singing the Gypsy songs a few nights a week. His first work in the United States was at a club called the Blue Angel, also the title of the 1930 film that made Marlene Dietrich an international star; occasionally, when she was in New York, she performed there, and that was how she and Yul first met.

Dietrich was forty-one years old, twenty years older than Yul, but their romance, which would continue off-and-on for two decades, was relentless and passionate. Her long association with director Josef von Sternberg had ended in 1935 after seven films. Hitler's government tried to lure Dietrich back to Germany; instead, she repudiated Fascism and in 1939 became an American citizen. By this time she had co-starred with Gary Cooper, Jimmy Stewart, and Cary Grant. Despite her many love affairs, by all accounts Yul was the love of her life; a biography by her daughter, Maria Riva, makes that clear. Over the years, she often helped Yul with theater and film connections and, from time to time, with money.

In Ridgefield, the Chekhov Company's days were divided between acting classes and rehearsals of the Shakespeare plays they performed for college audiences. Since Yul was new to the company and spoke so little English, he mostly drove scenery and costumes to colleges around the Northeast, ahead of the small bus that transported the troupe of fifteen-or-so actors and stage hands. At each stop he'd unload the Depression-era van and then help set up the scenery: that same night, after a quick rehearsal, the company would perform one of three or four plays. Until he learned sufficient English, Yul's only role was as a silent spear-carrier. Chekhov and Shdanoff conducted their classes, exercises, and rehearsals in English, and that was how, in large part, Yul learned the language of the English-speaking theater — though he also conversed with his two mentors in Russian. The fact that Yul became a distinctively *Russian* actor owed more to these years in America with Chekhov than to his birth in Vladivostok.

On December 2, 1941, the Chekhov Players opened at the Little Theatre (now the Helen Hayes) on Broadway with a limited run of Shakespeare's *Twelfth Night*, in which Beatrice Straight played Viola. The production was directed by George Shdanoff — known by this time as "the Doctor" for his ability to diagnose actors' problems. Yul played the small role of Fabian, a clown — albeit a very different sort from the clown he had created at the Cirque d'Hiver. He learned the Shakespearian text phonetically, much the way an opera singer learns lyrics in an unfamiliar language, and recited his lines by rote. Nonetheless, by the age of twenty-one, Yul hade made it to Broadway, less than a decade after leaving Harbin. His first Broadway credit listed him as "Youl Bryner."

Five nights after *Twelfth Night* opened, the Japanese bombed Pearl Harbor in a surprise attack that recalled to many their surprise attack on the Russian Navy at Port Arthur in 1904. As a result, the production closed a few nights later. Nonetheless, thanks to this small role, which also entitled him to a union ticket with Actor's Equity, Yul was signed by an agent named Margaret Lindley. She was not very encouraging about finding him work until his English improved, but she was willing to introduce him to the right people at her frequent house parties. It was there that he met a young starlet who, at twenty-two (a year older than Yul), had already co-starred in three major Hollywood films, and she offered to help him learn English. Her name was Virginia Gilmore, and they fell in love the moment they met.

Actually, the name given at her birth in El Monte, California, was Sherman Poole. She was of English and German extract; her grandmother had crossed from Missouri to California in a covered wagon, bearing several children along the way. A studio press agent, Richard Condon (later the author of *The Manchurian Candidate* and other novels), decided that "Virginia Gilmore" would be more stellar. She was a stunningly beautiful dark blonde of small stature and girlish demeanor, though hardly naïve. At seventeen she had been the girlfriend of the illustrious German director Fritz Lang, who had fled Nazi Germany for Hollywood; through him, she had met with other German émigrés. Indeed, when she had to pass her final exam in economics at Hollywood High School, she was tutored by

Lang's friend, playwright Bertolt Brecht; she failed the exam, and was accused by the teacher of being a Socialist. Already she was espousing left-wing causes.

Samuel Goldwyn declared Virginia "an honest-to-God American beauty with brains who even writes poems," and soon she was signed as a Goldwyn Girl. Because of her shapely legs, she was featured in *Life* magazine with the moniker "Gams Gilmore." By nineteen she had starred in Jean Renoir's first American film, *Swamp Water*, followed by the leading female role in Fritz Lang's *Western Union*. Onscreen she had flirted with Gary Cooper in *Pride of the Yankees*, and offscreen with Babe Ruth, who made an appearance in that film; Virginia went out on a few predictably uncomfortable dates with the Babe, a renowned lothario.

When Yul met Virginia, his spoken English was still riddled with errors, though a steady diet of Dashiell Hammett and Mickey Spillane murder mysteries slowly improved his idiomatic American. Since Virginia, nicknamed Gin, commuted between Broadway and Hollywood, their first two years together were interrupted by months apart.

After Pearl Harbor, Yul volunteered for the U.S. Army but was rejected because of scar tissue on his lungs, apparently from tuberculosis. So he volunteered his services to the Office of War Information, primarily broadcasting hourly news bulletins from New York in French to the Resistance movement across France; he also broadcast war-related news in Russian to the Soviet Union. This gave him a useful role in the war effort; it also introduced him to many of the pioneers of early radio who were already preparing for the new broadcasting medium: "picture radio."

During this time, Yul continued to live, work, and travel with the Chekhov Players. The company toured as far south as Louisiana. In Baton Rouge, Yul was stopped for speeding, and because the cops could not make sense of his English when he resisted arrest, they threw him into Baton Rouge's "coloreds' jail" for a night, providing him with a fresh and vivid insight into American society of the 1940s.

In New York he took any work he could find to cope with the mounting medical costs of his mother's treatments for leukemia: he sang in any style that was called for; he modeled for fashion photographers, including renowned English portraitist Cecil Beaton; he posed naked for art students and for artistic photographers of the "nude male form"; and even before he could speak reliable English, he went out on theater auditions. In one of her last letters, Marousia wrote to her sister in Harbin that Yul was so attentive to her needs that she was concerned for him.

Marousia died in hospital in the early spring of 1943; her ashes were buried in Cold Spring, New York. She had never recovered from her betrayal by Boris, the only love of her life. Both of her children were unashamedly relieved that her long years of grief and the suffering of end-stage leukemia were over at last, because they knew that was exactly how she felt.

Michael Chekhov was closing the Chekhov Players and moving to Los Angeles, where a number of film roles were waiting for him, most notably that of a Freudian psychiatrist in Hitchcock's *Spellbound* (1944), who counsels the hero, Gregory Peck's character, at the request of his protégé, played by Ingrid Bergman. Peck was also a student of Chekhov's; along with other Hollywood stars, Peck worked privately on each of his film roles with either Chekhov or Shdanoff.

Six months later, Yul boarded the Twentieth-Century Limited train to Chicago (a great improvement over the Trans-Siberian), and from there he rode the Sky Chief to Los Angeles. After two and a half years of courtship, Yul married Virginia at the Los Angeles County Courthouse in 1944, as announced inauspiciously by gossip columnist Louella Parsons, who made her opinion clear: "Virginia Gilmore and some Gypsy she met in New York will be married on September 6th."

In time Yul applied for U.S. citizenship, which was granted on the basis of his residence and his marriage to a U.S. citizen. That meant that he had to declare his "place of birth," not merely his Swiss "place of origin." Surprisingly, he declared that he was born in "Sakhalin, U.S.S.R.," which is not a city at all, but the enormous island serving as a penal camp that Anton Chekhov had investigated in 1890, before his visit to Vladivostok, and where new Soviet labor camps had been established by Lenin. There was good reason for Yul to falsify his birthplace: at the time of his birth, Vladivostok had been part of a country that no longer existed — the Far East Russian Republic. There was no telling what bureaucratic complications *that* fact might entail, so Yul simply mentioned one of the Russian regions where Bryner & Company had investments in mines. The official declaration on his U.S. passport represented one more effortless act of renunciation — otrecheniye — this time of his birthplace. It was at this time that he also changed the spelling of his name to "Brynner."

Gin had done a lot of work in Hollywood and on Broadway, and had met many influential people whom Yul was getting to know, even though he was often introduced as "Mr. Gilmore." At this point Gin was under contract with Twentieth Century Fox, and the studio was always unhappy when their contract ingénues got married. As punishment, between some significant roles, they cast her in numerous B pictures: by 1945, Virginia was known in the trade papers as "Queen of the Bs," having already appeared in fifteen films. On Broadway, she worked with renowned director and playwright Moss Hart, and then Harold Clurman, among others, establishing herself as a capable theater actress, not just another Hollywood blonde.

Yul and his bride settled into a small apartment on East Thirty-eighth Street over a dry cleaners and, with two irregular paychecks, struggled to pay the rent. Between Yul's infrequent gigs at nightclubs (his radio broadcasts for the Office of War Information were not paid) and Gin's work on stage, they were often seriously broke. Yul kept going to "cattle calls" and any other audition his agent could get him into, but he was just too foreign for wartime roles. It was only because he needed work so badly that Yul took a truly embarrassing "acting" job, but one that opened a whole new world. On a bulletin board at the Office of War Information radio he read about a job on television, still referred to as "picture radio."

Television had been developed by Philo T. Farnsworth, who obtained his first patent to the technology in 1927, but then lost proprietary rights in a litigious assault by David Sarnoff's Radio Corporation of America. RCA first demonstrated the invention at the 1939 World's Fair in New York. Just five years later Yul starred in one of the very first broadcast television shows.

There were only about three hundred television sets across the New York area when those first shows were broadcast, tentatively and experimentally, by the Columbia Broadcasting System from its studios on the top floor over Grand Central Station. There were no commercials — the broadcasts were not reliable enough yet — but these first steps into the future of entertainment gave CBS a fighting chance against the National Broadcasting Company, which had dominated radio programming since its inception in 1927.

The children's show that featured Yul was called *Mr. Jones and His Neighbors*. "Mainly," he later recalled, "it involved wearing a silly hat." The show only lasted for a few weeks, but for the record book, and for his résumé, Yul had starred in one of the world's first scheduled television shows, and the network executives now knew his unusual name. More importantly, he had become friends with many of the creative people who would soon become the pioneering producers and directors of commercial television. Emphasizing his association with Chekhov, Yul also let it be known that he was willing and eager to direct any TV show, anytime. Before long, the fact that he'd worked with television at its very start would prove useful, even though it had entailed wearing a silly hat.

17

Despite scores of theater auditions, Yul had not landed a single serious acting job. Most of the parts offered were conventional American roles for which he was obviously ill-suited, given his background. But for the rare exotic role, there were few actors in New York who could compete with him. Aside from his mysterious concoction of an accent, he had a slightly Asiatic look, inherited from his grandmother Natalya, accentuated by his wiry, muscular body. His thinning hair added at least five years to his age — and so did his agent, Margaret Lindley: when the right role turned up, she insisted that Yul was born in 1915, one of many inventions perpetuated in countless biographies.

The right role came along in the fall of 1945, just after Japan's surrender. Director John Houseman, who was Orson Welles' associate with the Mercury Players, was casting a new musical entitled *Lute Song*. It starred a young ingenue named Mary Martin — who in years to come, would also launch such classic musicals as *South Pacific* and *The Sound of Music* — and it featured lavish sets by a renowned designer. After one audition, Yul won the lead male role.

Lute Song was a highly stylized adaptation of an ancient Chinese myth, Pi-Pa-Ki, about an impoverished scholar who travels to the capital and wins elevation to glory . . . but only if he renounces his wife to marry a princess. The musical opened at the Plymouth Theatre on February 6, 1946, and though the audiences responded very emotionally, critics were tepid. "Miss Martin has a difficult part, and on the whole she does well," wrote Lewis Nichols in the *New York Times*. "Yul Brynner is the luckless husband and gives a satisfactory performance." In spite of such faint praise, Yul won Broadway's prestigious Donaldson Award as the most promising new star of 1946. Much later in life, when he had received many other awards, Yul still considered this the most important of his career, indisputably establishing his reputation as an actor at the age of twenty-six.

The brief bio that Yul wrote for himself in the playbill was the kind of fabrication that he would continue to give for the rest of his life. "Yul Brynner is partly Mongolian," it began accurately enough — his grandmother was part Buryat. But he went on to claim he had "served his theatrical apprenticeship in Prague, Riga, and Warsaw," which was not true; "thereafter with Georges and Ludmilla Pitoëff for six years" — true, for half that time — "appearing in plays of Pirandello, Ibsen, Claudel, and Chekhov" — well, he appeared in some of those.

All of this contradicted the brief biography in the show's ornate program, which offered a different blend of fact and fiction. "Yul Brynner, a Swiss citizen on his way to becoming an American, was born in Siberia, spent most of his childhood in China, was educated in France. . . . His background is as colorful as Joseph's coat, as complicated as government regulations and as fantastic as a story from the Arabian Nights." All true. But then the bio went on: "Yul's mother was pure Gypsy; his father, one of the wealthiest men in China, is principally Mongolian, partly Gypsy, and partly Swiss." Marousia would have been horrified to be called a Gypsy: her heritage was of Russian intelligentsiya, not Romany vagabondage. Both Veras — Yul's aunt and his sister — were enraged at this otrecheniye of his mother. It was accidental, Yul explained to them, a result of his poor English when he told the producer about his background.

Otrecheniye had a twin, wrote historian Meier: *samosvantso,* or self-proclamation. When the past is denied, a new past must be invented. According to *The Russian Idea,* by Nikolai Berdyaev, samosvantso is "a purely Russian phenomenon. . . . Someone who proclaims to be someone he is not is a *samosvantso*, a self-proclaimer, an imposter, a pretender." This "purely Russian phenomenon" may or may not help explain Yul's many myths; at the least, it puts his inventive biographies into the context of an identifiable cultural phenomenon.

Only a handful of people knew the fantastic trajectory that Yul's life had taken from Vladivostok to Broadway. Of course his sister, Vera, who was there for his opening night — between her own professional triumphs as a soprano — knew exactly where this mysterious foreigner had come from; and Virginia knew the long odyssey that had brought him there, too, if less precisely. The United States, and New York City in particular, are filled with millions of amazing tales of émigrés and refugees who made good: Yul's story was one of those tales, and it was only just beginning. But none of the adults who had raised Yul were there to cheer his triumph. His mother and his uncle Felix had both died three years earlier, his aunt Vera and cousin Irena were in Manchuria, and his father was under Soviet house arrest outside Vladivostok.

A few weeks after *Lute Song* opened, Virginia went into rehearsal for Maxwell Anderson's *Truckline Café*, directed on stage by Harold Clurman, the first U.S. director to teach Method acting. To co-star with Virginia, Clurman chose a good-looking twenty-one-year-old kid from Nebraska named Marlon Brando, who had thoroughly absorbed Stanislavsky. Years later, critic Pauline Kael wrote that she and her date arrived during the second act of *Truckline Café*, and that the gut-wrenching emotionalism of Brando's performance was so extreme she had to look away, believing the actor was having a seizure. The show garnered Brando a Theatre Critics' Circle Award as "Promising New Actor of 1946," matching Yul's Donaldson Award. *Truckline Café* closed after thirteen performances but as it happened, Virginia greeted the failure with relief: the week before rehearsals had begun, she and Yul had learned that she was expecting a child by the end of the year.

By the time their son was born on December 23, 1946, Yul had been touring most of the year. *Lute Song* closed after three months on Broadway and then played Chicago, Des Moines, and Colorado Springs before settling in at San Francisco's Curran Theatre. There, Yul received word of his son's birth and cracked open a bottle of Dom Perignon with his friend and backstage dresser, Don Lawson. Two days later, after a harrowing trip on a commercial DC-3 prop plane, Yul was at his wife's side and saw his son for the first time. Gin and Yul had not settled upon a name, but Mary Martin, still a close friend of the couple, insisted the name "Yul" should be preserved, and the infant given the same name as his father and great-grandfather. Yul agreed, explaining to Virginia that in the Bryner family the patriarch's name had been handed down, like a title. Virginia was reluctant, but after twenty-eight hours of labor and a breech birth, she really didn't care enough to resist. So on the birth certificate, they named their baby Yul Brynner, Jr. They made no arrangements for baptism in any church, Protestant or Orthodox; but a few months later, while attending the baptism of a friend's infant at St. Bartholomew's Church on Park Avenue, Gin managed to have her son baptized as Yul Brynner, Jr., and she named Mary Martin as the godmother.

A few months later, Boris, Katya, and their daughter, Catherine, came through New York after their release from Soviet detention and their trip through Moscow, Switzerland, and England. They spent most of a day visiting with Virginia and Yul Jr. Gin forever remembered her father-in-law as a gallant man and extremely handsome, though with a more stolid look than Yul's. Boris was delighted to see his only grandchild, and departed with fond memories of Virginia.

When *Lute Song* closed on the road, Yul returned to New York and devoted himself to his wife and child: friends considered him even then a doting father. But the most urgent thing he needed to do was to make enough money to move his family to an apartment that wasn't above a dry cleaner. He quickly found work directing for CBS; his greatest obstacle was his natural insubordination with the network executives and their minions, who tried to control even the creative aspects of the business. Suffice it to say, this was not steady work.

On his twenty-eighth birthday, July 11, 1948, Yul was directing a one-hour drama on *Studio One* when a telegram arrived with the news that his father had died suddenly of a heart attack two days earlier in Shanghai. The telegram came from Shura Ostroumov, Yul's uncle (by marriage to his aunt Nina). Katya was too distraught to function, so Shura promised Yul he would take care of everything, including the family finances: once all the residual assets of Jules Bryner's empire were dissolved, Shura would distribute them to Katya and Vera and Helen, the widows of Boris and Felix and Leonid.

News of his father's death came as a blow to Yul, though not one he could bear to reflect upon. He probably would not have wanted to attend his father's funeral, but in any case neither he nor his sister Vera could travel to Shanghai. Nevertheless, although he had long since turned cold toward his father, in years to come he was determined, he told Virginia, to assure his son the kind of reliable love he had never had from Boris.

But that meant bringing home a steady paycheck. So when the producer of *Lute Song* asked Yul to go to London with the production, he accepted even though it would mean a separation from his family. The play opened there at the Winter Garden Theatre on October 11, 1948, and received rave reviews; once it was clear that the run would last for a year or more, Virginia came to London with the baby and stayed for almost six months.

Post-war England was a nation in triumph and in distress; Yul and Gin both recalled their time there as mostly gray and sad. The ruins of buildings struck by German V-2 rockets were still teetering, and the city air was thick with coal and wood smoke. When *Lute Song* closed, Gin took the baby back to New York while Yul stayed on to star in *Dark Eyes*, a short-lived Russian comedy at the Strand Theatre about three Russian women and their life as refugees in New York: it was the first production to feature Yul's name alone above the title (thanks to his critical success in *Lute Song*). The play had run for six months on Broadway in 1943, but in London it closed abruptly, leaving him without a paycheck and only a BOAC airline ticket home . . . which he soon lost in a poker game.

Penniless, he got a ride to Paris by car and ferry, and found work with his old friends at the Cirque d'Hiver, where the Bouglione brothers welcomed him back for a "star turn" on the trapeze, generating a little publicity. That led to work through Maurice Carrère, the manager of Maxim's, the restaurant and enduring symbol of France's *belle époque*. With the help of Carrère, Yul found gigs in other clubs and cabarets.

But Paris, five years after the German Occupation, was not the city he had left in 1940. The Dimitrievitch family had fled to Argentina to escape the Nazis, who exterminated hundreds of thousands of Gypsies throughout Europe. The French economy was struggling, and bitter recriminations and retaliation continued against those accused of collaboration with German troops. Toward the end of 1948, when he could pay for a second-class crossing by ship, Yul returned to New York.

• • • • • • • •

For the next three years, Yul worked primarily as a television director for CBS. His training with Chekhov, together with his can-do-anything self-assurance and his pioneering experience with the medium were all that he needed to build a promising career. He had only to restrain his own insolence with the network executives and the floor managers, because of which they would not put him under contract as Virginia kept hoping. But since Yul was very good at what he did, he was constantly rehired, one show at a time, to direct one-hour dramas — a dozen or more over the next year.

He and Virginia also co-hosted the first husband-and-wife talk show, called *Mr. and Mrs.* Yul later described the experience in the *Saturday Evening Post*:

> It was hilarious. . . . Virginia and I were the producers, writers, directors and performers, although we occasionally had guests if we could hoodwink some unsuspecting celebrity. We paid our guests' taxi fare. The budget didn't allow more than that. Once we staged a meeting between Salvador Dalí and Al Capp. The conversation was so censorable I'm amazed we were allowed to stay on the air, but in the end they did something very charming. They both did a drawing on the same sheet of paper. It was during Al's Shmoo period, and he did a drawing of a Shmoo. While he was drawing it, Dalí drew a window in its stomach, showing a desert horizon and skeletons in the distance throwing long shadows.

Yul directed dramatic shows on *Studio One*, *Omnibus*, and *Danger*, working with a group of young directors who would become masters of film in the coming decades: Sidney Lumet (*The Fugitive Kind*, *The Pawnbroker*), Martin Ritt (*Hud*, *Norma*), and Yul's assistant, Johnny Frankenheimer (*The Manchurian Candidate*). He also directed and sometimes co-hosted *The Stork Club*, a talk show broadcast live during the day from a chic dinner spot of the era. This put Yul at the pinnacle of the New York social scene just as traditional class divisions began to overlap in the

"Power Elite," described by historian C. Wright Mills: "In café society, the major inhabitants of the world of celebrity — the institutional elite, the metropolitan socialite, and the professional entertainer — mingle, publicly cashing in one another's claims for prestige." That was *The Stork Club*, birthplace for the talk-show celebrity culture we know so well today.

In 1949 Yul landed his first film role, as the suave kingpin of a drug-smuggling ring, in *Port of New York*, a low-budget thriller that starred Scott Brady as the lead cop. It wasn't a piece of work that Yul ever looked back upon fondly or proudly: in fact, as he put it, he shot his role over a long weekend in between drinks. It didn't pay well, either, but his performance as an elegant, soft-spoken, snakelike murderer was work he could confidently show any future director in lieu of a hasty screen test. And, while still in his twenties, Yul had now become a film actor.

The fact that he was often broke was never obvious: like his father and grandfather, he was always dressed impeccably and stylishly in custom-made, monogrammed shirts. Even when he didn't have cab fare, Yul had a valet: his friend and "dresser," Don Lawson, stayed on, though for stretches of time Yul could not pay his salary. Don was also responsible for maintaining the expensive hairpiece that Yul had reluctantly bought at the insistence of his agent and some of the booking agents for his performances. The 1940s represented the heyday of American toupee-makers, and the millions of men who kept them busy succeeded mainly in keeping baldness something shameful, or at the least, comical. By his mid-twenties, Yul's hairline had retreated far past his forehead to form a thin, narrow widow's peak. The artificiality of even the best-made "rug" annoyed Yul more than he would admit, but the fact remained that he needed the work.

By 1950, Yul was a well-known figure among television and theater professionals, and had some public recognition in the towns where *Lute Song* had played. He was a U.S. citizen, so was free to work any job he could find — but as the father of a growing boy, what he needed was a steady paycheck. That had been driven home to him early on when he and Gin had had to give up their apartment, leaving them penniless and homeless with a young child in winter. Yul quickly proved himself an accomplished carpenter and paid some of his bills by making simple, attractive butcher-block furniture for his friends in show business: a coffee table he built for film composer Alex North that year is still intact after sixty years.

After that terrible winter, Gin urged Yul to give up acting and focus on a career in television, where his reputation was solid and growing. In 1950, a steady job opened up at CBS for a floor manager (staff producer) for the new TV studio on Broadway and Fifty-second Street, later renamed the Ed Sullivan Theatre. Virginia pleaded and then demanded that Yul take the job. He refused, but promised to seek steady work directing. That was a promise he kept, even after another opportunity arose.

After *Lute Song* with Yul, Mary Martin had a triumphant run in *South Pacific* by Richard Rodgers and Oscar Hammerstein. When she heard that the composer and playwright/lyricist had been commissioned by British actress Gertrude Lawrence to write a musical adaptation of *Anna and the King of Siam*, she insisted that the only actor for the role was her former co-star.

For this audition, Yul ignored the advice of his new agent, Ted Ashley, and instead of wearing his hairpiece used electric clippers to trim his hair close to the scalp. The historical King Mongkut I had been almost sixty years old during the events depicted and had spent time in a Buddhist monastery where the monks shaved their heads. In the end, however, his choice was aesthetic, not historical.

Years later, Richard Rodgers described Yul's audition. "Out he came with a bald head and sat cross-legged on the stage," wrote the composer. "He had a guitar, and he hit this guitar one whack and gave out with this unearthly yell and sang some heathenish sort of thing, and Oscar and I looked at each other and said, 'Well, that's it!'" That "heathenish sort of thing" was his trademark folk song, "Okonchen Poot."

The plot of *The King and I* derived indirectly from two ostensibly accurate historical chronicles by Anna Leonowens, *The English Governess at the Siamese Court* (1870) and *The Romance of the Harem* (1873); but even these original documents were largely fanciful, starting with the original title. Leonowens was hired as a teacher, not a governess, which would have given her much higher status in the royal court. In all, what she offered was a highly fictionalized account of her time as schoolteacher for the dozens of offspring that Siam's king had fathered with his wives and concubines. It also recounts how her own influence upon the king's political strategies altered the history of Southeast Asia in the 1860s by safeguarding Siam from Britain's imperial intentions. Her account, widely accepted as factual, was all the more daring since it discussed the private life of Siam's late, beloved monarch.

But while researching a book about Anna's son, historian W. S. Bristowe discovered that Anna had distorted or fabricated many salient facts about her life; these included the date and place of her birth (1831 in India, not 1834 in Wales), the identity of her parents (Edwards, not Crawford), and the rank of her husband (private, not major). A good deal of Leonowens's description of the royal palace in Bangkok, first published two years after she left Siam for the United States, was sensationalist fantasy, including underground dungeons — in a city built on stilts in watery marshes. Even her prize student, Chulalongkorn (later crowned King Rama V), took her to task: in a stinging letter to the press, his royal secretary wrote that Leonowens "has supplied by her invention that which is deficient in her memory." Seventy years later an English writer named Margaret Landon compounded Leonowens's inventions in a new book, *Anna and the King of Siam*, in which she assembled a new version of the original works, and added variations. Landon's book was then further adapted as a black-and-white, nonmusical film starring Rex Harrison and Irene Dunne. Although Rex Harrison was utterly unconvincing as an Asian monarch, the film was a big hit, and it convinced English star Gertrude Lawrence that the role of Mrs. Anna on stage would be perfect for her.

Rodgers and Hammerstein romanticized the story even further, as Richard Rodgers explained in the *New York Times* four days before the play opened at the St. James Theater. "We have not been slavishly literal in following the book, nor completely conscientious historically," he wrote. "But in spite of whatever factual compromises we have seen fit to make, we have tried very hard, within our own romantic medium, to present the King and Anna as the genuine and fascinating man and woman we believe they were. The strength of their story lies in the violent changes they wrought in each other. Yet their life together bears unmistakable implications of deep mutual attraction — a man-and-woman relationship so strong and real and well-founded that it seems in some ways more than a love affair, more than a marriage."

Be that as it may, what *is* historically certain and significant in the story of *The King and I* is that, under the rule of King Mongkut and his son, King Rama V, Siam was the only country in Southeast Asia that did not succumb to colonization, owing to the wily manner in which King Mongkut played the European powers against each other. This was exactly how the emperor of Korea had tried to regain control of his country: by personally selling a vast timber concession to Jules Bryner to give Russia a vested interest in Korea's independence from Japan.

Yul brought his own white heat to a majestic role that launched his career like a guided missile. The character of the King — his willfulness, his innocence, his noble ambitions — was there in the script, but the stature, power, and urgency all came from Yul, who brought everything he had experienced to every moment he had on stage. Foremost was the technique he had learned with Michael Chekhov and George Shdanoff; especially valuable for this role was Chekhov's emphasis upon physicality. Even the King's regal, barefoot prowl projected the animal power Yul had developed as a trapeze artist in the circus. His years in the nightclubs had prepared him as a confident and powerful singer as well, albeit with a style unlike anything Broadway had ever heard. Yul had never visited Siam (renamed Thailand in 1939, after becoming a constitutional monarchy), but his childhood had given him a deep familiarity with Asian reticence and deliberate inscrutability. And acting an Oriental role was hardly new to him after *Lute Song*.

Dancing, however, did not come naturally to him, and in the key romantic moment of the play, "Shall We Dance?" Yul had to lead Gertrude Lawrence in a passionately energetic waltz (technically, a polka), pitching the actress out of his arms and across the stage. They were lucky enough to have the finest Broadway choreographer of all time, Jerome Robbins, who designed the enduring dance step-by-step. Robbins also created the immortal ballet-within-the-musical of *Uncle Tom's Cabin*, presented in traditional Siamese costumes, masks, and movements.

Choreography aside, Yul had a hand in almost every aspect of the production. In a biography of Rodgers and Hammerstein, Frederick Nolan wrote that "Yul Brynner proceeded to make the part of the King — and indeed, much of the play — his own. The director of *The King and I* was John Van Druten, but Van Druten wasn't tough enough to handle Gertrude Lawrence, who was insecure and temperamental. Brynner had directed on Broadway and in television. . . . When he spoke, Lawrence listened. Rodgers confesses that they would have been in a lot of trouble had Brynner not been around."

Under the creative guidance of Rodgers and Hammerstein, the original production of *The King and I* achieved the status of a work of art; it was still possible to conceive of a Broadway musical as *art* in the 1950s, rather than commercial entertainment. The potential upside and downside of a production weren't as enormous as they became, and the bottom line did not govern every decision; aesthetic goals often trumped financial ambition. The orchestra was much larger than that of today's productions, and when costume designer Irene Sharaff ordered custom Thai silk to be woven for her color schemes, the producers acceded to the considerable cost. Even the makeup that Yul designed for his role challenged conventions in its Kabuki-like, exaggerated ferocity — effectively placing him on a different plane because every other actor on stage wore naturalistic theater makeup.

The production had many things going for it. The story itself was popular, thanks to the book and the first film, and Rodgers and Hammerstein had proven that they were at the top of their game with *Oklahoma! Carousel*, and *South Pacific*. They were not infallible, but they had a lot of experience, and they knew how to use their golden reputation: even before opening night, Frank Sinatra had recorded three of the show's songs and made them hits.

When the play opened, the only name above the title was Gertrude Lawrence's. Her performances had always guaranteed satisfaction for her fans; that is why she was guaranteed 10 percent of the *gross* ticket sales. Born in 1898 in England, "Gertie" had been starring on stage in London and New York for more than twenty-five years and had tremendous drawing power in the theater, especially after her collaborations with Noël Coward, who soon became a good friend of Yul's. She was the only actress with sufficient standing to commission Rodgers and Hammerstein to write a musical for her — all the more surprising because she could barely carry a tune and now was introducing such songs as "Getting To Know You," "Hello, Young Lovers," and "Shall We Dance?" In the first program for the show, Yul's credit was well below the title along with the rest of the cast's, as stipulated in Lawrence's original contract.

But that changed after opening night, March 29, 1951. The play had a triumphant reception and passionate word-of-mouth acclaim for the exotic, bare-headed, bare-chested man who played the King of Siam. Though the *New York Times* critic Brooks Atkinson was only tepid in his overnight review, in the Sunday paper a few weeks later he was forced to eat crow. "Mr. Rodgers and Mr. Hammerstein have got way beyond the mechanical formulae on which musical shows are founded," he acknowledged, "and are saying something fundamental about human beings. . . . *The King and I* is literature, and since the literature is expressed largely in music, it is tremendously moving. . . . Always a charming woman, Gertrude Lawrence plays the part of Anna with force and intelligence. . . . Yul Brynner's vehement, restless, keen-minded King is a terse and vivid characterization with a blazing spirit and stylized ruthlessness of manners and makeup." Within weeks, Yul's name was on the theater marquee next to Gertie's.

The unique and original character that Yul created was the unforeseen element of the show's overwhelming success: the willful autocrat who, over the course of each performance, gradually revealed the struggle between the better angels of his nature and the demons of his willfulness. The King's intensity, his mercurial humor, the juxtaposition between his clever mind and pidgin English, and his raw masculine appeal absolutely seized the audience's attention, so different was he from the domesticated masculinity of other contemporary leading men: William Holden, say, or Gregory Peck, or even newcomers like Paul Newman and Marlon Brando. A willful, irascible tyrant, a gentle father figure, and prolific sire to a small village of sixty-eight offspring, he was an innocent who struggled with the paradoxes of life, reluctantly accepting the invaluable help of an educated woman. To women the King offered an appealing image of the dominant man as a willful little boy at heart, dependent upon Anna's wisdom. To men he represented virility itself, full of swagger and domineering power.

And he was as mysterious and exotic a figure as they had ever fixed their eyes upon, moving with the lithe, deliberate swagger of a Siberian tiger, and disclaiming in a powerful voice with an indefinable accent.

The King and I ran for more than two years in New York, for a total of 1,246 performances. It was the biggest hit on Broadway. As Otis Gurney effused in the *Herald Tribune*, "Musicals and leading men will never be the same. . . . Brynner set an example that will be hard to follow. . . . Probably the best show of the decade."

Gertrude Lawrence died of lung cancer in 1952, three weeks after her last performance. She was replaced by a succession of Mrs. Annas, but only Yul's name was above the title. The production then set out on a ten-city tour of the country that lasted another eighteen months, by the end of which he was a nationally known star. Every night after the curtain came down, a throng of fans waited for a glimpse of Yul Brynner between the half dozen cops on horseback sent by the city to guard his stage door. This was like the fervor that Frank Sinatra had induced among bobby-soxers a decade earlier; in fact, several of the same mounted police had guarded Sinatra, too.

Stardom comes as a shock even to those best prepared: it is transformative because it is such an unnatural social experience, derived from the distortions of theater, film, and publicity. The superstar who arrives in a hall filled with random strangers suddenly becomes their organizing principle, and as the swarm begins to coalesce, they no longer *act* like individuals: at first they politely steal glances, before gawking unashamedly, then collectively acknowledging that they are all fans. They radiate a peculiar fervor, the delusion of complete strangers all convinced that they are intimately familiar with their idol. This casual group of people mutates into an inconsiderate throng or, at its worst, a dehumanized mob that will crush small children and little old ladies just for an autograph.

No one had the faintest idea where this new star had come from — and that suited Yul fine. The Bryner family history was too complicated for any of the entertainment reporters to get halfway correct; that much he had already learned. And since a number of reporters had already noticed discrepancies in his past biographies, he playfully began providing a new life story in each interview, just as the Dimitrievitch family had always done, inventing new variations of their past with every telling. But the Gypsies weren't doing it in print.

Yul's background was obscure enough to avoid trouble, but suspicion of "Russkies" had only grown after the Soviet Union tested its first nuclear weapon in 1949; the arms race added real chill to the Cold War. Toward the end of 1950, U.N. forces crossed the thirty-eighth parallel from the south, and by the end of October they approached the Yalu River. That is when North Korean troops counterattacked, and two hundred thousand Communist Chinese "volunteers" streamed south across what once had been Jules Bryner's timber concesssion. They seized most of the Korean peninsula, until the U.S. Army landed at Inchon, liberated Seoul, and drove Communist troops back north above the thirty-eighth parallel — just a few hundred miles from where Yul and Boris had hunted tigers fifteen years earlier with the Yankovskys. In the U.S. Senate, Joseph McCarthy was alleging that Communists controlled Washington and summoning witnesses, under threat of subpoena or blacklist, to "name names" of anyone who had attended left-leaning gatherings. In a time when Americans were being warned "there's a Red under your bed," it was remarkable that Yul avoided all suspicion.

Perhaps the most surprising aspect of Yul's early stardom was the least noticed: even as he was performing eight shows a week, he continued to direct television dramas, exactly as he had promised Virginia. He directed *live* hour-long shows of *Danger*, *Studio One*, and *Sure as Fate* — in one episode of which he cast Marlene Dietrich, with whom he was still romantically involved; in another, he cast her daughter, Maria Riva. He also appeared on *Omnibus* as the fifteenth-century French poet François Villon. Often he would race down Broadway with a police escort from the CBS Studio to the St. James Theater — next door to the theater where the Chekhov Company had performed *Twelfth Night* — arriving just in time to apply his intricate stage makeup.

Yul's stamina was inexhaustible in those years. He rarely slept more than four hours, and now that all sorts of new doors were opening to him, he wanted to walk through every one. His tireless curiosity and creativity drove him to one new project after another, while his unceasing hunger for life remained insatiable. Most nights after the makeup came off, Yul was at one of the jazz clubs on Fifty-second Street, usually Eddie Condon's; or uptown at the club owned by his friend, boxer Sugar Ray Robinson. He rarely got home before sunrise; most Sundays before dawn he would go fishing for striped bass in the Long Island Sound with his friend Jerry Dannenberg.

With a steady paycheck, he was able to move his family to a larger apartment at Central Park West on 104th Street, on the tenth floor: not the best part of the park, but a dramatic improvement after years above a dry cleaner. Settling in, Yul would stay up nights installing one of the world's first "high-fidelity sound systems" into a closet, or building butcher-block furniture for the kitchen. He also constructed an enormous toy train set that filled the dining room, to the dismay of his wife and the delight of his six-year-old son. He told me then that he had always been fascinated with trains because when he was a boy the longest railway in the world stopped right outside his home. No one else believed him when he told stories about pirates in the Orient, or Siberian tiger hunts, or the railroad that his grandfather Jules built . . . but I always did.

Despite his commitment to family, Yul continued to see Marlene Dietrich, as well as other women. Unbeknownst to Gin, he took a small apartment near the theater, organized by Don Lawson: there he kept some of his wardrobe and had occasional romantic assignations. On some weekends he would leave me there to nap during the evening show, before taking me out fishing at four in the morning. Sometimes during the afternoon, Yul would ask Marlene to babysit for me — our secret from my mother.

With the play's success, Yul began meeting all the stars and personalities who visited New York, many of whom were curious enough to come backstage to shake his hand: dignitaries from Albert Schweitzer to Eleanor Roosevelt, and entertainers like Frank Sinatra and Joe E. Lewis. Bona fide monarchs, including Queen Juliana of Holland, were happy to welcome Yul to their ranks, at least in jest, well aware that Yul's real-world power had drawn them there. Adults, even General Douglas MacArthur, usually became intimidated backstage. Children, however, always felt comfortable with the King because of the love he showed for the children on stage — and, in fact, wherever he encountered them, Yul radiated a natural adoration for kids.

He remained a wonderful and devoted father to me. He gave me a strong bond: a sense that he and I alone shared a destiny that was fundamentally different from everyone else's. We were both gypsies, he often explained, while teaching me Aliosha's songs on the diminutive guitar he brought me when I was eight. Like him, I had traveled from the time I was born, as part of our touring troupe; and, like him, I found out very young how to adapt and improvise. Above all, Yul never let me doubt that I was the most important person in the world to him: that never wavered. While I rarely spent evenings with him, in the morning and daytime we frequently took off alone together, sometimes to go fishing, but most often to water-ski. That was our sport, from our rented summer home on Long Island Sound at Wilson Point, in Connecticut, and later, as we traveled around the country and around the world.

Yul and I were so thoroughly engaged in our shared interests — from model trains to speed boats to water skis — that we often didn't need words to communicate. An article in *Cosmopolitan* magazine reported that "a hostess who entertained the Brynners for a weekend . . . was impressed by Yul's relationship with his son, then about six. 'The little boy was a carbon copy of his father, same chunky build, same intense, dark eyes. They played together with a special understanding, a wonderful, intimate rapport.'"

Twentieth Century Fox had secured an option on the film rights of *The King and I* by investing in the Broadway play, but before Yul was signed to star in that film, a visitor came to see him backstage during intermission. As Yul later described it,

> I was spending hours creating an illusion of character, and everything I worked for would be destroyed for anyone who came backstage to see me in the middle of the performance. I couldn't talk to a visitor in the character of the King, because

> Rodgers and Hammerstein had written no dressing-room dialogue for me to use on visitors. However, one evening when the curtain came down after the first act, someone said, 'A man who claims to be Cecil B. DeMille wants to see you.' I couldn't refuse to see a man of his stature — a man who has created far more illusion than I ever dreamed of. So I said, 'If his illusion about me as the King is destroyed, that's his problem. Show him in.' When he was ushered in he said, 'How would you like to play in a picture which your grandchildren will be able to see?' I said, 'I'd like it very much. . . .' He told me about Rameses, and . . . before he left, I accepted the part and we shook hands. From then on, it didn't matter what the business people did about the contract."

The Ten Commandments was to be a remake of DeMille's silent 1923 black-and-white blockbuster; filming would not begin for a year.

DeMille was seventy-two years old, a short, dapper, bespectacled man with a white fringe of hair and an authoritarian swagger. Although he looked like a milquetoast bank clerk, he behaved like a general at war, or more exactly, like an absolute autocrat, which he was, within his field; it was no coincidence that DeMille was also committed to an archconservative political agenda. While many of Yul's friends (and even more of Gin's) had been blacklisted — including our neighbor, composer Sol Kaplan — DeMille was pressuring every director in Hollywood to sign a loyalty oath or lose Guild credentials. It was tantamount to an auxiliary witch hunt for the House Un-American Activities' Committee hearings, still in progress. The proposed oath was voted down resoundingly by Guild members, who recognized DeMille for what he was, politically: a right-wing extremist who had failed to carry off a midnight putsch.

But DeMille was also unquestionably the founding father of Hollywood. In 1914, he had directed the first feature-length film, *The Squaw Man.* DeMille, D. W. Griffith, Charlie Chaplin, and a handful of other men had helped build Hollywood from the ground up, much as Jules Bryner and his associates had created Vladivostok, thirty years earlier. DeMille had constructed the first Hollywood movie studio, before establishing Paramount Pictures.

This was a man Yul could admire deeply, and the chance to play the pharaoh of Egypt in the biggest film production in history was irresistible — and a far cry from his only previous film, *Port of New York*.

In 1953, the Brynners set out on tour across the United States with *The King and I.* The actors, dancers, stage hands, and key orchestra musicians numbered about sixty, and the company leased its own train cars for the tour, including freight cars for the costumes and scenery, and a "private varnish," a deluxe car, for Yul and his family; a tutor, Ernest Painter, came along to teach the children traveling in the company, including myself. The small, errant kingdom of Siam set forth: Washington, Philadelphia, Cincinnati, Cleveland, Detroit, Milwaukee, St. Louis, New Orleans, Atlanta, Kansas City, Fort Worth, Chicago, Denver, Salt Lake City, Portland, San Francisco, and on to Los Angeles.

Most stops were for just two weeks or a month. The strain on Gin was evident from an article she published later about the challenges of being a mother on tour.

> Hotels that sounded fine and conveniently located turn out to be firetraps, miles from the theater. Restaurants become such a perilous gamble that if kitchen facilities are not available, out comes the illegal hot plate, which must be hidden from the cynical-eyed maid after each meal. By the time you have located a convenient shopping center in one town, you are ready to leave for the next engagement. Laundry accumulates in perplexing quantities and can't be sent out because you are leaving shortly; consequently, the bathroom becomes a damp, hazardous crypt, strung with wash that refuses to dry. Finally, when the day's work is over and you have the leisure to sit quietly with your husband, he is not there. He is gone to work, and you find yourself alone in a strange city. Since you are never in one place long enough to make friends or find any continuity

> to living, loneliness and a sense of isolation from the rest of the world become your bitter enemies, which have to be fought continually and with any weapon at hand. . . . The wife is left to face a series of empty hotel rooms in a string of unfamiliar cities. She is alone, often after a physically tiring day, absent from her friends and the familiar belongings of home. Unless she takes great care, she soon builds up a desperate state of mind about what to do in the evenings.

This was a far remove from Virginia's public and personal image as a glamorous, artistic actress in her own right. Periodically, as the tour progressed, her drinking became problematic, but that would have been likely under any circumstances.

In late 1954, when *The King and I* settled into a six-month run in Chicago, we moved into a small rented house in suburban Evanston so that I — nicknamed "Rocky" by that time — could attend third grade in an excellent public school and at least sample the experience of a normal life. For Virginia it was a much-needed break in the touring routine: she quickly made friends with neighbors and took delight in the very ordinariness of life, however short-lived.

Yul took advantage of this time to return to university. His restlessness and curiosity condemned him to boredom without some constant challenge; and while he had attended some classes at the Sorbonne in Paris, he was acutely aware that he had not had a university education. So he enrolled for a course in photography and a master's seminar in philosophy at Northwestern University, in Evanston on the way to his theater in downtown Chicago. Yul studied philosophy with Dr. Paul Schilpp, whose farm we visited on weekends. When asked by a reporter for his assessment of Yul as a student, Schilpp replied that Yul "not only did all the required reading for classes, but a great deal more. It is my deliberate judgment that he is one of the most brilliant students I ever had."

A few years later Yul explained to a reporter for the *Saturday Evening Post* why he chose to study philosophy, and offered a revealing self-portrait. "Most interviewers are afraid to report a man's philosophy," he noted. "It's the most direct approach to his character. It motivates his whole way of life, his actions. All my life, I've had a certain understanding. It's this: in the realest sense you live your life alone; in essence you are born, live and die alone. If you can learn to live with yourself, the relations you acquire with other people, be they close or casual, are gravy." Over the course of his whole life, Yul almost never chose to be alone.

The philosophy Yul put forward resonated with the world of uncertainty and abandonment he had grown up with in the Russian Far East.

> I grew up with another conception too. . . . Death is an integral part of everyday life. You know when your birth was, but your death is not predicted. What makes you think it will be ten years from now? What makes you think it won't be tonight? But if I knew I was going to die tonight, with what care I would live this day! How much more clearly I'd hear the songs sung around me. How much deeper would I look into the faces of my friends. That is what I mean when I say, if you could really know your life for even one minute, in that minute you could have it all. . . . A philosophy professor [Schilpp] asked me if I'd mind if his class asked me a few questions. "Why not?" I said. So one young man asked, "Mr. Brynner, can you explain the terrible compulsion which drives you, a man who has already arrived, into attending a university in your spare hours? You're doing eight performances a week and commuting, yet in the few hours which remain to you, you study and seek new goals. What's eating you?" I said, "Only when I am dead and buried will the time come when I would like to have it said of me, 'He has arrived.' If you are stupid enough to think you have arrived before that, you are dead already. From then on there can be only stagnation. You're merely animated meat." . . . What drives me is not compulsion. . . . It's more because of something someone once said of me: "Yul has an extra quart of champagne in his blood."

I remember reading that interview as a child and wondering if I too was born with an extra quart of champagne in my blood. As I read it now, I am struck by how essentially Russian my father's philosophy was, in its character and its consequences: "If I knew I was going to die tonight. . . ."

The day *The King and I* closed in Chicago, Yul left to shoot his first scenes for *The Ten Commandments* in Egypt, where DeMille had constructed the largest film set in history for the exodus of the Jews. In fact, all the film's statistics were enormous, starting with a budget of 13 million dollars.

DeMille's influence on Yul's professional life was second only to Michael Chekhov's, and eventually surpassed it. Although DeMille was never close with his actors, his relationship with Yul was different. Sam Cavanaugh, a cameraman on the film, observed them together. "I knew from experience that [DeMille] wouldn't tolerate the slightest interference. Why, he'd stomp off the set if anyone dared to raise their voice. But it was very different in the case of Brynner. It was as if DeMille was paying close attention to a very intelligent, favorite child. . . . The old man took [Yul's] advice without a murmur. Later the script called for a mob to try and tell Pharaoh its troubles — almost one at a time. Yul thought it would be more striking if they all babbled simultaneously. DeMille agreed and reshaped the entire scene."

Yul was always proud to acknowledge the father-son relationship that developed and endured between the two men. In one interview Yul allowed that "the reason why I felt so close to Mr. DeMille was that he thought like me, on a grand scale"; he *always* referred to the director as "Mr. DeMille." DeMille returned the compliments: "Yul Brynner is the most powerful personality I've ever seen on the screen: a cross between Douglas Fairbanks, Sr., Apollo, and a little bit of Hercules."

Both men were committed to their own convictions, generally arrived at by methodical analysis, including consultation with *the* established authority in a given field. Both held in contempt anyone they found to be irresolute. And both could behave like absolute autocrats, deliberately keeping everyone in their orbits on their toes. Wherever DeMille was on the set, for example, he made a practice of sitting down suddenly, without warning; one assistant had the job of being ready to slip a stool under him in time, lest Mr. DeMille fall flat on his ass. DeMille thought this helped keep everyone on the set more alert. Yul recounted this and many other DeMille anecdotes with glowing pride. He also learned from DeMille everything he could about working in front of a camera, most especially how to use dramatic lighting to his advantage, lessons that would serve him throughout his film career.

Yul got along well enough with Charlton Heston, who had top billing. Heston was among the second generation of top Hollywood stars of the talkies, after the first wave of Clark Gable, Gary Cooper, James Cagney, Spencer Tracy, Jimmy Stewart, and Cary Grant — all of whom were still giving some of the best performances of their careers in the 1950s. The second generation tended toward broader chests and shoulders, ever since the Hays office, which dictated onscreen morality, had begun allowing men (Gable in *It Happened One Night*) to take their shirts off. The most prominent of this new wave were Burt Lancaster, Kirk Douglas, Robert Mitchum, Anthony Quinn, Charlton Heston, and with *The Ten Commandments*, Yul Brynner.

Yul's success thus far resembled the earlier phenomenon of Rudolph Valentino more than the public appeal of his contemporaries. He seemed to belong to a different species from Gregory Peck, Ray Milland, William Holden, or Glenn Ford, so exotic that he stood aloof and apart: no director ever had to choose between Cary Grant, Jack Lemmon, and Yul Brynner. His exotic masculinity tapped different chords, promising the danger and excitement of all that was uncommon. In that respect, the romantic persona that Yul embodied was the quintessential foreigner of indefinite origins: not just a well-bred gentleman, but an earthbound avatar. Maybe that is what Hedda Hopper meant in her gossip column when she wrote: "What totally bald actor regards himself as being too good for his peers?" In fact, Yul came to feel varying degrees of genuine affection and begrudging respect for many of his peers, though when he was younger he was not always so generous. But if any competitive situation arose, no matter when, where, or with whom, Yul *always* felt compelled to win.

Most of his work in Egypt turned out to be action footage on the precarious "royal chariot," since he agreed with DeMille that the audience should

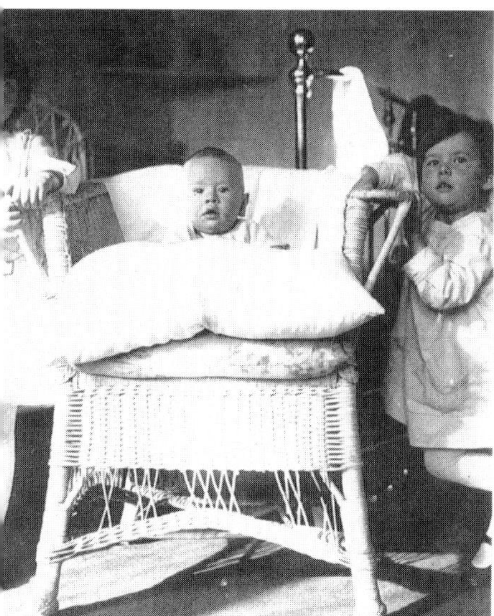

ner received a great deal of attention from his 'era, and his double cousin, Irena, both of adored him.

A tireless, willful, and clever child at age three, at Sidemy he learned to love swimming, fishing, and boating.

ter 1923, when Boris abandoned Marousia, Yul and Vera lived with their uncle Felix, aunt Vera, and usin, Irena.

Yul and his sister Vera were raised against a continual backdrop of revolution in the streets and in their own home. For both, imagination provided a means to escape sorrow.

Yul's first acting role was as a squirrel in the family Christmas play in 1925.

Yul, Vera, and Marousia moved from Vladivostok to Harbin, China, in 1927. They never returned to Russia.

Yul attended the well-respected YMCA school in Harbin for four years.

By the time he was sixteen, Yul had been working in Paris nightclubs and the circus for four years. His self-assurance was palpable.

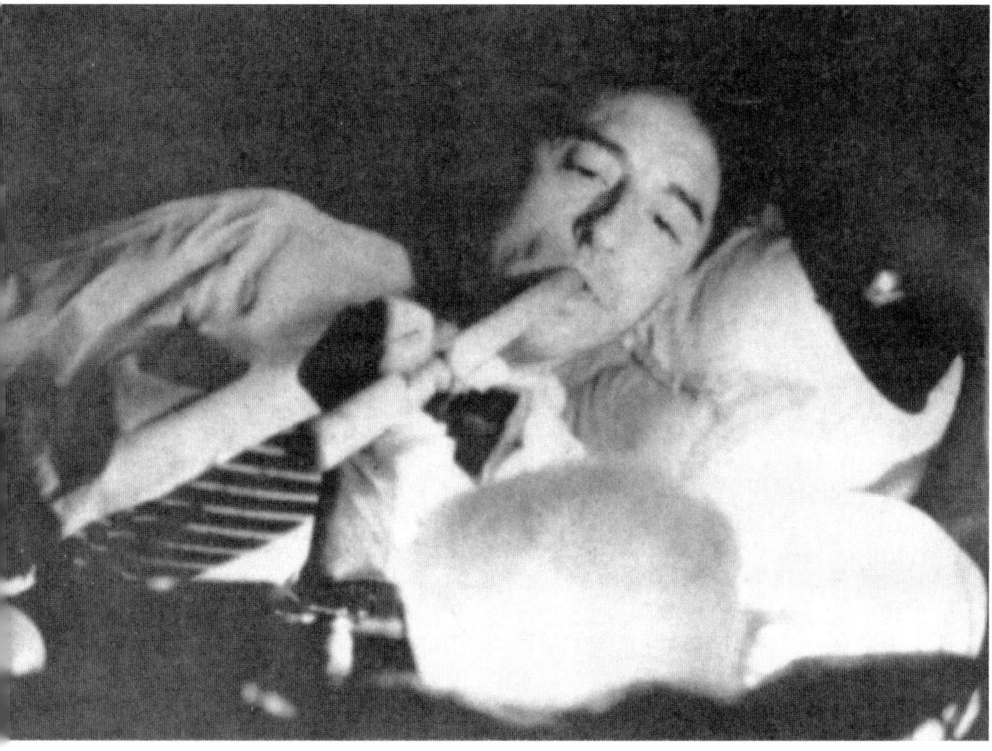

the 1930s, in Paris, Yul was supplying opium he had brought from Harbin to Jean Cocteau, whom met at the nightclub Raspoutine. *(Cecil Beaton, Sotheby's).*

In 1938 Yul and Boris hunted with the Yankovskys in northern Korea.

Back in Paris, Yul worked in the circus by day...

...and in the Russian nightclubs that had proliferated around Paris, performing with the Dimitrievitches, his adopted Gypsy family.

Yul at his aunt's home in Lausanne, Switzerland, in 1938, where he stopped smoking opium.

ul played guitar every day, learning new songs herever he traveled. At twenty-one, he was ired by the first New York nightclub he audi-oned for, the Blue Angel.

It was there that he met Marlene Dietrich, who remained his lover for almost twenty years. For a time she became my babysitter. (*Corbis Images*)

Virginia Gilmore was a well-known starlet when she and Yul fell in love. Upon their marriage in 1944, Yul was described in the Hollywood press as "some Gypsy she met in New York."

In 1946, Yul won the lead role in the Broadway musical *Lute Song*, co-starring with Mary Martin. Set in ancient China, it reflected much about the Far East that he had known in his own childhood.

While Yul was in *Lute Song*, Virginia was co-starring with Broadway newcomer Marlon Brando in *Truckline Café*. She was pregnant at the time; I was born in December.

Yul, at twenty-six, designed his makeup for *Lute Song* to emphasize the faintly Asian look he had inherited from his grandmother Natalya.

Yul's teacher, Michael Chekhov, in the role of a psychiatrist in Hitchcock's *Spellbound*.

In 1949, after *Dark Eyes* closed in London, Yul returned to the Cirque d'Hiver in Paris, where he had been an acrobat in the 1930s.

After returning from Europe, we spent much of the summer of 1949 on the beach at Rye, New York.

Yul's first film was a B picture called *Port of New York*, in which he played a suave drug dealer and strangler.

Yul was one of television's first directors. Using Chekhov's techniques he directed dozens of dramati shows on *Studio One*, *Danger*, and *Omnibus*.

Yul had fished in his childhood at Sidemy, and with his father on the Sungari River in China. In the early 1950s, he often fished in Long Island Sound.

While performing eight shows a week on Broadway, Yul directed and acted on live television. Here, during the second year of *The King and I*, he played François Villon on *Omnibus*.

A journalist wrote that my father and I "played together with a special understanding, a wonderful, intimate rapport."

The defining pose of the King of Siam.

The other characters in the musical had "realistic" makeup. Yul alone wore a Kabuki-like mask that took him an hour to apply.

TO THE ACTOR's "mentor"

ith fondest love

rom The Actor

Yul. 1954

Yul's handwriting was unique; this is his inscription to mentor George Shdanoff's copy of Chekhov's book, which Shdanoff passed on to me when I studied acting with him.

In March 1957 Yul received the Academy Award for best actor in *The King and I*.

One month later we were in Mexico, water-skiing every day. At thirty-six, Yul was jumping at competition level.

Yul played a Soviet officer in *The Journey* (1958), filmed in Vienna, where he spent almost six months at the end of his marriage to Virginia.

Yul helped produce, and appeared in, Jean Cocteau's last film, *The Testament of Orpheus* in 1960.

A portrait sketched by Cocteau in 1961.

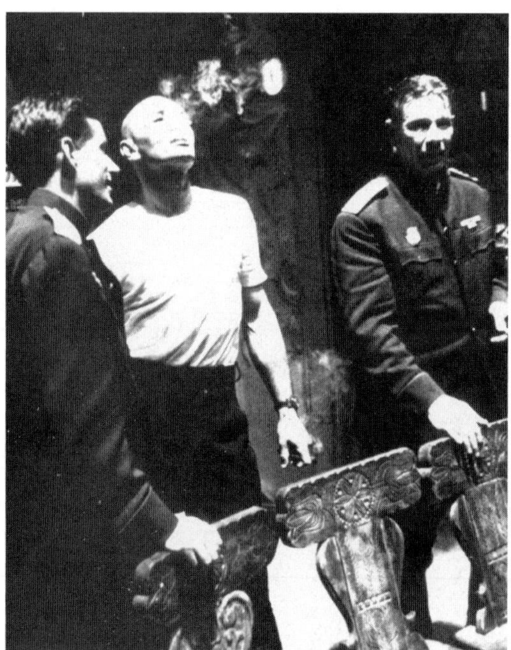

As a youth, Yul had developed dozens of manly skills. In 1958, he showed off his talent for blowing smoke rings to great effect.

To the grandmother of his daughter, Lark, he inscribed this picture: "Dear Jane, though Brynner rhymes with 'Sinner,' I know to you I'll always be a 'Saint.' Yul"

In 1959, as consultant to the UN's High Commissioner for Refugees, Yul (seen here in Austria) visited numerous camps in Europe and the Middle East.

Yul married Doris Kleiner in 1960. At the party on the set of *The Magnificent Seven*, I was at their side with Steve McQueen.

Victoria was born to Doris and Yul in 1962. A cheerful, beautiful child, she filled the lakeside home in Switzerland with delight.

Cocteau provided designs for the letterhead of Yul's film company, Alciona.

In 1962 Yul played the Russian Cossack warr
Taras Bulba. The experience marked a turni
point in his film career.

For more than a decade Yul and I water-skied around the United States and Europe. Here, on the Geneva lake in front of our home, we skied all summer.

ᶠrank Sinatra was one of Yul's closest friends for
ılmost twenty years. During the Rat Pack era,
ny father and I spent many vacations with
ᶠrank all over the world.

In 1965 Yul recorded the Gypsy songs he had learned with his "big brother," Aliosha Dimitrievitch, when they were teenagers thirty years earlier.

ı September 1971 Yul married Jacqueline Thion
e la Chaume, with whom he had been in love
ır several years. (I am in the background.)

Jacqueline and Yul adopted their daughters, Melody and Mia, photographed here in 1980.

For his last fifteen years, Yul's home was a historic, sixteenth-century manor in Normandy named Criquebeuf.

In 1979 Yul took his revival of *The King and I* to London, where Queen Elizabeth II greeted him and co-star Virginia McKenna backstage after a Royal Variety performance.

see that he really was leading a hundred mounted soldiers on a chariot in hot pursuit of Moses. That was challenging enough without the pharaoh's blue metallic helmet that weighed almost twenty pounds and magnified the blistering desert heat. One bad bounce on the chariot could break his neck or throw him out into the path of hundreds of stuntmen driving chariots close behind. This scene and the subsequent pursuit of Moses were all Yul had to do in Egypt; the rest of his scenes were shot on the Paramount sound stages in Hollywood.

As soon as he had finished working with DeMille, Yul started filming *The King and I* at Twentieth Century Fox Studios in Westwood, where Century City stands today. He still bore a strong resentment toward the Fox executives, who had done their best a decade earlier to prevent Virginia from marrying "some Gypsy from New York" when she was under contract to the studio. Knowing that Fox would not find any other actor to attempt the role after his own nationwide triumph on stage, he was difficult, demanding, and sometimes demeaning to "the suits" who ran the studio, as he often described them. In a cover story on Yul in *Newsweek* magazine after the film was released, his friend director Richard Brooks explained that "Yul is suspicious of studio people, but he doesn't take on the little fellows, just the big ones. He becomes violent about the mendacity of what he calls the parasites of the business. He feels that producers, agents, studio personnel are making no contributions, and whenever one of them is caught in a deceit, he gloats, justified that they were really as bad as he knew or hoped they would be."

According to the *Newsweek* cover story, "An executive at Twentieth Century-Fox, which Brynner often refers to as Nineteenth Century-Fox, recalls: 'At a party one night, Yul drank a lot and had nothing to say unless the conversation was on a subject he hated. Then he ranted like a boor. He was pleasant enough to me until he learned I was with the studio. Immediately his lynching spirit came out. I've never received such a going-over. In his opinion, all studio officials are untalented dunces.'" Another friend told *Newsweek*, "He is so full of hate for incompetence, that he often becomes downright violent." Charles Brackett, the producer of the film, told the magazine that Yul would goad him and "threaten to walk off the set if his ideas weren't instantly adopted. In story conferences he'd always have the last word. The moment he'd squat on the floor like a baseball catcher I could be certain I was in for a lecture." Finally, *Newsweek* reported, Yul became exasperated with producer Charles Brackett and told him, "You don't know it, but you died several years ago."

What had provoked so much anger from Yul were the studio's plans to fundamentally alter the nature and the story of *The King and I*, which he himself had helped to develop during the original rehearsals five years earlier with Rodgers and Hammerstein. In order to "make the musical more visual on screen," the executives at Twentieth Century Fox wanted the King's death to be the result of a struggle with a white elephant, rather than the implied heartache of self-realization provoked by Mrs. Anna's harsh criticism.

Yul fought them every step of the way, won almost every battle, and succeeded in virtually co-directing the film. To begin with, in his contract he had demanded casting approval, so he began by choosing, as his co-star, Deborah Kerr, whom he admired and adored. But given his experience in the theater with Michael Chekhov, in live, two-camera dramas at CBS, and finally with the implacable Cecil B. DeMille, Yul had his say in virtually every aspect of every film angle. The film's director of record, Walter Lang, was later quoted as saying that "if you didn't agree with Yul, you could expect to be called a bloody fool or lots worse. He would claim that he was really the picture's director, that I wasn't needed. That without him calling the shots the movie would wind up being second rate." Leading lady Kerr later told a journalist that "Yul's imaginative suggestions and instructions were responsible for turning *The King and I* into a great movie. If not for him it would have wound up being just another pleasant Hollywood musical. He had a wonderful way of handling actors — got things out of them they never realized they possessed. Nothing escapes him — he was interested in the most minor scene. I will always be grateful to him for making me look better than I really am."

Nonetheless, the film of his signature role remained forever a disappointment to Yul: he saw only what was wrong with it. First, because of the noisy new Cinemascope camera, *all* the dialogue in the film had to be dubbed after the shooting, dulling the spontaneity of the performances. Certain camera angles and some of the editing annoyed Yul to no end. Still, he was perfectly confident that the film would be a hit.

In 1955, while shooting one film after another in Los Angeles, and with more scheduled, Yul bought a modest home in Brentwood, near Beverly Hills, at 223 North Layton Drive, near where the Getty Museum now perches. Yul needed to be reasonably near the film studios and, at the age of eight, I needed a steady school routine and a neighborhood where I could find companions. It was a small ranch-style house with only two bedrooms, hardly more than a bungalow, but it had a small backyard that led to a secluded arroyo where Yul enthusiastically planted an herb garden.

In the basement he built a darkroom: since studying at Northwestern University, he had become devoted to the art of black-and-white photography, mostly but not only portraits, and he developed all his own work himself, though he soon allowed me to enlarge and print some of his photographs. As with other "hobbies" he cultivated wherein his perfectionism combined with his curiosity, photography became his obsession and amateur standing was never good enough. Within a year he was a member of Magnum, the elite photographer's agency (representing, among others, Henri Cartier-Bresson, Ernst Haas, and Inge Morath, all of whom became Yul's friends) and just as *The King and I* opened across the country, Yul's color stills of the film appeared in *Life* magazine.

Although our home was modest, there were touches of dramatic flare. The small dining alcove was dominated by a red throne-like chair with a silver-handled bullwhip from *The Ten Commandments* hanging from its high back; the dinner table was the actual five-foot-wide face of a clock from the railway station in Rheims, France, seated upon an authentic woodstove from a French caboose. And in the master bedroom, the floor was covered in a soft white fur; the "floating" king-sized bed that faced a fireplace was actually suspended from the ceiling by polished brass elephant chains from India, with the head of the bed secured to the wall. In the backyard there was a full-sized trampoline that Yul had bought — still rare in the 1950s — because I wanted to learn the acrobatic routines he had performed on the trapeze at the Cirque d'Hiver.

• • • • • • • •

Even before his film career was established with the regal characters of Asian king and Egyptian pharaoh, Yul sought to broaden the spectrum of roles he would be offered; he was all too aware of the danger that, like Rudolph Valentino, he would be relegated by studios executives to exotic, sword-and-sandal roles. At the same time, his accent and his persona were so unmistakably foreign that no studio would have even considered him for a role in a Western.

It's not surprising that Yul began looking for Russian characters he could play even as he continued to foster a deliberate enigma about his exact origins; he steadfastly preferred to be a man of mystery rather than explain the unique intricacies of Bryner family history. But it was natural that he began developing a number of Russian works for film, including Dostoyevsky's *The Brothers Karamazov* and Gogol's *Taras Bulba.* He also was approached by a brilliant Russian director whom he admired and liked immensely named Anatole Litvak. In his early fifties, Litvak was a short, handsome man with prematurely white hair and a strong, indefinable accent. Ukrainian-born, he had begun in the theater in St. Petersburg at about the time that Boris met Marousia there; he then worked as a film editor for Pabst in Germany. Litvak had had his greatest successes in France and England, including *Mayerling* (1936), before emigrating to the United States and rising to the rank of colonel during World War II.

Litvak proposed *Anastasia* to Yul. Adapted from a Broadway play, it was a fictional account of a true story based on a misrepresentation, not unlike *The King and I.* For some years a German-speaking woman named Anna Anderson had claimed that she was in fact Anastasia, daughter of Tsar Nicholas II, saying that she had mysteriously escaped the slaughter of the rest of the Imperial family in 1918 in the basement where they had been imprisoned by Felix Dzerzhinsky's secret police. The film was set in Paris in the 1930s, when Yul had lived there; his role was that of a corrupt White Russian general, a Svengali who recruits and trains a homeless amnesiac, played by Ingrid Bergman, to impersonate Anastasia and inherit the Imperial fortune — on behalf of wealthy White Russian émigrés who have put up the money to prove her claim.

It was filmed in Paris and London in 1956: my mother and I joined Yul in Europe for the summer. It was an opportunity for Yul to take his wife and son to the Cirque d'Hiver to meet the acrobats, clowns, and lion trainers that he had worked with in his youth. He took us to visit Cocteau at his home in Milly-La-Forêt, southwest of Paris, where Jean declared himself my "spiritual godfather." Jean also said to me, very seriously, that "Yul Brynner must be mad to imagine that he could be Yul Brynner." (Some years later I discovered that he was adapting his well-known remark about Victor Hugo, *Hugo était un fou qui se croyait Hugo*: "Hugo was a madman who believed he was Hugo.") The previous year, Cocteau had been elected to the Académie Française, the panel of forty *immortels*, the ne plus ultra of France's traditional literary high culture. To the avant-garde, his acceptance of this honor from the classical establishment proved that the "enfant terrible" of Parisian culture had always been a conservative.

One night that summer I stayed up late to meet the Dimitrievitch family at the club where they sang. Aliosha and his family had only recently returned to Paris from Argentina, where they had fled the Nazi Occupation. For *Anastasia*, Yul hired the Gypsy family who had adopted him to appear in the nightclub scenes, modeled after one of the actual clubs where Yul had performed with them. Somewhat more cautiously, he introduced my mother and me to his co-star, Ingrid Bergman, with whom, it was rumored in the press, he was having an affair.

Ingrid, seven years older than Yul, had already starred in more than thirty films; but in the early 1950s she had fallen into "disrepute," according to the prurient U.S. press, by abandoning her Swedish husband for Italian film director Roberto Rossellini, with whom she soon had three children. *Anastasia* was to be her first American-made film since the marital brouhaha — which she herself took very lightly; but a further scandal with Yul would have defined her as a serial home wrecker.

The *annus mirabilis* of Yul's career was 1956, when his first three major films all opened, catapulting him to the peak of his profession, the leading male star in the world. All three films were critical and box-office successes, and were quickly touted for a variety of Academy Awards. The songs from

The King and I filled the airwaves alongside Elvis Presley's first national hits, and "Anastasia," Pat Boone's recording of the theme song from the film, made the Top Ten for weeks.

Yul Brynner became an icon even *before* his work had been widely seen, by virtue of his name and shaved head. He was shocked at how much attention his bald pate received. It speaks to the culture of the time: the fifties were governed by appearances and by shame: men were *supposed* to be embarrassed about baldness, not flaunt it as Yul did. A slew of bald jokes about Yul Brynner suddenly appeared in the press, which annoyed him . . . though he too would crack bald jokes about himself, if they were funny.

With sudden fame came renewed interest in the press about Yul's private life, which he was loathe to discuss. But he did not mind talking about his appetite. An article in *Redbook* began this way:

> At precisely five o'clock every morning, in a small redwood house in Los Angeles, a bald-headed man in his thirties wakes up with the tormenting conviction that he is starving to death. This is the fabulous Yul Brynner . . . who is being widely hailed as the most exciting male on the screen since Rudolph Valentino. At five o'clock Brynner stalks his kitchen and begins his day. His breakfast consists of a large steak, sometimes two, washed down with coffee. Before nine o'clock, tigerish hunger smites him again and he tides himself over until 12 o'clock lunch with a few large meat sandwiches. For lunch he has chops, steak, turkey, or roast beef, and this may get him by until two o'clock when he sends out for sandwiches and cake. In the afternoon he refreshes himself several times with snacks. At dinner Yul eats large helpings of roast beef, with bread, potatoes and dessert. He has a snack before bedtime and goes to sleep at once. He would take a nap after lunch, he says, but can barely doze off before hunger disturbs him. This preoccupation with eating does not affect Brynner's remarkably photogenic physique. He stands just under six feet, weighs 180, and is muscled like an athlete.

Most of the articles focused on the question of Yul's *exact* origins, and the plethora of discrepancies in past biographies. Yul's ambivalence toward both his parents continued to reverberate through his fictions. As his own marriage to Virginia became less happy in its second decade, he seems to have sympathized somewhat more with Boris for abandoning the melancholic Marousia: perhaps leaving behind an unhappy marriage might be the *right* thing to do. That put his own abandonment as a child in a very different light.

According to *Redbook*, Yul was "part Mongolian, part Romanian Gypsy and part several other warm-blooded nationalities, depending on his mood. Several years ago he was part Russian, and was born in Russia, but he changed his mind about that. He prefers now to be born on the island of Sakhalin, off the east coast of Siberia." But according to *Collier's* magazine, Yul's father "was a Mongolian who had been born in Switzerland, attained Swiss citizenship and studied mining engineering at the University of St. Petersburg; in Switzerland Brynner *père* adopted the name of Brynner, a fairly common Swiss one, substituting it for his real Mongolian name, Taidje Khan."

To a reporter from the *Saturday Evening Post*, Yul offered several options:

> "In one story I was born in Sakhalin. In another my father was a Mongolian who chanced to be born in Switzerland, thus qualifying him for Swiss citizenship. There is still another story that my father borrowed the Swiss name Bryner, and substituted it for his real name, Taidje Khan, and that I added another 'n' to it. Some of the stories have it that my name at birth was Taidje Khan, too, although they do not make it clear whether I am supposed to be Taidje Khan, Jr., or my father's name was really something else. Still another story runs that my mother was a Romanian Gypsy, and in my eighth year my mother's mother took me with her to live in Europe and not long after our arrival there she died. Why don't you use one of those versions?"
>
> Looking me squarely in the eye — and when Brynner looks you squarely in the eye, there is a noticeable impact, you

> can almost hear a click — he said, "If you took the trouble to trace those stories, you'd find that none of them was really told by me. They came out of conversations someone is supposed to have had with me, but when writers come to me to verify them, I tell each of them, 'Yes, that's true.' Because no matter what story I tell them, writers invent things about me, and once they've invented them they believe them. They tell these tales at a dinner party, and they become part of the Brynner story. I don't want to embarrass anyone, so who am I to take the trouble to deny all this fiction? In fact, I enjoy it. . . . They may not get the story they came for, but they'll get a story that's not dull."

Just teasing the gaje . . .

For the few who had known him since his childhood, Yul's worldwide recognition came as no surprise, but merely confirmed his exceptional nature, which no one had ever doubted. His sister's career as a singer was also advancing remarkably: Vera starred (as alternate lead) in the premier production of Giancarlo Menotti's opera *The Consul* and had the title role in the first live broadcast of an opera on television, *Carmen*, conducted by none other than Arturo Toscanini; she was also the gentlest, most feminine figure I had ever known, second only to my own mother. Marousia's sister had moved with her daughter, Irena, to San Francisco, and though largely blinded by cataracts, the older Vera genuinely enjoyed Yul's national triumph, having detected his ambition for stardom when he was twelve.

Yul generously helped all his family members, for whom, it turned out, his success and assistance was critical. His uncle by marriage, Shura Ostroumov, who had undertaken to distribute the remains of Jules Bryner's assets, had not done right by Felix's widow, Vera, or by Boris's widow, Katya; they received next to nothing from the substantial, final dissolution of Jules' empire. Until Irena established herself as a jeweler, she and her mother depended largely upon Yul. So did Katya, who was near death from cancer in London just as Yul was filming *Anastasia* there. Yul cared for his stepmother to the end, and also became the legal guardian for her daughter, Catherine, eighteen years old, when she was threatened with becoming a penniless ward of the court. Yul also regularly helped his sister, Vera: although doing well professionally, she and her second husband, a former navy man named Roy Raymond, were struggling financially. Yul helped put Roy through electrical engineering training just as Vera gave birth to her daughter, Laura.

In short, Yul was broke as a result of taxes, overhead, and the family and staff he supported, including his loyal dresser and English-born secretary, not to mention agents, lawyers, and more. As his fame grew, so did his own small, expanding empire . . . but his slim savings did not. Of course, Yul's extravagance was a significant factor. For the most part, Virginia was quite frugal, because even as alcohol and despair beclouded her judgment, she was determined to emulate the average American housewife and mother, however unsteadily. She was constantly concerned about long-term financial stability in the unstable world of Hollywood. Yul, however, was quick to insist that he really did not value money — or, therefore, frugality. He had been raised in a family of industrialists, accustomed to luxury: summers at the country estate at Sidemy, with boats and cars and private homes spread out from Vladivostok to Harbin to Shanghai. After very real financial hardship in his teenage years, he had been groomed for stardom by such big spenders as Marlene Dietrich and Cecil B. DeMille.

Besides, however little money he had in the bank, Yul's agents, Ted Ashley and Ira Steiner, were negotiating contracts for three or four films ahead, worth hundreds of thousands of dollars apiece. "Every studio wanted him," Ashley was quoted as saying. "They were willing to pay tremendous prices. Never have I known another star so sought after." So Yul was utterly unconcerned about such mundane issues as savings accounts: he continued to spend like a drunken sailor . . . and to catch hell from his wife for his extravagance. His extensive personal wardrobe included custom-built shoe trees for his custom-made John Lobb shoes, and a dozen black leather Gucci suitcases. He kept his collection of Havana cigars in the humidor rooms of Dunhills in several cities. And while shooting *Anastasia* in Paris, he had purchased the new Mercedes 300 SL sports car, best remembered for its gull-wing doors.

When the Academy Award nominations for 1956 were announced, Yul's films had captured two nominations for best picture (*The King and I* and *The Ten Commandments*), two for best actress (Deborah Kerr and Ingrid Bergman), and the best actor nomination for him in *The King and I.* He was competing against Kirk Douglas in *Lust for Life*, James Dean (posthumously) for *Giant*, and Sir Lawrence Olivier, often described as the greatest actor in the world.

That only made it sweeter for Yul when he won the Academy Award. At the age of thirty-six, the odyssey that had begun in Vladivostok had brought him to the top of the Hollywood food chain. His acceptance speech was short. "I hope there isn't a mistake," he said with a big smile, as he was handed his Oscar, "because I'm not giving it back."

In 1956, Nikita Khrushchev inherited most of the powers of Stalin, who had spent a quarter century perfecting a thuggish, totalitarian autocracy under the thin veneer of Communist ideology. So it was astonishing when Khrushchev began his own reign by denouncing Stalin, his mass murders, and the imprisonment of millions in the labor camps. Overnight, monuments vanished and hundreds of streets were renamed, as were dozens of cities. De-Stalinization enraged the KGB leadership and other entrenched Stalinists, but until they were well enough organized to challenge Khrushchev, they waited for an opportunity to bring him down.

The decade of Khrushchev's rule brought some relief to the suffering Russian people, along with new woes. These included a disastrous attempt to shift the agricultural economic base from wheat to corn, for which neither the farmers nor their equipment were prepared. On the other hand, with the launch of Sputnik, the world's first satellite, in October 1957, the USSR appeared to have become the most advanced and powerful nation on earth just as Lenin had predicted forty years earlier.

Tension mounted between the superpowers as they advanced from atomic to thermonuclear weaponry, tension that Eisenhower was not well equipped to deal with, medically, after two heart attacks; nor was Khrushchev, temperamentally, after numerous public tantrums. The baby-boom generation was too young to remember Stalin, so for us, the short, stocky son of a Russian coal miner became the face of Communism. In 1960, when the USSR shot down the American U-2 spy plane, Eisenhower's refusal to apologize for violating Soviet airspace further enraged the earthy, intemperate Khrushchev, who displayed his Russian anger by removing his shoe and pounding on the podium in front of the UN General Assembly. "Puts shoe to new use," read the *New York Times* headline. "Premier Khrushchev with his shoe before him. He waved and banged with it." He also baffled the CIA and the world by shouting an ominous threat: *Ya pokazhu vam kuzkinu mat!* The mystified UN translator rendered this literally: "I will show you Kuzma's mother!" which is a folk idiom that means, roughly, "I will show you what-for!" But it left the CIA and military planners around the world scrambling to discover the identity of Kuzma, not to mention his mother — exactly the effect Khrushchev had intended. The following year, when the Soviet Union tested its first thermonuclear bomb, it was named "Kuzma's Mother."

Khrushchev's outbursts might have seemed just plain silly had he not been one of the two men on earth dedicated to a policy of mutually assured nuclear destruction, with the power to trigger it or prevent it. Tensions would finally peak in October 1962 with the Cuban missile crisis.

To the Soviet leadership, the domination of its "satellite nations" — Poland, Lithuania, Estonia, Latvia, East Germany, Czechoslovakia, Bulgaria, Albania, Hungary, Yugoslavia, and others — was a prerogative based upon the "natural superiority" of Russia. To sustain that illusion of superiority, Stalin had cordoned off his empire from cultural contact with the world; so, too, did Khrushchev at first. Only a handful of old American films (in 16-millimeter prints) circulated in the USSR, most of them obtained from allied U.S. troops. Soviet citizens knew next to nothing about American culture. And although the biggest movie star in the world was Russian-born, almost no one in Yul's homeland had heard of him. Even reports of the Academy Awards were muted by the Soviets.

During this same era, curiously, Russian influence over American culture had been on the rise. In addition to the celebrated classical musicians who had defected from the USSR, the Bolshoi and Kirov were the most admired ballet companies in America. Even at the height of the Cold War, well-educated Americans recognized the distinction between the Russian culture and the Soviet threat. But the greatest impact Russian art had on America was in the theater, specifically with the acting techniques pioneered at the Moscow Art Theatre thirty years earlier.

In the 1930s, Harold Clurman's Group Theatre had developed along the lines of the Stanislavsky "system," especially in the left-leaning works of such playwrights as Clifford Odets. But it was Lee Strasberg, the director, acting coach, and teacher of the Actor's Studio who, along with colleagues Stella Adler, Sandy Meisner, Herbert Berghof, and Uta Hagen, brought Stanislavsky's "method acting" (a term coined by Strasberg) to the forefront of American theater and film through the work of Marlon Brando, Kim Stanley, Jessica Tandy, and many others. By the end of the twentieth century, three generations of American actors and directors had been profoundly influenced by Stanislavsky's approach.

Michael Chekhov, on the other hand, was known to only a handful of actors and directors who had worked with him, including Gregory Peck, Gary Cooper, Anthony Quinn, and — together with Yul, his most famous student — Marilyn Monroe, who began working with Chekhov early in her film career and remained devoted to him. In his workshop she played Cordelia to Chekhov's King Lear; it's a shame that scene wasn't filmed. Monroe once gave Chekhov a portrait of Abraham Lincoln with the message, "Lincoln was the man I admired most all through school. Now that man is you."

A year before his death in 1955, Chekhov published an essential guide to his approach, *To the Actor: On the Technique of Acting*, and he turned to Yul to provide the preface. Yul wrote that, after first seeing a Chekhov production in Paris,

> I came out with the deep conviction that through you and through you only I could find what I was working for — a concrete and tangible way to reach a mastery of the elusive thing that one calls the technique of acting. I tried to join your group when you first started the Chekhov Theater at Dartington Hall in England. Then I heard that you had moved to America with most of your group to continue your work in Connecticut, and it took me several years, through all the world events to finally come to America with the sole purpose of at last working with you.

Monroe studied Chekhov's book religiously and relied upon his technique in every role. When she missed a lesson, she was wracked by remorse: one note she wrote to him said, "Dear Mr. Chekhov, please don't give up on me yet — I know (painfully so) that I try your patience. I need the work and your friendship desperately." After his death, his colleague George Shdanoff took over as her coach. So when she heard that Yul was preparing to make a film of Dostoyevsky's classic, *The Brothers Karamazov*, she carefully read the novel that Chekhov had told her was the greatest work of literature, and while working on *The Seven-Year Itch* with director Billy Wilder, she volunteered herself for the role of Grushenka. Her interest was reported in the Hollywood press, and widely mocked. Wilder (who later directed her in *Some Like It Hot*) reportedly replied that he'd be happy to direct Monroe in "a whole series of *Karamazov* sequels, such as *The Brothers Karamazov Meet Abbott and Costello*." The studio that had her under contract, Yul's old nemesis, Twentieth Century Fox, announced that it had no intention of permitting her to play the role. Nonetheless, the project led her to a meeting with Yul, and a brief romantic interlude.

Yul was prepared to gamble his new star power on *The Brothers Karamazov*, knowing that Americans would not rush to see a soulful, anguished classic about a Russian family's degeneracy — not in the age of *Gidget* and *I Love Lucy*; nor, for that matter, in the time of the arms race and Khrushchev. Richard Brooks, the director, was a man Yul liked and admired; they agreed to a couple months' fishing in Acapulco, Mexico, to revise the screenplay together. "When we were working out his character in *Karamazov*," Brooks later said in an interview, "Yul must have asked three hundred questions a day. He was constantly aware of the importance of the picture and of himself in it."

Meanwhile we got in a lot of waterskiing in Acapulco; after a few weeks practicing on the ski jump, Yul came literally within spitting distance of the world record. At thirty-seven, Yul was still very athletic and loved the sheer exhilaration of flying again, as he had on the trapeze.

The Brothers Karamazov was published in 1881 near the end of Dostoyevsky's desperate life and years in debtors' prison. The novel recounts the relationship between a degenerate old man, Fyodor Karamazov, his four sons, and the large fortune that his deceased wife has bequeathed to them. Dostoyevsky dissects the souls of the brothers, foremost of whom is Dimitri, Yul's character, whose innocent spirit is a blank slate for God to write what He will upon; like Job, Dimitri is a litmus test for the power of God. *Karamazov* is also a novel about money, and about unethical transactions made with fistfuls of rubles, often for the favors of warm-blooded women.

Casting the central role of Grushenka was the biggest challenge: she is a nightclub owner with the smile of a virgin and the avarice of a madam. While she is still Fyodor's mistress, she seduces Dimitri. The role went to the little known Swiss actress Maria Schell; she had the smile, all right, but she never caught fire. One can only imagine Marilyn Monroe in the role, and what that would have done for the film.

British actress Claire Bloom brought a positive luminescence to the aristocratic Katya, who must either possess Dimitri or destroy him. It was obvious to all that she found working with Yul an exhilarating, liberating experience: as she told *Newsweek*, "He is a tremendously subtle actor. Without any tricks or outward gestures, he can convey a thought precisely as he wants to. He's the most exciting man I've ever worked with, and I'd give my eye teeth to do something with him again."

Yul's performance as Dimitri fused Dostoyevsky and Chekhov. He created an idealist, a character struggling to transcend what is basest in himself to reach what is highest. The performance is bathed in innocence, even when Dimitri is filled with hatred and wishing for his father's death. "There are fathers," says Dimitri, "and then there are animals who merely sire you." Much of the story is set in Mokroie, the very same Gypsy village outside Moscow where the Dimitrievitch family had lived and performed for Rasputin before fleeing Russia for Paris. The musical theme of the film is one of the old Gypsy songs, "Inokhodetz," and the Dimitrievitch family sings it on the soundtrack, in exactly the way they had sung it when Yul first met them in Paris in the 1930s.

The movie has a sumptuous look and feel, rich with dark velvets and drunk with exhilaration; it was Hollywood Dostoyevsky à la 1950s, to be sure, but the result was about the best they could have hoped for. The whole film was shot in Los Angeles using plastic snow: economics forbade any alternative. That is never apparent to the eye, nor is the discomfort of the actors as they trudge through the summer of 1957 wearing heavy wool coats.

Nor is it evident that Yul had broken his back on the first day of shooting: filming a scene on horseback, he had cracked two vertebrae. On the next day, Friday, he missed work, but he was in front of the camera first thing Monday morning. Scar tissue along his vertebrae already made it difficult for doctors to decipher his x-rays, given his circus injuries. With boyish defiance, he tackled the challenge of physical pain as if he relished it: pain was something he could compete with, and defeat. To the end of his life, Yul regarded his work in *The Brothers Karamazov* as his finest performance on the screen.

A volcanic rage had become the distinguishing feature of Yul's persona, a trademark that carried over from king to pharaoh to Anastasia's Svengali; Dimitri Karamazov was also filled with anger, if not as thoroughly possessed by fury as his other early characters. Yul was also a smoldering romantic presence in each film, including *The Buccaneer*, produced under the aegis of DeMille and directed by Anthony Quinn, when the actor was married to DeMille's daughter. For *The Buccaneer* — in which his co-stars were Claire Bloom and Charlton Heston (cast as Andrew Jackson, but apparently still playing Moses with a drawl added) — Yul wore a full wig under a pirate's scarf as Jean Lafitte, the French-born historical privateer who helped Jackson win New Orleans in the War of 1812. As shooting began, he told me and my mother that his grandfather Jules had worked on a pirate ship that took him from Marseille to Shanghai; he'd heard that from his father Boris and from the rest of the family, so he had always been fascinated by pirates. After his years in France, Lafitte seemed an ideal role for him. The film was visually stunning, morally mischievous, and also did well at the box office.

Playing an all-American character, which had always eluded Yul, was the opportunity provided by his next film, a screen adaptation of William Faulkner's novel *The Sound and the Fury*, directed by Martin Ritt, with whom Yul had worked side by side at CBS. Developing a mild Southern drawl, Yul carried it off, demonstrating that he was not limited to exotic roles. Like *Karamazov*, this was a daringly uncommercial undertaking: it was no surprise that the film flopped at the box office.

••••••••

In October 1956, an uprising had swept across Hungary against the oppressive Soviet authority and its puppet Hungarian leadership. There had been union meetings to discuss grievances before the uprising, but it was mostly a spontaneous outpouring of anger and frustration, partly inspired by anti-Soviet movements in Poland.

The next eighteen days saw the most significant resistance to Soviet authority since the Civil War had ended in Vladivostok, thirty-four years earlier. Finally, Soviet tanks crushed the ill-prepared insurrection: in three weeks, Soviet troops killed some twenty thousand Hungarians and suffered thirty-five hundred casualties themselves.

A well-known Hungarian writer, George Tabori, quickly wrote a story entitled *The Journey*, set in the midst of the uprising, which he sent to Yul and to Ukrainian-born director Anatole Litvak. It was a love story somewhat along the lines of *Casablanca* — between a Soviet border officer, Major Surov (Yul), and an Englishwoman (Deborah Kerr) who helps a leading insurrectionist (the first film role of Jason Robards, Jr.) to escape into Austria on a bus full of tourists. Yul's character was a variation on "the bastard with a heart of gold" that he liked most to play. Shot mostly in Vienna and other Austrian locations, the film was a deliberate slap at heavy-handed Soviet imperialism.

In May 1958, *Newsweek* published a cover story titled "Yul Brynner — Real and Fancied: Bald but Big Box Office"; the cover photo showed only his scalp and his eyes, and the headline of the article was "Yul Brynner — Golden Egghead." Two years after he had won the Oscar, a national magazine was still treating him like an oddity for shaving his head. It slowly began to dawn on him that the attention to his baldness might *never* evaporate, a fact that began gnawing at his innards. But the article itself was the most serious attempt yet to identify his origins. It began:

> "I was born out of wedlock in Sakhalin, an island east of Siberia, on July 12, 1920," Yul Brynner said last week, offering yet another highly romanticized version of his fantastic life. "My father was a rich Russian, my mother a Gypsy, and I lived with her until I was

> 10, when she died. My father, who was then living in Peking, refused to see me. But his real wife, who was separated from him and later divorced him, accepted me as her own son. During the Manchurian war she decided to leave Asia and took my half sister Vera and me to Paris. The years there were difficult. We had little money. My exotic appearance, my physique, and my restlessness came in handy. Learning always came easily, and I spent my days studying philosophy at the Sorbonne and my nights alternating between jobs in the circus and in nightclubs."

But the *Newsweek* reporter, Michael Mackay, also interviewed his sister, Vera. When she learned that Yul was disowning their own mother, Marousia, and declaring Vera his *half*-sister, she erupted, and *Newsweek* printed the result. "That must be variation number nineteen," she said with a sigh. "I love Yul, and I don't mind anything he concocts until he brings the family into it. Our father was a Swiss businessman working in Manchuria. Our mother was a Russian actress-singer. They were married before we were both born."

Had Yul truly been as alone in the world as he felt, all the myths he told in his life would not have had hurtful implications to his mother, his sister, and others. Much as Yul might have wanted to be a Dimitrievitch, his mother was no Gypsy. Yul could not understand why Vera would disavow his little "games" with the press, and, as a result of Vera's "betrayal," Yul did not speak to his sister again until she was on her deathbed.

There was much more in the *Newsweek* cover story that enraged him. Yul had behaved with hostility toward the reporter, who now returned repeatedly to the subject of Yul's scalp, and even related it to his biographical discrepancies:

> Brynner created his visual trademark, the bald-as-a-lie head he has since electric-shaved every day. Although his hairline was only receding a bit by the time the king role was offered, he decided to appear with the gleaming pate because he felt it was more suitable to the appearance of a barbaric Siamese. It was an immediate hit, particularly to women. "He's ugly magnetic,"

> one ardent feminine fan said recently, and added with savage glee, "Look at his face. The bone structure suggests cruelty and women love it. There are very few male animals like him. . . ." "You can look into his eyes and go back centuries. . . ." "He would be the most attractive man alive even if he grew grass on his head."

The article went on to examine his personal character in terms he had never seen printed before.

> "He has to be top man," says a close friend. "He won't admit that he is not a perfect person. . . . If you level with him you come out second best and only get contempt for your inadequacies. When I think of Yul I think of reputations tumbling, balloons being pricked, façades being torn down — the Brynner Wrecking Co. always at work. But he is so honest and unafraid in this dishonest and frightened town that I find what he says and does is refreshing. At times he can be gentle and even chivalrous." [He is] impossible about setting to rights the true record of his childhood. His bizarre and often conflicting accounts of his early life have trapped writers for years.

In fact, everything about the article enraged Yul.

By this time his marriage with Virginia was beginning to fall apart. Between his barely disguised infidelities and her drinking, and with their son now in boarding school two hours from home, the atmosphere at home grew rancid. Gin had joined Yul in Austria throughout much of *The Journey* shoot, and there she studied cellular mutations that might lead to cancer and became a qualified lab cytologist. But during that stay she became aware that Yul was having a protracted affair with an Austrian teenager named Frankie Tilden, and she returned to Southern California enraged and distraught.

Cavalier though Yul was about his romantic affairs, he nonetheless struggled to save his marriage, if only because of the memory of Boris's conduct toward his mother and its effect upon his own childhood. Yul knew that my life, at the age of eleven, would be thrown into chaos by divorce.

Their marriage ended in November 1958. What actually triggered their separation was an extraneous event: in Spain, actor Tyrone Power died while filming a biblical extravaganza, *Solomon and Sheba*. The studio's insurance company offered Yul one million dollars to finish the role, after salvaging only a few over-the-shoulder shots of Tyrone Power. This was much more money that any actor had ever been paid for any film, and Yul was under financial pressure; at the zenith of his career, he was in debt for $100,000. A key factor was the punitive level of U.S. taxation — approaching 90 percent for large salaries in the late 1950s.

For some time Yul had been considering moving to Europe, which would, if he were an overseas resident for a three-year period, entitle him legitimately to significant tax benefits. He had asked Virginia to bring me to Switzerland for just that time to attend the International School of Geneva; she refused, insisting it would be both disruptive to my schooling and unpatriotic.

Yul was in many respects American: a Dodgers fan, jazz aficionado, and ardent Democrat. But at a deeper level, his essence was that of a man without a country. That's not surprising, given the vicissitudes of history that had shaped his early life and his family background. The time he had spent in Europe lately reminded him how he missed the Old World and its less Puritanical mores. So over Thanksgiving weekend, 1958, Yul took me for a walk and explained that he was moving to Europe and leaving my mother, that I'd be able to visit him in a few months, and that I could reach him by phone any time of day. Numb, I declared I was sure he was doing the right thing.

Virginia had been twenty-two years old when they had met in 1941, and his abandonment — otrecheniye — left her in ruins. Yul remained the only love of her life. Already teetering on the brink, she succumbed to the alcoholic impulse deep within, the impulse that Yul insisted had condemned their marriage.

After sixteen years together, Yul never saw Virginia again.

In December 1958, Yul took up legal residence in Lausanne, Switzerland. The last time he had been there was in 1937, when his aunt Vera had cared for him during his withdrawal from opium. Distraught at the end of his marriage, he soon admitted himself to a clinic for a ten-day period of intensive rest.

Lausanne has always been an exquisitely dull Swiss city: that is part of its charm, when one is in need of dullness. Situated on Lac Léman not far from Geneva, it has a beautiful vista of Evian, five miles across the lake, and the snowy summit of Mont Blanc beyond; Yul could not help but notice the resemblance to the view from Sidemy. Lausanne, where Jules Bryner had sent Felix to learn French, was just a few hours' travel from where Jules himself had been born, near Geneva, in the country that had saved Boris from the gulag. It is a temperate region, very warm in the summer and moderate in winter, though foggy and damp.

The Swiss were too civil to behave rudely toward Yul. Since dominating the covers of magazines, he had been unable to walk down the street in any city without being ogled or mobbed. Of course, he had sought such recognition, but no one can be prepared for the relentless intrusions of fame. Elsewhere, people suddenly stopped their cars in front of his to take a picture; men would ask for his autograph at a urinal. For the rest of his life, Yul experienced shocking incivility every time he was in public. What he saw of human behavior in groups was unnatural and inconsiderate, and I was often right beside him, experiencing this weirdness. The Swiss, though, were different: after a prolonged glance, most politely guided their gazes away. With this faux anonymity, Yul soon felt truly at home and came to love his new life.

There was a dizzying logic to his relocation. A century earlier, Jules had set out eastward from this landlocked European country for Asia and settled in

Vladivostok, where he died at home just months before Yul was born in the same house; almost forty years later, Yul left our home in California, continued eastward and settled near the place where Jules was born, completing the Brynners' circumnavigation of the planet.

He leased a small apartment in the lakeside neighborhood of Ouchy, and promptly left for Madrid to make his worst film to date. "It was all I could do to keep a straight face," he said later. Italian actress Gina Lollobrigida played Sheba, with a ruby in her naval, and a decrepit George Sanders emulated a potent warrior. Yul's only consolation was that Michael Chekhov was not alive to witness this awful biblical behemoth that paid him more money than any other film he ever made.

Next Yul went to Paris to film a comedy that had recently closed on Broadway, *Once More, with Feeling!* with Kay Kendall. Almost everyone associated with the film was, like Yul, a tax fugitive from the United States or England — and so was the whole project. Between Hollywood's union requirements and U.S. tax policies during the arms race with the USSR, dozens of U.S. films — "runaway productions" — were being shot in Mexico, Spain, Italy, or France, saving millions of dollars. This suited Yul perfectly, and later in 1959 he went to Greece to shoot *A Gift from the Boys*, co-starring his old friend Noël Coward, but with disappointing results. Both these films, directed by Stanley Donen, were evidence that Yul's imperious persona was not well suited to comedy.

In January 1959, Yul's young girlfriend from Vienna, Frankie Tilden, gave birth to a baby girl, whom they named Lark. He had offered her the option of terminating the pregnancy, but Frankie wanted to raise her daughter by herself, with or without his assistance, and he was content to respect her wish. Lark grew up in Austria, developing a thick skin and a wonderful sense of humor to cope with life's vicissitudes.

While Yul moved to Europe, my mother moved to New York to restart her acting career on the stage and to find a good Eastern prep school for the following year, when I would turn twelve. That left me alone in boarding school in California. Most weekends I would spend with the family of film composer Alex North in Beverly Hills. I was happy to be away from my unstable mother.

True to his word, Yul stayed in touch with me, mailing something or other almost every day from wherever he was: Madrid, Lausanne, Paris, or London. When I started a stamp collection, he began looking for more exotic stamps, always in corner blocks (four stamps from the corner of a sheet, prized by collectors). As with other hobbies that we had started, my little stamp collection soon became *his* principal preoccupation; using all his contacts, he collected corner blocks from every country in the United Nations. Then he sent these to each of the heads of state and, with sheer star power, convinced them to autograph the stamps from their nations. Every single one complied willingly — the only exception was Khrushchev. This was the only time in his life that Yul asked anyone for an autograph. Within a year, it was no longer my little stamp collection, but a unique archive worth many thousands of dollars. Before long, Yul auctioned the stamps in order to collect, as he put it, some slightly larger pictures . . . by Cézanne, Dufy, and other impressionists.

But our collection of United Nations stamps had launched an even larger undertaking. The UN had designated 1960 as World Refugee Year and issued postage stamps to focus global attention upon the millions of people warehoused in camps from Austria to Jordan to Hong Kong; when we began collecting them, Yul wrote to UN High Commissioner for Refugees Dr. Auguste Lindt, and, well, one thing led to another. As Yul began to study the refugee issue, he could not help but identify very personally with the problem of displaced persons.

Yul was appointed special consultant to the high commissioner for refugees, and was issued a U.S. diplomatic passport as well as a United Nations *laissez-passer*. He spent much of the next year photographing refugee camps around the world for a book entitled *Bring Forth the Children: A Journey to the Forgotten People of Europe and the Middle East.* He also made a television documentary with Edward R. Murrow for CBS, *Rescue, with Yul Brynner*. After being driven from their homes, most of these refugees could not leave their concentration-camp-like barracks because no country would accept them. His empathy was sincere for these helpless people trapped in bureaucratic purgatory with no government to assist them: it arose from his earliest experiences as well as from his empathy for the Gypsy culture he had adopted. I never saw my father prouder than when he handed me the first copy of his book and showed me the dedication on the first page: "This book is dedicated to Rocky, my son, in the hope that he will observe, learn, and give something of himself in order to earn his place in society." The book's photographs, by Yul and by Inge Morath, documented the refugee camps: there were more than thirty-two thousand refugees in Europe then, mostly from the Soviet satellite countries. The desolation that scars these abandoned faces defines those who had stumbled into the gaps between nations. In his preface, Yul explained that

> When I was fifteen, and a circus performer in Paris, we gave a matinee for orphans. I worked as a clown and an acrobat at the same time, flying as an acrobat but dressed as a clown. I still remember the day because of the contact, the rapport I had with those youngsters. . . . Though I was at first asked only to assist in the making of a documentary film, and to give some advice about the postage stamps that were to be issued during the World Refugee Year . . . I entered a two-year contract with the Office of the High Commissioner.

Yul wrote the text himself, in collaboration with UN experts, and painted a poignant and prescient description of what the future held for the political lepers living out their entire lives in camps. "The refugees did not choose their lot. They are the result of our world's madness. . . . Every day when my work in the camp was finished I wanted to wipe my eyes on a piece of clean landscape — anything, after the drabness of those barracks, the hopelessness that strikes you almost physically whenever you look down a camp street." This was not the disengaged voice of a lame-brained celebrity popping in for some charity gig. With real human solidarity he chronicled the plight of ten thousand Tibetan refugees, devotees of the Dalai Lama who had just become a refugee himself, as well as more than one million refugees from Communist China encamped along the edges of Hong Kong.

> Nearly 15 million refugees around the world still need assistance.... As long as we live in a world that indulges in war and the kind of rivalry and strife that substitute for war, I feel that we really have to make ourselves responsible for the results.... It is important that we do not simply develop a bad conscience about them and let it go at that. These are our fellow human beings, displaced and deprived of their means of making a living, through no fault of their own.... There is no disgrace in being a refugee, but there is certainly disgrace in trying to forget that refugees exist.

Writing about the teenage Palestinian refugees he met, Yul could foresee that the absence of any hope in their lives would leave them only one option:

> Take a youth of seventeen who lives in a camp and is unable to go on to a vocational school. He has time on his hands. All he does is think about his hatred and his desire: his hatred for the people who have deprived him of his homeland, his desire to push them into the sea.

That was half a century ago. In the television documentary Yul insisted that if these young men were not given some peaceful way to change their circumstances, they would be *driven* to terrorism. And in fact, by the time those young men reached their thirties, many had joined the Palestinian Liberation Organization, Hamas, or Hezebollah. "More than 500,000 of these people are in Jordan," Yul wrote. "When I visited King Hussein in his palace in Amman, he pointed out that more than one-third of the people in his kingdom are refugees.... The Middle East refugee clings to the belief that one day he will go home." Fifty years later, that remains true. Yul admired the twenty-four-year-old Hashemite king, believed to be a direct descendent of the prophet Muhammad. Don Lawson, who went along as *aide-de-camp*, told me that King Hussein made a joke about "a summit meeting between Jordan and Siam.... He came pretty close to calling Yul

'Your Majesty.'" After watching Yul's documentary on television, poet Marianne Moore published a tribute in the *New Yorker* in May 1961, which ended: "Yule — Yul log for the Christmas-fire tale-spinner / Of fairy tales that can come true: Yul Brynner."

In Paris, Yul fell in love with a woman of extraordinary beauty and charm. Doris Kleiner was born in Yugoslavia, but culturally she was Chilean, having grown up in Santiago. In her early twenties she made her way to Paris, where she became connected with the crème de la crème of European society. At twenty-eight, she was eleven years younger than Yul when they met at a formal ball given by Paul-Louis Weiller, a wealthy industrialist, and within months they were inseparable. She was a cheerful, spirited companion who quickly made fast friends with all the people Yul worked with, and much of the temper Yul showed, on film sets and off, dissolved with her teasing and mirth.

Yul and Doris spent a good deal of time in Paris, often overlooking the Louvre from the Hôtel Meurice, which fifteen years earlier had been the residence of the Nazi high command during the Occupation. But now the Meurice was Salvador Dalí's residence in Paris; he and Yul resumed the friendship they had started twenty years earlier, when Dalí was his talk-show guest on CBS. Home, however, was in Switzerland, where Yul and Doris, tiring of the Lausanne apartment, began looking for a house on the lake, where Yul felt deeply content. By this time, work seemed like a sure thing, thanks to runaway productions that now filled the film studios in London, Paris, Madrid, and especially Rome, where the biggest runaway of all, *Cleopatra*, was in production.

While his move to Europe brought Yul a measure of tranquility, it also reinforced his sense of displacement; the United States had been his home since 1940, and now he was in voluntary exile. This sense was augmented by the milieu of wealthy expatriates that he and Doris now belonged to. In Switzerland, a growing number of pilgrims settled along the lake, from Geneva to Gstaad, creating a small subculture called the "jet set," thanks to the new Boeing 707 and Caravelle. American and British transplants included Charlie Chaplin, Noël Coward, Charles Lindbergh, Elizabeth Taylor, Richard Burton, William Holden, and Audrey Hepburn, to name some of our best-known neighbors and friends.

Europe's highest society held some fascination for Yul. He had played guitar for some of these same people in Paris clubs during his adolescence, including several Rothschilds, Ali Khan, Prince Rainier, Prince Michael of Romania, Gianni Agnelli of Fiat, Porfirio Rubirosa of the Dominican Republic, and other knights of industry, arts, and entertainment. At the pinnacle of this social pyramid reigned Wallis Simpson, duchess of Windsor, and her husband, formerly Edward VIII, the abdicated king of England. Yul's attitude toward this crowd was ambivalent; he liked the understated elegance of these bona fide aristocrats, though they included the very gaje he had teased and ridiculed with the Dimitrievitches. But dismissing his own past was a survival technique Yul had adopted at a very young age.

The Magnificent Seven was adapted from *The Seven Samurai* (1954), Akira Kurosawa's four-hour masterpiece. How the idea of adapting samurai into cowboys first arose has been the subject of debate; I can only say for certain that in late 1956 Yul took me to a screening of the Japanese original, and afterward we talked about his plan to adapt it as a Western. Anthony Quinn later sued, claiming that the adaptation was his own idea, but lost in court.

The plot seemed highly original at the time: an American gunslinger is persuaded to recruit a half dozen gunmen to protect a village of poor Mexican farmers from a gang of fifty *bandidos,* not unlike the hunghu'tze that had beseiged Sidemy. The recruitment of the gunmen became almost a genre of its own, from *Ocean's Eleven* (1960 and 2003) to *The Dirty Dozen* (1967). Yul's contract with the producers and United Artists gave him script and cast approval and much more. He recommended the casting of Steve McQueen (whom I suggested, because I liked him on television in *Wanted, Dead or Alive*), Charles Bronson, James Coburn, and the four other gunslingers recruited by Yul's character, Chris.

To prepare for the gunplay in *The Magnificent Seven*, Yul studied quick-draw from a holster with the world champion, Rodd Redwing. Redwing, a Native American, had trained Steve McQueen, along with many other Hollywood actors. McQueen practiced hours each day and at his peak could fire two rounds into a square-foot target in a tenth of a second; my father reached a speed of twenty-five hundredths of a second.

Yul had rented an exquisite villa in Cuernavaca, Mexico, notable for its mosaics by Diego Rivera, some distance from the hotel where the cast stayed. Since Yul had selected these actors, his position of leadership was secure. McQueen made some deliberate efforts to steal the audience's gaze from Yul by fidgeting while they were on-camera together, but came away with considerable respect for Yul, which he expressed to me years later.

On March 30, 1960, Doris and Yul were married in Mexico, four days after his divorce from Virginia became final. I was present, along with a small handful of friends. After the vows, a fiesta erupted in the plaza of the Mexican village film set with mariachis, fireworks, and tequila all around, adding to the warm atmosphere on location, and a casual, good-natured mood that was not always present on Yul's movie sets.

Significantly, Yul was playing a laid-back, friendly, and unflappable character in what became one of the first "buddy" Westerns. Yul cut his own dialogue to the bare bone: the Man of Few Words was already an established cowboy tradition which Yul, as Chris, took to the limit. In his opening scene, Steve McQueen as Vin asks him, "Where did you ride in from?" Chris points with his thumb back over his shoulder. Vin asks, "Where are you headed?" Chris aims his forefinger straight ahead.

The film was not an instant hit with the critics, mainly because of its deliberate pacing. The *New York Times* review called it "a pallid, pretentious and overlong reflection of the Japanese original." Notwithstanding the added remark that "Mr. Brynner just is simply not a cowboy," *The Magnificent Seven*'s popularity grew steadily by word of mouth, and within a year or two the film had become hugely profitable, especially outside the United States, where it opened in 1961 just as President John F. Kennedy took office.

The golden era of Yul's film career came to an end with *The Magnificent Seven*, though that was not yet apparent. In five years he had released eleven films, four of which — *The King and I*, *Anastasia*, *The Ten Commandments*, and *The Magnificent Seven* — are considered enduring classics.

The Kennedy inauguration provided a brief warming between the Cold War adversaries. During this window of opportunity, Premier Khrushchev offered improvements in cultural exchange as a gesture to the new president. Since 1959, when a young Texan named Van Cliburn won the Tchaikovsky Competition in Moscow, the two governments had been willing to trade cultural tokens even as they prepared to wipe each other off the face of the earth: the Red Army Chorus and Band and many Russian ballet companies toured American cities, while Russian theater welcomed a Broadway musical, *How to Succeed in Business without Really Trying* — capitalism laughing at itself — and a handful of American films were distributed in the USSR. Among the first of these was *The Magnificent Seven.*

No American film was ever so treasured and respected during the Soviet era, and that affection remains today. *The Magnificent Seven* became a national obsession in the Soviet Union: people thronged to see the movie again and again. It was especially popular with teenage boys who, like Vladimir Putin, are today in their fifties and could recite every line of dialogue: after the first year, Soviet authorities prohibited children under sixteen from seeing the film, reportedly because so many boys started shaving their heads. It was already a secular rite of passage for fathers to take their sons to see the film, and thanks to DVDs, that continues today. By now, *The Magnificent Seven* is more a part of the cultural heritage in Russia than it is in the United States. Recently, a renowned actor in the Moscow theater spoke to me with tears in his eyes, insisting that "*only* a Russian could have made a great Western like *The Magnificent Seven.*"

Yul was a Russian actor not because of his genes but because of his technique, born at the Moscow Art Theatre. There is an intensity to Russian acting that one does not find in other cultures. The finest British actors, Yul used to remark, often seem emotionally detached, as if offering an intellectual overview of their characters rather than fully inhabiting them. Russians were delighted that the star of this American masterpiece was born in Vladivostok, but that did not account for the film's lasting success. More important was the way the plot resonated with socialist idealism: a self-appointed band of fair-minded warriors go to the assistance of helpless farmers simply because it is the right thing to do. The leader of the gunmen is *of* them, not above them, a colleague more than a boss.

The initial success of *The Magnificent Seven* owed mostly to Stalin: thanks to him, it was the first Western to be seen across Russia, where many assumed it was the *only* Western ever made. In this one film, Russian audiences experienced all the roguery, romance, and self-reliance of the American frontier. From cowboy hats and boots to quick-draw holsters and Western saddles, set in the landscape of the Texas borderline and a poor Mexican village: this was an exotic world for the Soviet imagination, a place where noble vagabonds followed a virile, socially minded leader of few words in black working-man's clothes, with a casual style and cynical humor. The Russians loved the story, the style, the characters, the camaraderie, the humor, and everything else about it. And for all they knew, the entire genre consisted of this one film.

Others may have thought this was Yul Brynner's only film. Most of his work was not seen in the Soviet Union until twenty years later, when the first videotapes began to circulate illegally, along with underground *samizdat* journals and rock 'n' roll albums, from which many Russians learned colloquial English. Then some of Yul's other films were seen, though others, like *Anastasia* and *The Journey*, were considered subversive by Soviet authorities: owning copies of those was to risk a crime against the state.

My father had remained in touch with Jean Cocteau and, like many of the poet's friends, often helped him out financially. When Yul started up his production company, Alciona, to make *The Magnificent Seven*, he paid his old friend a premium to design the company logo — certainly a unique Hollywood artifact. And when Jean prepared to shoot his last film, *Le Testament d'Orphée* (1960), Yul helped him raise the necessary capital. Yul made a brief appearance in the film together with Pablo Picasso and other old friends of Cocteau's to commemorate the poet's career. As a metaphor for Cocteau's former opium supplier, Yul was cast as a formal usher who repeatedly obliges Cocteau to wait before "seeing the princess." That summer, Yul and Doris were warmly received by Picasso at his *atelier* in the south of France, where the painter presented Doris with a small drawing. Yul remained impressed by the free-spirited creativity with which Picasso approached his work each day, in a studio filled with disorder.

The relationship between father and son was often a central theme in the films Yul chose, and never more so than in *Taras Bulba*, the Russian classic by Nikolai Gogol about a fearsome Cossack leader. It was the film that broke Yul's heart and, like *Solomon and Sheba*, changed the course of his career.

Whether or not this theme reflected his relationship with Boris — or with me — the paternal trait suited the authoritarian characters he had played ever since the king of Siam, with his crown prince and scores of offspring. Gogol's sweeping epic, spanning thirty years, presents the ultimate parable of authoritarianism: a devoted father murders the beloved son who betrays him. Yul worked hard to create a rich, robust character for Taras, whom he described in one interview as a mythical figure. "In my mind he is fifteen feet tall, in order to make the things he does convincing. He has the facility to mesmerize his Cossacks into doing what he wants them to do. He has a great love for his son. Taras has a peasant streak in him, but even though he kills Andrei, his son, for betraying the Cossack cause, he learns something from Andrei. His world is changed, broadened, he places more value on people." Clearly Yul's unusual interpretation of *Taras Bulba* did not place much value on Andrei's life.

Yul had never made a film he cared about more. He wanted to track this character over the decades, revealing how autocratic Russian nationalism outstripped even Taras's paternal instinct. He wanted the movie to be filmed strictly in sequence: that way, when he was playing Taras as an old man, he could have the caps taken off his front teeth. It might have been the best performance he ever gave on the screen. But in the end that didn't matter — because *Taras Bulba* turned out to be a terrible movie.

Many factors contributed to this bitter failure, including phony dialogue and terrible painted backdrops. Yul's carefully crafted performance was edited without regard for the timing and emphasis that he and the director had planned in detail. Finally, when the studio lost all faith in it, the film was butchered in the editing room to make it short enough to fit on a double bill. But the single decisive blow was the casting of Tony Curtis, just five years younger than Yul, as his son. Curtis had given excellent performances in *The Sweet Smell of Success* and *The Defiant Ones*. But at the age of thirty-seven, Curtis was just not credible as a teenager; he seemed more like a childish adult. This performance alone condemned *Taras Bulba* to oblivion, because Tony Curtis was not only *in* the film, he was nominally its star. Yul had accepted an extra hundred thousand dollars or so to take second billing. So even though Yul gave his all to the title role, *Taras Bulba* became a bad Tony Curtis movie.

When Yul saw the final cut, something inside him broke. The finished film was so far from his original dream as to be unrecognizable, and for several nights thereafter he could not sleep. In some irrecoverable way, his aesthetic trust had been violated by the film, much as his filial trust had been violated by Boris, and Yul decided he would never again lay his heart on the line for the film industry and the "suits" who ran it. "I can't go on being the only one who cares," he said more than once. "It's star power that brings people into the theaters; but as the star, I can't insure the quality of a Yul Brynner film. In fact, because of the director's control over editing, I can't even guarantee the quality of my own performance. From now on, I'll just take the money and run."

Yul appeared in another two dozen movies in his career. He co-starred with an array of great actors, and gave several electric performances in a few memorable films. But not one of these could be called unforgettable, nor do any belong in a class with *The King and I*, *Anastasia*, *The Brothers Karamazov*, or *The Magnificent Seven*. While his other performances are informed by the teachings of Michael Chekhov, few are inspired.

American society was gradually transformed from the prudish anxiety of the 1950s to the libertine daring of the 1960s by a combination of rock 'n' roll, the Beatles, *Playboy*, the contraceptive pill, and the rise of a cultural "global village" in the new jet age. The greatest symbol of this evolution came with the passing of the torch from the failing, grandfatherly Eisenhower to the boyish and exuberant John F. Kennedy. Eisenhower's first inaugural had had "more hoop skirts than *Gone With the Wind*," according to the *New Yorker*; by contrast, Kennedy's inaugural ball was organized by Frank Sinatra.

That same year, Yul and Frank became fast friends, and over the next decade we shared many holidays, travels, and adventures with Sinatra and his crowd. Frank was a bachelor most of that time, and while he was especially fond of Doris, treating her with respect and affection, most evenings it was a closed circle of high-spirited men setting out to "get the booze, get the broads, and get the hell out of here." It was the first time Yul had reveled in male camaraderie since his New York friendships of the early 1950s; in many ways, Frank was probably the closest friend Yul had had since Aliosha Dimitrievitch. But Yul never once sang with Frank, or for him. Most of the music Frank listened to was Sinatra.

Frank was near the zenith of his long career. The boyish star of the bobby-soxers in the war years suffered a string of public setbacks before becoming the mature saloon singer of the 1950s and winning the Academy Award as best supporting actor for *From Here to Eternity* (1954) and a nomination for best actor for *Man with the Golden Arm* (1957). It was Humphrey Bogart who had named Frank and his friends the Rat Pack, including Sammy Davis, Jr., Dean Martin, Peter Lawford, Joey Bishop, Don Rickles, and a few other pals with whom Frank sustained a playful, unsteady lifestyle of hedonistic hilarity — while never failing to deliver as professionals. Frank welcomed Yul warmly among them, and gave him his new moniker: the Chinaman.

Since I was almost always with my father when I wasn't in school, from the age of fifteen I too was often a part of this movable feast: in Beverly Hills, Palm Springs, Las Vegas, Acapulco, New York, London, Paris, and Tel Aviv, I was the only teenager in the crowd. Early on I began making myself useful by refreshing the adults' drinks, which gave me something to do with my hands while my eyes and ears absorbed the banter and general revelry. Before I was sixteen, I was pouring most of the drinks whenever George Jacobs wasn't around — he was Frank's loyal and beloved houseman. Pouring drinks lent a certain *raison d'être* to my presence, and I was delighted to play bartender. That was no small job in a crowd whose motto was, "I'd rather have a bottle in front of me than a frontal lobotomy."

His second wife, Ava Gardner, once described Frank as "so wild, so full of love and energy, that he is like three men rolled into one. But behind the front of a big drinker and party giver, he is highly sensitive and intelligent, and he has a heart of gold." Over the years I saw most all of Frank's facets, and I loved him at his best and his worst, which could be pretty terrible. By virtue of the treatment he received as a star, he felt entitled to behave in ways he would never have tolerated from anyone else, often giving himself license to treat others without respect or consideration.

Back then, Frank's mean streaks, like my father's, seemed to me justified by his unique stature as an artist. Traveling with either of them, what one experienced was an aggressive if well-meaning public that could suddenly swell into a turbulent crowd jabbing out at eye level with pens and other sharp objects. When situations became genuinely menacing, they were not easily forgotten. Frank and Yul were both young men when they required cops on horseback at the stage door nightly; the hateful view of strangers which that fosters helps to make celebrity a slow-acting poison. For all but a few well-grounded individuals, stardom produces an artificial and unbalanced relationship with the rest of humanity. Psychologically, the relentless attention of complete strangers is abnormal, and gradually induces a state of perpetual self-consciousness — not self-awareness, but self-centeredness. It is not surprising that stars feel *entitled* to exceptional treatment when privilege is constantly reinforced by acquaintances and strangers alike, and stardom seems to overrule civil conventions. In the midst of such exceptionalism, the golden rule is easily suspended.

It wasn't surprising that Yul was drawn to Frank, whom he regarded as the greatest saloon singer of all time, which is all Frank ever claimed to be. They shared the same passion for revelry along with the same impatience and intolerance with studio executives and other guys Frank called "brown shoes." And they could both tap into deep wells of unreleased anger with little or no warning — and later delight with pride in describing their acts of rage. There was never any competition between them: they deferred to each other's supremacy in separate arenas. Yul often stayed at Frank's Palm Springs house beside the Tamarisk Golf Club, where he took up golf for a few years, more for the companionship than for the sport. Frequently he was there just with Frank and his parents, Dolly and Marty, an erstwhile mayor and a former firefighter of Hoboken, New Jersey. Marty always cooked the pasta and Yul always cleaned the platter.

Then he and Frank would sit up long into the night, downing respectively the Johnnie Walker and Jack Daniels on the rocks that I often poured, and sharing stories of the strange roads they had traveled. Frank was five years older than Yul, but much less worldly, which he freely admitted, admiring the *savoir faire* with which Yul and Doris seemed to move through life. On the other hand, Frank had his roots in New Jersey and remained famously connected with the "businessmen" who had owned the saloons where he performed, from Jersey to Miami to Vegas. Yul did not share Frank's fascination with the mob, but over the years came to know some of the less savory figures, like Sam Giancana, longtime Chicago Mafia boss, whom we first met in 1962, about the time he and Pete Roselli were being consulted by the Kennedy administration on the planned assassination of Fidel Castro.

In November 1962, my sister Victoria was born in Lausanne, after an anxious pregnancy for Doris and Yul. A confident and ebullient child, her face seemed to combine aspects of her mother's beauty and of Yul's sister's. By then we had settled into a home directly on Lac Léman, an hour's drive from Geneva. Chanivaz, as it had long been named, was not an enormous house, though it required a large staff to maintain the perfectionism that Yul and Doris expected. Most importantly, the property had a beach and boathouse. Each summer we skied around the lake behind an enormous 350-horsepower boat that Yul had custom designed, named *Seven* after the film that paid for it. That was soon followed by a lithe, swift sailboat, an Olympic class 5.5 meter, which Yul methodically learned to race. He had wanted to sail, he told me, ever since watching regattas at Sidemy with his uncle Felix.

In the *salon* and *petit salon* at Chanivaz, a small but substantial collection of impressionist and post-impressionist paintings began to flourish: Cézanne, Utrillo, Dufy, Braque, Modigliani, Van Dongen, and Picasso hung on the walls, and a half dozen bejeweled *objets* by Fabergé adorned the exquisite coffee tables. In the garage, a bronze convertible Bentley Continental sat beside the chauffeured, midnight-blue Rolls Royce, a rare Silver Wraith.

Five years earlier, we had lived in a modest bungalow beside an arroyo in West Los Angeles, where my mother drove about in a station wagon. Now, we were living much like the authentic European royalty who lived or vacationed in Switzerland. And though Yul had earned a fortune very suddenly, he spent it, not like a *nouveau riche*, but like old-family aristocracy, and with much the same sense of entitlement. Forty years after Jules lost his empire to the Bolsheviks, Yul had created his own formidable realm, and enjoyed a level of luxury that his father Boris had known only as a young prince of Primorye.

But at the end of 1964, Yul learned that the IRS had denied the legitimacy of his residence in Switzerland and was demanding back-taxes of more than a million dollars. Though his lawyers were convinced he would win his case in court, the IRS threatened to freeze all his U.S. assets, including future earnings, until the case was settled, a processs that could take years. Reluctantly and angrily, Yul paid the millions in taxes that he did not owe according to the laws he had meticulously obeyed. It was blackmail, he insisted, and as long as he was a U.S. citizen, the IRS could lay claim to any amount of money they chose.

Six months later, in July 1965, Yul abandoned his U.S. citizenship with a formal renunciation at the American embassy in Bern, Switzerland. Otrecheniye. He had become a naturalized American in 1945 with his marriage to Virginia; now twenty years later he returned to the Swiss citizenship he had inherited from Jules. To the American press, he explained briefly that he was taking this measure, not out of disloyalty, but only to ensure that in time of war he could not be separated from his family, who were now Swiss nationals. The announcement went largely unnoticed: the press, it seemed, had long ago decided that Yul Brynner was *sui generis*, a law unto himself in matters of national origin.

After *Taras Bulba*, Yul continued to make one or two films a year, playing an assortment of exotic figures: an Arab in *Escape from Zahrain* (1962) and a Native American in *Kings of the Sun* (1964); a Nisei Japanese in *Flight from Ashiya* (1964) and a dark-skinned Creole in *Invitation to a Gunfighter* (1964). He played a Nazi sea captain and a Jewish general, and later a sultan from India as well as a freedom fighter from Yugoslavia. He worked with top-caliber actors: Marlon Brando (*Morituri*), John Wayne (*Cast a Giant Shadow*), Kirk Douglas (*Light at the End of the World*), Christopher Plummer (*Triple Cross*), Robert Mitchum and Charles Bronson (*Villa Rides*), Henry Fonda (*The Serpent*), Orson Welles (*The Battle of Neretva*), and Katherine Hepburn (*The Madwoman of Chaillot*). In each of these films he gave a sterling performance and was well paid. Some were better than others, but none were considered a work of art, even by Yul; not one was a commercial hit.

Yul still occasionally pulled out his seven-string guitar at parties, and when he was in Paris he visited the restaurants and clubs where his Gypsy "brother," Aliosha, still played: Tsarevitch, Raspoutine, and Chez Vodka at the Grande Sévérine. Aliosha, now in his early fifties, urged Yul to record the songs they had started singing together in 1935. So Yul approached Vanguard Records in New York, a company that recorded historic figures such as Mississippi John Hurt for the sake of preserving their work rather than for profit, and Vanguard offered to produce an album of Gypsy folk songs.

After some weeks of rehearsal in Paris, they went to Vienna to record the album in an ideal acoustic setting: a nineteenth-century chamber where Chopin and Liszt once performed. Although bass guitar was added later, in Vienna it was only Aliosha and Yul, just as they had thirty years earlier. A few of the songs, like "Two Guitars," were Gypsy variations on Russian songs, but others were the oldest known songs in Rom, some ("Khassiyëm") dating back three hundred years. These were the songs that Aliosha's father had sung for Rasputin half a century earlier.

For the album, released in the United States as *The Gypsy and I*, my father asked me to write the liner notes. I was eighteen and had spent many evenings of my own with Aliosha and the Dimitrievitch family, though I never played or sang publicly with them. But I tried, in my first published work, to identify and describe the powerful undercurrents that made this music so unique. While I was writing about the Romany people, I might as well have been writing just about my father.

> The Gypsies' here is now, their permanent address is the present. When they move, the only baggage they carry is in their hearts: their desperate ecstasy, their laughing remorse, and their musical love; all that will be needed at their next encampment. . . . What is sung for money is not sung for themselves. They would no more pour out their souls to the nightclub *gaje* than read the palm of another Rom. The difference between what they sell and what they keep forever is sharp: properly, the verb "to sing" is intransitive; "singing to" is finance, "singing out" is expression. . . . Aliosha was nineteen years old, Yul was twelve, when they first met in Paris. Yul became a part of their Kumpania. . . . Aliosha is the impetuous, tough little boss; so he is also the clown. . . . Yul is the energy and inspiration, the voice that demands an echo; but Aliosha trained that energy. Yul's words are foreign to us, the pain and bursting joy are not. Trust, all the explosions and burning pain are his own: he sings them as he has lived them.

The album's release went unnoticed except by Yul's most ardent fans, but a few copies made their way surreptitiously to the Soviet Union, where they were soon bootlegged. A decade later, when cassette players became available, copies of the album spread quickly across Russia.

In 1964, director Sergio Leone made *A Fistful of Dollars*, the first "spaghetti Western," proving that a cowboy movie shot in Italy with locations filmed in Spain could capture the global market for frontier shoot-'em-ups, whether or not the film succeeded in the United States. Using cut-rate Italian actors with their English dialogue dubbed by cut-rate American actors, good editing, and a snappy sound track produced crowd pleasers. All that was needed was *one* handsome American to play the lead: in this case, Leone cast an unknown young TV actor from Los Angeles named Clint Eastwood. Two years later, Yul made *Return of the Seven* in Alicante, Spain, and Rome, Italy, the first of seven Westerns he would shoot in Europe. Some were American productions, others were bona fide spaghetti Westerns in which the other actors pretended to speak English. None of these films was memorable.

It was an unsettling time in Yul's professional life. Since ceasing to invest himself emotionally in films after *Taras Bulba*, he found little satisfaction in work; now, he was making movies that he and his friends would not choose to see. While he remained absolutely professional in all his work habits — and demanded that everyone else do the same — at the end of the day, he was simply picking up his paycheck and going his way. He never lost his dignity in these roles, and he brought to them a stature they otherwise did not deserve. But he had moved further and further away from the dramatic art he had studied with Chekhov and Shdanoff.

Switzerland was still Yul's home, but he was gradually spending less time there. When he wasn't away shooting a film in England, Spain, or the United States, he was often visiting Sinatra. Gradually his relationship with Doris became more strained, and in November 1967, they separated. Doris continued to live at Chanivaz with Victoria, while Yul and I set out for Palm Springs to spend Christmas, and my twenty-first birthday, with Frank. Two years after renouncing U.S. citizenship in favor of his Swiss birthright, Yul abandoned Switzerland altogether, and never lived there again.

The following month Yul's sister, Vera, died of breast cancer. Only in the last year had Yul learned of her illness and begun speaking to her again. He was quick to help her family financially so that she could go to the Long Island shoreline, look out at the ocean, and recall Sidemy. I was there at their reconciliation, which held no trace of recrimination. Though it had been a decade since they had seen each other, brother and sister sounded like children resuming yesterday's games. But Vera was gravely ill, and only morphine kept her free to joke and to laugh.

After Vera passed away, there were only two people left whom Yul had known since childhood. He remained close with Irena and her mother, Vera, whom he cherished as the woman who had brought him up; he never failed to visit them when he passed through New York. Vera, blind and utterly dependent upon Irena, was always in high spirits when my father and I visited. She still did not speak English and I spoke almost no Russian, but there was no doubting the abundance of love she showed Yul and offered to me as well.

But my father had little attachment to his past worlds. It would never have crossed Yul's mind to drive by the apartment where he had first lived with his mother in Paris; or, in New York, to notice the dry cleaner's he and Gin had lived over; or, in Los Angeles, to make a detour to see our old Brentwood home. In some ways he regarded his entire past the way he regarded Vladivostok, as a place long gone that could never be visited again. Since he could not reasonably yearn to return to his birthplace, why should he yearn for any of his former lives? "Don't look back" was Yul's motto, long before Bob Dylan came along.

In the late 1960s, Yul recast his life again. He gradually moved all his belongings to Paris, where he kept an elegant business office at 18-20 Place de la Madeleine, nevertheless spending much of his time shooting films in "swinging London" of Beatles-era Carnaby Street, and the first miniskirts. Most often he lived at the Dorchester Hotel overlooking Hyde Park, and spent evenings in supper clubs like Annabelle's or the Aretusa, before proceeding to the hot new *discothèques* like Sybilla's or Tramps. In some men this might have signaled a midlife crisis, but Yul was simply returning to the world he'd known since his teens. Though he would later make it a trademark to consistently wear black, in 1967 Yul was experimenting with all kinds of original clothing, including futuristic jewelry designed by his cousin, Irena, which Sammy Davis, Jr., began wearing in lieu of a necktie.

From younger friends like actress Mia Farrow (by now the former Mrs. Frank Sinatra) and Roman Polanski, as well as from me, he got some sense of popular culture and even experimented with marijuana. In 1968, he made a brief appearance in a film starring Peter Sellers and Ringo Starr, *The Magic Christian*. I had already become friendly with the Beatles a few years earlier, but nothing had prepared me for Yul's plunge into sixties' culture . . . in drag. Yet there he was, in a long blonde wig and gold lamé dress, singing Noël Coward's "Mad about the Boy." In his own judgment, this brief, good-humored adventure in cross-dressing proved he'd be "one ugly broad."

By 1968 Yul was no longer hiding the fact that he had fallen in love. Jacqueline Thion de la Chaume had grown up in Paris through the Nazi occupation, raised a daughter, Sophie, and had recently been widowed. Her aristocratic and feminine bearing, together with her Gallic beauty, enhanced the pleasure of her sharp mind and fierce loyalty. Doubtless Yul and Jacqueline shared great passion, but most of all they nourished a passionate friendship. Their attunement was so strong that, if they sat quietly side by side, one hesitated even to speak to them for fear of interrupting their silent dialogue. For two years Yul made his home in a suite at Jacqueline's apartment beside Place de la Concorde, only a mile or so from where he had first lived after leaving Harbin. Life in France was utterly familiar and natural to him; he loved the quirks and contrariness specific to the French.

He and Jacqueline had found a house in Normandy where they wanted to live, an ancient manor almost five hundred years old. Yul had always retained happy memories of his summers as a teenager in Deauville. The original structures of the Manoir de Criquebeuf were two stone guard towers, some forty feet apart, built during the Hundred Years' War. In the early 1500s, the towers were conjoined by a three-story beam-and-mortar structure that resembled a castle. It was a house with enormous charm and personality: through the centuries the beams, some almost two feet wide, had warped slightly around each other, creating the strong, unpretentious atmosphere of an organic structure, shaped over generations. And the location of the house was convenient, since most of Yul's film work was in Paris or London.

It was in Deauville that Jacqueline and Yul were married on September 23, 1971. I was present at the ceremony and at the small reception afterward at Criquebeuf, and so can attest that my father was as happy as I had ever seen him. Jacqueline offered me her sincere and enduring friendship, despite some egregious misbehavior on my part during my most ungainly years. And she offered Yul her devotion, without ever compromising her allegiance to her daughter, Sophie, whom Yul also loved dearly.

In the fall of 1974, Yul made the first of two flights to Saigon. He and Jacqueline, eager for children, had decided to adopt a daughter from the orphanage where Mia Farrow had found her first adopted children. Yul returned from Vietnam with a daughter, whom they named Mia. A year later, in the last months before the final surrender of South Vietnam, Yul returned to Saigon to arrange for the passage of my youngest sister, who then miraculously survived a disastrous crash during an airlift of orphans; when she arrived in France safely, they named her Melody. With Mia and Melody, their home was suddenly all laughter and merriment: a houseful of children and pets.

Film roles were becoming scarce for an entire generation of stars, from Henry Fonda to Kirk Douglas to Yul Brynner. So it was to his good fortune when a promising young writer-director named Michael Crichton invited him to reprise his character from *The Magnificent Seven* . . . but as a robot. *Westworld* (1973) was filmed in Hollywood on a miniscule budget in just seventeen days, and was directed somewhat ponderously. But Yul's performance as a killing machine — foreshadowing Schwarzenegger's *Terminator* — remains interesting and durable. So does the motif of a theme park populated with submissive robots, who run amok and begin killing guests; Michael Crichton resurrected the same plot for the dinosaurs of his novel and film *Jurassic Park* almost two decades later.

Yul was disgusted with his career, composed mostly of spaghetti Westerns at this point. He was casting about for new options in his professional life. He had often considered film directing; after his experience at CBS, he had much more experience than other actors who turned to directing — most notably the star of the first spaghetti Western, Clint Eastwood. But he had had angry confrontations with most of the studio heads in Hollywood, and he never did seriously seek out a project he could direct.

By 1974, Yul was prepared to return to the theater. He was approached by his old friend and mentor George Shdanoff, who invited Yul to star in a production of *Othello* — first in Los Angeles then for a limited engagement on Broadway — and Yul accepted. I had asked him before if he would consider going back on stage, and he had scoffed at the idea; after twenty years in film, he really didn't feel like returning to the tortuous routine of eight shows a week. But *Othello* would provide an opportunity to remember what he loved about acting, and to return to the foundation of his art under the trusted hand of "the Doctor" who had directed his first play in the United States, the Chekhov Company's *Twelfth Night*. I was very excited for him at the prospect of this collaboration.

But though Yul did return to the theater, his Othello never came to life. When word got out that he was coming back to the stage, he received other offers and quickly agreed to star in a musical of Homer's *Odyssey* by the team that had created *Man of La Mancha* a decade earlier. The plan was to tour the United States for six months before opening on Broadway in late

1975. Yul only accepted the role on condition that he receive the lion's share of the revenue.

As for the production of *Othello*, Yul refused to discuss the matter further; in fact, he never spoke to Shdanoff again. Gregory Peck, who continued to work with Shdanoff on every role, said many years later that the cancellation of *Othello*, which had already been booked into theaters, had broken Shdanoff's heart and spirit.

Odyssey opened in Washington, D.C., in January 1975. There were many things about the production that did not work: the leading lady was too operatic for show tunes, and the adaptation from Homer by Erich Segal (author of *Love Story*) was laughably bad. The Broadway dancers playing Greek warriors were embarrassing, and the songs were forgettable. Still, for Yul it was an exhilarating and transforming experience. He delighted in the process of developing the production together with the director and the composer/producer, as well as with the rest of the cast. Though a far cry from his work with Chekhov, it was still much more creative than his recent filmmaking. And in the end, the performance he gave was remarkable. As Odysseus returning to his palace in Ithaca disguised as an old beggar, he created a touching, comical character. Comedy, as Edmund Kean noted on his deathbed, is hard; and eight shows a week is very hard. Yul brought all his dynamic energy to the effort, but it was not enough to save the show. On the road, before the musical reached Broadway, it was renamed *Home, Sweet Homer*; the cheap wordplay was not a good omen. Finally, on January 4, 1976, the production opened on Broadway and closed on the same night. The reviews, which announced the closing, were at best charitable.

But by then Yul had already made the decision to revive *The King and I*, twenty-two years after his last performance as the King of Siam.

In June 1976, Yul and a new company of *The King and I* began rehearsals in Indianapolis for the production, which was scheduled to tour for six months before opening on Broadway. The production was directed by Yuriko, the choreographer who in 1951 had danced the role of Eliza, which was now being performed by her daughter, Susan Kikuchi. The role of Mrs. Anna was played by Constance Towers, who brought great warmth to the English schoolteacher.

Shortly before rehearsals began, a precancerous growth was detected on one of Yul's vocal cords. This was scraped clean, leaving him hoarse for several days and in some pain, but by the first rehearsal, he felt terrific as he began to play the King again, and swept up in his old role, he left the other actors dumbstruck with the power of his voice. The next day Yul had no voice at all: just a deep, guttural growl with what sounded like the gurgle of blood. The next day it was worse. He was unable to speak at all during the first week of rehearsals, and the second week was no better. His vocal cords were not healing.

When I arrived in Indianapolis to visit a few days before opening night, the situation was dire. For three weeks Yul had mimed his way through rehearsals. His voice doctor insisted that he remain seventy-two hours without so much as whispering, but he had no understudy: the producers knew that audiences would not stay to see a substitute. Tickets to the final previews had been offered to the public, and any cancellation of performances could endanger the production's subsequent theater bookings.

It took a lot of gall, but I offered an unlikely solution: I would sit beside the orchestra conductor and supply the vocal performance of the King, while Yul mimed the role on stage. Having grown up backstage at the St. James Theater, I still knew every syllable and inflection, and my voice had much the same resonance and timbre as Yul's. He was unconvinced until we tried it out in his hotel suite. Then, smiling for the first time in weeks, he agreed to try it.

That night, after announcing our plan to the audience, we gave the first known father-and-son performance, and a few thousand ticketholders shared a unique moment in the theater. It was as close, perhaps, as he and I could ever become, as Yul heard his own character performed by the voice that was his legacy. Twenty-five years after the original dress rehearsal, Yul and his son created the King together, and for that one night we shared the throne of Siam.

The King and I opened on Broadway in May 1977. It was not certain how sophisticated New York audiences would respond to the first revival of a musical with its original star, and there was skepticism about whether the play would have any appeal in the disco era of *Saturday Night Fever*.

The *New York Times* led by declaring that *The King and I* was a "Reminder of a Golden Age" for New York theater. The review began:

> Yul Brynner is a great actor — or at the very least a great acting presence — not because of what he does but because of what he is. He strides on a stage caught in the invisible spotlight of his personality. He gestures, gesticulates, and moves with the certainty of an automaton and the grace of a dancer. Often he is very still, his body seemingly carved out of time. . . . He dominates . . . but also charms. He is a Genghis Khan in a Savile Row suit and a Maserati.

And how did he look a quarter of a century after his first opening night in the role? According to the *Times*, "Mr. Brynner grinning fire and snorting charm is as near to the original as makes little difference." As another reporter put it: "Mr. Brynner, who says he is fifty-six years old but appears to be in a state of eternally lean, trim fitness, said he felt more right for the part now than he did the first time around." The character of King Mongkut had always been near sixty years old, even when Yul was thirty;

so this was an actor growing into a role, not like an aging Shakespearean playing a teenage Hamlet.

Now, a whole new generation discovered Yul Brynner. Each night the audience comprised many ladies from the suburbs who had had a crush on him since 1951, but now they often brought their grown daughters, instead of their husbands, to swoon along beside them. On Wednesday matinees, the atmosphere could be positively lubricious.

Yul's health required maintenance. By this time, the back injuries he had suffered as an acrobat and the vertebrae he had cracked in 1957 while filming *The Brothers Karamazov* put him in continuous pain. His vocal cords required special care: every room he spent time in had humidifiers. And although he had stopped smoking in his early fifties, he was prone to shortness of breath. Still, he was rejuvenated as he relived, sometimes deliberately, his first rocket to stardom.

Henry Fonda and his wife Shirley rented the Brynners their brownstone on the Upper East Side. With Mia, Melody, and their nanny, it made for a warm, stable household: they had been on the road nonstop for almost three years, with rare visits to their home in Normandy. Yul needed to spend fifty weeks on the road to maintain the expensive property for his annual two-week visit. Still, it was his home, and he loved it there.

Performing eight three-hour shows a week — six nights each week, plus two matinees — involves a disciplined routine, as Jacqueline already knew. Yul's day was planned around 6 P.M., when, after a light supper, he arrived at his dressing room to begin two hours of makeup, wardrobe, and preparation, while making phone calls or watching the evening news. After the curtain came down at eleven, he would shower and meet with backstage guests before going out on the town for a few hours, burning off energy at Studio 54 or the other hot spots of the era. He would be asleep by three, and wake at eleven to a large breakfast. He would then have a few hours to take care of chores before repeating the whole routine. On tour, when matinees were on Saturday and Sunday, the company performed for twelve hours in a span of just thirty-three hours *every* weekend; and their only day off, Monday, was reserved for travel to the next city. With only a rare hiatus, that is how Yul lived for the next ten years.

• • • • • • • •

The King and I played to sold-out houses in New York for eighteen months, closing at the end of 1978; a few months later, Yul began rehearsals for an entirely new production at the Palladium Theatre in London, with British film actress Virginia McKenna as Mrs. Anna. Yul had never played his signature role in London; his last performance there had been in the short-lived *Dark Eyes* thirty years earlier. In England, the musical opened to even greater acclaim, and was included in the Royal Variety Show, at which Yul, in royal costume, greeted Queen Elizabeth II backstage.

For the next two years, Yul and Jacqueline settled into a cozy house near the Chelsea Embankment. From London, it was possible for the family to fly to Normandy by charter plane on Sunday night and return to London Tuesday. That was an especially welcome treat for Mia and Melody, then about seven and six years old, as well as for Jacqueline. For Yul, it meant visiting the dozens of pairs of white pigeons he had collected in recent years, in the luxurious *pigeonnier* he had had custom-built, and enjoying his customary enormous breakfasts in the small room he had designed for that purpose in one of the *manoir*'s fifteenth-century towers.

It was there that Yul's family gathered on July 11, 1980, to celebrate his sixtieth birthday. I was there for the occasion with my wife, Elisabeth, from our home in upstate New York, along with Victoria, 17, who still lived near the lake in Switzerland, and Jacqueline's oldest daughter, Sophie, whom Yul had always treated as his own; my sister Lark, in Austria, who visited Yul from time to time, was not with us.

Yul was not aware that 1980 marked another milestone: one hundred years earlier, Jules had established his company in Vladivostok.

During the run of the play in London, Yul became the honorary president of the International Romany Union (IRU), an organization begun almost a decade earlier that aimed to achieve political rights for the Gypsies of Europe. Until this time, Gypsies had spurned any political representation, but by refusing to trust the gaje, their situation remained perilous everywhere they roamed, from the tinkers of Ireland to the large but uncertain numbers of Central European Gypsies in Hungary, Czechoslovakia,

Romania, and beyond. Yul helped finance a school for England's tinkers and spoke out forcefully on their behalf. Working with the IRU, he helped unify Gypsy interests in Europe, aiming to persuade the UN to formally designate a Counsel for the Romany People. Before that happened, though, the different clans (Sinti, Manouche, Kaale, and Romanichels, among others) fell out with each other, achieving little.

By the time *The King and I* closed in London, Yul had spent almost seven years (since the *Odyssey* tour began) playing eight shows a week, but he was ready for more. After a few months' break, he started up a new U.S. touring company — but this time he owned the production together with his partner Mitch Leigh, composer of *Man of La Mancha*. As Yul explained it to me, they got a private bank loan for about half a million dollars with which to start the TV advertising: thirty-second spots in local markets, beginning in Washington, D.C. Money began rolling in from advance ticket sales, which after repaying the bank loan completely, raised the startup costs of the production — sets, costumes, salaries, and so forth — before opening night. It was a brilliant and unprecedented means of financing without paying interest to a bank or other lenders.

Now, as co-owner of the production he starred in, Yul felt as if he had at last freed himself from the suits, the "brown shoes," and the "financial bloodsuckers" with whom he had done battle since the start of his career. But now his boss was . . . Yul Brynner. If he were unable to perform, he would not only lose all his income, but would also have to pay the running cost of the production — the "nut" — which was about $200,000 per week. The new arrangement compelled him to keep on performing, even when the pain in his spine and legs became almost intolerable. "The show must go on" had become a merciless mandate.

Yul had taken on the traditional European role of actor-manager. In his lifetime the best known of these had been the Shakespearean Donald Wolfit, depicted in Ronald Harwood's *The Dresser*, who toured England with his own troupe, starring in every play; Yul had seen Wolfit's *Macbeth* in 1938. Michael Chekhov had also played leading roles with the Chekhov Players, which, as a touring company, was modeled upon Wolfit's. Now, once a month, Yul held corrective rehearsals for his whole cast, even after years on the road; he checked the sales of programs and T-shirts; he oversaw the company's payroll.

Like some vagabond tribe, the Kingdom of Siam once again scooted around America. In some cities, like Pittsburgh and Philadelphia, Yul was playing the King for the fifth and sixth time.

In the summer of 1981, Yul abandoned his marriage to Jacqueline; even more painfully, perhaps, he ended the friendship from which he had drawn great strength for more than a decade. He remained thoroughly devoted to their daughters, Mia and Melody.

In the continual grind of his years on the road, the Russian heritage that had suffused Yul's childhood and youth was long gone from his mind. He never picked up the guitar anymore, and he had almost no occasion to speak Russian; all the family was dead except Irena, with whom he rarely communicated after her mother Vera had died, and he was no longer on speaking terms with Shdanoff. Besides, what was there left to recall of the Russian Far East except a few dim memories? There was never any question of visiting Vladivostok. For sixty years Soviet totalitarianism had suppressed or eradicated Russia's cultural traditions, razed Orthodox cathedrals — including Uspensky, where Yul had been baptized — and renamed its cities, as if that would solve anything. What could he have found there except fear, mistrust, and a fierce denial of history?

Early in the Cold War era, the naval harbor of Vladivostok had become the base of the Soviet nuclear fleet in the Pacific, and so was declared a "closed city," one that could not be visited even by ordinary Russians, much less Western movie stars. And, *The Magnificent Seven* notwithstanding, the Communist regime was not about to invite Yul or otherwise highlight the contributions of his bourzhoy forefathers to the development of the Far East. Commemorating the Bryners might even have been construed as a crime. Now the Soviet state owned the Bryner shipping company and operated the Tetukhe mines, renamed "Dalnegorsk," which had produced critical supplies of lead for bullets during World War II.

The early 1980s were still the era of Brezhnev, successor to Khrushchev, who had succeeded Stalin: since 1928, *only these three men* had ruled the Soviet people. And they had run the country into the ground, partly with grandiose military budgets in the nuclear arms race with the United States (long before President Reagan proposed his Strategic Defense Initiative) and partly with imperial adventurism in Afghanistan, a failed foray not unlike the *aventure* of Tsar Nicholas II along the Yalu River. But Central Planning, more than any other single failure, brought down the Soviet economy, one Five-Year Plan at a time. Every business in the country had to be supervised by Moscow; even a kiosk could not be owned privately, but had to be controlled by a gargantuan Communist bureaucracy, where corruption further doomed the social experiment. This massive, totalitarian state rested upon the broken bodies of millions of Russians who had been sent to the gulag.

Like most Russians scattered around the world during the diaspora, Yul had long since renounced any hope of seeing his birthplace.

Not long after his divorce from Jacqueline, Yul married again. His fourth wife, Kathy Lee, was a twenty-five-year-old Malaysian-born dancer from the London company of *The King and I*, who by this time was performing the lead role of Eliza in the ballet of *Uncle Tom's Cabin*. They were wed in San Francisco on April 4, 1983; she brought him pleasure and comfort.

Five months later, in Los Angeles, Yul celebrated his four thousandth performance as the King, a record never equaled on the American stage. A tribute, entitled *A Toast to the King*, was planned for the occasion — a gala soirée hosted by the widows of the play's composer and playwright, Dorothy Rodgers and Dorothy Hammerstein.

That same day Yul learned he had inoperable lung cancer. A few hours later he was on stage as usual, performing the King's death scene.

Yul had smoked two to four packs of cigarettes a day from the age of twelve until he turned fifty: Gauloises, mostly, but also Old Golds and Camels. He had collected and smoked thousands of Havana cigars, and even enjoyed a prolonged phase of pipe smoking thanks to director Richard Brooks. He was always holding a cigarette in the photos he chose for his publicists to distribute to fans, and whenever possible smoked on screen as deliberately as Humphrey Bogart, who also contracted lung cancer.

The treatment chosen was radiation rather than chemotherapy. He continued performing, but ticket sales plummeted when word got out that he had cancer. He went on hiatus to see how the lung tumor, which was too near his heart to remove surgically, would respond. In the interim, he and his young bride retired to Normandy. He also visited a doctor in Bremerhaven, Germany, who prescribed a diet Yul adopted that relied heavily on carrot juice.

With all the power he had left, Yul fought a valiant battle, and when he achieved a temporary remission, he interpreted this as his conquest of cancer. His imagination joined with his willpower to convince himself that he would not succumb. His new friend Michael Jackson, who had just released the album *Thriller*, offered to co-host a party at Studio 54 to publicize Yul's "triumph over cancer" and to announce, unbelievable as it seemed, a farewell tour of *The King and I* beginning in March 1984, to be followed by a final six-month run on Broadway. At the age of sixty-three, and with inoperable lung cancer in remission, Yul went ahead with partner Mitch Leigh to schedule a further eighteen months of performance.

Lung cancer had barely changed his professional routine, or the choices he made. To concede defeat suddenly and retire to Normandy in illness, alone with his young wife who spoke no French, isolated from the television shows he was used to, the medical attention he would require, and the few friends he still enjoyed seeing: that might prove even tougher than grinding out eight shows a week. He told one journalist, "Growing up in the Far East helped me. There was an idea that you go to bed not knowing if you'll have a tomorrow and you must be thankful for every tomorrow and make the most of it. It affects everything: how carefully you listen; how you taste things. I couldn't see myself going to bed and waiting to see what would happen with my illness. I preferred to play to 2,000 or 3,000 people and standing ovations. The choice is quite simple."

As often as possible, Yul arranged visits from his daughters Mia and Melody, as well as from Victoria in Paris. He was always gentlest at these times. He made a point of being soft-spoken when I visited with him in San Francisco, and again in Boston in September. By now, his day was becoming so filled with medical rituals that — combined with six hours of makeup, performance, and cleanup — there wasn't a whole lot of time for anything else.

His makeup had become one of the hardest parts of the job: during the hour each night that he painstakingly reinvented the King's face, he felt the full weariness of four thousand performances. And surrounded by mirrors and bright lights, he was most aware of the changes taking place in his face and body. So it was in a melancholy moment while doing his makeup in Boston that Yul found my eyes in his mirror and said with a deep sigh, "You know, Rock, the only time I'm ever happy now is on stage."

But that was only part of the truth. He was doing exactly what he had chosen to do and he wouldn't have had it any other way. For me, and some others who loved him, his pain and discomfort often made it difficult to watch.

In March 1984, Yul flew from Baltimore to attend the opening of New York's Hard Rock Café. I had first introduced Yul to the Hard Rock in the early seventies in London, where I had been its manager not long after my friend Isaac Tigrett created the café with his partner, Peter Morton. Now I invited Yul to invest in the New York venture, and he graciously made the effort to participate. He spent much of that opening with Lauren Bacall, an old friend, and with Walter Cronkite, whom he had hardly seen in the thirty years since working with the CBS newsman. He also shared some laughter with Danny Akroyd, Eddie Murphy, and other contemporary young stars.

The farewell tour brought *The King and I* to the Broadway Theater for its opening night on January 7, 1985, followed by another party at the Hard Rock Café. In honor of the premiere, beacons swept the skies over the Manhattan skyline, and mounted police guarded Yul's path from the backstage door, just as they had done in 1951.

The headline in the Sunday *New York Times* read, "When an Actor Is Taken Captive by a Single Role." The article, published just before the Broadway opening, featured a full-page Hirschfeld cartoon of Yul as the King.

> Thirty-three years after originating the role, Mr. Brynner returns. . . . [He] has played on occasion to three generations of the same family — grandparents who saw the original production, parents who saw the revival in the late 1970s, and children.

> . . . And there is a note of finality, of a circle come complete . . . Mr. Brynner has called it his farewell engagement, an unsettling double-entendre, given the actor's well-publicized treatment for cancer last year. Mr. Brynner says that he is in "complete remission" now as a result of radiation therapy, and he appears remarkably robust for a man in his mid-60's, muscular in the chest and arms, his voice deep and resonant.

Reviewing the production in the *New York Times*, Frank Rich wrote that:

> Yul Brynner's performance in *The King and I* — the longest running theatrical star turn of our time — can no longer be regarded as a feat of acting or even endurance. After 30-odd years of on-and-off barnstorming . . . Mr. Brynner is, quite simply, The King. . . . Man and role have long since merged into a fixed image that is as much a part of our collective consciousness as the Statue of Liberty. One doesn't go to Mr. Brynner's "farewell engagement" at the Broadway to search for any fresh interpretive angles — heaven forbid! One goes to bow. . . . The performance is ritualistic, all right, but the high stylization the actor brings to every regal stance, arrogant hoot, and snarling declaration of "etcetera" has the timelessness of Kabuki, not the self-parody of camp.

Most of the reviews were less generous toward the production as a whole, but that did not affect ticket sales, which beat every show in town including the hottest new musical, *Cats*. And most critics agreed with the *New Yorker*'s laconic review: "Attendance is mandatory."

At the Tony Awards that spring, Yul was given a special lifetime achievement award. He did not thank the cast, or Rodgers and Hammerstein, or Chekhov and Shdanoff, or his family. His complete acceptance speech was brief. "I just want to thank Yul Brynner. He turned out pretty good after all."

The last performance of Yul's career came on June 30, 1985. It was the 4,633rd time he had played the role. For much of the audience it was a transcendent night of theater history, followed backstage by a final toast that I proposed to the cast and friends assembled afterward on stage: "Long Live the King!" The next day, before returning to his home in France, he flew to Los Angeles to visit a close friend, Edie Goetz, as she succumbed to cancer. It was a painful trip for Yul to make, physically and emotionally, and left no doubt of the devotion he still felt for a few friends. After, he and his wife Kathy flew back to Normandy.

But the following month they returned to New York to receive better treatment for his pain. He was admitted to New York Hospital in early September, where he lingered for a month. He slipped away on October 10, 1985, just over one hundred days after his last performance. His wife and most of his family were in the room. I was holding my father's hand when he died.

A few months later, the American Cancer Society began airing a public service announcement on all the networks. It featured Yul, who fixed his gaze at the camera and said, "I really wanted to make a commercial when I learned that I was that sick, saying simply, 'Now that I'm gone, I just want to tell you: Don't smoke. Whatever you do, just don't smoke.'" The commercial aired for three years, and it seems that thousands of people gave up smoking cigarettes after hearing Yul speak from beyond the grave. Twenty years later, the *New York Times* commemorated the commercial in an article entitled, "In Unforgettable Final Act, a King Got Revenge on His Killers."

Yul lived and died without regret. He had moved and inspired many millions of people, known countless beautiful women, lived in scores of magnificent homes, and earned and spent a fortune. By means of his art, Yul had crowned himself king, and was acclaimed by the world as the absolute autocrat of an illusory empire.

PART FOUR
ROCK BRYNNER

I'm only everyone I've ever known . . .

— Red Hat the Clown (1972)

The odyssey that began with Jules Bryner did not end with my father.

Most of my childhood was spent traveling. I was seven when we went on the road with *The King and I*, but we had already traveled with *Lute Song*, including to London when I was two; that is where I first began to speak, with a British accent. Still, "home" referred to the Upper West Side of Manhattan. That is where I began school and where I gained an undeserved reputation as a prodigy, primarily because I was good enough at chess to win a few games against the old men who played in Central Park, delighting my dad.

My mother goaded my curiosity about the world in every way she could, and as an only child, I was a voracious young reader. She encouraged all my explorations to teach me that I could learn anything I wanted. As a toddler watching Yul build furniture, I had a fascination with tools, so my mother bought broken radios from a secondhand store, and I spent hours taking them apart; by the age of eight, with help from my aunt Vera's husband, I assembled a Heathkit transceiver and earned my novice license as a ham radio operator, able to communicate instantly with friends and strangers around the world, forty years before the Internet made that commonplace.

I loved hearing my father singing with his guitar. The mysterious Gypsy language reminded me how different his childhood was from my own, the same realization made by millions of immigrants' children. When I was six years old, I performed with a group of children on television's cultural magazine, *Omnibus*, when renowned maestro Leopold Stokowski conducted an orchestra of children in Haydn's *Toy Symphony*: I was charged with playing the cuckoo (ocharina) prominently featured in the score. As reported in the *Daily News* the next day, Rocky "brazenly informed the temperamental maestro that . . . the cuckoo would sound more convincing in a lower register." Stokowski shrugged when I "tendered this musical lèse-majesté. 'You think this would sound better?' asked Stokowski, trying hard not to grit his teeth. 'Maybe it wouldn't,' said Rocky calmly, 'but it sure would be a lot easier to play.' 'That will be fine,' he said, handing it back to the triumphant Rocky." Yul could not have been prouder.

My nickname, "Rocky," was acquired on my first day at school. The bus driver who picked me up at the corner of Central Park West and 104th Street asked Virginia my name. She worried that "Yul" would seem too exotic in a busload of kids named Johnny and Billy and Bruce, and that, because I was younger than the other boys, I would be a target for bullies; so she told the driver I was called Rocky, after former middleweight champion Rocky Graziano, and since I liked the name, I kept it. Decades later I got to know Graziano, born Rocco Barbella, a sweet and funny man who had heard that I was named after him; he, in turn, had been named after San Rocco, a fourteenth-century saint.

Like most post-war babies, I was raised by the book, and the book was by Dr. Benjamin Spock, who helped raise an entire generation . . . and later repudiated his approach to parenting as overindulgent. Virginia was devoted to me and to her responsibilities as a mother beyond anything else, and she did her best to provide me with a conventional American upbringing in public schools and with experiences that would resemble my classmates': Coney Island, summer camp, bowling. Yul, on the other hand, wanted me to have the most exceptional upbringing possible — to see and do amazing things, and to know the most interesting and influential people — so I was included in most social occasions and grew accustomed to being the only child in a room full of adults, with whom I soon interacted more comfortably than with kids. Mature behavior was my ticket to adult company and praise, which, apparently, was just what I wanted.

I understood that my parents were creative artists who played characters on the stage. I had a better sense of what that meant after seeing *The King and I* in a theater filled with adults shrinking from my father's ferocity and sobbing at his death. I saw the impact he had upon the crowds at the stage door, and I was as proud of my father's accomplishments as any other son. Since he took all the commotion for granted, so, naturally, did I.

We lived just eight blocks away from my aunt Vera, who, with her husband Roy, usually cared for me when my parents were traveling. Vera told me about her childhood and Yul's, and I learned the foreign names of Vladivostok, Sidemy, and Harbin. My aunt confirmed many of my father's least believable stories: how the longest railway in the world stopped in front of their house; about tiger hunts, and the circus, and the Gypsies in nightclubs with whom he sang. She taught me a little more Russian every time I visited, and explained to me about the tsar and the Bolshevik Revolution, and how my grandfather had been imprisoned by the Soviets. When she performed the title role in *Carmen* in television's first broadcast opera, I was there in the studio. Vera showed me great love throughout my childhood, and I always looked forward to visiting her . . . until my father stopped speaking to her because of the *Newsweek* interview in which she debunked his fictional history. That was when I stopped speaking to her, too, out of loyalty to my dad: it broke my heart, and hers, but I apparently needed to demonstrate that I could be as cold and manly as my father.

When Vera wasn't free to look after me, I spent time with Don Lawson, Yul's valet, and sometimes with the dramatic blonde German woman who was very entertaining when she cooked my favorite dish, potato soup. I learned that her name was Marlene Dietrich . . . and that I must never mention her to my mother.

It seemed as if the life awaiting me was some kind of fable, a parable that meant something. I hope that all kids feel the same, and I know many who do; like everyone else, I had to figure out just what myth it was that I was meant to incarnate. Yul had always taught me to think on a grand scale, and because he was taken for King, I was often taken for Prince. I was six when I asked him about Buddha, to whom the king of Siam prayed each night on stage. It's not surprising that I identified with the tale my father told me: Prince Buddha was raised in a palace where all misery, poverty, and disease had been eliminated. One day, from the palace wall, the prince saw a diseased beggar on the street; baffled, he could not understand why there was suffering and deprivation in the world. So, with only a beggar's bowl and the clothes on his back, the prince set out from his father's palace to begin a journey to wisdom and to learn about the world.

I was seven when we set out across the country with *The King and I.* When we weren't on the train, we were living in hotel rooms, which soon became, for me, more "normal" than a home. My mother took me all over each city, from the Mormon Tabernacle in Salt Lake City to the Schlitz plant in Milwaukee (she couldn't find much else for us to do there); I fished for trout outside Denver and explored the Museum of Science and Industry in Chicago; I learned about cattle at the Texas State Fair and saber-toothed tigers at the La Brea Tar Pits; and everywhere we went, we water-skied. Through the unofficial headquarters of this new sport in Cypress Gardens, Florida, Yul could always find local fanatics who invited us to ski on lakes or rivers around the country, providing a spectacular introduction to the variety and grandeur of the United States.

We spent the summer of 1956 — Yul's *annus mirabilis* — in Paris and Saint-Jean-de-Luz, in the Basque region, and by autumn I could speak some awkward French. I also saw London for a week, during which Yul was presented to Queen Elizabeth II for the first time, at the British premiere of *The King and I.* More and more I noticed how often my father was treated like actual royalty. To me, he was something much greater than a king: he was an artist. I knew that that was not a title that could be handed down, but then, I never wanted to be king, or even a star. I wanted to become a writer.

I was nine years old when I was sent to boarding school. My parents could not have made a better choice for my education; nonetheless, to an overprivileged only child, boarding school seemed tantamount to banishment, like reform school. The day my mother left me there, something inside of me went cold for years to come. I spent the first week in a state of betrayed solitude and abandonment. Eventually I came to love Chadwick School, where I made many friends, but the sense of betrayal lingered.

Many of the students at Chadwick School were also Hollywood brats, including Liza Minnelli, who was my age and had lived a similarly disjointed childhood on the road. Liza was the first girl I ever kissed, as we danced to "Tammy"; years later we learned that while Yul was on tour with *Lute Song* he had had an affair with her mother, Judy Garland. Together, Liza and I were watched with fascination by adults.

Culturally, I was a typical baby-boomer kid who loved Elvis Presley and

James Dean and Marilyn Monroe; the difference was that I had actually met them — each at the peak of fame that, in different ways, killed all three. In fact, I could meet almost anyone I wanted, because my devoted dad was not above using his fame for my benefit. When I read Neville Shute's novel *On the Beach*, its description of a post-nuclear world left me badly shaken; after Yul made a few phone calls, a three-star air force general turned up for dinner at our house. General Bernard Shreiver was attached to the Strategic Air Command and oversaw the air force's development of intercontinental ballistic missiles. He was delighted to have dinner at Yul Brynner's home, even if it meant being grilled by his precocious ten-year-old son. In April 1958, Van Cliburn won the Moscow International Tchaikovsky Piano Competition and became my musical hero: I loved Russian culture as much as I feared Soviet bombs. By August, Van Cliburn was in our living room, playing Tchaikovsky on my small spinet.

At the end of my parents' marriage, when I was eleven, I wrapped myself in protective layers of sophistication: most of my school friends were children of divorce, and it seemed like a club I was sure to join. I didn't believe anyone would have been better off if my parents had stayed together, but what their divorce would mean for my own life was uncertain.

At thirty-eight, Virginia was a doting single mother, a sensitive intellectual, and a functional alcoholic struggling to maintain a facade of sobriety. When Yul left her for his new life in Europe, she returned to New York City to resume her career on Broadway, where she co-starred with Henry Fonda in *Critic's Choice*. I was in boarding school, thousands of miles from any family. Because of my mature demeanor, everyone assumed I could handle the situation; so did I. On long weekends my surrogate home was with film composer Alex North (*A Streetcar Named Desire*, *Cleopatra*, *Who's Afraid of Virginia Woolf?*) and his wife, Sherle. Since their son Steve was away at the International School of Geneva, his room became my own. I was actually relieved to be away from my mother, who was often morose, angry, and tearful, and who drank too much in the evenings. It was hardly a coincidence that, soon after my twelfth birthday, I started drinking too, on the sly: at the Norths' home there was a perpetual party and a broad selection of drinks to sample. Besides, both my parents and all their friends drank heavily. So whether or not I was born with an extra quart of champagne in my blood, I knew that I wanted to drink like my dad.

The choice I had to make at thirteen was between my stable, delightful father in Europe or my impaired mother in New York; finally I persuaded Virginia to allow me to transfer to the International School of Geneva, where I entered tenth grade. The International School was founded in 1924 to accommodate children of the first diplomats at the Geneva-based League of Nations, forerunner of the United Nations. The student body truly was international, and the atmosphere was distinctly more mature and cosmopolitan than at American high schools. Europe was still a deadly serious place: when I settled there, it was just fifteen years after the Third Reich ended. Our Student United Nations was conducted in the actual chamber of the League of Nation's original Assembly, complete with simultaneous translators. Living side by side with children from around the world completely dissolves stereotypes and prejudices, as they are proven erroneous day after day.

My three years there nurtured a great burst of intellectual growth, thanks largely to the influential teaching of an Australian-born aesthete named John Mawson. By the end of the fifth form (eleventh grade), Chaucer, Shakespeare, Blake, Sterne, Wilde, and Ibsen had become unintimidating and accessible. I dived into Dante and Pirandello, Goethe and Mann, Rabelais and Camus . . . and Cocteau, my self-appointed godfather. I read Shakespeare and Joyce, and became devoted to the work of Samuel Beckett after seeing the premiere production of *Fin de Partie* (*Endgame*) with actor Roger Blin, to whom Beckett had dedicated the play. Most of the time I spoke French, and I eventually changed the spelling of my name to "Roc," which was more conventional in Europe.

I was soon fully settled in Switzerland, and considered it my only home. Thanks to Jules, I was even entitled to a Swiss passport, just for the asking. Once or twice a year I visited my mother in New York, though these were often dreary, angry get-togethers that left us both emotionally drained: by seven in the evening, after her second glass of wine, my mother became bitter and hostile; often I provoked her subtly and in general I handled these situations hurtfully. Out of solidarity with my dad, I continued to reject my aunt Vera and did not see her again until she was on her deathbed. My rejection — my otrecheniye — of this delightful, loving woman who had helped raise me hurt her terribly, and the thought of it still shames me. But at the time, it was easy, since I had already been forced to exile my mother from my heart, because of her drinking.

I tried to spend all my vacations with my father and his friends, and by the time I left high school, I'd already taken a big bite out of life and let the juices run down my chin. I had been with Sinatra in the studio when he recorded with Count Basie, discussed Tchaikovsky with Van Cliburn, and received metaphysical advice from Jean Cocteau. At fifteen I had been seduced by the wife of a famous Caribbean playboy, and given my heart to Suzy Parker, Coco Chanel's protégée and the world's first supermodel; at twenty-nine, Suzy delicately declined my passion, but gave me her heartfelt friendship for many years. I had swapped jokes with Milton Berle, poured drinks for the Rat Pack, and been the designated driver for a Mafia don.

"Sam Giancana was one of the most powerful criminals of the mid-twentieth century," according to Sinatra biographer Anthony Summers. First arrested for murder at eighteen, by the 1940s Giancana was right-hand man to Al Capone's heir, Tony "The Big Tuna" Accardo. In those days, "the Chicago crime empire controlled myriad clubs, jukebox rackets, elements of the movie industry, gambling in Las Vegas, and enterprises in Cuba. And in 1957, when Accardo stepped aside, the power passed to Giancana." Five years later, I spent Christmas with my father in Acapulco at a "house party" in the pink-and-white bungalows of the Las Brisas Hilton, organized by Sinatra. One of those invited was a fellow who called himself Dr. Moony, a crude, ugly man, then fifty-two years old. We all knew he was Giancana.

On New Year's Eve, all the guests flew to Merle Oberon's home in Cuernavaca; since I chose not to go and Giancana was not invited, I was recruited to drive "Dr. Moony" around the clubs of Acapulco, looking for loose women. At sixteen, without a learner's permit (what the hell, this was Mexico), I was still clumsy with the stick shift of the pink-and-white hotel jeep — especially after a few drinks. Grinding the gears mercilessly, I damn near killed the Mafia don by bashing his head against the windshield a half dozen times. Still, Giancana pretended to like me, and I was grateful for that . . . and even more grateful that I never saw him again.

• • • • • • • •

After graduating from the International School, my first choice was to attend Trinity College, Dublin, where Samuel Beckett had studied. But I had also been accepted at Yale University, and so I enrolled there in the fall of 1963, when I was sixteen years old. Yale was still an all-male school that year, when Kingman Brewster became the university president. From the time I arrived back in the United States, I was technically under my mother's uncertain authority, which did not bode well. But if my experience at Yale was not a happy one, that was mostly because of my own snobbish immaturity.

Less than three months after I arrived, President Kennedy was assassinated. I was in a friend's dorm room that Friday afternoon, and because the radio was on, we heard the news from Dallas instantly. Within minutes, as I crossed the campus, young men sat weeping on the cold ground. But some Yalies cheered, aping their families' conservative attitudes; others seemed mostly annoyed that the Harvard-Yale football game that weekend was canceled.

The initial assumption was that the Soviets had ordered the assassination, probably in connection with the Cuban missile crisis the previous year that had undermined Khrushchev's authority with Stalinist hard-liners. Lee Harvey Oswald's experience in the USSR was soon reported in the press, and for a time it seemed likely that President Johnson would retaliate, possibly triggering an all-out nuclear exchange. It was all the more unsettling when, that Sunday afternoon, millions of us were watching on live television when Jack Ruby shot Oswald to death.

The next day I applied to transfer to Trinity College, Dublin. I was accepted there for the following autumn. I had felt alienated in the United States after six years in Europe, and the assassination of JFK, while not the decisive factor, prompted me to recoil from the violent disposition that seemed inherent in American culture; after all, no Swiss leaders had been assassinated lately. Whatever the concoction of personal and cultural motives that took me back to Europe, I did not expect to live in the United States again.

I have always been driven by an insatiable and often indiscriminate curiosity. And it seems I never did anything the right way until I had first explored every possible alternative. I never aimed to become rich or famous, though I probably expected my achievements to assure it; what I wanted was to experience *everything*, and not only from the limited perspective of a movie star's son. I wanted to become not only a writer, but a Renaissance man, pretentious as that sounds, knowledgeable about myriad things, like the Russian intelligentsiya I had learned about as a child. My biggest obstacle was that I didn't have the first clue about how the *real* world — out there beyond theater, literature, and Hollywood — operated. For all the intellectual abstractions that filled my head, it would be years before I could go out and find an ordinary job and pay my own rent.

I had chosen Trinity College because of the writers who had studied there: Jonathan Swift, Lawrence Sterne, Oscar Wilde, and J. P. Donleavy, whose recent novel *The Ginger Man* painted a picture of earthy ribaldry at Trinity that appealed to the budding alcoholic in me; and most of all Samuel Beckett, whose novels and plays were so inspiring they left me mute. Dissimilar as these authors are, their fiction shares a fierce humanism and ironic detachment that reaffirms proudly, in the lilting phrases of the Celtic heritage, that where there's life, there's mud. The shadows of Yeats, Synge, O'Casey, and Behan (recently deceased, from the bottle) still enlivened the Dublin pubs where, like most everyone, I spent hours each day. Even the newsboys who shouted the headlines were poets, and the *Irish Times* had a weekly column by one of the greatest comic novelists of all time, Flann O'Brien (*The Third Policeman*, *At Swim-Two-Birds*), under the byline "Myles na Gopaleen." Self-invented eccentrics from every social stratum haunted the streets, each one rich in passionate convictions and personal dramas, most of them living from farthing to farthing. Dublin was a far cry from Yale and from Hollywood.

The Ireland I knew was an endless carnival of gritty roustabouts and epic poets, down-and-out philosophers, God-fearing fanatics, and bitter *raconteurs* sipping poteen from shaky hands. In 1964, Ireland was still trapped in a post-war economy: Woodbine cigarettes could be bought one at a time from barrels, and a woman with a cow was selling fresh milk just off Grafton Street. It was still respectable to have a drink or two in the morning; not a few did, and that included me at seventeen, stopping on my way to class from student digs in Rathgar, and later from a mews behind Fitzwilliam Square. I knew my way around Dublin before even I arrived, just from a close reading of *Ulysses*.

I entered the Trinity honors program known as Mental and Moral Science, studying philosophy exclusively. I did not major in literature because I was doing that anyway; hell, I was living it. For four years I read the philosophers intently, concentrating especially on the immaterialism of Berkeley (a Trinity alumnus), the categories of Kant, and the dynamics of dialectic (winning the McCran Prize for Hegelian studies).

My mother visited me for a horrific stay, the only time we drank seriously together, with my friends, at Bailey's, Neary's, McDaid's, and the Old Stand. The experience of seeing her eighteen-year-old son drunk every evening left my mother distraught and afraid, and the impact altered her life. A few weeks thereafter she began her recovery at a meeting of Alcoholics Anonymous. As her future unfolded, one day at a time, she never had another drink in her life.

A few months after arriving in Dublin, I had a nervous breakdown, caused either by the pressure of exams or alcohol poisoning, or both. I was treated at the Clinique Cécile in Lausanne, near the place where my father was detoxified for opium when he was also seventeen. Returning to university, and supplied with a brand-new drug called Valium, I modulated my lifestyle into something more sustainable and applied myself diligently to Wittgenstein, Heidegger, and the early structuralists.

By 1964, the Cold War had found its expression in a proxy war in Vietnam between a Communist insurgency in the south fought by the North

Vietnamese Army and their best-trained troops, the Viet Cong — formerly the Viet Minh, who had defeated the French in 1954 at Dien Bien Phu; they were equipped and supplied by the Soviet Union, under Leonid Brezhnev, and by Communist China under Mao Tse-tung. Presidents Eisenhower and Kennedy had progressively increased the number of U.S. military "advisers." In August 1964, President Johnson, facing re-election against the ultra-hawkish Republican Senator Barry Goldwater, rushed the Gulf of Tonkin resolution through Congress, based upon distorted information about an attack on a U.S. ship; contravening the U.S. Constitution, this allowed U.S. troops to "repel any armed attack against the forces of the United States" without a congressional declaration of war. Thereupon, the Johnson administration increased the U.S. troop commitment in 1964, and again the following year. In October 1965, the first major engagement of U.S. troops began at Ia Drang, as described in the book (and the Mel Gibson film) *We Were Soldiers Once . . . and Young*.

One month later in Dublin, I received orders from the U.S. Selective Service to report to a base in Germany for a physical exam, after which I would be inducted into the army. The automatic college deferment from military service did not apply to philosophy students enrolled in universities overseas. I had applied for and been denied conscientious objector status. The choices before me were the same that millions of Americans faced: either to be inducted and, in all likelihood, sent to Vietnam, or to refuse induction and face criminal trial if I ever returned to the United States to visit my mother.

But because of Jules Bryner, I had one other choice. By the Swiss law of "paternal privilege," I could revert to Swiss nationality and renounce my U.S. citizenship, exactly as my father had done six months earlier. For most people, nationality is an inherent component of their being and identity. Given Yul's background and adopted Gypsy traditions, it's not surprising that he perceived nationality as little more than gaje paperwork, of no real meaning. As a devoted teenage son, I could not feel differently.

I would be proud today to claim that I was among the earliest anti-war draft resisters or "refuseniks," many of whom fled to Canada and were granted amnesty by President Carter in the 1970s, but I would be lying. After the first battle at Ia Drang, there wasn't even a war yet, much less an anti-war movement. My reasons for refusing to fight were complicated, but they were not ideological. The most salient reason was simply that I was terrified. I was more afraid of failing out of boot camp and humiliating myself and my renowned father than I was of dying in Vietnam. I was not merely accustomed to the soft life, I was dependent upon it. By then I was smoking three packs of Gauloises a day and drinking much more than anyone knew. But it was also true that Switzerland, not the United States, had been home to me and my father since I was twelve years old.

In December 1965, shortly before my nineteenth birthday and just after receiving my first Swiss passport, I went to the U.S. embassy in Bern, Switzerland, and formally renounced my U.S. citizenship. I explained, exactly as my father had done in the same office earlier that year, that I wanted to have the same passport as my father, in the event of war; as far as that went, it was true.

In Paris, I came to know an editor named George Belmont who had been close friends with Samuel Beckett since the late 1920s, when they had attended Trinity College and the Ecole Normale Supérieure together. One afternoon, when I met with George near the Jardin du Luxembourg, Beckett showed up and joined us for lunch.

Beckett was above all else a sensitive, compassionate man who could not bear to be ungracious, even to the admirers who stalked him near his apartment on Boulevard Saint-Jacques. This was three years before he was awarded the Nobel Prize for literature, but he was already "damned to fame," in his own words, something he handled very differently from my father. He was especially considerate to young idolaters, like myself, because he had been one himself, in utter awe of James Joyce. Over lunch, I learned that Joyce had given Beckett a pair of his shoes, which the younger man often wore for inspiration on his long walks through Dublin at night, before hobbling home . . . because Joyce's shoes were much too narrow for his feet. Many of Beckett's sad-sack heroes, starting in *Waiting for Godot*, suffer from shoes that pinch.

Sam, as he was known, was eager to hear the results of Trinity's latest cricket match, but I had to disappoint him: I had no idea. He was also interested in the productions we were mounting at the Trinity Players Theatre, where I was preparing to direct *Marat/Sade*, and he sent his greetings to various professors whom he had known, especially Skeffington and French. At fifty-nine, Beckett's craggy, weathered looks owed much to the years in the French Resistance that he never discussed, sleeping rough in farmhouses of the Vaucluse, always on the run. Serious as he was, he was also gently playful, though even his laughter hinted at the bleak metaphysical outlook that he could not help but espouse. I learned over lunch that he kept on his writing desk this handwritten admonition: FAIL. FAIL AGAIN. *FAIL BETTER*. Most of all, the kindness in Beckett's silver eyes and the warmth of his voice were genuinely encouraging.

In 1968, when he learned he'd won the Nobel Prize, Beckett was in his country house, which was surrounded by reporters. He called George Belmont for advice, crouching below his window where he couldn't be seen. Shunning recognition, he was also one of the only Nobel winners in history to decline to attend the ceremony in Stockholm. And despite all the attention he received, he ever remained compassionate toward his fellow man.

This was the age of the Beatles and the "English Invasion" of popular music by the Animals, the Who, Clapton (still with the Yardbirds), and of course the Rolling Stones. I remained devoted exclusively to classical music . . . until May 1966, when Bob Dylan played the Adelphi Theatre in Dublin. After the intermission, he was joined by a band — actually, The Band, including guitarist Robbie Robertson. I'd heard Dylan, of course; by then everyone had. A week before I entered Yale, the poet and folksinger from Hibbing, Minnesota, was the "opening act" for Dr. Martin Luther King, Jr.'s speech, "I Have a Dream," at the March on Washington. Like most people, I was awed by his lyrics but I couldn't stand his voice. There were other folksingers like Dave van Ronk and Ramblin' Jack Elliott whom I liked better. Until that night.

This was just before the Royal Albert Hall concert, and Dylan was performing new songs from *Highway 61 Revisited* and *Blonde on Blonde*, mostly solo, including "Visions of Johanna," "Desolation Row," and "Mr. Tambourine Man." Now I finally got it: he was a poet, uniquely gifted, who had turned to rock 'n' roll because it expressed our culture; if this had been the age of Mozart, Dylan might have gone with the minuet. He was still writing folk songs, mostly narratives with a plot; but the folk that these songs were about inhabited an urban culture of rock 'n' roll, and Dylan was talking to them — to us — where we lived. I also finally understood that he was a *brilliant* singer: his delivery and phrasing were as deliberate and expressive as Dietrich Fischer-Dieskau's, but what he was expressing was very different, and for those snarling, biting lyrics, his timbre was exactly right. Complaining about his voice was like criticizing the penmanship in a suicide note. He was, as Robbie Robertson once put it, "a powerful singer and a great musical actor with many characters in his voice. . . . the rebel rebelling against the rebellion." A lot of folkies that night were booing Dylan's conversion to rock 'n' roll, as they'd done throughout this world tour, but I was thunderstruck. "Like a Rolling Stone" spoke directly to millions of pampered college kids with a self-important sense of entitlement, much like myself.

After the concert, I crashed a party at the Gresham Hotel where the musicians were staying and spent an hour chatting with bass player Rick Danko and pianist Richard Manuel, though I didn't know their names yet. Dylan came and left, radiating weird vibes, and I didn't talk to him. A month later, he had a motorcycle accident in Woodstock, New York, and he never again sang those songs that way. During the months he spent in a hammock mending his injured spine, his band started recording without him, producing the songs that would become *Music from Big Pink* and the eponymous *The Band*. At nineteen, listening to those musicians in Dublin, I could never have dreamed that a decade later I would play a key role in their final performance together.

I was also ushered into the "youth revolution" through my friendship with Tara Browne, a member of the Guinness family of Ireland and Britain, producers of Guinness stout. Through him I became acquainted with "swinging London" *before* it turned into a cheap parody of itself. Tara was an effete, aristocratic type with curly blond hair and a knowing smile. By the age of twenty, through his investments in small businesses, he was widely credited with fostering the Mod foppery that was key to the King's Road fashions, from the Chelsea Antique Market to Granny Takes a Trip. It was Tara who first shared hashish with John Lennon and the Beatles, and I hadn't known him more than a day before I was smoking it myself for the first time. It was new and different, but as much as I liked it, it couldn't replace alcohol.

In London I often stayed with Tara and his wife, Nicky, in Eaton Row, and I came to know a number of their friends; eventually I decided to settle there after university. By then Carnaby Street had already turned into a tasteless conspiracy of knock-off fashions for tourists, but in 1967, London was still, well, groovy. It was at Sybilla's, a club Tara had invested in, that Yul and I got stoned on marijuana together for the first time, and became friends with Ringo Starr of the Beatles and Brian Jones of the Rolling Stones.

Two years after we met, Tara died in an accident at the wheel of his Lotus. On their next album, *Sgt. Pepper's Lonely Hearts Club Band*, the Beatles paid tribute to his short, swift life with "A Day in the Life": Tara had indeed blown his mind out in a car when he didn't notice that the lights had changed.

As deeply as Tara's death affected me, I did not recognize it as a warning.

When I turned twenty-one in Palm Springs, California, Frank Sinatra threw a party and sang "Happy Birthday." It was 1967, and Yul and I were there for Christmas. Sinatra then sent me in his Learjet to Las Vegas, where Sammy Davis, Jr., was performing. Sammy toasted me from the stage, and when I got to my hotel room near dawn, there were two attractive young women waiting — Sammy's "birthday presents," they explained. It was one hell of a way to become an adult.

But the most enduring gift came from my father: a compressed two weeks of daily acting lessons with George Shdanoff. I had asked Yul for this opportunity not because I wanted a career as an actor, but to consolidate what I had learned growing up in the theater and directing in Dublin. I had read Chekhov's *To the Actor*, which was dedicated to Shdanoff, and I wanted to understand how to make use of what he taught. With Shdanoff I studied the principles of drama, along with concrete techniques for exercising the imagination to discover and express a character's fundamental nature and deepest motives. The gruff, magical George Shdanoff, who had worked with Stanislavsky, Meyerhold, and Reinhardt, as well as Chekhov, had an uncompromising belief in the power of the theater to transform souls.

With my degree in philosophy, I settled in London in 1968, and in the absence of any "Philosopher Wanted" ads in the classifieds, began working on an idea I'd had, a play based upon Jean Cocteau's *Opium, Journal of a Cure.* In the early 1930s he had kept this journal during his detoxification in a clinic, describing addiction and withdrawal, along with the bohemian life of Paris in that era. Ironically, it was the failure of his detoxification that led him to my father, from whom he began buying his opium. I translated and adapted the notebook into a play for one character that I would perform myself, first in the familiar setting of the Dublin Theatre Festival. The director who helped transform the text into real theater was Ranald Graham, my closest friend from Trinity.

The Dublin premiere received terrific reviews, but what mattered to me most that night was how my professional debut took Yul by complete surprise. As a show of support, he brought half a dozen close friends from Paris to see the two-hour performance. He was completely astonished as he watched me, alone on a mostly bare stage, playing his old friend, with whom he himself had smoked opium, performed according to the principles of his own mentor, Chekhov.

Three months later I performed *Opium* at the Hamstead Theatre Club in London. Yul, feeling very much the proud father, made all our friends aware of the production. I received opening-night telegrams welcoming me to the acting profession from Elizabeth Taylor and Richard Burton, Frank Sinatra, Kirk Douglas, Julie Christie, Warren Beatty, Faye Dunaway, and my lifelong friend, Liza Minnelli.

The social world I inhabited briefly included many of the elite young artists of London who were not only raising the cultural profile of Britain, they were changing its balance of trade. I spent several days with Keith Richards while he was working up the riffs on *Let It Bleed*; with Ringo Starr and his wife, Maureen; and on the Burtons' yacht in the Thames River (where their dogs could stay with them without six-months' quarantine). At Kenneth Tynan's weekly *salon*, I spent time with playwright Tom Stoppard, director Michelangelo Antonioni, folksinger Arlo Guthrie, actress Ava Gardner, and Princess Margaret, sister of Queen Elizabeth II; and that was just one evening at the Tynans'.

In October 1970, *Opium, Journal of A Cure* opened on Broadway at the Edison Theatre, just blocks away from where my father had performed in *Twelfth Night*, *Lute Song*, and *The King and I*; because it was an established production from Europe, I was allowed a U.S. work permit. At twenty-three, I was alone on stage performing a play I had written. Yul couldn't attend my opening night this time: he was shooting a film in Yugoslavia, where I phoned him to read the *New York Times* review, which called the production "an excursion into a man's central nervous system, viscera and soul. . . . Brynner impressed one with this sensitively observed portrait of the artist as a young addict. . . . An evening of distinctive interest."

Most of the reviews, however, were not so kind, and ticket sales remained flat. The play closed after twenty performances. As impresario Sol Hurok once said, "When the audience doesn't want to see your show, you can't stop 'em."

I returned to London devastated, having anticipated only triumph as young men are wont to do. I had sublet the mews house I rented near Sloane Square, and though I had some monthly support from my father, reality quickly set in: without a work permit, I was not going to find employment — without which, I could not get a work permit. The same was true everywhere but Switzerland, where I no longer had a home. I had put myself in this situation, and I was beginning to learn that when you shoot yourself in the foot, it hurts every bit as much. I had achieved something remarkable with *Opium*, but I really had no interest in becoming a second-generation star. Many of my Hollywood cohorts did just that: Jane and Peter Fonda, Liza Minnelli, Michael Douglas, Jamie Lee Curtis, Carrie Fisher, and others. But that was never my ambition. In fact, I wanted to remove myself as far as possible from that world.

Having spent my young life in the milieu of Yul's fame and wealth, I set out on my own as a street performer and spiritual pilgrim named Red Hat the Clown: a long-haired, wandering minstrel with a large hoop earring, a twelve-string guitar, and a Victorian doctor's bag containing "the first step toward solving any problem in the world" (the *I Ching*, the *Whole Earth Catalog*, a ball of string, a bottle cutter, green tea, and marijuana). I tried to adhere to a few strict rules: to hurt no one, to spread laughter and warmth, and to free myself from the blessings and burdens of being a movie star's son. Even my drinking retreated into temporary remission. I was an anonymous hippie, learning how the world lived and worked. Through Red Hat, I became a character of the streets, a "ragged clown" in search of a Tambourine Man . . . the global village idiot.

My ambition was still to become a Renaissance man, but now I needed to leave behind the ivory tower. I wanted the life experience that would make me a jack-of-all-trades, one of those people who could survive by his wits whichever way the breezes blew.

Having tuned in, turned on, and dropped out, at twenty-four I hit the worldwide trail of vagabonds and urchins. A creature of my own imagination, living by a set of half-cocked principles and half-crocked notions. But by renouncing my own identity — otrecheniye — I broke free from the safety of my father's enchanted kingdom and, for the first time, felt relieved of adult responsibilities. As Tom Robbins wrote, "It's never too late to have a happy childhood."

The "red hat" was a maroon Borsalino, and when asked why I always wore a hat, I explained that it was good for my head. I carried all the exotic paraphernalia of a Euro-hippie: loose white garb, henna-red hair, patchouli, Tibetan prayer bells, twelve-string guitar, and an appetite for six-paper, London-style joints. I drank only a little wine and lived on a vegan diet. I stayed with old friends and new, most of whom I met through a network of vagabonds, and earned whatever cash I needed day by day. With my bottle cutter I could transform a dozen empty wine bottles into handsome glass mugs in under an hour: I used the proceeds at a flea market to buy old silverware — dinner forks — and over a fire curled their tines outward, then hammered them into bracelets; these could be traded for large silk scarves, which I stitched into a "Gypsy dress" that I could sell for a few hundred francs. When I was ready to move on, most often I just stuck out my thumb.

I traveled south, staying mostly in small towns and villages through France and Switzerland, Spain and Morocco, and back through Italy, planting California wildflowers all along my crooked trail. As Red Hat the Clown I traveled across the United States on a visitor's visa, taking a variety of menial jobs and driving scores of trucks, vans, buses, and last-gasp jalopies. Along the way, I had a few other jobs, too, including the most unlikely of all: I became Muhammad Ali's bodyguard.

In 1971, I briefly joined the European leg of the Rolling Stones tour as a roadie, driving equipment from Paris to Zurich. The concert organizer in

Switzerland, Hans-Rudi Jaggi, wanted to promote a fight there for Muhammad Ali, but didn't speak enough English to make the offer, so he recruited me. A week later I was at the Houston Astrodome meeting one of my greatest heroes.

Yul and I had rooted for Cassius Clay to win the Olympic gold medal in 1960, and in 1964, when the odds were 7–1 against him, I had bet a month's allowance that he'd win the title from Sonny Liston. And I had cheered him in 1967, when he was stripped of his title and his boxing license for refusing induction into the U.S. Army. Ali had been denied conscientious objector status while insisting that he was exempt from military service as a Muslim minister, observing that "No Viet Cong ever called me 'nigger.'" In sworn testimony that the U.S. Supreme Court later cited in its decision, Ali had pulled no punches.

> The Government has admitted that the police of Los Angeles were wrong about attacking and killing our brothers and sisters and they were wrong in Newark, New Jersey, and they were wrong in Louisiana, and the outright, everyday oppressors and enemies are the people as a whole, the whites of this nation. So, we are not, according to the Holy Qur'an, to even as much as aid in passing a cup of water to them, even a wounded. I mean this is in the Holy Qur'an, and as I said earlier this is not me talking to "get" the draft board, or to dodge nothin'. This is there before I was borned and it will be there when I'm dead but we believe in not only that part of it, but all of it.

On June 28, 1971, the U.S. Supreme Court ruled in *Cassius Clay aka Ali v. United States* that Muhammad Ali had indeed been legitimately entitled to the status of conscientious objector, and that the Selective Service had been misled by the Department of Justice in this matter. "It is indisputably clear," read the judgment, "that the Department was simply wrong as a matter of law in advising that the petitioner's beliefs were not religiously based and were not sincerely held."

The moment the Supreme Court decision was handed down, Ali's boxing license was restored. The first step toward Ali's attempt to regain the heavyweight title was organized at the Houston Astrodome a month later against Jimmy Ellis; it was in that Texas setting that I arrived in full hippie regalia to propose a Zurich fight.

The man who had made our meeting possible was Harold Conrad, a historic promoter and booster in the boxing world, going back to the days of his personal mentor, Damon Runyan. I got in touch with him from Zurich. Harold, who had put together a number of fights for Ali, arranged for me to sit down with Herbert Muhammad, Muhammad's principle business manager. Herbert was a son of the founder of the Nation of Islam, Elijah Muhammad, who had first inspired both Malcolm X and Muhammad Ali to join the Muslim faith. It took several days for the meeting to transpire, and three minutes to conclude our business. With a handshake, the fight was tentatively set for December against Karl Mildenburger, a German boxer who had gone the distance with the undefeated Ali five years earlier. (Mildenburger was later replaced by Jörgen Blin after being injured in a car accident.) Harold Conrad made it all happen.

When Ali and I met, it was love at first sight. My strange appearance as Red Hat suggested that I didn't take myself too seriously, something Muhammad liked right away. He understood that I was living out some kind of cockamamie parable, and he liked that, too. The fact that I was named after his pal Rocky Graziano tickled him to no end, since I looked quite unthreatening. It wasn't until our second or third day together that Herbert Muhammad mentioned to him that my father was Yul Brynner, and Ali was thrilled: he was a big fan, although they had never met, and he became his most boyish when I dialed Dad's number and put them on the phone together.

A few days later I walked with Ali and his corner-men — trainer Angelo Dundee, Dr. Ferdie Pacheco, and poet-jester "Bundini" Brown — to the last training session before the fight, at a gym a few hundred yards from the Astrodome Hotel. Ali was delayed posing for snapshots, and when a large Texan redneck started shouting insults — "Hey, Nigger, go back to Hanoi!" — I realized that all of the entourage had gone on ahead. The redneck kept coming after Ali even when the champ danced away. Obviously, if Muhammad defended himself, he might lose the boxing license he'd just had restored by the Supreme Court. That is why, when it was clear that the redneck really meant to hurt Ali, I leapt into the fray. The guy never noticed me until I grabbed his fist with both my hands and bent two fingers back till something broke. He dropped to the ground moaning. I'd never done anything like that before, but the situation was unambiguous, and I didn't hesitate. Muhammad danced off toward the gym, where I caught up with him. He turned to me with a big grin and said, "Who'd a ever have thunk that the son of the Pha-raoh of all Egyp' would be protectin' a little black boy from Louisville!"

"From then on," wrote Dave Hannigan in his biography of Ali:

> Brynner was Ali's bodyguard. It was a loose arrangement that suited everybody involved. There was no salary, no contract. Nothing as coarse as that. When a fight was on, Brynner answered the call and everything else would already be in place. A plane ticket at the airport. A hotel room when he arrived. He spent more than four years traveling the globe as a member of the extended Ali family. Not one of those who were there at the beginning or at the end. Just somebody who found himself in a peculiar situation and hitched along for the most unbelievable ride.

The most delightful part of that ride came a year later, when Harold Conrad and I decided to promote a fight in Dublin, of all places. Four years after graduating from Trinity College, I found myself walking into the same old pubs; but now, Muhammad Ali was with me . . . and I was his bodyguard. When the greatest fighter in the world needed protection, he called on me! It was surreal, especially to friends who had known me as a devout intellectual. In fact, it made front-page news in my college town.

> Face to face with Muhammad Ali's bodyguard and press liaison officer, Roc Brynner, one is confronted with the deep penetrating look of his bald-pated father, Yul Brynner. But there the

> resemblance comes to an abrupt halt. Roc is the guitar-playing, slightly built opposite to his father. . . . With one gold earring, a mauve floppy hat, multi-colored shoes . . . he has made an odd sight even in a company which is not noted for its lack of colour. For a bodyguard, he seems to do very little guarding and does not appear to carry a weapon. Instead, he plays a guitar in the lobby of the hotel and sings quietly. . . . Roc is no stranger to Dublin and recently received, in absentia, his master's degree in Philosophy from Trinity College.

At a press conference organized at Dublin Airport when Ali and his party arrived (wearing matching green blazers for the occasion), I prompted one reporter to ask Muhammad if his mother's maiden name wasn't Grady. And did that mean he himself was an Irishman? The whole press conference tittered, but Muhammad acted very serious, as he usually did — especially when he was cracking a joke.

"Well, back in the slave-ownin' days," Ali answered softly, "Massuh often snuck down to the slave quarters an' had his way with the women. That's how things was on the Grady plantation, and so . . . Yes, I am Irish! That is a part of what makes me the greatest fighter of all time!" It was amazing: right there, before everyone's eyes, Muhammad Ali had become an Irishman.

The most astonishing thing was that it was true. Muhammad Ali's great-grandfather was born in County Clare, a plasterer's son named Abe Grady. In the 1860s — about the time Jules Bryner sailed out of Europe as a cabin boy — Abe Grady shipped out of Ireland to New Orleans, where he sailed up the Mississippi to Kentucky, and there married a freed slave. So began the family odyssey that had now brought Muhammad Ali back to Ireland.

On July 19, 1972, Ali won the Dublin fight by a technical knockout in the eleventh round over a sweet-natured ex-con named Al "Blue" Lewis. It took place at a packed outdoor park at sunset, as flocks of geese passed overhead. Thousands of the spectators had sneaked past the gates without paying for tickets to see their hero, the most famous man on earth. The promoters lost their shirts on that fight, but the experience remains one of the many providential blessings of my life.

Over the next few years I joined Ali whenever I could, in New York, Las Vegas, or San Diego. As my life took me in different directions, I had to miss some of his greatest bouts, including the "Thrilla in Manila" with Joe Frazier, and the "Rumble in the Jungle" with George Foreman. I never was a fan of the sport, even though I had a boxer's nickname; I was just a fan and a friend of Muhammad Ali's. He is still my friend today, and for all the hardships that Parkinson's disease has inflicted, Ali still considers himself the luckiest men who ever lived. He made the whole world his empire by using physical power to serve a higher cause, without compromising his moral authority or his love for humanity.

In June 1971, the first Hard Rock Café opened in London. It was launched and owned by two very dissimilar characters: my friend Isaac Tigrett, from Jackson, Tennessee, and Peter Morton from Chicago, Illinois. At the time there wasn't a good American restaurant in Europe, and their idea was to create a playful, rock 'n' roll atmosphere, and to provide quality steaks and hamburgers with authentic American cocktails. Within a week there was a line of people waiting to get in. It was a completely original phenomenon, and thanks to the clean, bold beauty of the logo, buying a Hard Rock T-shirt at the restaurant soon became a mandatory errand for tourists. Desperately in need of a job that would pay me under the table, I settled in at the Hard Rock, and after a few months of on-the-job training, I was a manager. Focused upon making sure that everyone who came into the place had a good time, I was no longer Red Hat the Clown: soon enough I was known as the Easy Rock of the Hard Rock Café. Back then, the restaurant was owned by a Bermuda-based holding company named Don't Let Your Meat Loaf, Ltd. Recalling those scruffy early days of the Hard Rock, it is amazing that today it is a chain of more than one hundred restaurants around the world — a very corporate, global empire.

By that time, my drinking had progressed as far as it could go before it killed me. At the age of twenty-six, I could no longer disguise the fact that I was a physical and psychological wreck. The last days of my active disease do not need to be examined here; nor does a brief, wrongheaded marriage in 1973. My alcoholism and a parade of drugs had taken me to places I never thought I would go, and only sobriety could end the nightmare. I did not want to die, and I could dimly perceive that that was not necessary . . . thanks to the shining example of my mother, who had been sober for eight years.

In this story of the Brynners, my mother, Virginia, has received short shrift, but it was from this time forward that her love and counsel became most precious to me. Virginia had been a wonderful mother in my childhood when it mattered most, and then a sad, bitter figure when her marriage ended and drink overcame her. But then, in sobriety, she transformed her own life. With little money from her divorce settlement, she learned to live within her means, since emphysema limited her capacity for work and obliged her to seek the climate of Montecito, California. There was another strong lure for her there: the spiritual guidance of a holy and wise man. Swami Prabhavenanda, a devotee of Vedanta, also translated the Vedas, the Bhagavad-Gita, and other ancient Sanskrit texts, whose teachings are described in Christopher Isherwood's *My Guru and His Disciple*. With his guidance, Virginia, the former starlet "Gams" Gilmore, now set out on the path of the Vedas. She settled in a home beside the Vedanta convent and temple in the hills overlooking the Pacific Ocean, and dedicated herself to a spiritual life.

It was thanks to her example that I knew where to go when I realized that I had either to change or to die. I went to my first AA meeting in London on November 5, 1973, and that evening ended my career as an active alcoholic. Though there were brief slips later on, alcohol never again controlled my life.

That left me with little choice but to become a responsible human being, a frightening prospect; it also meant deciding where I belonged. I had lived on the road since infancy, and expected always to do so, but now I needed some measure of stability and a sense of belonging. Both my parents were in the United States.

After several months' sobriety, I decided to return to the country where I was born, and to make every effort to restore my American citizenship.

In 1975 I settled in Southern California and began a long legal process to become a naturalized American. Knowing that it would be some time before I could work legally, I decided that I wanted to learn a well-paid, down-to-earth profession that I could practice anywhere, while continuing to write plays and fiction. I became a computer programmer and systems analyst. This was long before the birth of personal computers, and the programming languages included COBOL, FORTRAN, and Basic Assembly Language, the most elementary binary coding. With six months' training, I landed my first job as a programmer with Bank of America. But that same week a much more exciting possibility arose, and in no time flat I found myself on the road with The Band.

Since I had seen them with Bob Dylan in Dublin a decade earlier, The Band had become one of the most beloved and respected groups in the world. While the rest of rock 'n' roll was moving into the era of psychedelia and lurching toward the heavy-metal sound of Led Zeppelin, these five men went back to the roots of contemporary music, recording songs that could only be described in traditional terms: ballads, ragtime, blues. Having played together since they were teenagers — they came together in 1960 with Arkansas rocker Ronnie Hawkins, then spent years playing with Dylan — by the time their own first album, *Music from Big Pink*, came out in 1968, they were accomplished musicians. Robbie Robertson was lead guitarist and principal songwriter; Richard Manuel, Rick Danko, and Levon Helm were the singers who played piano, bass, and drums, respectively, with Garth Hudson on organ and saxophone. Levon was American, but the other four were from Canada; nonetheless, it was the American past that their music evoked, reaching as far back as the Civil War for "The Night They Drove Ol' Dixie Down." Their best-loved song, "The Weight," is also the most portentous, with its mysterious, doleful refrain: "Take a load off Fanny and . . . you put the load right on me."

Their ballads are enigmatic, soulful evocations of common American life, usually among the dirt-poor characters who make up an off-kilter community — like the sad-sack worlds of Winesburg, Ohio, and Tobacco Road set to four-four time. Their songs depict an "Invisible Republic," in Greil Marcus's words, of eccentric, flawed and eminently *human* heroes that embody American individualism, which he explores in *The Old, Weird America: The World of Bob Dylan's Basement Tapes*, about The Band's collaborations with Dylan. Princeton historian Sean Wilentz recently wrote that the ballad is "perhaps the major form through which Americans told each other about themselves and the country they inhabited." Ballads, like the Dimitrievitch folk songs, constitute the very soul of a country's culture, and given the chance to go on the road with The Band, I jumped at it.

When I had first seen them in Dublin, these guys already seemed much older than their years: still in their twenties, they were more like world-weary sidemen than glittery young rock stars. The unstudied raggedness of their vocal harmonies and refrains took them years to perfect, but it bespoke the down-home individuality of the five men and their musical tradition.

I met them through friends in the mid-1970s, when we all lived north of Malibu, California, at Point Dume — in the shadow of Dylan's new home with the copper dome, where he lived with his five kids and his wife, Sara. In nearby Trancas, The Band owned a recording studio named Shangri-la, a former bordello spread out ranch-style, with a dozen small suites. I'd spent a few evenings there shooting the breeze when their road manager, Sandy Mazzeo, asked me to drive a bus up to a concert The Band was giving in Santa Barbara that Saturday to kick off to a national tour for their new album, *Northern Lights, Southern Cross*. "Sure," was all I said.

Well, one thing led to another, and by the following week I had apparently become indispensable, and The Band was willing to pay me under the table because Immigration still hadn't given me a green card. Next thing I knew, I was touring America again, just as I'd done as a child with *The King and I*: suddenly I'm flying to Miami to pick up a customized tour bus and driving it overnight to New York, where I'm meeting The Band and driving them to Pittsburgh, Philadelphia, and Boston, after which I'm driving them straight to Texas — Boston to Austin, nonstop — in time to set up for an outdoor concert for two hundred thousand together with the Steve Miller Band and some other groups, before driving to New Orleans. Those were just my first five days on the job. With the tour bus and two tractor-trailers carrying all the equipment, we caravanned across the country on a cloud of hilarity and exhaustion. And, as a Band Aid, no matter how battered up I got over the months, I spent the evenings listening live to my favorite band. It was as exhilarating as it was debilitating.

The most damaged of our entourage on that tour was Richard Manuel: with his gruff phrasing and fragile falsetto, his was the most dramatic voice in The Band. By then Richard was drinking two bottles of Grand Marnier a day and snorting anything white, in the hope that it was cocaine. In those days, the "Devil's Dandruff" was something just about everyone in popular music either used or abused — now there's a distinction without a difference. The routine of recording an album and then touring never gave Richard an even chance at sobriety, even after rehabs and lithium; and he certainly didn't want to know about Alcoholics Anonymous. As our tour meandered from New Orleans to Hattiesburg, Mississippi, to Anniston, Alabama, it was obvious that Richard's life was in jeopardy.

By the end of the tour, Robbie Robertson and I had become good friends, and he invited me to stay at his family's home in Malibu while he figured out what The Band should do next under the circumstances. At thirty-five, Robbie was bone-tired with the routine of touring. Two years earlier, when Dylan and The Band had finished playing to packed stadiums around the country, Robbie had had enough of live shows. It was always the old hits that their fans wanted, and replaying them had lost Robbie's interest completely. By this time he was happily settled with his three children and wife, Dominique, and had solid prospects in the music world without The Band. In recent years he had been writing almost all The Band's new songs; and more than once, when he and I drove up to the studio for a scheduled recording session, none of the other musicians showed up. It just wasn't fun anymore.

In September 1976, Muhammad Ali fought Ken Norton for the third time, and Robbie and I saw the fight on closed circuit. Ali won by decision — but it was a sad, dispirited match, and Ali was so far from his best that it hurt to watch. Robbie and I sat glumly contemplating The Band's prospects after a tour that was as dispiriting as the boxing match we'd just seen.

The goal for bands back then was to break even on the road and make a profit from album sales. But that had changed, along with the nature of rock 'n' roll itself, after the OPEC oil embargos in 1973 and 1974, which had increased all travel-related costs, even hotels and meals. The latest tour had actually cost The Band out-of-pocket. The same thing was happening to many of the biggest groups. Unless a band could fill a football stadium, a tour could barely break even. Now promoters began looking for spectacular acts that would draw in even younger audiences. The result was the birth of packaged and produced bubblegum rock shows. Alice Cooper, Kiss, Elton John in drag, and Peter Frampton appealed to kids in junior high and, sadly, that set the tone for acts to come, which ever since have focused more on marketing than on music. Punk rockers rebelled against this trend until they too were swept up in it. Meanwhile, revered idols of the 1960s soon found themselves back where many of them had started out, on the folk-music circuit. It was hard to picture that happening to the guys in The Band . . . but not impossible.

"We can't keep this thing going forever," Robbie said that night. "We aren't the Mills Brothers."

Robbie Robertson is a deep and complex man whom I rank highly among the artists I've known, and for a time he was a big brother, just as Aliosha had been to my father. He'd known Richard Manuel since they were teenagers, and he understood that Richard would need years off the road and away from the studio to get a grip on sobriety. We talked about musicians who could replace Richard, especially their good friend from New Orleans, Mac Rebennack, known as Dr. John; he certainly had the musical skills, but not Richard's voice, which had been a large part of The Band's identity from the first track of their first album, "Tears of Rage."

Finally, Robbie said quietly to himself, "It's over." I was stunned to realize that he was talking about the end of The Band. "I don't want us to wind up playing dives and pool halls." He went silent again for a long while. "But I'd love to go out with a big bash."

"And invite other musicians to celebrate the end with you," I suggested, unnecessarily. "That would be worth filming."

"Of course," he replied.

When it came to finding a name for The Band's final concert, Robbie later explained what happened. "Rock and I were bouncing things back and forth . . . I'm naming things off: 'Last Dance.' The old song title, 'Save the Last Dance for Me,' 'The Last Waltz.' And Rock goes, 'That's it! That's it! Say nothing else, I'm telling you!' He's the one who raised the flag, who said, 'You have to call it *The Last Waltz*.'"

The event unfolded less than two months later, on Thanksgiving 1976, at Winterland in San Francisco. Eight years earlier, the musicians had given their first concert there as The Band; now, Martin Scorsese was there with five camera crews to document their swan song, in a film produced by Robbie. The concert itself was organized by legendary promoter Bill Graham, who borrowed the set of *La Traviata* from the San Francisco Opera for the occasion, including giant chandeliers. The concert began in mid-afternoon when all five thousand in the audience sat down at long tables for Thanksgiving dinner while a twenty-piece orchestra played and most everyone danced. Then the concert itself lasted almost eight hours, as The Band was joined by one musical guest after another: Ronnie Hawkins, who had given them their first job; Dr. John, representing their Dixieland musical roots; Neil Young and Joni Mitchell, close friends and fellow Canadians; Eric Clapton, whose guitar duel with Robbie left the audience breathless; Muddy Waters, who brought along the blues tradition reaching right back to Robert Johnson; Van Morrison, the mystical, Celtic wild man; Paul Butterfield, whose harmonica had moved the blues harp into rock 'n' roll; and Bob Dylan, with whom The Band had first been booed and then revered. My old friends from London days, Ringo Starr of the Beatles and Ronnie Wood of the Rolling Stones — patriarchs from the bipolar 1960s — joined all the other artists on stage at the end for an emotional shout-out of Dylan's "I Shall Be Released."

I was road manager for *The Last Waltz*, together with Sandy Mazzeo, who first hired me. I worked closely with Robbie and Marty Scorsese in preparing the song list (there were finally fifty-four songs in the concert) and an actual shooting script of each song, so the camera crews would know which soloist to focus on. On the lighter side, Bill Graham built a closed cubicle in the wings where some of the artists could snort their cocaine privately just before going on stage. The cubicle was equipped with three small cassette players playing looped tapes of snorting noises to disguise those of the artists; Graham mounted plaster molds of noses on the walls of the cubicle, just for the surreal effect. Together, we named it the Cocteau Room.

By the time the concert began that November night, my work was done, and I was free to listen and watch and imprint this emotional moment in American musical history in my mind.

Why did *this* music matter any more than the foxtrot, or a good rumba? Mick Jagger once defined rock 'n' roll as "three chords and a lot of energy," which is pretty good as far as it goes. But it also gave a voice to the largest generation in American history, to the civil rights and anti-war movements. Anti-establishment demonstrators in the United States, France, and Czechoslovakia had all listened to the Beatles, the Stones, and Pink Floyd; and at the end of the decade, when their aspirations were crushed by Kent State, Paris, and Prague, they were listening to The Band. "The Night They Drove Ol' Dixie Down," which Robbie wrote, discovered emotional parallels between the 1960s and the 1860s, reflecting the mournful mood of dissident Americans after the election of Richard Nixon. Rock music provides a direct, honest expression of its era as surely as the Dimitrievitches music did half a century before; Yul drew that parallel himself the first time he heard The Band.

Wynton Marsalis makes the argument that jazz is the archetypal American art form, because it can be produced by a handful of musicians from different backgrounds who may never have met before, but who can sit down together and improvise something altogether new by calling upon shared traditions. Similarly, *The Last Waltz* was a melting pot of those traditions, and three decades later, there still hasn't been a concert to equal it.

I'd met Dylan several times while I lived with Robbie and after, but we didn't have a serious conversation until a couple years later. By then I had helped open the first sushi bar in Malibu, a place called Something's Fishy, on the Pacific Coast Highway just north of Topanga, that is still there today. Dylan used to come in, sometimes when I was playing guitar in the dining room. I sure had a lotta gall: I sang "Visions of Johanna" for him, "Tambourine Man," and "Don't Think Twice, It's Alright." Bob was real polite about it.

In 1978, he had just finished the long Rolling Thunder tour and recorded a new album, *Street Legal*. By that time I had traveled a ways with Ramblin' Jack Elliott, the folksinger who, as Dylan later wrote, "had actually traveled with Woody Guthrie, learned his songs and style firsthand and had mastered it completely. . . . Elliott had indeed already gone beyond Guthrie, and I was still getting there." Jack is still the master of the talkin' blues, and can spin a yarn better than anyone: they don't call him "Ramblin' Jack" just because he travels a lot. His whole life has been composed of complex, convoluted tales, miniature *Tristram Shandy*s reflecting the commonalities of American life. Jack had gone along on Rolling Thunder, and through him I got to know Bobby Neuwirth, Dylan's old friend, a singer, songwriter, and artist of formidable talent.

One afternoon, waiting for Neuwirth to show up at Dylan's studio in Santa Monica, I ended up spending a couple hours alone with Dylan instead. He had been at low tide since the mid-1970s and not ashamed to admit it, or even sing about it. "I've been double-crossed too much / Sometimes I think I've almost lost my mind. / Ladykillers load dice on me / Behind my back, while imitators steal me blind"; that was how he put it in the original lyrics of "Idiot Wind" a couple years earlier. His long marriage had just ended, and he seemed to be standing on a corner wondering which way to turn.

We spent the afternoon chatting comfortably. I told him how my great-grandfather went to China on a pirate ship, and built and lost an empire; how my father, who had sold opium to Cocteau, had started out singing folk songs, too, and that his first gig in America was playing Gypsy guitar around downtown New York. And I recounted some of the adventures I'd had along my own crooked mile: with the Dimitrievitches around Paris and with Sinatra around the world; during my Dublin days, and later, as Red Hat the Clown, looking for Tambourine Man and finding Muhammad

Ali instead; and later still, on the road with The Band. I thanked him for the influence his songs had had on my life, and Bob liked that fine, and he told me a few things, too. But when I noted the impact he'd had upon his era, and he shrugged and turned to leave. Dylan detested that stuff the way Yul hated the rudeness of fans.

"Don't mention it," Bob replied, halfway out the door, and he meant every word.

In 1978, I fell in love with a wonderful woman, Elisabeth Coleman, who at the time was press secretary to the governor of California, Jerry Brown. In December of that year we were married and moved east: Elisabeth wanted to return to journalism in New York, and since I had completed much of my first novel, I wanted to be near the city. Elisabeth had grown up in Dutchess County seventy miles north of Manhattan, where her parents still lived, and her father found us a small house among the horse farms of Pawling, New York. Our marriage lasted only a few years, although our friendship endures.

I am still in Pawling today, at the top of Quaker Hill, a long way from Broadway, Hollywood, and the demimonde of rock 'n' roll. I have lived here for almost thirty years now, rooted in the same small community, an experience neither my father nor grandfather had. The gypsy life I had inherited came to an end when I decided to make my stand here in this hilltop forest, where God lost His shoes. Henceforth, my restlessness — the Brynner restlessness — would have to content itself with intellectual adventures. For me, the family odyssey had ended, or so I imagined.

My first novel, *The Ballad of Habit and Accident*, was published in 1981. It is a picaresque, fictionalized account of my own misspent youth in Dublin and beyond, written in "the Irish mode" and echoing the comic strains of the writers who inspired me. It is the first of six books I have published, and remains in some respects my favorite child. Perhaps that's all the more true because I have no flesh-and-blood children — which is not something I regret. I was never prepared to be a parent: it would have been a selfish exercise. In 1984, I married Susan Shroeger, but we too proved to be better friends than spouses. Given the marriages I witnessed growing up, it's no surprise that I wasn't very good at partnership. My life has largely been guided by a dozen great loves, but it really didn't make much difference whether or not I found the right woman, because I was never the right man.

Yul never read *The Ballad of Habit and Accident* or any other work of mine. He had always encouraged me to become a writer, but by the time I was published, he was too busy to read, he explained. Nonetheless, when the *Wall Street Journal* critic likened his son to "a modern Dante," he took pride in the compliment. We had, by that time, overcome a cold and strained patch in our relationship that had lasted several years. Is such conflict between generations inevitable? Why do two people who are so resonant to each other punctuate a lifetime of mutual care to confront each other head-on over the very qualities they share?

> *I'll tell you the reason, won't cost ya a dime:*
> *'Cause the young want more room, and the old*
> *want more time.*

But in the last year of Yul's life, we saw each other almost every day for the first time in decades. I would sit with him in his dressing room during his hour-long makeup, just as I had as a little boy.

My father's death in October 1985 was a protracted ordeal that allowed his family to feel greatly relieved for him when he breathed his last. But the experience, which left me reeling, was quickly followed by the reality that my mother, Virginia, was also near the end of her life; after years of struggling with emphysema, she died at her home in Santa Barbara, California, in March 1986.

The loss of both parents left me stunned and rudderless, but my decision to return to academia to study U.S. history provided a measure of stability. In 1993, at Columbia University, I defended my doctoral dissertation, "'Fire Beneath Our Feet': The Constitutional Impact of Shays' Rebellion." This work presented evidence I had found in archives across the Northeast, demonstrating that the Massachusetts uprising in 1786–7 was an indispensable event in the establishment of the United States national government; that nothing less than the specter of widespread insurrection in the new country would have persuaded the states to sacrifice their sovereignty to create a central government.

My passion for history grew out of my predilection for philosophy. It is the *unfolding* of events that captivates my curiosity, whether examining the founding of American democracy or the collapse of the Russian Empire. Each of these vast events was produced by the free choices made by millions of flawed individuals. Yet, when we reflect upon history, it is unbearable to think of the chain of events as merely one thing happening after another. The language skills of our species compel us to search for some underlying, transcendental logic provided by Destiny, or Chance, or God. And, of course, we usually find the things we set out looking for, owing only in part to our dogged determination; we generally find the patterns we seek because we see the world through lenses we grind for ourselves, over the courses of our lives. And so our belief in, say, astrology, or Hegel's dialectic, or Christian eschatology, is self-reinforcing.

During five years of Constitutional research, I also wrote a beautiful and bittersweet memoir entitled *Yul: The Man Who Would Be King*, which chronicled my father's life and my own at his side. There I sketched out for the first time the history of the Brynners, with the help of Yul's cousin, Irena, and the information I had elicited from Yul and his sister years before. But I knew only the vague outlines of the early Bryner story. In the 1980s I could not visit Vladivostok, and Soviet archives were inaccessible.

In 1989, almost a quarter century after I had followed my father's example of renunciation, my U.S. citizenship was restored. Life rarely allows us to rectify our most egregious mistakes, even if we have found the courage to admit to them. The day I regained my birthright remains one of the brightest of my life.

In those years I also became a pilot, fulfilling a dream I had nurtured since childhood, and because my doctoral research required a good deal of travel, it was also a convenience, flying myself from Maine to Ohio, from Vermont to Florida. Of course, those who had known me as a young intellectual alcoholic now glanced to the skies with newfound apprehension. I was not obvious pilot material, admittedly, but the few years I spent flying without mishap suggest how I had changed in sobriety. To pay for my passion for aviation, I invested in a twin-engine Beechcraft Baron and started

ıt twenty-six, Virginia and Yul were devoted and diligent parents.

ɫy mother, stage and film actress Virginia ilmore, was more inquisitive than beautiful, ıd even more sensitive. Midway through her ̃e she took a path to great wisdom and ›odness.

No matter how broke, Virginia and Yul always found a way to spend a few weeks at the beach. Yul still loved to swim in the ocean.

By the age of six, I had a reputation as a chess prodigy among the old men who played in Central Park.

My hero in 1958 was Van Cliburn, who had won the Moscow Tchaikovsky Competition. At our home, he played on my spinet.

By 1959, I usually traveled alone to Paris, where Yul would meet me. I've always wor a hat. It's good for my head.

fter we settled in Switzerland, our neighbors and friends included Charlie Chaplin; our families acationed together in France in 1960.

as fifteen when I fell in love Suzy Parker, ice my age. Coco Chanel's protégée, the first permodel, she was my true friend. Our mock gagement portrait was taken in Kyoto in 1962.

"Sam Giancana was one of the most powerful criminals in America." As his driver, at sixteen, I almost killed him.

I joined my father on almost every film set. Here, in 1967, I played a scene in *Villa Rides* with Robert Mitchum, with whom I spent a lot of time, and Charles Bronson, whom I'd known on *The Magnific Seven.*

Yul and I became good friends with Sammy Davis, Jr. Here, Yul was giving him a necklace made by Irena a few weeks before I turned twenty-one, when Sammy would welcome me to Las Vegas.

Samuel Beckett inspired me to study at Trinity College, Dublin, where he returned in 1959 to receive a D. Litt. I met him five years later.

My sister Lark was the daughter of Yul's Austrian sweetheart, Frankie. She and I got to know each other years later.

Opium is the one-character play I adapted from Cocteau's journal when I was twenty-two. I played Jean Cocteau in Dublin, London, and on Broadway in 1970.

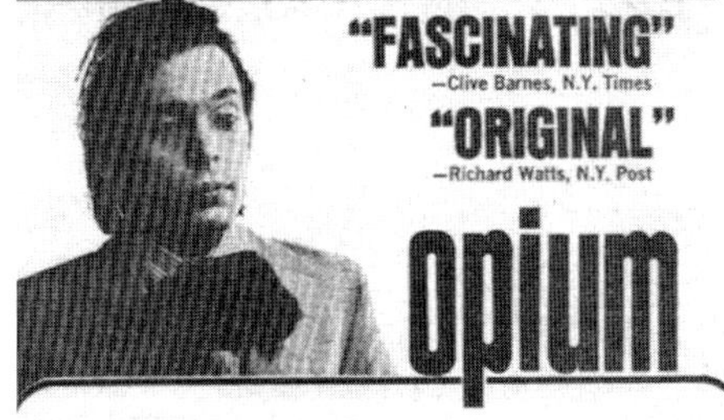

"THIS EXCURSION INTO A MAN'S CENTRAL NERVOUS SYSTEM, VISCERA AND SOUL, AN EXCURSION SOLEMNLY, AND YET WITH POMPOUSLY EXHIBITIONISTIC THEATRICALITY, TRANSFORMING ITS HONEST OBSERVATIONS INTO A BLEAK EGO TRIP, IS FASCINATING. AN EVENING OF DISTINCTIVE INTEREST. ROC BRYNNER IMPRESSED ONE WITH THIS SENSITIVELY OBSERVED PORTRAIT OF THE ARTIST AS A YOUNG ADDICT."—Clive Barnes, N.Y. Times

"ORIGINAL, WELL-ACTED. BRYNNER IS AN ATTRACTIVE AND OBVIOUSLY TALENTED YOUNG FELLOW." —Richard Watts, N.Y. Post

"A RARE DELIGHT." —William Glover, Associated Press

"ROC BRYNNER DOES A MAGNIFICENT JOB. A SINGULARLY FINE ACTING SKILL." —John Schubeck, WABC-TV

"FASCINATING AND DISTURBING. A BRILLIANT PERFORMANCE BY BRYNNER. I ADMIRE HIS COURAGE IN BRINGING 'OPIUM' TO THE STAGE." —William Raidy, Newhouse Newspapers

"A REMARKABLE YOUNG MAN IN A REMARKABLE THEATRICAL PRESENTATION. ROC BRYNNER MAKES THE WHOLE THING COME ALIVE WITH STRENGTH AND CONVICTION." —Leo Mishkin, Morning Telegraph

"FASCINATING! IT HAS WIT AND IMAGERY. REWARDING TO SEE AND HEAR, THANKS LARGELY TO THE BRAVURA AND CONVINCING PERFORMANCE OF ROC BRYNNER." —George Oppenheimer, Newsday

"AN AMAZING NIGHT. A SHOW OF STRIKING MERIT. EXTRAORDINARY. REMARKABLE. THE TURNING INSIDE OUT OF A HEAD, WHICH ALL CONTEMPORARY HEADS CAN'T HELP BUT APPLAUD."—Larry Cohen, Hollywood Reporter

"VIVID FLASHES OF HUMOR AND INTELLIGENCE." —Peggy Stockton, WMCA Radio

Two hours alone on stage confirmed that I had learned something studying with George Shdanoff.

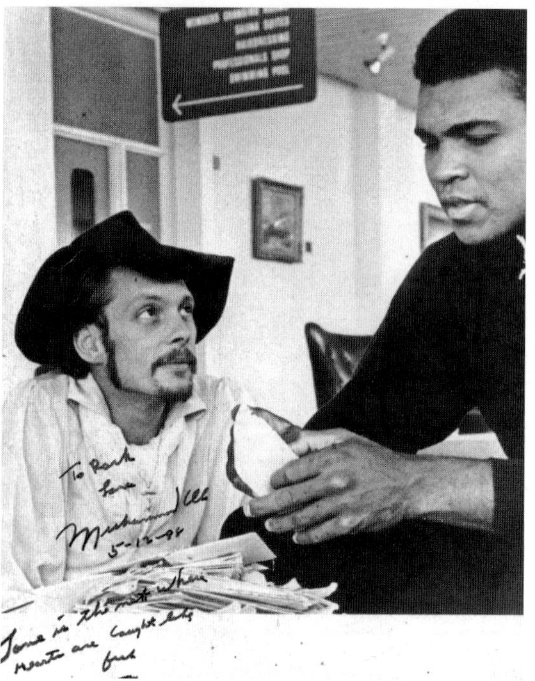

In 1971, I became friends with Muhammad Ali, then, unexpectedly, his bodyguard. Over the next three years I often traveled with this spiritual giant.

Summer is here at last!

The weather experts say we are at last in for a spell of warm sunny days, with temperatures right up in the seventies or thereabouts. In a summer that so far has left us "cold" and in a deep depression with no seeming letup the sun has burst through in all its glory, and ... our days though the weathermen are even talking of a week.

FORECAST—Dry and sunny. A few haze or fog patches in some coastal areas; light variable winds with sea breezes, very warm inland; a little cooler on the coast. OUTLOOK—Some fog patches tonight; sunny again tomorrow

Yul's son is Ali's guard

... to face with Muhammad Ali's bodyguard and press relations officer, Roc Brynner, one is confronted with the deep penetrating look of his famous bald-pated father, Yul. But there the resemblance comes to an abrupt halt.

Roc, is the guitar playing, slightly built opposite to his father. He travels with the Muhammad Ali party but not always with the former heavyweight champion. Generally Roc precedes the arrival of Muhammad Ali at his various appointments, mainly his training sessions for the fight next Wednesday night with Al 'Blue' Lewis.

COLOURFUL

With one gold earring, a mauve floppy hat, multi-coloured shoes and blue elephant-flared denim trousers, he has made an odd sight even in a company

INJURED

The men broke a glass pa... in the door, giving Mr. Mc... a hand injury. ... daughter, Breda, who'll be ... soon, arrived home a short t... afterwards. It was a good th... she didn't come back a ... minutes sooner, or she mi... have got caught up in this thi... he said.

BANDSTAND

Manslaughter verdict in Lynskey case

SUMMER to and from DUN LAOGHAIRE—HOLYHEAD

Currently until 2 September 1972

15 July until 2 September

DUN LAOGHAIRE—HO...

When I arrived in Dublin with Ali, it was front-page news in my college town.

At the 600-year-old Gypsy gathering at Saint-Marie-de-la-Mer near Marseilles, the clans of the Rom were joined by hippies from across Europe, including Red Hat, always with a Gladstone bag.

I spent a couple years as a stoned hippie named Red Hat the Clown. I'm not sure how I survived; but I always wore the Russian Orthodox cross made for me by Irena.

After eight years' sobriety, I published my first novel in 1981, a fictional account of my life. My lifelong pal, Liza Minnelli, gave a star-studded publishing party.

A year after this photograph was taken in 1984, my father died in New York City, on the far side of the world from Vladivostok.

By 1990, I was flying a twin-engine Beechcraft Baron every day. *(Marianne Barcellona)*

I especially loved flying down the Hudson River corridor at 1,000 feet, passing the World Trade Center. *(Marianne Barcellona)*

I was road manager for The Band's final concert together, *The Last Waltz*, where Bob Dylan joined Robbie Robertson. *(Neil Preston, Corbis Images)*

Robbie Robertson, The Band's guitarist and principal songwriter, has remained a good friend in the decades since *The Last Waltz*.

My close friend Ramblin' Jack Elliott is still touring all around the United States.

'd known Ronnie Wood in London before he oined the Rolling Stones. Many musicians of hat era aren't around anymore, but some have hosen sobriety over death.

In 2003 I was invited to Vladivostok, where I gave a series of academic lectures sponsored by the U.S. State Department. One lecture was at the Far East State Technical University that Jules had founded on a hill over the Golden Horn harbor.

ЭЛЕКТРОННАЯ ВЕРСИЯ ГАЗЕТЫ В СЕТИ ИНТЕРНЕТ - http://www.vladnews.ru
ПОСЕЩЕНИЙ ЗА НЕДЕЛЮ- 132199

Владивосток

ЛАСТОЧКА

16 СЕНТЯБРЯ 2003 ГОДА ВТОРНИК № 139 (3133)

415-625 - ОТДЕЛ ОПЕРАТИВНОЙ ИНФОРМАЦИИ, 415-660 - СОЦИАЛЬНО-ЭКОНОМИЧЕСКИЙ ОТДЕЛ, 226-857, 266-037 - ДИРЕКЦИЯ РЕКЛАМЫ. ИНДЕКС ПОДПИСКИ - 53414. ТИРАЖ ВО ВТОРНИК - 30850, СРЕДУ, ЧЕТВЕРГ - 30900, В ПЯТНИЦУ - 41950. ЦЕНА - СВОБОДНАЯ.

ЧАЙ ДЛЯ ПОХУДЕНИЯ
Северное чудо

Куда ведут звездные дороги...

PACIFIC

ТИХИЙ ОКЕАН СВЯЖУТ С АДРИАТИКОЙ

Роль Транссиба растет на Западе и Востоке

На проходящей в Санкт-Петербурге 3-й Международной евроазиатской конференции по транспорту обсуждается предложение Венгрии продолжить международный транспортный коридор №5 через Киев до Москвы с выходом на Транссиб.

Как сообщает РИА «Новости», первый заместитель главы МПС России Владимир Якунин положительно отнесся к такому проекту, который позволит связать побережье Тихого океана с Адриатикой. Он также заинтересованно отозвался о предложении Казахстана сформировать новый транспортный

Международный кинофестиваль во Владивостоке стартовал

Едва прилетев сеульским рейсом в пятницу во Владивосток, один из самых долгожданных гостей фестиваля Рок Бриннер сразу попросил свежий номер «В», в котором аккурат в этот день было опубликовано его интервью. Развернул газету, удовлетворенно хмыкнул, сел в ожидавшую машину и помчался на торжественную церемонию открытия.

Проход по так называемой звездной дорожке известных киноактеров - славная традиция

I did not expect my arrival would be front-page news, or anticipate how meaningful it was to Vladivostok that I had “returned” to the city that my forefathers Jules, Boris, and Yul had, in different ways, put on the map.

The striking, art nouveau Bryner Residence. Yul was born in the room behind the balcony where I stood in 2003.

The Bryner Residence (red arrow on the left), 15 Aleutskaya Street on Tiger Hill, still stands out abo harbor square, seen here from Svetlanskaya Street.

Today the Bryner home belongs to FESCO, the Far East Shipping Company established by Jules 125 years ago. They warmly welcomed my visit.

In 2003, at the First Vladivostok Internati Film Festival, I presented the first Yul Bry Award. I promised myself then that I wou return the following year.

In 2004 I visited the Bryner mines in Tetukhe, now Dalnegorsk. This old mine shaft, started by Jules and operated by Boris, survived into the Soviet era before shutting down. There are still three major shafts in operation.

From the upper mines here the ore was loaded onto the original Bryner railroad and carried twenty miles down to Pristan Harbor. . .

. . . beneath the lighthouse Jules built on what is still called Cape Bryner.

This 1994 ruble features Cape Bryner.

The narrow Vladivostok peninsula features hills that rise above bays and harbors. The old town is still much as Jules knew it.

Although winters are harsh in Vladivostok, autumn is especially clear, warm, and beautiful.

In 2004, I was invited to speak about the Bryners and Russian history at the Kennan Institute for Advanced Russian Studies, first in Washington, D.C., and later in Moscow (above).

At the Russian Film Festival of New York in 2003, I accepted an award on behalf of my father, and sang "Okonchen Poot."

Returning to Vladivostok, I fell in love with Olya Vigovskaya, who accompanied me to the Second Vladivostok International Film Festival.

Together we visited Sidemy, where Olya spent many of her summers as a teenager. She showed me the estate where my father grew up, and the tomb that Jules had built for our family.

a charter business, Flights of Fancy, Inc., which flew out of Danbury, Connecticut, near my home. The business allowed me to fly all over the Northeast, conducting research in Boston and Springfield, Massachusetts, and at the National Archives in Washington, D.C. Ultimately, flying cost more time and money than I could afford, and the environmental heedlessness was unacceptable; but the pleasure and poetry of aviation remain a vivid memory. I loved flying at low altitude above the hilltop where I live and down the Hudson River to the city where I was born, back in the days when my father was in *Lute Song* and my grandfather was under Soviet arrest. Flying past the World Trade Center in 1989, it was utterly impossible to imagine the horrors that would come in 2001.

The last work I published, before the book you are holding in your hands, was *Dark Remedy,* the medical, legal, and social history of the most reviled pharmaceutical product of all time: thalidomide, distributed in the 1950s as a tranquilizer until its use was connected to thousands of severe birth defects. Thanks to my co-author, Trent Stephens, I was given the privilege of researching and writing about this important episode in modern medicine.

By 2003, I was lecturing on U.S. history at Marist College in Poughkeepsie, New York, and other nearby institutions, while working on a variety of historical and literary projects. I had lived alone on a hilltop for most of the preceding twenty years, having learned, the hard way, that it is better to live alone than to *wish* you did. This wasn't exactly the life I had planned on, but, as a wise man once said, "If you want to make the gods laugh . . . just tell them your plans." And while I haven't raised any children, neither have I left any behind.

Certainly, nothing could have been further from my plans than traveling around the world to Far East Russia. But that was just what came next.

The First International Vladivostok Film Festival invited me to come and present the "Yul Brynner Award." The e-mail that bore the invitation came from one of the Festival's organizers, Alexander Doluda, offering an air ticket via Moscow and accommodations. It concluded with this intriguing note: "In Russian, your name, 'Rock,' means 'Destiny,' and it is your destiny to come to Vladivostok."

The festival was scheduled for the first week of September, which would have meant missing my first four lectures of the semester, and that was not acceptable. But rather than decline immediately, I dithered, allowing myself to daydream about visiting Vladivostok, which had never in my life been an option. Now, I could only go if I could shave two days off the itinerary by traveling the other direction around the world, over the Pacific, but that air ticket cost double the Russian route via Moscow, and the festival could not afford it.

I received another invitation from Doluda, followed by phone calls from a Russian friend of his in the United States, urging me to accept. Finally, without regard for the consequences, I accepted. I also asked Doluda to contact the U.S. Consulate there and extend my offer to give some talks or lectures during my visit; in the past I had given a handful of lectures in Amman, Jordan, and Berlin, Germany, with the help of the U.S. embassies.

Within days I received a phone call from the public affairs officer with the U.S. consulate in Vladivostok, Tara Rougle, inviting me to lecture there under the auspices of the State Department. The Speaker's Tour Program is one of the last remnants of what was once a robust effort in public diplomacy, communicating directly to the people of other nations rather than to their governments. I submitted a proposal, and a week later the State Department formally invited me to visit Vladivostok on behalf of the U.S. government, to present a series of lectures on "The Ideological Origins of the United States Constitution" and other subjects at the Far East State University and other venues, while also attending the film festival. When told that I could travel westward and save two days' travel, I accepted immediately.

That the State Department would engage me as an emissary signaled an unexpected development in my life. Almost forty years after I had renounced my citizenship, the United States government was sending *me* to introduce the Russian people to the Constitution. I took this not as a vindication of my youthful error but as a validation of the paths I chose later: sobriety, return to the United States, my restored citizenship, and a doctorate in history. It was as a result of those choices that I was invited to visit my father's birthplace on behalf of my birthplace, and to bring my family's odyssey full circle.

Once I had been invited to Vladivostok, I only had to say one word — yes — and the rest fell effortlessly into place. Completing my family's global odyssey did indeed seem like destiny: I did not make this trip happen, it happened *to* me. If I had spent years trying to arrange a lecture tour in Far East Russia, it never would have worked out. Instead, the Brynner odyssey itself seemed to demand resolution. The trip was neither a longstanding goal of mine nor a sudden whim: it was a blessing delivered, apparently, by the same historical forces that had transported my family through these four generations.

Doubtless the Brynners had endured on wits and nerve, curiosity and perseverance; but it was the great winds and waves of history, mostly Russian history, that had determined our family's long voyage. When the tsar established a naval port at Vladivostok, Jules moved to Russia and built an empire, which he lost as a result of the timber concession that provoked the Russo-Japanese War, triggering the revolution that laid the foundation for the Bolsheviks. Boris, born a prince of Primorye, nearly ended his days in a Soviet labor camp. Had Yul not been driven from Russia by the Soviet regime as a child, he could not have achieved worldwide recognition, and until that regime collapsed, I could not have traveled to Far East Russia.

My arrival in Vladivostok was front-page news, taking precedence over the Russian stars who had come from Moscow and St. Petersburg for the festival. I was met at the airport by Tara Rougle, a pretty woman in her thirties, a career foreign service officer. She escorted me to the Hotel Versailles (pronounced "Fersal" in Russian), the most comfortable in the city, which had been commandeered as the headquarters for the fearsome Cossack, Ataman Semyonov, during the Intervention, the same year Yul was born at the Bryner Residence around the corner.

Vladivostok today is a city of some 700,000, but the population is shrinking quickly, as it is in cities across Russia. It looks much like European port cities, with a thriving merchant-marine economy, based on timber, fish, and fur, spread out along the edges of its complicated bays and natural harbors. Admittedly, many roads are in disrepair, though not much worse off than some approaches to Manhattan, and some neighborhoods look shabby, but not so different from parts of the Bronx. Throughout the city, clusters of uniformed men — soldiers, sailors, and police — seem to be loitering: most have been laid off from the services, and wear their old uniforms while guarding buildings and businesses; their presence is welcome.

Because Vladivostok is once again "the wild East." The Soviet regime was very effective at suppressing crime, enforcing a safe, if repressive, society. But with *perestroika* (reconstruction), all that changed. Gorbachev's new set of guides — "socialism with a human face" — was blamed for the upheavals that followed the collapse of Soviet authority, which included an explosion of criminal activity at every level of society, from street drunks state authorities.

During my visit, I began to learn how deeply post-Soviet Russia has been shaped by what happened in its first months and years: the privatization of all the property in the country. Until 1991, there were no private businesses and no private property: *everything* belonged to the Soviet state. Then, overnight, every piece of property was claimed by someone: every apartment and every apartment building; every market and supermarket, every factory and industry; every barrel of Russia's vast oil reserves and every mining operation . . . including Tetukhe. How legitimate were these claims? And who would decide which were legitimate, after the Soviet courts shut down? Did a family that lived in an apartment for three generations have a claim? Was their claim inherently stronger than that of a thug whose armed goons simply seized the building? The old Soviet laws did not address these questions, and the new laws had not been written; as yet there wasn't even a consensus on what the laws should be or who should write them. In fact, there was no consensus whatsoever in Russia.

All these issues arose in the absence of an independent judicial *system*. For seventy years, Soviet judges did what they were told by the men who appointed them, and many of those appointed by Yeltsin to replace the old guard were corrupt cronies with no interest in the law, except as a basis for graft. This corruption filtered all the way down to traffic cops. Even today, when a driver receives a violation, it is only a pretext for a negotiable bribe. On a day-to-day basis, that culture of corruption *is* Russia's judicial system. While Vladivostok is in many respects a world unto itself, the "process" of privatization was no different there.

During the Soviet era, wrote historian Andrew Meier, "the architects of the Gulag turned Vladivostok into a seething entrepôt in the archipelago of camps," and "sprawling transit camps grew up on the rough northern outskirts"; that is where the poet Osip Mandelstam died in 1938 and where my grandfather, Boris, was held with his wife and daughter by the KGB. After the Soviet fall, city leaders "envisioned . . . forming a bridge to the Asian markets close by [to] join arms with the Pacific Rim, and, in a case study of globalization's fruits, arise from its post-Soviet slumber." The First International Vladivostok Film Festival was part of that effort, inviting filmmakers from the Pacific Rim nations — the United States, Canada, Japan, Russia, and both South and North Korea — to exhibit their latest works. Whether or not the festival would become an annual event remained to be seen.

The first post-Communist governor of the Maritime Region was Yevgeny Nazdratenko who, through the 1990s "made Primorye his personal duchy. . . . 'Nasty' Nazdratenko local U.S. diplomats dubbed him." As a display of his capricious power, he publicly presented the illegal skin of an endangered Siberian tiger to Belarusian dictator Lukashenko. The citizens of Primorye paid a terrible price for the excesses of this homegrown autocrat. "For years," wrote Meier, "Nazdratenko so mangled the region's delicate energy policy that millions spent the winters without heat. The combination of mismanagement, embezzlement, and political brinksmanship was stunningly callous. . . . Like so many millions of Russians, the hardy souls of Primorye relied on a long tradition of self-preservation." Not long after Putin came to power, Nazdratenko was offered another profitable post — as minister of fisheries — and was quickly replaced by the new elected governor of Primorye, Sergei Darkin.

A few hours after I arrived in Far East Russia, the thirty-nine-year-old governor and his wife, actress-singer Larisa Belobrova, welcomed me warmly to the opening of the five-day festival. Naturally, like all the residents, they were great fans of Yul Brynner, who is, after all, Vladivostok's only "hometown boy" to become world-renowned. Governor Darkin, a large, strong man with a boyish smile, took personal pride in Yul's career. Russians love Yul possessively, and claim for their own culture his virile bravado, ironic humor, and the intelligence in his eyes. But fans in Russia treat artists with respect rather than with the frenzied adoration my father generally received in the United States; and it rarely occurred to them to remark upon his shaved head.

More importantly, the abiding image of Yul in Russia is that of an egalitarian, matter-of-fact American cowboy, not the scowling, imperious king of Siam. Everything about *The Magnificent Seven* appeals to the social conscience of socialist and post-socialist Russians: a man of the people leads warriors to the defense of impoverished farmers. Some of Yul's other films have been available on videotape and DVD, but none were ever shown in theaters. For that reason, with the U.S. consulate's assistance, we presented the Russian premiere of *The King and I* while I was there, almost half a century after it was made. We also held a screening of *The Brothers Karamazov*, with a number of Dostoyevsky experts in the invited audience. They all preferred *The Magnificent Seven*.

Months before this trip was planned, my sister Victoria sent me a very sweet gift: the cowboy boots Yul wore in *The Magnificent Seven*, which she had found on eBay. After Yul's death his widow, since remarried, had shamelessly sold off almost all of his personal belongings; sadly, he had not bothered to bequeath a single possession to myself or to my sisters. Although he carefully specified bequests to his lawyer and his agent, Yul's heritage to his own children did not include a single keepsake of his empire. Otrecheniye. My father's guitar, acquired long before stardom, is the only personal item I have of his, along with these cowboy boots. My feet had always been a half-size smaller than his; twenty years after his death, I have literally grown into my father's boots. I wore them in Vladivostok; while Yul never again walked the streets of the city where he was born I made sure his boots did.

My father left another legacy for which he is remembered every day across Russia, one that I had never guessed at, which has nothing to do with his movies. From St. Petersburg to Vladivostok, thousands of Russians listen regularly to Yul's Gypsy songs, performed as he had perfected them long before he was a star. Cassettes of his album with Aliosha Dimitrievitch, bootlegged in the Soviet era, have been replaced with CDs today.

One of the artists invited to perform at the Vladivostok Film Festival was the well-known singer and songwriter Alexander Skliar, with his rock group, Va Bank. He introduced himself to me on my second day there. A thin, intense man in his early forties with a deep baritone, he explained that he had come to Vladivostok because he learned I would be there: he wanted to tell me how much Yul's recording had influenced him — persuaded him, in fact, to become a musician. Skliar had been trained as a diplomat, hoping perhaps to be stationed in Paris or Rome; instead, in the 1980s he had been attached to the Soviet diplomatic mission in North Korea. But after hearing Yul's Gypsy songs, he had had an epiphany and given up his career in the foreign service for music. Today, Skliar and Va Bank are among the most serious, ironic, and imaginative musicians in Russia, while Skliar remains a dedicated rocker — the only rock singer I know who sings *basso*. An hour after we met, guitars in hand, Skliar and I were singing "Okonchen Poot" together. He is the only musician I know who sings Yul's trademark song.

It was Sasha (Alexander) Doluda who had persuaded me to make the trip, and called it my destiny. Sasha is two years younger than I, slim and muscular, with long, neatly tied hair that hangs halfway down his back. An artists' representative, he was one of the organizers of the festival, and he quickly became my Russian brother. I had assumed that his efforts to bring me to the Far East were driven by admiration for Yul, but in fact they had more to do with Jules. As a young man, Sasha had lived for a time in Tetukhe, and there, just beneath Cape Bryner, Sasha first met Natalya, who became his wife many years later. That was the special bond that made him so determined to "bring me home to Vladivostok."

I was frequently greeted with the same phrase, in English or Russian: "We are happy you have *returned*!" — to a place I'd never been. And unfamiliar as Vladivostok was, I did indeed feel as if I were returning. If I started to tell acquaintances about my family's roots in the Far East, they often cut me off; they already knew the story because my great-grandfather is in the schoolbooks, and the family history is on display at the regional museum.

In fact, the Arsenyev Museum resides in the original 1880 home of Bryner & Company, built by Jules at the corner of Svetlanskaya and Aleutskaya streets in the heart of the Old City. Since one of my lectures was scheduled at the museum, I arrived early to introduce myself. There I saw the display about the Brynner family, which included photographs, letters, and even a copy of my memoir about Yul. The origins of the most mysterious movie star of all time were perfectly well known to the city's oldest museum and to its expert on his family, Iraida Klimenko, who has been a great help with my research. The Arsenyev even had recent photos of me; I was surprised to learn that my life was being tracked by a museum.

Although I am Jules' first male descendent to visit Vladivostok in the post-Soviet era, I am not the only one alive; Leonid's descendandts thrive in the northwest United States, from San Francisco to Seattle. And I was not the first Bryner to make the trip. In 1992, just a year after the collapse of Soviet authority, Irena had visited. Yul's cousin was then seventy-four years old; sixty years had passed since the night Felix and Vera had sneaked out of the harbor with her and sailed to freedom aboard the *Glinifer*. Upon her return, Irena visited Sidemy, which she had often described to me vividly, gave a concert of songs by Tchaikovsky and Mussorgsky, and contributed to the Arsenyev Museum several pieces of her hand-worked jewelry. She already had permanent displays at the Cooper-Hewitt Museum, the Louvre, and the Hermitage, formerly the tsar's Winter Palace, in St. Petersburg, where her mother and her aunt had fallen in love with the Bryner brothers in 1915. Irena's visit was nothing less than a mystical experience for her. Having returned under her own steam, she was no longer the hapless pawn of vast historical forces; against daunting odds, she had survived to make it back to where she had begun. Accomplishing this crowned her life's story with wholeness and shape, a sense of earned integrity that lasted until her death in New York City in 2003, just before I was invited to Vladivostok. Now, it fell to me to scatter her ashes from a three-masted schooner into Amur Bay; with that, her journey was complete.

At the Far East State University, which my great-grandfather had helped to establish, I spoke about the ideology behind the U.S. Constitution to some two hundred students of U.S. history, political science, and literature. They followed closely, responding immediately and warmly to the casual manner in which I lecture, very different from the dry formalistic style of most Soviet-trained professors. My interpreter, Evgenia Terekhova, is an esteemed professor herself, and a member of the Far East branch of the prestigious Academy of Sciences. Evgenia enjoyed this opportunity to display her dramatic talents, interpreting my gestures and jokes as well as my words and ideas. I gingerly addressed the new Russian Constitution, which divides the country into ninety-three regions, some as small as the heavily populated Moscow area.

With their animated questions afterward, these students made it clear how engaged they are in exactly the constitutional issues that I had raised. Higher education in Russia, during Soviet times and since, is rigorous, and the majority of the younger people I met in Vladivostok were fluent in English, and with the Internet; they will never be in a closed city again. Even here, at the end of the Trans-Siberian Railroad, which still crosses the country in a week, *Spiderman* opened on the same day as it did in Times Square, dubbed into Russian. They also get Russian MTV and *Izvestia* from Moscow; whether the news they receive is full and accurate is beyond my ken to judge, but they can read the *New York Times* if they choose.

The topics of my other scheduled lectures varied from global warming — "Is Humanity Suicidal?" the subject of my 1998 novel, *The Doomsday Report* — to "The Social and Political Impact of Rock 'n' Roll," given at the

Gorky Library, where I contributed to the film collection five DVDs — Yul's favorites of his career. As well, Tara Rougle arranged a seminar of historians at the U.S. consulate, for whom I outlined my doctoral work.

The most emotional event came at the Arsenyev Museum. There I spoke at length about the family odyssey that had unfolded since my great-grandfather had constructed the building we were in. The hall was packed, and I came to realize that these were not just Yul Brynner or even Jules Bryner fans. Many were there *in search of a usable past*, a familiar phenomenon since the fall of Communism. After three generations in a totalitarian state that had erased, distorted, renamed, or outlawed any honest history, most Russians now dismissed the failed Communist ideology by means of a familiar psychological mechanism: otrecheniye. Renouncing the entire Soviet system, from Central Planning to the Gulag Archipelago, was difficult for some and impossible for others, but as a result, Russians individually and collectively are now desperately eager to recover their pre-Soviet history, rather than have no history at all. By my visit to Vladivostok, I unwittingly provided its citizens with a chance to reconnect with their own past. It was important that they reveal to me, to other Russians, and most of all to themselves, the memories they had kept alive secretly, hidden from Soviet authorities. A dozen or more people brought me photographs of Sidemy (which I did not have time to visit on this trip) and other souvenirs of the Bryner past. My arrival provided them with a pretext to reflect on the founding of their city long before Stalin, and to recall their own origins.

For decades, families who had been ordered to live in squat, anonymous blockhouses around the port would visit the Old City just to recall what society had been like before the Soviets seized control in 1922. Bolshevik partisans had been declared heroes for having liberated Russia from industrial capitalists like Jules Bryner; still, the citizens never forgot the founding fathers, even when mentioning their names had been forbidden.

People waited for me in the lobby of the Hotel Versailles to recount anecdotes about the Bryners: "My grandfather was an accountant for Bryner & Company, and he was shocked when he saw that Jules's widow, Natalya, had cut her daughter-in-laws, the Blagovidovas, out of her last will and testament." "The Bryners were friends with the American, Mr. Gray. Actually, his name was Mr. Black, but when he married a Miss White, they changed their name to Gray." Others presented me with letters citing similar random anecdotes about my family; some brought mementos they had prepared. What was most striking was how much it meant to them to deliver these fragments of history, as if it fulfilled a commitment to their own ancestors.

Another reaction I did not expect was the pride they took in the eclectic adventures of my life. When they saw a photo of me with Muhammad Ali, for example, I became a direct link between their city and the most famous man in the world, a champion they admire. And *The Last Waltz* has become a big hit among the older rockers around town. The people of Vladivostok, who have always counted Yul as their own, now became possessive about me as well. Again and again, the feeling was reinforced that I was not just *in* Vladivostok, I was *of* Vladivostok.

The climate throughout Peter the Great Bay is very mild in autumn, quite hot by day and comfortable in the evenings; the long, bitter winters are something else. Walking about the city, as I did for several hours each day, I was struck by the layers of history represented by the buildings and statues. There remain imposing reminders of pre-Soviet grandeur: the one Orthodox church that was not torn down, the baroque grandeur of Kunst and Albers, and the arch commemorating Tsarevitch Nicholas's visit to Vladivostok in 1891 when he laid the cornerstone for the train station, together with the city fathers. But now, directly across the street from the train station stands a giant statue of Lenin on a pedestal, thirty-five feet high. In the main square stands an enormous bronze monument to the Red Army soldiers of the Civil War. And in front of the Gorky Theater there is a bust of the Bolshevik partisan Sergei Lazo, burned alive in the furnace of a Trans-Siberian locomotive. It is as if, all across Russia, the monuments to autocracy and communism are still engaged in a motionless war with each other.

On my third day, I was invited to visit the Bryner Residence. I was accompanied by Tara Rougle and by U.S. Consul General Pamela L. Spratlen, with whom I had already spent enough time to consider a friend.

Pamela was much loved all around Vladivostok, and it was easy to see why: she had previously been posted in Paris and Moscow. There is a sharp intelligence in her eyes and meticulous, fluent Russian at her command. Pamela was engaged in geopolitical issues relating to post–Cold War disengagement between the U.S. and Russian Pacific fleets; doubtless, the enigma of North Korea, one hundred miles to the south, was not far from her mind.

The Bryner Residence is now the corporate headquarters of Jules' Far East Shipping Company, or FESCO, and its directors were delighted to welcome me; in fact the company's CEO, Mr. Ambrosov, who works from his Moscow office, timed his visit to coincide with mine. The executive offices are in the Residence, while the larger Bryner building next door, where Jules and Natalya lived, houses the operational offices.

The Residence is a pleasing and unusual building that faces east on a twenty-foot-high embankment, with trees and a garden separating it from Aleutskaya Street. It is painted a light yellow, with a decorative, checkerboard trim. Its asymmetry is surprising, as is the deliberate panache of its art nouveau design. I knew from Irena that Yul was born on the third floor, below the arched roof and decorative "bow." Climbing the broad stairway, I tried to imagine Interventionist troops sleeping on these steps in *this* hall. The separate Bryner apartments are now configured as offices, and I can't say that what I experienced there was spiritual communion: the walls did not speak to me, even in the room where my father was born. I only felt awe at the *fact* that I was there. I admired the building, and loved the Old City as a whole, but I think anyone would feel the same fondness for Vladivostok, given such a warm welcome.

Being in Russia gave me the opportunity to wonder how much of my father's emphatic phrasing and broad gesturing, for example, was characteristic of Russian behavior, and how much was pure Brynner. By knowing Yul's sister, aunt, and cousin, I had detected subtle, specific mannerisms — an arched eyebrow, a wicked grin, an explosive hoot of derision — that I assumed were distinct to the Brynner family. Of course, I did more than identify these expressive characteristics; some of them I had also acquired as a child. Now, I began to recognize some of these expressions in Vladivostok, mannerisms I did not detect on later visits to

Moscow and St. Petersburg. That much, at least, felt a little like "discovering my roots."

Throughout this adventure, I did feel as if Yul were traveling with me: not gazing down from above, but looking out from within me. I do not believe in any afterlife beyond the profound ways in which the past lives on within us, offering counsel and forewarning if only we pay attention to subtle extrapolations. Since my parents passed away, I have sometimes invoked their memories and "conjured them up," if you will, though I do not for a moment believe their ghosts are hanging around, waiting to be summoned. But by calling up their memories at significant moments and "sharing" the changes in my life, I can inform and update my own images of them. So, at least the Yul who lives within me knows that I completed his odyssey.

But I also carried within me another person who made this trip possible, who had never been to Russia: without the example of my mother's sobriety, I would never have outlived the Soviet regime. So I arranged to attend two AA meetings in Vladivostok with an interpreter. Alcoholism is rampant in Russia, with an enormous impact upon its society and economy. And under the Soviet regime, the country experienced *state-sponsored* alcoholism: often, when dismal economic results had to be announced, the government first lowered the price of vodka across the country, muting any widespread discontent. Gorbachev, on the other hand, alarmed by the loss in productivity caused by alcohol, severely restricted its legal consumption. He had even less success than American Prohibition in the 1920s, and generated resentment that hampered other reforms. In 1991, when Gorbachev and the Soviet Union were replaced by Boris Yeltsin and the new Russian Federation, it was impossible to ignore the irony that the new premier — the greatest hope for self-government in all Russian history — was often a stumbling drunk.

The Vladivostok AA meetings were no different from those in other countries, but the gatherings were new and isolated, barely surviving in a culture which has not yet understood that alcoholism is a disease for which the treatment — abstinence — is a proven possibility through a program that has saved millions of lives since 1935. I heard the same horrific stories of destructive behavior and destroyed lives, and only a modicum of hope that their lives could really be changed by attending these gatherings. My encouragement meant a lot to the group: they had seen my picture in the newspaper when I arrived, and two days later I was gathered there with them, listening to their experiences and sharing my own, and echoing some of the thousands of success stories I have heard at meetings over the past thirty years.

Consul General Spratlen invited me to join her at lunch with the mayor of Vladivostok, Yuri Kopylov. A short man, strong as a bull, with a thick neck and eyes that expressed a kind of threatening humor, the mayor was anxious to meet me, apparently, since I had been formally presented to the governor. Kopylov was running for re-election the following year, I'd heard, and was already busy shoring up support. Still, he caught me off guard when he offered me, in front of the U.S. consul general, the deed to the Bryner Residence.

"You like the house?" Mayor Kopylov asked. "I will give it to you! I can do that! You sign two documents and it is yours!" Surely, he was joking. But Kopylov wasn't smiling, and when he added that he would like my support for his re-election, I was speechless. Finally, I suggested that the people at FESCO would not be happy to hand over their property to me. "So," replied the mayor, "I will give you the shipping company as well!" This time I felt sure he was joking, and the consul general laughed nervously while I gratefully declined the offer. The following June, Kopylov lost the mayoralty in an election that featured a hand grenade aimed at his predecessor, Cherepkov.

But the mayor's playful offer raised a serious issue: in the lawless "process" of privatization, no one in the world had a more legitimate claim to all of the Bryner's property and businesses than I did. That may explain why the CEO of FESCO was in Vladivostok for my visit. Certainly I could have lodged a valid claim in court; in the absence of an independent judiciary, the outcome would be determined by political connections, competitive bribery, and threats or violence. That is why I had jokingly reassured the CEO that I was *not* in Vladivostok to reclaim the Bryner empire — and why he evinced some signs of genuine relief.

The same occurred when I met the CEO of Dalpolymetall, the company that now owns the Bryner mines at Tetukhe. Vasily Usoltsev is a member of the regional Duma, a tall, good-looking fellow in his thirties; we met in the office of local business developer and historian, Vladimir Khmel, and Usoltsev presented me with a beautiful quartz crystal taken from the Bryner mines, which still operate today. To him as well I joked that I had no ambitions in the production of lead, zinc, and silver, but that it did my heart good to know that Jules' business was still providing work for thousands of people in the small town of Tetukhe, now called Dalnegorsk. Usoltsev invited me to tour the mines on a future visit, and I accepted.

Because by then I had already decided that I would have to return to Vladivostok. One week was not enough time to see and do all the things that had engaged my voracious curiosity. And there was another reason why I was eager to return. I had only been in Russia for a few hours when a woman of breathtaking beauty had smiled warmly and captivated my imagination. At many of the events I attended that week I saw the same stunning brunette, Olya Vigovskaya, an expert in the native tribal cultures of Amur, who worked with an atelier full of friends preserving the native crafts of the region, designing dresses with the exquisitely detailed embroidery that is Olya's specialty, evoking the patterns of the Nanaï and Udege tribes. Admittedly, it wasn't very sensible to fall in love with a woman who lived nine time zones away from my home, was significantly younger than me, and spoke little English. But for the first time since having my heart broken by a dishonest vixen in my own hometown, I felt an attraction that I could not dismiss. Olya provided another strong motive for returning to Vladivostok.

"Why is it," I asked my friend Sasha Doluda, "that so *many* of the women here are fantastically beautiful?"

"Because Vladivostok was a closed city for fifty years," came his explanation. I nodded thoughtfully. But that didn't really make sense: evolution certainly hadn't had enough time to have a hand in it. What Sasha meant was that many of the most beautiful women might have gone to Moscow during those decades, if they had had the option.

Internal emigration toward the jobs and opportunities of Moscow and St. Petersburg has become one of the foremost problems in capitalist

Russia. With the declining population of the country as a whole, the unrelenting drain of ambitious workers toward the metropolitan region is devastating smaller cities across the country. The concentration of wealth is remarkable: in 2004 Moscow had the largest number of billionaires of any city in the world — some thirty-four — as well as the only vibrant job market in the country. Independent young Russian women are drawn there as much as the men. The official population of Moscow is ten million, but estimates range as high as twelve million. Recent laws require internal émigrés to have fixed addresses and incomes before they are allowed to register as Moscow residents, providing new opportunities for corruption.

The beauty of Vladivostok's women has a more fundamental explanation that is cultural, not economic. Wary as I am of such generalizations, I think that Russians are noticeably self-possessed, and that in women this is a particularly appealing quality — at least, to me. Most often, if one glances at a single Russian woman in the street, she does not gaze away shyly: she looks you right back in the eye, unashamed and fearlessly flirtatious, even when it means nothing at all. It seems that Russian women appraise their looks objectively, make the most of them very effectively, and take pleasure in using their charms to taunt men. This bold, feminine bravado seemed familiar; it was much later that I realized I was often reminded of Yul's sister, Vera.

On the final night of the First International Vladivostok Film Festival, the awards were presented. Since there were separate awards for best film, best actor, and best director, that afternoon I asked Sasha Doluda exactly what was the Yul Brynner Award that I was presenting.

"I don't know," Sasha admitted, "but the jury has already chosen the winner."

That evening the festival held its Gala Awards Ceremony. Produced with enormous ambition and energy, no expense was spared to make it a dazzling event, with lasers, streamers, and confetti. The evening began with a performance by Governor Darkin's wife, Larisa Belobrova, of a song, "Pacific Meridian," specially commissioned for the event.

Toward the end of the gala, I went on stage and presented the Yul Brynner Award, won by a film that had not been completed or released — a film, in fact, that the jury had not even seen. It was a Russian work, *The River*, the filming of which was cut short by the death of its star, a much beloved actress. I found deeper significance in this choice. Forty-five years earlier, when Tyrone Power died during the filming of *Solomon and Sheba*, Yul had decided to complete his role for a million dollars. With that, my father left his marriage, and the United States, and began choosing his films more for the money than for the art. Now, the first Yul Brynner Award was given as a tribute to a film that was *not* completed when its star expired. It seemed to me perfectly fitting.

What has become of the "Russian Idea"? The phrase was coined by Dostoyevsky in 1877, when Russia laid siege to Turkey. In the words of one historian, Dostoyevsky anticipated the "denouement of the drama of world history. He predicted the conquest of Constantinople (the original seat of Eastern Orthodoxy) and the unification of the Slavs under Russia's political domination, to be followed by an apocalyptic confrontation in which the dying civilization of Europe would be saved and all nations united in brotherhood by means of the 'Russian idea,' contained in Russia's Orthodox religion."

In 1996, after having narrowly defeated a resurgence of the Communist Party, Boris Yeltsin established a government commission aimed at determining the essence of the Russian Idea: is it a matter of ethnic identity or of shared ideology? What remains the underlying, distinguishing characteristic of the Russian people after both tsarism and Stalinism have been relegated to the trash heap of history? Is the country's unique sense of destiny always rooted in imperial ambition, as when Tsar Nicholas II felt destined to seize Korea along the Yalu River in 1904, or as Stalin felt compelled to dominate Eastern Europe in 1945? Is the Russian character even compatible with the practice of democratic self-government? All these unanswered questions and more swirl about the country today; Yeltsin's commission never could arrive at a consensus. Perhaps that's because, as homespun humorist Will Rogers remarked in the 1930s, "Russia is a country that, no matter what you say about it, it's true."

I subscribe to Ernest Renan's jaded view that "A nation is a group of people united by a mistaken view about the past and a hatred of their neighbors"; I am suspicious of sweeping generalizations about heterogeneous cultures. My perception of nationalism is a product of twenty-first-century realities: today, all the greatest threats we face — and the solutions — are global.

Pandemics, famines, climate change, tsunamis, terrorism, economic interdependence, currency valuation, outsourced labor, information technology, a moral response to genocide: these issues can only be addressed effectively by the global community, through international institutions. It is not just one side of the earth that is endangered by global warming, any more than it is just one end of a ship that sinks. Besides, what is the character of *any* given nation? I can think of no simple "Swiss Idea" or "Irish Idea," let alone some single identifying characteristic for a mosaic of immigrants like the United States. Russia is also a vast tapestry of ethnic identities, woven together by historical layers of imperial conquest. It is accustomed to being ruled by force because that is how it was assembled; in a crisis, nations revert to their founding myths. And while the rebirth of Orthodoxy after seventy years of enforced atheism was nearly miraculous, a nationalist religion is unlikely to provide the glue that will hold Russia together.

The one constant in Russian history is the heavy-handed governance of a single leader: the Romanov autocracy was carried on by Stalin, "the Red Tsar," and today the Russian people are more wary than ever of democracy. That word does not mean self-government to most Russians I have met: rather, "democracy" connotes the corrupt and frenzied decade of Boris Yeltsin, under whose shaky hand their country was stolen by thugs and oligarchs in a greedy free-for-all with the polite name of "privatization." *That* is how "democracy" is identified by many in Russia, and the results of that shameful era will not be undone by the imprisonment of a few billionaires like Khodorkovsky.

As for self-government, it is apparent that for the time being most of the Russian people do not trust their neighbors to govern the country through the ballot box. While recent elections have lacked the essential elements of democracy, starting with a free press, there is no question that the majority of Russians support Putin, believing he needs a free hand, that is, all the autocratic powers he asks for. The most critical element in democracy, a judicial system that is *independent* of the governing party, is rarely even discussed. If one raises that issue in Russia, many, like President Putin, are quick to point to the Supreme Court's embarrassing role in the U.S. presidential election of 2000.

No one can foretell how Russia will evolve. Putin has called for "a *new* Russian Idea" that blends "universal humanitarian" and "traditional Russian" values. In that effort, I can only hope that he succeeds, for the sake of the people of Vladivostok and for the collective soul of Russia.

Epilogue

Since my first visit to Vladivostok, I have made five more trips to Russia, as one event after another gradually compelled me to write this book.

In early 2004, I was invited to speak at the Kennan Institute for Advanced Russian Studies, part of the Woodrow Wilson International Center for Scholars in Washington, D.C. Acknowledging that my fields of expertise as a historian did not include Russia, I proceeded to recount the Bryners' saga in the Far East. The lecture was very warmly received, and soon after I was invited back to the Institute by its chairman, Dr. Blair Ruble, to celebrate the one hundredth birthday of George Kennan, the renowned diplomat who in 1946 had initiated the U.S. policy of "containment" toward Soviet ambitions.

After my Kennan lecture, Bella Pak, a Korean scholar who had been listening attentively, introduced herself: she is a specialist in Russo-Korean history like her renowned father, Professor Boris Pak, and she offered to share with me documents relating to Jules Bryner they had uncovered in their research at the State Archives in Moscow. Soon after, she sent me the secret report on Jules' activities in Korea, written in 1896 by an undercover agent for Finance Minister Sergei Witte. Equally valuable, Ms. Pak sent me the account written by Jules himself, explaining why he first explored the Yalu River, as well as his logistics for marketing its estimated six and a half million tons of processed timber; his explanation discloses none of the territorial ambitions that Tsar Nicholas II would later attach to the ill-fated acquisition of Jules' concession in Korea. These two documents, which only came to light because of my Kennan lecture, persuaded me that this book would have to sketch a history of modern Russia, if only to put my family's story in context.

I visited St. Petersburg in the summer of 2004 on a privately sponsored lecture tour, speaking to students and faculty in a variety of academic settings, including Smolny College at St. Petersburg University and the historic Mayakovsky Library, thanks to a U.S. consular program that sponsors an "American Corner" in major libraries across Russia — a well appreciated and cost-effective contribution to U.S. public diplomacy.

Post-Soviet St. Petersburg is a far cry from its triumphant days as the Imperial capital, but it is still glorious — especially during the "white nights" of the summer solstice, when the sun merely dips below the horizon. At midnight, I went to the banks of the Neva River to watch the drawbridges rise and fall, as I'm sure that Boris and Marousia did ninety years earlier, after they met there as students under the rule of Tsar Nicholas.

Along the northwest embankment of the Neva River stands the Gorny Institute, the mining school founded by Catherine the Great in 1773. I was not sure what years Boris had been a student, but I stopped by there one day without advance notice, and soon met with the director of the Institute's museum. Their unique geological collection was also initiated by Catherine, upon the advice of her friends Voltaire and Diderot, the Enlightenment *philosophes* who had liberated knowledge from religion and compiled the first encyclopedia.

Like many of Russia's institutions, the Gorny Institute lost most of its records in the throes of revolution and its aftermath. Nonetheless, the director, Jeanna Polyarnaya, produced an archive listing all the Institute's graduates; Boris Bryner was listed for his master of science degree with honors in 1916. When I mentioned that our family had created the mines at Tetukhe, the amazed museum officials took me to the well-guarded room where their collection of Fabergé's bejeweled *objets d'art* are kept; there, a wall-sized glass cabinet displayed a collection of rare stones taken from the Tetukhe mines, obtained by the museum during the Soviet era. The Institute was unaware that this special collection came from the mines of their graduate, Boris Bryner.

In St. Petersburg on Bloody Sunday, 1905, protesters to the war with Japan were descending upon Winter Palace Square when hundreds were massacred, an event that helped replace the Russian Empire with the Communist Soviet Union. Ninety-nine years later, in the same square, Paul McCartney performed the Beatles' 1970 hit "Back in the U.S.S.R." more than a decade after its demise. Across the country such ironies are too commonplace to be noticed: many buildings are adorned with both the Communist hammer and sickle *and* the double-headed eagle of Imperial Russia, while monuments to the tsars rub shoulders with statues of Communist heroes. This tolerance is selective: though Lenin is still revered, Stalin is rarely mentioned in polite society, and some statues — like that of Felix Dzerzhinsky outside KGB headquarters in Moscow — have been removed. Nonetheless, Putin himself has ominously described the collapse of the USSR as "a genuine tragedy" and "the greatest geopolitical catastrophe" of the twentieth century. As Peter Baker remarks in his perceptive new study, *Kremlin Rising: Vladimir Putin's Russia and the End of Revolution*, Russia today is concerned with "glorifying its lost empire rather than exulting in the downfall of dictatorship." "Nationalism mixed with Soviet-era symbolism," writes Baker, "was the perfect balm to the collective bruised ego." Meantime, directly opposite Lenin's tomb, Dior and Vuitton now dominate Red Square with capitalist iconography, and the giant bomb shelter beside the Kremlin, built to protect the Soviet leadership, today houses a deluxe shopping mall. Moscow has adopted capitalism with a vengeance, unimpeded by the ethical constraints that Adam Smith took for granted in *The Wealth of Nations*.

I spent several weeks in Moscow delivering lectures and conducting research for this book. I presented *The King and I* at the renowned film school known as V-GIK, and spoke at the Moscow branch of the Kennan Institute, which is under the auspices of the Academy of Sciences. At the Moscow Art Theatre, the director of archives was delighted to share facts and anecdotes about Mikhail Chekhov, Katya Kornakova, and Boris, along with a videotaped lecture that Yul's discarded mentor, George Shdanoff, gave there during a visit before his death.

I returned to Vladivostok in September 2004 as a guest of the second Vladivostok Film Festival, rather than the U.S. State Department, and it felt even more remarkably like a homecoming. Upon my arrival, Olya Vigovskaya and I fell in love and were together throughout my stay. After I arrived with Olya at the Film Festival Gala, feeling for all the world like a prince of Primorye with his princess, our love story was reported in the press, and by now is known across Russia. Since then, Olya has spent three months with me in the United States, and I have visited her a fourth and fifth time. But she undoubtedly belongs in Vladivostok, and I belong on my hilltop in upstate New York. So . . . we will have to do a lot of traveling.

Not one of my paternal forefathers reached the age of seventy. As I approach my sixties, to become a father against those odds would be irresponsible. And as I search my very soul, I accept with complete equanimity the fact that I am the end of the line connecting me to Yul and Boris and Jules. I contemplate mortality with aplomb precisely because I will not leave behind a grieving child. Besides, "I'd rather die happy than not die at all"; that's what The Band used to sing. And I am enjoying the happiest time of my life, which I hope may last for decades.

Olya and I visited Sidemy together, crossing Amur Bay by boat with Sasha Doluda. The peninsula settled by Mikhail Yankovsky and Jules Bryner had been used as a Pioneer Communist Youth Camp for decades, during which thousands of Primorye children had vacationed there; in the 1990s, after the Soviet era, Olya spent many of her summers there with family friends. So it was my sweetheart who showed me around the property and the beaches where Yul, and Boris before him, had spent childhood summers. It is a beautiful spot, rising from a rocky beach to the field where the Bryner house used to stand; now, only the foundation remains. But on a low bluff over the beach, the walls of the honeymoon cottage are still standing, and below the floor are crawl spaces where the family sometimes hid the children from wolves and tigers, *hunghu'tze* and other bandits, and later from Bolshevik partisans. In 1882, Jules and Natalya had spent their nuptials in this cottage, and in 1915, Boris and Marousia came to stay here after their wedding in Petrograd. Yul paddled in these waters when he was seven, and developed the passion for sports that made him a lifeguard in Normandy, and an acrobat in Paris. That passion enlivened my own childhood, as we water-skied across America and Switzerland.

I paid a visit to the Bryner mines at Tetukhe when the new company, Dalpolymetall, was gracious enough to invite me. It was a three-hundred-mile drive north through the Sikhote-Alin mountains to the town of thirty thousand that is now known as Dalnegorsk.

After lunch with the managing director, we went to the first mine that Jules had opened in 1897, on the very spot that Chinese ginseng traders had brought him with a geologist, though how they made it there on horseback in winter is unimaginable. The Upper Mine, no longer operational, is at the top of an eight-hundred-foot hill; from here the first silver, zinc, and lead ores were lowered to the narrow-gauge railroad that Jules had imported by sea from Europe. I followed the Bryner railroad, powered by diesel locomotives half the size of passenger engines, as it wound its way to the refinery; from there the ore continues through the valley by rail some twenty miles to the small port of Pristan on the Sea of Japan. The train proceeds out onto the narrow Bryner Pier, where the carloads of refined ore are dumped onto barges that carry it to ships waiting in the natural harbor below the lighthouse high above on Cape Bryner. The complex operation still proceeds exactly as it did when Jules designed Tetukhe more than a century ago. And right after the fall of the Soviet Union, Cape Bryner appeared on the thousand-rouble bill of the Russian Federation.

The next day I was escorted down one of the operational mine shafts, worked by the thousand or so employees of Dalpolymetall. My guide was a man I admire immensely: Leonid Sinevitch has worked in the Bryner mines (as he still calls them) for almost fifty years; notwithstanding, he is very hearty. Leonid did not know the Bryners, but the town never forgot the family that had carved this isolated community out of the taiga. The adults Leonid had known as a boy in the 1940s were personally acquainted with Boris, and shared many stories of Jules as well. He is remembered as a generous and compassionate patriarch, so concerned with his workers' well-being that he built a clinic and distributed free food and clothing that he imported because Tetukhe was only accessible by sea. This is not how most Russian mining communities remember their private employers.

After suiting me up in mining gear, Leonid took me a thousand feet down in the shaft by elevator; from there we climbed down rickety ladders another two hundred feet to the main level of operations, where we walked for several miles observing the different stages of the work, and discussing its history all the while. Clearly, the remote location and challenging conditions made this an audacious undertaking of Jules' from the start. I had never been deep inside the earth before visiting my family's mines, and the experience was a powerful lesson in the courage and perseverance of human endeavor.

Today, Dalnegorsk is suffering. The Communist regime had served the interests of the miners well, and though there was much that was not popular in that era, incomes and pensions were good for the "salt of the earth": prices under Socialism made travel — even an air ticket to Moscow — affordable. With privatization, government projects, including a half-built cement factory, were halted, and later sold off for scrap metal. And though paychecks were not cut, the basic cost of survival increased dramatically. It is not clear how this town will survive another century.

By the autumn of 2005 I had spent a total of two months in Vladivostok and come to feel very at ease in the city. I've made a lot of friends there among entertainers, environmental groups, academics, recovering alcoholics, and dedicated artists, and given public talks and lectures to hundreds of university students and involved citizens. I began advising the History and Humanities Institute on texts and teaching approaches for their U.S. history program; this is a department of the Far East State University that began as the Oriental Institute, with scholarships from Jules, in 1899; it seems only natural that I should try to help out. The damn Russian language remains baffling, with its too-large alphabet and millions of rules and exceptions, but I am working on it. I have a mobile phone when I'm there, and I can get around the city by bus. And while I wouldn't choose to leave my hilltop in New York, I feel very at home when I visit Vladivostok.

Before the end of the Soviet era, I could never have reassembled the story of our family. And before e-mail existed, locating relatives and documents would have been a more daunting enterprise. But it was through friends that I located Valery Yankovsky, the grandson of Jules' partner at Sidemy and the son of Yuri, "the greatest tiger hunter in the world," with whom Yul and Boris went hunting at Novina, in North Korea.

Valery Yankovsky is now ninety-four years old, and lives in remarkably fine health and clear-minded independence with his wife of fifty years, Irina. A respected writer and historian, he is only distantly my "uncle": his grandmother was the cousin of my great-grandmother, Jules' wife, Natalya;

but also, his mother's cousin was Katya, Boris's second wife, stepmother to Yul. Valery's home is three hours from Moscow by train, where I visited him in June 2005, during my fourth trip to Russia.

Valery is the only person alive today to have known four generations of my family, the four subjects of this book. He knew Jules as an elderly man, Boris as an avid hunter in his prime, and Yul as a "young pup" with boundless energy at Sidemy. Now, eighty years later, I appeared from New York, reasserting the Bryner bond with the Yankovskys.

The first half of Valery's life was filled with such intense adventures that, I believe, he needed the second half of his life to absorb and record it all. In that respect our lives have been remarkably parallel, but there all resemblance ends. Valery was eleven years old in 1922 when he and his family fled the Bolsheviks from Sidemy: "eight Holland cows and seventy people" on barges riding the Pacific waves to northern Korea, where they built Novina — Boris and Katya owned a dacha that they visited every summer there, which Yul had visited at seventeen. Valery spent many years hunting tigers, wolves, and wild boar through the Russian taiga, the hills of North Korea, and the mountains of Manchuria. He lived under the rule of the last tsar of Russia, the king of Korea, and the Japanese mikado, and has spoken a half-dozen or more languages fluently. His English is still remarkable.

Valery Yankovsky was also in Pyongyang in 1945 when the Soviet Army wrested North Korea from Japanese control, which Imperial Russia had failed to accomplish so disastrously forty years earlier along the Yalu River. He was ordered to work as an interpreter for the KGB's counterespionage unit, SMERSH (the Russian acronym for "Death to Spies," familiar to James Bond fans), and in October 1946, he witnessed the arrival of Kim Il Sung in Pyongyang on the very afternoon that his tyranny over North Korea began; today his son, Kim Jong Il, still rules.

A few months after Kim Il Sung seized power, Soviet authorities imprisoned Valery on trumped-up charges of having aided the Japanese enemy, and after a mockery of a trial, he was sent to the gulag, transported as "human cargo" to work in labor camps for the next ten years in the deadly Siberian mines near Magadan, north of the Arctic Circle. Released in the mid-1950s, he and Irina settled near Moscow because of their son's asthma.

Valery and I had read each others' memoirs, and though we only had a few hours to spend together, there was no doubt that we became very close. He told me about my family, and clarified a number of details I had not resolved. He was surprisingly fond of my great-grandmother, Natalya, though unaware of her Buryat ancestry, established by family records. He had been especially close with Boris during their summers hunting together in northern Korea, and it was especially valuable to hear that my grandfather was a man of notable charm and gallantry.

I also had something of value to offer Valery: I brought him the key documents about Jules' activities in Korea, along with the earliest manuscript of this book. These documents — Jules' contract with the king of Korea, his research along the Yalu River, and the report on his activities from the secret agent Pokotilov — had never been available during the seventy years of Soviet rule, and the fact that Jules Bryner was the catalyst in the Yalu River affair was omitted in Soviet accounts. Thus it has somehow fallen to me to restore the key to this decisive event to the history of Russia.

Now Valery is adapting and translating my work to provide Russian readers and historians with the first detailed account of Jules Bryner's role in triggering the war with Japan that produced the Revolution of 1905, setting the stage for the Communist Revolution that produced the Cold War. Whatever first brought me to Vladivostok — curiosity, history, destiny, or still some other power — less than two years later I felt blessed to provide this courageous old man with documents explaining events that had shaped his world and his life. And, embracing as we said goodbye, we acknowledged with awe that the forces of history which had torn our family apart had now brought us together.

Appendix

Text of the Korean forest concession, given by the Korean King to the Vladivostok merchant of the First Guild, Ju. I. Bryner, 28 August 1896.

His Majesty, the Korean King, who is engaged in the introduction into Korea of correct forest management and the development of timber using European methods, agrees to conclude the following agreement:

1. Jules Ivanovich Bryner, a Russian subject and Vladivostok merchant of the First Guild, is permitted to form a company under the name of "The Korean Forest Company."
2. The Korean Forest Company receives the exclusive right to conduct forest operations for a period of twenty (20) years on the government lands in the upper reaches of the river Tumen and along its right tributaries in the Mushinskij area and also on the island of Djazhalet (Ul' leng-do) in the Japanese Sea. In addition, after establishing itself in these areas, The Korean Forest Company has the right to explore the forest areas along the Yalu river system on Korean territory with the help of experienced people, and after that will have the right to expand its operation to relevant areas, carrying out activities on the same basis as in the Tumeskij area. If activities along the Yalu river system are not begun within 6 years from the date of the signing of the present agreement, then The Korean Forest Company loses all rights to this area.
3. Within the above-mentioned borders, the designated company has the right to do whatever is necessary to create roads and horse railways, and to clear the rivers to allow

for the floating of logs, and also to build houses, workshops, and factories.

4. For the duration of the contract, the designated company accepts the responsibility for hiring and maintaining a forestry/logging specialist from the corps of Russian foresters, who has completed a course of study in a forestry institute, and in the same manner, a sufficient number of Russian assistants for him.

   Forestry management and the development of timber resources must be carried out in a correct manner under their guidance, namely:

   a) Trees younger than 30 years old must not be cut down, and they must be allowed to grow with the appropriate oversight and care.
   b) Care must be taken for the growth and re-development of trees in the wood-cutting area where the company is active. For approximately every hundred trees that are cut down, at least one of the best trees must be left untouched for reseeding.
   c) Strong measures must be taken for the prevention and control of forest fires. The local administration will issue regulations for this purpose forbidding the burning of clearings in the forests and their surrounding areas. The forestry specialist and his assistants will monitor the execution of these regulations with the help of local officials.
   d) The cutting down of trees by the company must not take place everywhere, but only in places designated as annual tree-cutting areas. To this end, every year around the 15th of September an area will be set aside for the year's tree-cutting, the borders of which will be marked with embankments and ditches. In this way, the forest areas selected by the company will be gradually divided into 20 wood-cutting parcels. Work in each of these wood-cutting parcels must not continue for more than 2 winters and 1

summer, and furthermore, the cutting and transporting of timber is allowed only from the 15th of September to the 15th of May.

5. For the development of the forest, the company may build steam-driven lumber-cutting factories either on the Russian bank of the Yalu River, or on the Korean side, whichever is more convenient. The timber products obtained in this manner can be shipped abroad or sold locally.
6. The forestry expert appointed by the company will be available to the Korean government for the drawing up of forestry regulations and the introduction of the same into the Kingdom, and especially for the education of Koreans in practical forest management, in methods of seeding in the areas of tree-cutting, in methods of disseminating new trees, and so on. The Korean government will also have the right to assign government functionaries and young people to the company's lumber factories for them to become familiar with lumber manufacturing equipment and the methods of selling/marketing of lumber in general.
7. The Korean government will afford the company every kind of assistance in its relations with local residents, and in everything that concerns the hiring of workers or meeting transportation needs. The government will supply foreigners working for the company with passports and will afford them all protection.
8. Most of the work will be carried out by Koreans, but in case of non-performance on their part, the company will have the right to replace them with Russian or foreign workers.
9. Generally the company will buy provisions for the workers locally, but if there is a price increase during a famine or there is no harvest, provisions will be obtained abroad and distributed to the workers using delivery channels specially set up to the location. Provisions, instruments, materials,

and machines needed for the forestry work will be imported from abroad free of duty; similarly there will not be any duty imposed on timber products obtained by the company and shipped abroad.

10. Jules I. Bryner will amass all the capital needed for the successful conduct of the business of the above-mentioned company.
11. Jules I. Bryner will provide the Korean government with a document, confirming that the government will be the owner of all the company's property without any expenditure on its part, and that it will have the right to receive one quarter of the entire net profits of the company, in consideration of which no duty or taxes will be levied against the company for the use of the forest.
12. The main headquarters of the company will be in Vladivostok with a subsidiary in Seoul or Chemul'po. Once a year there will be a general meeting of shareholders or their representatives either in Seoul or Chemul'po. At this meeting, each share will be the equivalent of one vote. Any questions or issues that are not included in the text of this agreement will be decided by a majority of votes of the shareholders of the company. The company's books will be kept in Vladivostok, as the closest location to the place of the work, and copies certified by a notary will be submitted to the general meeting in Seoul or Chemul'po for review.
13. His Majesty the King can appoint an official who will reside where he thinks it most convenient to look after the interests of his government and control/monitor the quantity of cut and shipped lumber, that is, near the lumber depot(s) where all the lumber is concentrated in one area. This official has the right to conduct an audit of the books from time to time. In addition, an official of the local administration might be appointed who would pro-

vide rafting tickets for all the cut and shipped lumber, on which would be written the name of the person to whom the tickets were given, the date and place of the cutting down of the wood, and the quantity and measurements of the lumber (or timber). If by the 15th of November, through circumstances caused by the will of God, the lumber referred to on the tickets has not been rafted, then the tickets will be returned to the official that issued them and he will replace the tickets with other documentation indicating the place of origin of the lumber, the quantity of lumber, and the reasons that it could not be rafted. With this documentation, the shipment could be sent the following year.

14. The portion of the net profits due to the Korean government will be paid yearly in Seoul through a Russian-Chinese bank, where Mr. Bryner will maintain a permanent security deposit in the amount of fifteen thousand (15,000) rubles in silver, as a guarantee of the timely payment of the Korean government's portion of the profits. If the amount of the net profits increases, the amount of the deposit will increase accordingly.
15. This contract will become void if work in the forests has not begun within one year from the date of its signing, assuming of course that the delay is not the result of war or another similar cause out of the control of the company. In the latter case, by mutual agreement between the Korean government and the above-mentioned company, the deadline for the beginning of work will be extended.
16. In the case of the death of Mr. Bryner before the end of the period of the present contract, his rights will be transferred in full to his heirs and successors. Mr. Bryner has the right to transfer this contract to any trustworthy Russian individual or organization.
17. An exact translation into Chinese will be attached to the

Russian language text of the concession. However, in the case of any misunderstandings, the Russian text will be considered primary.

Jules Ivanovich Bryner
Vladivostok Merchant of the First Guild
Seoul, 28th August, 1896

I hereby certify with the seal of the Imperial Mission the signatures of the Vladivostok Merchant of the First Guild, Jules Ivanovich Bryner, and the Korean minister of foreign affairs, I Van Eng, and the minister of Commerce and Trade, Chzho Ping Chik. Seoul, 29 August, 1896, No. 70.

Vice Consul Poljanskij

Translated by Peggy Troupin

Notes

Introduction

1 **History is neither** Samuel Beckett, "Dante, Bruno, Vico, Joyce," in *Our Exagmination Round His Factification For Incamination of Work in Progress* (London: Faber, 1929).

Part One

10 **with the Danzas Company** From documents in the Bryner file, Möriken-Wildegg Archives, Public Records Office, Aargau, Switzerland, where Jules' birth was registered.

10 **galley boy on a privateer** Irena Brynner, *What I Remember* (New York: 1st Books, 2002), 13. Also, extensive conversations and recorded interviews with Irena, her mother, Vera, and other family members.

12 **"Take away your opium** F. L. Hawks Pott, *A Short History of Shanghai: Being an Account of the Growth and Development of the International Settlement* (Shanghai: n.p., 1928), 34.

17 **"We saw the officers' house** Arsenyev Primoski State Museum, ed., *Old Vladivostok* (Vladivostok: Utro Rossii, 1992). Much of the early account of Vladivostok comes from this and other regional archives and collections.

19 **Gustav Kunst and Gustav Albers** Lothar Deeg, *Kunst & Albers Wladiwostok* (Essen, Germany: Klartext-Verlag, 1996).

19 **"about 50 public and private houses** Arsenyev, *Old Vladivostok.*

20 **"We have nothing to conquer** Andrew Malozemoff, *Russian Far Eastern Policy, 1881–1904* (New York: Octagon Books, 1958) cited in David Wolff, *To the Harbin Station: The Liberal Alternative in Russian Manchuria, 1898–1914* (Stanford, Calif.: Stanford University Press, 1999), 42.

21 **a note signed** From documents in the Bryner records in the Public Records Office of Möriken-Wildegg, Aargau, Switzerland. Jules' gift was a Japanese picture roll from 1765 that today is kept in the Public Record Office of Aargau.

22 **"It was an encyclopædic store,"** Maria Lebedko, "An Online Walking Tour of Vladivostok," http://www.wsulibs.wsu.edu/Vladivostok/.

22 **"The clerks were multi-lingual,"** John J. Stephan, *The Russian Far East: A History* (Stanford, Calif.: Stanford University Press, 1994), 85.

24 **"As Yankovsky, Bryner, and Shevelev** Donald N. Clark, *Living Dangerously in Korea: The Western Experience, 1900–1950* (Norwalk, Conn.: EastBridge, 2003), 149.

25 **at the Uspensky Orthodox Church** From the Uspenskaya Cathedral register, Vladivostok, provided by Tatiyana Kushnareva.

28 **"We didn't occupy** Stephan, *Russian Far East*, 79.

28 **"The Trans-Siberian Railroad** Steven G. Marks, *Road to Power: The Trans-Siberian Railroad and the Colonization of Asian Russia, 1850–1917* (Ithaca, N.Y.: Cornell University Press, 1991), 27. Much of my account of the Trans-Siberian Railroad is indebted to Marks, the only authoritative source in English.

29 **"the frantic post-1880 jostling** Paul Kennedy, *The Rise and Fall of the Great Powers: Economic Change and Military Conflict from 1500 to 2000* (New York: Vintage Books, 1987), xviii.

29 **"London expected to make use** Marks, *Road to Power*, 33.

31 **"shaped by an axe,"** C. L. Seegar, ed., *Memoirs of Alexander Iswolsky, Formerly Russian Minister of Foreign Affairs and Ambassador to France* (London: Hutchinson, 1920), 113–114.

31 **"an expression of patience"** John Albert White, *The Diplomacy of the Russo-Japanese War* (Princeton, N.J.: Princeton University Press, 1964), 12, 15.

32 **"a desolate frontier town** Robert K. Massie, *Nicholas and Alexandra* (New York: Atheneum, 1967), 22.

32 **"Witte's spending** Marks, *Road to Power*, 129.

32 **"One day in deepest mourning,** Massie, *Nicholas and Alexandra*, 44.

35 **"cold salmon with mayonnaise** Mrs. Eleanor Pray, personal letter, June 1917, cited in Birgitta Ingemanson, "A Paradise Lost: The Novogeorgievsk Estate, 1892–1922", 8. Ms. Ingemanson, a luminary among scholars of the Russian Far East who teaches at Washington State University, has been very generous to me with this project. She was given access to Mrs. Pray's letters by Patricia Silver, a descendant, and in numerous books and articles has examined the social and political history of the region.

36 **also specified in their agreement** The entire contract in Russian is reprinted in A.I. Gippius, *O Prichinakh Nashei Voiny s Iaponiei. C. Prilozheniiami Dokumenty* (St. Peterburg: Tip A.S. Suvorina, 1905), microfilm, 49–52; translated into English for me by Peggy Troupin.

37 **"Bryner's efforts were crowned** Letter from D. Pokotilov to P. M. Romanov, Seoul, Sept. 25, 1896. This document was found in the Russian State Archive in Moscow by historians Boris Pak and Bella Pak.

38 **"When we were** V. I. Gurko, *Features and Figures of the Past: Government and Opinion in the Reign of Nicholas II* (London: Oxford University Press, 1939), 262.

39 **"ill-balanced faculties** V. M. Vonliarliarsky, "Why Russia Went to War With Japan: The Story of the Yalu Concession," *Fortnightly Review*, n.s., 521 (May 2, 1910), 816.

39 **"itself the key** White, *Diplomacy*, 33.

39 **"It pleased His Majesty** V. M. Vonliarliarsky, "Why Russia," 825.

42 **"Bryner's official connections** White, *Diplomacy*, 32.

42 **"Witte, contradicting himself** Alexander Solzhenitsyn, *August 1914: The Red Wheel* (London: Bodley Head, 1989), 677, 680.

43 ***Russia's entire Far Eastern policy*."** White, *Diplomacy*, 40 (my italics).

43 **"he was deluded** Gurko, *Features and Figures*, 264.

43 **"The Japanese Prime Minister** Ibid., 265.

44 **"Drawn on by ambition,"** Ibid., 274.

45 **Although Japan** Massie, *Nicholas and Alexandra*, 73.

46 **On the evening of February 8,** Stephan, *Russian Far East*, 79.

46 **"Chinese civilians were shot like partridges."** White, *Diplomacy*, 36.

47 **1 million men** Richard Harding Davis et al., *The Russo-Japanese War: A Photographic and Descriptive Review of the Great Conflict in the Far East* (New York: Collins, 1904), 97.

48 **"at the very moment** Marks, *Road to Power*, 202. I owe most of this account of the war effort at Lake Baikal to Marks and to Davis *et al.*

49 **"You have wished us victory,** Massie, *Nicholas and Alexandra*, 74.

49 **"The Russians were outnumbered** Davis, *Russo-Japanese War*, 97.

50 **"I treated everybody** Massie, *Nicholas and Alexandra*, 91.

50 **"with Mamiya Strait in our grasp** *Japanese Times*, July 11, 1905, cited in White, *Diplomacy*, 224.
51 **"Sire, Russia has been drawn** White, *Diplomacy*, 210.
51 **"the number of working days** Gurko, *Features and Figures*, 314.
51 **"'Bloody Sunday,'"** Massie, *Nicholas and Alexandra*, 97, 99, 100.
52 **"if a state overextends itself** Kennedy, *Rise and Fall, xvi.*
54 **"Wartime Vladivostok** Stephan, *Russian Far East*, 101.
55 **"Complete anarchy"** Ibid., 102.
57 **a light-gauge rail system** I owe much of this account to C. A. (or A. C) Kidd's unpublished account of the mines, "Tetiuhe: A History of the Tetiuhe Mine In Siberia" (London: 1980), which Mr. Kidd's family has kindly allowed me to cite. I was first given a copy made from the London School of Economics Archives by Johnny Veeder, QC of King's College, University of London, to whom I am deeply indebted for much of my information about Tetukhe, thanks to research for his paper, "The Tetiuhe Mining Concession 1924–1932: A Swiss-Russian Story (Where the Arbitral Dog Did Not Bark)," in *Liber Amicorum Claude Reymond: Autour de l'Arbitrage* (Paris: Edition Juris-Classeur, 2004).

As well, Dalpolymetall, the current owners of the Tetiuhe concession, gave me an extended tour in the mines and the region in 2004, where I heard many local accounts.
59 **"The word 'partisan'** Stephan, *Russian Far East*, 123.
60 **"Yesterday afternoon** January 24, 1918. Historian Birgitta Ingemanson found this citation among Mrs. Pray's letters and kindly forwarded it to me. Previously the Bryners had lived at Svetlanskaya 55/1, Feodorovskaya 3 and 8, and Vsilkovskaya 13.
60 **By 1897 the population of all Far East Russia** Stephen Kotkin and David Wolff, eds., *Rediscovering Russia in Asia: Siberia and the Russian Far East* (Armonk, N.Y.: M.E. Sharpe, 1995), 27.
60 **By 1914 the total population of all Siberia** Felix Patrikeeff, "Russian and Soviet Economic Penetration of North-Eastern China, 1895–1933," in *Essays on Revolutionary Culture and Stalinism*, ed. John W. Strong (Columbus, Ohio: Slavica, 1990), 57.
62 **no one dared speak to the tsar** Paul Rodzianko, *Tattered Banners: An Autobiography* (London: Seeley Service, 1934), 100.
65 **recovered consciousness and began to scream** Ibid., 124. Rodzianko, grandfather of my friend Paul, was dispatched by General Kolchak a few months later to investigate the assassinations in Ekaterinburg.
66 **a "Special Board" hearing** Veeder, "Tetiuhe Concession."
67 **"the ribbon of steel** Stephan, *Russian Far East*, 109.
67 **"unlike the Reds,"** Ibid., 137.
68 **"he moved about in his famous armored railcars** John Albert White, *The Siberian Intervention* (Princeton, N.J.: Princeton University Press, 1950), 197.
69 **The Japanese financed** Canfield F. Smith, *Vladivostok Under Red and White Rule: Revolution and Counterrevolution in the Russian Far East, 1920–1922* (Seattle: University of Washington Press, 1975), 28–29.
69 **Vladivostok was a world unto itself,** Stephan, *Russian Far East*, 132.
70 **Morphine, cocaine, prostitution,** Ibid., 126.
70 **6 percent of the AEF** Ibid., 134.
73 **"kept two flags** Smith, *Vladivostok*, 108, 149.

Part Two

78 **the 2,824th degree** The museum director of St. Petersburg's Gorny Institute, Jeanna Polyarnaya, found Boris's official designation in the Gorny archives.

80 **"This war is madness,"** Witte, cited in Maurice Paléologue, *Turning Point: Three Critical Years, 1904–1906,* trans. F. Appleby Holt (London: Hutchinson and Co., 1935), I, 122–3.

81 **the first woman licensed as a doctor** According to her daughter, Irena, in conversation.

83 **"in his capacity as a Tsarist army officer** Irena Brynner, *What I Remember,* 16–17.

83 **Lenin struck me as a happy man.** Arthur Ransome, *Russia in 1919* (New York: B.W. Heubsch, 1919), 124.

84 **"'ten days that shook the world'** Stephan, *Russian Far East,* 152.

85 **"Three weeks before** Anne Applebaum, *Gulag: A History* (New York: Doubleday, 2003), 5.

86 **"The Tetukhe mine, however,** This account of the business dealings is drawn from Veeder's research, which he generously shared with me.

87 **as a White officer** Irena Brynner, *What I Remember*, 25.

89 **Four such members** Smith, *Vladivostok*, 53, 199n40.

90 **"As entrepreneurs** Veeder, "Tetiuhe Concession."

90 **By 1922, industrial production in Russia** Kidd, "Tetiuhe," 14.

91 **"fulfilled a political** Stephan, *Russian Far East*, 164–65.

93 **tertiary syphilis** According to a recent article in *The European Journal of Neurology* (June 2004), and *The Moscow Times*, June 23, 2004, 4.

95 **ardently courted** Conversation with the director of the Moscow Art Theatre Museum, July 4, 2004.

96 **"The program for our undertaking** Konstantin Stanislavsky, *An Actor Prepares* (New York: Theatre Arts, 1939), 8.

97 **My dear Mamulinka,** Boris's original letter is with the Smithsonian Museum's collection of Irena Brynner's works in Washington, D.C. It has been translated into English by Carol Anschvetz. The endearments Boris uses here emphasize Marousia's role as a mother, not as his wife.

99 **Accordingly, Boris received a divorce** This and many other facts about Boris and Katya were provided by their daughter, Catherine Bryner, of Guilford, Australia.

99 **"I remember how she paced the floor,"** Irena Brynner, *What I Remember*, 33.

101 **a city of 150,000** Kidd, "Tetiuhe," 88. This account of Tetukhe owes much to the writings of Kidd.

103 **In the first fifteen months** Ibid., 91.

103 **"Boris spent** Ibid., 31.

104 **Stalin's peculiar cruelty** Retold in Dimitri Volkogonov, *Stalin: Triumph and Tragedy* (London: Weidenfeld and Nicholson, 1991), 74.

104 **"The Stalin myth** *A Brief Biography of Stalin* by Laura Detloff, Dickinson College, Carlisle, PA, at http://www.dickinson.edu/~history/dictators/stalin_dictator1.html (accessed January 2004).

105 **"while I fully appreciate** *Mining World*, October 10, 1927.

106 **And in letters** *The London Times*, January 1, 1932; February 17, 1932.

107 **"The attitude of Soviets** Leonid Bryner to the Swiss Consul General of Shanghai, Nov. 2, 1945. Letter obtained by V. V. Veeder from the Bern Archives of the Swiss Department of Foreign Affairs.

108 **"The waves were higher now,"** Irena Brynner, *What I Remember,* 73–75.
109 **"Boris heard** Kidd, "Tetiuhe," 31.
111 **"To cover the fruits of aggression** Stephan, *Russian Far East,* 183.
112 **"Like excised tissue** Stephan, *Russian Fascists,* 43.
113 **twenty years before Churchill** Though Churchill has always been credited with inventing the "iron curtain" simile in his 1946 speech in Missouri, it actuallly first appeared in Swedish, as "*järnridå,*" in the title of a 1923 Swedish travel guide by Per Emil Brusewitz, *Bakom Rysslands järnridå: På motorcykel från Petrograd till Tiflis* [Behind Russia's Iron Curtain: By Motorbike from Petrograd to Tiflis] Stockholm: Hugo Gebers fölag, 1923). Historian Birgitta Ingemanson of Washington State University discovered this historical find and generously volunteered the fact for inclusion here.
113 **"We left on our ice-breaker** Valery Yankovsky has described their escape from Sidemy and the lodge at Novina to me in letters and conversation, as well as in his book, *From the Crusades to Gulag and Beyond,* trans. Michael Hintze, 2nd ed. (Sydney: privately published, 2001).
114 **"There were orchards** Clark, *Living Dangerously,* 152.
117 **validated each other's** Hannah Arendt, *The Origins of Totalitarianism* (New York: Harcourt, 1951).
119 **"The invasion of Harbin** Catherine Bryner to author, October 17, 2004. The remainder of the chapter includes citations from this and other letters.
120 **"the abduction by force** Leonid Bryner, November 2, 1945. From the archives of the Swiss Department of Foreign Affairs; obtained by V. V. Veeder.
121 **to exchange Soviet spies** For more on the spy exchange for Boris Bryner, see Christine Gehrig-Straube, *Beziehungslose Zeiten: Das schweizerish-sowetische Verhältnis zwischen Abbruch und Wiederaufnahme der Beziehungen, 1918–1946, aufgrund schweitzerischer Akten* (Zürich, Switzerland: Verlag Hans Rohr, 1997), 445–5, 457–8.

Part Three

131 **"He declared that he no longer** Irena Brynner, *What I Remember,* 38.
131 **"Yul was a lively and naughty boy,"** Ibid., 87.
132 **"Harbin remained a major center** Stephan, *Russian Fascists,* 40, 86.
133 **"when Yul had a fever,** Irena Brynner, *What I Remember,* 50–51.
134 **"There was panic** Ibid., 88.
134 **"every time her ex-husband** Ibid., 81.
140 **"I pretended to be an old hand** *Collier's,* July 6, 1958, 38.
141 **"I flew and cried,"** *Redbook,* May 1957, 96.
141 **"a handsome young man** Irena Brynner, *What I Remember,* 102–3.
145 **"Russians have long** Andrew Meier, *Black Earth: A Journey through Russia after the Fall* (New York: Norton, 2003), 341. Aleksandr Panchenko cited in Meier.
149 **"I never stopped wondering,"** Michael Chekhov, Charles Leonard, ed., *Michael Chekhov's To the Director and Playwright* (New York: Harper and Row, 1963) 39.
150 **"When you are a pianist,"** Preface by Yul Brynner in Michael Chekhov, *To the Actor* (New York: Harper and Bros., 1953), *x.*
150 **"The body of an actor** Ibid., 2.

158 ***samosvantso* is "a purely Russian phenomenon** Berdyaev cited in Meier, *Black Earth*, 341.
162 **"It was hilarious** *Saturday Evening Post,* November 22, 1958, 78.
165 **"Out he came with a bald head** Richard Rodgers cited in Frederick Nolan, *The Sound of Their Music: The Story of Rodgers and Hammerstein* (London: Unwin Paperbacks, 1979), 170.
166 **"has supplied by her invention** *Appletons' Journal: A Magazine of General Literature,* August 30, 1873, 288.
166 **"We have not been slavishly literal** Rodgers cited in the *New York Times,* March 25, 1951.
167 **"Yul Brynner proceeded** Nolan, *Sound,* 170.
168 **guaranteed 10 percent** Ibid., 168.
169 **"Mr. Rodgers and Mr. Hammerstein** *New York Times,* April 8, 1951.
170 **"Musicals and leading men** *New York Herald Tribune,* March 30, 1951.
173 **"A hostess who entertained the Brynners** *Cosmopolitan,* May 1958, 37.
173 **"I was spending hours creating an illusion** *Redbook,* May 1957, 34.
174 **a right-wing extremist** Farrow, *What Falls,* 25.
177 **"Most interviewers are afraid** *Saturday Evening Post,* November 22, 1958, 80.
179 **I knew from experience** *Newsweek,* May 19, 1958, 101
181 **"An executive at Twentieth Century-Fox,** Ibid., 102.
186 **five o'clock every morning,** *Redbook,* May 1957, 32.
187 **"was a Mongolian** *Collier's,* July 6, 1956, 36.
191 **"Puts shoe to new use,"** *New York Times* headline, October 13, 1960.
193 **"I came out with the deep conviction** Brynner, in his preface to Chekhov, *To the Actor,* ix.
197 **"I was born out of wedlock** *Newsweek,* May 19, 1958, 100.
203 ***Bring Forth the Children*** The citations that follow are from Yul Brynner, *Bring Forth the Children: A Journey to the Forgotten People of Europe and the Middle East,* photographs by Inge Morath and Yul Brynner (New York: McGraw-Hill, 1960).
208 **"A pallid, pretentious and overlong reflection** *New York Times,* November 24, 1960.
212 **"In my mind** *Seventeen,* October 1962, 172.
214 **"more hoop skirts than *Gone With the Wind,*"** Philip Hamburger, *New Yorker,* Feb. 1953.
215 **"so wild, so full of love and energy,** Farrow, *What Falls,* 104.
225 **Gregory Peck, who continued** In conversation with the author, April 1991.
229 **"Yul Brynner is a great actor** *New York Times,* May 30, 1977
237 **"In Unforgettable Final Act,** Barron Lerner, *New York Times,* January 25, 2005.

Part Four

241 **"brazenly informed** *New York Daily News,* April 13, 1953.
247 **"Sam Giancana** Anthony Summers and Robbyn Swann, *Sinatra: The Life* (New York: Random House, 2005), 252.
254 **"a powerful singer and a great musical actor** Robbie Robertson in *Rolling Stone,* April 15, 2004.
258 **"an excursion into** *New York Times,* October 6, 1970.
260 **"The Government has admitted** Ali, cited in the Supreme Court decision, 403 U.S. 698 (decided June 28, 1971).

262 **"From then on,"** Dave Hannigan, *The Big Fight.* (Dublin: Yellow Jersey Press, 2002), 2.

262 **Face to face with Muhammad Ali's bodyguard** *Dublin Evening Press*, July 15, 1972.

267 **"perhaps the major form** Sean Wilentz and Greil Marcus, eds., *The Rose & the Briar: Death, Love and Liberty in the American Ballad* (New York: Norton, 2004).

270 **"Rock and I** David Fricke, "On *The Last Waltz* Twenty-Fifth Anniversary" (4-CD booklet, 2001), 39.

272 **"had actually traveled with Woody Guthrie,** Bob Dylan, *Chronicles, Volume One* (New York: Simon and Schuster, 2004), 251–52.

277 **The last work I published** Rock Brynner and Trent Stephens, *Dark Remedy: The Impact of Thalidomide and Its Revival As a Vital Medicine* (Cambridge, Mass.: Perseus, 2002).

281 **"the architects of the gulag** Meier, *Black Earth*, 240, 242.

281 **"made Primorye his personal duchy** Ibid., 243.

294 **"denouement of the drama** Aileen Kelly, "The Two Dostoevskys," *New York Review of Books*, March 27, 2003.

299 **"a genuine tragedy"** *New York Times*, April 26, 2005.

299 **"glorifying its lost empire** Peter Baker, *Kremlin Rising: Vladimir Putin's Russia and the End of Revolution* (New York: Lisa Drew, 2005).

303 **"eight Holland cows and seventy people"** Valery Yankovsky, in private correspondence.

Bibliography

Applebaum, Anne. *Gulag: A History*. New York: Doubleday, 2003.

Arsenyev Primoski State Museum, ed. *Old Vladivostok*. Vladivostok: Utro Rossii, 1992.

Baker, Peter. *Kremlin Rising: Vladimir Putin's Russia and the End of Revolution*. New York: Lisa Drew, 2005.

Beckett, Samuel. "Dante, Bruno, Vico, Joyce." In *Our Exagmination Round His Factification For Incamination of Work in Progress*. London: Faber, 1929.

Beveridge, A. J. *The Russian Advance*. New York: Harper and Bros., 1904.

Brashler, William. *The Don: The Life and Death of Sam Giancana*. New York: Harper & Row, 1977.

Brynner, Irena. *What I Remember*. New York: 1st Books, 2002.

Bristowe, W. S. *Louis and the King of Siam*. London: Chatto and Windus, 1976.

Brynner, Yul. *Bring Forth the Children: A Journey to the Forgotten People of Europe and the Middle East*. Photographs by Inge Morath and Yul Brynner. New York: McGraw-Hill, 1960.

Callow, Philip. *Chekhov, The Hidden Ground*. Chicago: Ivan R. Dee, 1998.

Carter, James H. *Creating a Chinese Harbin: Nationalism in an International City, 1916–1932*. Ithaca, N.Y.: Cornell University Press, 2002.

Chekhov, Anton. *Island: A Journey to Sakhalin*. London: Century, 1987.

Chekhov, Michael, *To the Actor*. New York: Harper and Bros., 1953.

———. *Michael Chekhov's To the Director and Playwright*. Ed. Charles Leonard. New York: Harper and Row, 1963.

Clark, Donald N. *Living Dangerously in Korea: The Western Experience, 1900–1950* Norwalk, Conn.: EastBridge, 2003.

Cocteau, Jean. *Opium, Journal d'une désintoxication*. Paris: Stock, 1930.

Crowe, David M. *A History of the Gypsies of Eastern Europe and Russia*. New York: St. Martin's Press, 1994.

Davis, Richard Harding, et al. *The Russo-Japanese War: A Photographic and Descriptive Review of the Great Conflict in the Far East*. New York: P. F. Collins, 1904.

Deeg, Lothar. *Kunst & Albers Wladiwostok*. Essen, Germany: Klartext-Verlag, 1996.

Dylan, Bob. *Chronicles, Volume One*. New York: Simon and Schuster, 2004.

Farrow, Mia. *What Falls Away*. New York: Doubleday, 1997.

Gehrig-Straube, Christine. *Beziehungslose Zeiten: Das schweizerish-sowetische Verhältnis zwischen Abbruch und Wiederaufnahme der Beziehungen, 1918–1946, aufgrund schweitzerischer Akten*. Zürich, Switzerland: Verlag Hans Rohr, 1997.

Gippius, A. I. *O Prichinakh Nashei Voiny s Iaponiei. C. Prilozheniiami Dokumenty*. St. Petersburg: Tip A.S. Suvorina, 1905.

Gurko, V. I. *Features and Figures of the Past: Government and Opinion in the Reign of Nicholas II*. London: Oxford University Press, 1939.

Hannigan, Dave. *The Big Fight*. Dublin: Yellow Jersey Press, 2002.

Ingemanson, Birgitta. "Mrs. Dattan's Tea Circle (1890s–1920s)," a lecture at the Dattan Seminar (Sept. 21, 2004) at Far East State Technical University, Vladivostok, Russia.

———. "Vladivostok: Russia's Frontier Town on the Pacific." in *The Siberian Saga*, Eva-Maria Stolberg (New York: Peter Lang, 2005), 119–30.

Kennan, George. *Siberia and The Exile System.* 2 vols. New York: Century Co., 1891.

Kennedy, Paul. *The Rise and Fall of the Great Powers: Economic Change and Military Conflict from 1500 to 2000.* New York: Vintage Books, 1987.

Kidd, C. A. (or A. C.). "Tetiuhe: A History of the Tetiuhe Mine In Siberia." Unpublished. London: 1980.

Kotkin, Stephen, and David Wolff, eds. *Rediscovering Russia in Asia: Siberia and the Russian Far East.* Armonk, N.Y.: M.E. Sharpe, 1995.

Malozemoff, Andrew. *Russian Far Eastern Policy, 1881–1904.* New York: Octagon Books, 1958.

Marks, Steven G. *Road to Power: The Trans-Siberian Railroad and the Colonization of Asian Russia, 1850–1917.* Ithaca, N.Y.: Cornell University Press, 1991.

Marowitz, Charles. *The Other Chekov: A Biography of Michael Chekov, the Legendary Actor, Director and Theorist.* New York: Applause Theater & Cinema Books, 2004.

Massie, Robert K. *Nicholas and Alexandra.* New York: Atheneum, 1967.

Meier, Andrew. *Black Earth: A Journey Through Russia After the Fall.* New York: Norton, 2003.

Nolan, Frederick. *The Sound of Their Music: The Story of Rodgers and Hammerstein.* London: Unwin Paperbacks, 1979.

Paléologue, Maurice. *Turning Point: Three Critical Years, 1904–1906.* 2 vols. Translated by F. Appleby Holt. London: Hutchinson and Co., 1935.

Patrikeeff, Felix. "Russian and Soviet Economic Penetration of North-Eastern China, 1895–1933." In *Essays on Revolutionary Culture and Stalinism*, edited by John W. Strong. Columbus, Ohio: Slavica, 1990.

Pott, F. L. Hawks. *A Short History of Shanghai: Being an Account of the Growth and Development of the International Settlement.* Shanghai: s.n., 1928.

Ransome, Arthur. *Russia in 1919.* New York: B.W. Heubsch, 1919.

Riva, Maria. *Marlene Dietrich.* New York: Knopf, 1993.

Rodzianko, Paul. *Tattered Banners: An Autobiography.* London: Seely Service, 1934.

Seeger, C. L., ed. *Memoirs of Alexander Iswolsky, Formerly Russian Minister of Foreign Affairs and Ambassador to France.* London: Hutchinson, 1920.

Smith, Canfield F. *Vladivostok Under Red and White Rule: Revolution and Counterrevolution in the Russian Far East, 1920–1922.* Seattle: University of Washington Press, 1975.

Solzhenitsyn, Alexander. *August 1914: The Red Wheel.* London: Bodley Head, 1989.

Stanislavsky, Konstantin. *An Actor Prepares.* New York: Theatre Arts, 1939.

Stephan, John J., *The Russian Far East: A History.* Stanford, Calif.: Stanford University Press 1994.

———. *The Russian Fascists: Tragedy and Farce in Exile, 1925–1945.* New York: Harper and Row, 1978.

Summers, Anthony, and Robbyn Swann. *Sinatra: The Life.* New York: Random House, 2005.

Sumner, B. H. *Tsardom and Imperialism in the Far East and Middle East, 1880–1914.* Hamdon, Conn.: Archon, 1968.

Thubron, Colin. *In Siberia.* London: Penguin, 2000.

Veeder, V. V. "The Tetiuhe Mining Concession 1924–1932: A Swiss-Russian Story (Where the Arbitral Dog Did Not Bark)." In *Liber Amicorum Claude Reymond: Autour de l'Arbitrage.* Paris: Edition Juris-Classeur, 2004.

Volkogonov, Dimitri. *Stalin: Triumph and Tragedy.* London: Weidenfeld and Nicholson, 1991.

Vonliarliarsky, V. M.. "Why Russia Went to War with Japan: The Story of the Yalu Concession," *Fortnightly Review*, n.s., 521 (May 2, 1910); n.s., 522 (June 1, 1910).

Weatherford, Jack. *Genghis Khan And the Making of The Modern World.* Pittsburgh, Pa.: Three Rivers Press, 2004.

Wells, Spencer. *The Journey of Man: A Genetic History.* Princeton, N.J.: Princeton University Press, 2003.

White, John Albert. *The Diplomacy of the Russo-Japanese War.* Princeton, N.J.: Princeton University Press, 1964.

———. *The Siberian Intervention.* Princeton, N.J.: Princeton University Press, 1950.

White, Stephen. *Britain and the Bolshevik Revolution: A Study in the Politics of Diplomacy, 1920–1924.* New York: Holmes and Meier, 1980.

Wilentz, Sean, and Greil Marcus, eds. *The Rose & the Briar: Death, Love and Liberty in the American Ballad.* New York: Norton, 2004.

Williams, Albert Rhys. *Through the Russian Revolution.* London: Labour Pub. Co., 1922.

Wolff, David. *To the Harbin Station: The Liberal Alternative in Russian Manchuria, 1898–1914.* Stanford, Calif.: Stanford University Press, 1999.

Yankovsky, Valery. *Potomki Nenun.* Moscow: Eksmo, 1986.

Index

NOTE: Photo locations are shown by a letter, which indicates a section of photos (A, B, C, or D), plus a number, which is the page within that section where the photo can be found.